D0855409

Becoming Roman

The Origins of Provincial Civilization in Gaul

Under the emperors' rule, the cultural lives of all Rome's subjects were utterly transformed. This book is a study of this process – conventionally termed 'Romanization' – through an investigation of the experience of Rome's Gallic provinces in the late Republic and early empire. Beginning with a rejection of the concept of 'Romanization' it describes the nature of Roman power in Gaul and the Romans' own understanding of these changes. Successive chapters then map the chronology and geography of change and offer new interpretations of urbanism, rural civilization, consumption and cult, before concluding with a synoptic view of Gallo-Roman civilization and of the origins of provincial cultures in general. The work draws on literary and archaeological material to make a contribution to the cultural history of the empire which will be of interest to ancient historians, classical archaeologists and all interested in cultural change.

Greg Woolf is Professor of Ancient History at the University of St Andrews. He is co-editor, with Alan K. Bowman, of *Literacy and Power in the Ancient World* (1994).

Becoming Roman

The Origins of Provincial Civilization in Gaul

Greg Woolf

CAMBRIDGE
UNIVERSITY PRESS

PUBLISHED BY THE PRESS SYNDICATE OF THE UNIVERSITY OF CAMBRIDGE
The Pitt Building, Trumpington Street, Cambridge CB2 1RP, United Kingdom

CAMBRIDGE UNIVERSITY PRESS
The Edinburgh Building, Cambridge CB2 2RU, United Kingdom
40 West 20th Street, New York, NY 10011–4211, USA
10 Stamford Road, Oakleigh, Melbourne 3166, Australia

First published 1998

Printed in the United Kingdom at the University Press, Cambridge

Typeset in 10/12pt Plantin [GT]

A catalogue record for this book is available from the British Library

Library of Congress cataloguing in publication data

Woolf, Greg.
    Becoming Roman: the origins of provincial civilization in Gaul /
Greg Woolf.
        p.   cm.
    Includes bibliographical references and index.
    ISBN 0 521 41445 8 (hardback)
        1. Gaul – Civilization – Roman influences.   2. Romans – Gaul.
3. Rome – History – Empire, 30 BC–AD 284.   4. Cities and towns,
Ancient.   5. Rome – Provinces – Administration.   1. Title.
DC33.2.W66   1998
944–dc21
                                                        97–47263 CIP

ISBN 0 521 41445 8 hardback

To the memory of my father

Contents

Illustrations

Preface

This book is a study of the origins and nature of the culture of the provinces of the early Roman empire. The creation of provincial cultures is not an obvious sequel to Rome's conquest of the Mediterranean world and its continental hinterlands. To illustrate the point we might imagine another – counter-factual – Roman empire, created in much the same way as the real one by armies led out on campaign by aristocratic generals to defend and extend Roman power, and to win booty, prestige and territory. As the campaigns become grander, the armies grow larger and fight further and further away from home until expansion ceases and there is peace in the provinces of this imaginary Roman empire. Taxes are paid and the odd rebellion essayed and suppressed but otherwise life goes on much as it did before in the cities of the Greeks, the villages of Gaul, the temples of the Egyptians and so on. If Counter-Rome's subjects farm a little harder and fight a little less, the day to day rhythm of their lives is unchanged, they speak the same languages as before, worship the same gods, inhabit the same houses and eat the same foods off the same pottery as they had always done. And when the empire withers away or collapses, as all empires – imaginary or real – must do, all is exactly as it was and no traces of it remain. Gauls and Greeks, Jews and Egyptians once more go their separate historical ways, untouched by their shared experience of imperial rule.

This book is an exercise in differentiating that imaginary, counter-factual, empire from the real one. As a matter of fact the provinces of the Republican empire did bear some resemblance to those of our counter-factual model, but under the emperors the cultures of Rome's subjects were transformed utterly. Cities sprang up where there were none before, new temples were raised to new gods, and even the most intimate details of life were refashioned. In Gaul men literally came down from the hills, shaved off their beards and learned to bathe themselves. Nor did these changes affect only the richest and most prominent. The humblest altars and the cheapest pottery vessels testify to the creation of a new civilization. Changes of this sort might be documented from all over Rome's empire, but did not result in a culture of imperial uniformity. Rather each region witnessed the creation of distinct civilizations – crudely described today as Romano-British, Gallo-Roman and so forth – that reflected their various predecessors but nevertheless converged on, and formed part of, an imperial whole. For this reason, and to allow the process to be studied in the detail it deserves, this study is based on the provincial cultures of just one part (albeit a large part) of this empire, Rome's Gallic provinces.

Roman Gaul covered a vast and varied swathe of territory that today comprises the whole of France and much of Switzerland, Germany and the Low Countries. At the end of prehistory all this area was inhabited by late iron age populations, who shared broadly similar arts and technologies, but combined them in intensely local manifestations. Roman armies conquered all these societies in the second and last centuries BC and brought them into an empire already based on the Mediterranean world. Gallo-Roman civilization emerged from the subsequent confrontation between iron age cultures and the civilizations that we call Classical. This study poses the questions of why did this happen and why did it happen in the ways that it did? The subject, then, is the various processes usually summed up in the term Romanization, although, for reasons that will become apparent, that term is in many ways unhelpful.

The aim of this book is not, therefore, to provide another history of Roman Gaul, nor to provide a comprehensive account of Gallo-Roman archaeology.[1] It does, however, aim to offer an analysis of Roman civilization in early imperial Gaul. The subject is enormous and might be studied through any number of media, and in a variety of ways. I am very conscious of the paths not trodden: there is little here on art and architecture, less on numismatics, nothing on gender. The silences are not, of course, all of my choosing, but I have often selected among alternatives so as to treat each theme once, and to keep the work to manageable proportions. In selecting topics for detailed discussion, I have been guided sometimes by what seems central – urbanism, for example, and cult – and sometimes by the availability of recent high quality studies. In this respect, this study has only been possible thanks to the excellence of so much recent archaeological work in France and neighbouring countries, to the extent that it would have been impossible to write a book of this sort twenty years ago. The technical proficiency

---

1 The fullest overall account remains that of Jullian (1908–26). Up to date accounts are offered to the history by Drinkwater (1983), and to the archaeology by King (1990a). The best short English introduction is provided by the chapters contributed by Goudineau to *Cambridge Ancient History* volumes X (1996) and XI (forthcoming).

of this research and its systematic nature have transformed our knowledge of Roman Gaul, and I make no apology for asset-stripping the
best results of these labours, although I do so conscious of the immense
debt I owe to them. Archaeologists are necessarily painfully aware of
the incomplete nature of their findings, and the provisional nature of
any conclusions. Yet that problem will be with us as long as the science
survives, and arguably there is little point accumulating data if analytical syntheses of this sort are not to be attempted. Historians and
classicists are less worried by the provisional nature of interpretation,
seeing it as inevitable within any living intellectual discipline. It is pro-
foundly to be hoped that new understandings of Roman cultural history
and further archaeological research, both in fieldwork and in theoretical
debate, will all contribute to the superseding of my arguments and conclusions. That is inevitable in any case, but it is better to embrace the
future than to attempt (futilely) to ward it off.

Gauls were not alone in becoming Romans. The argument therefore
begins (chapter 1) with an exploration of how best to approach the general intellectual issues involved, couched as a discussion of Romanization,
long the dominant paradigm in such investigations. Important contexts
for these changes are the nature of Roman imperialism and Roman
notions of civilization, both in theory and in their impact on practice.
Those subjects are treated in chapters 2 and 3. I have avoided attempting to provide a thumbnail sketch of the salient features of pre-Roman
culture and society in the region, partly because I have discussed some
aspects elsewhere,[2] but mostly because it seemed better to integrate discussion of each aspect with that of its transformation under Roman rule.
Chapter 4 provides a brief sketch of the geographical and chronological
contours of change, viewed through one particularly sensitive medium,
epigraphy. The discussion then moves on to consider central features of
Gallo-Roman civilization, beginning with the most public manifestation,
the creation of Gallo-Roman cities (chapter 5), and moving through the
transformation of the countryside (chapter 6) to the establishment of
new patterns of consumption (chapter 7). That progress also lead from
discussion of public and collective acts of cultural transformation, through
more private manifestations of cultural change and from the activities
of the new aristocracies of Roman Gaul to the gradual dissemination of
Roman styles and tastes throughout the population. The final substantive chapter (chapter 8) deals with a central issue, religion, often (but
wrongly) thought of as the last bastion of pre-Roman identity and culture.

2 Woolf (1993a) (1993b) (1993c). The best account of the archaeology of the late La
  Tène is Collis (1984).

I conclude (chapter 9) with some comments on the sort of civilization created and enjoyed in Roman Gaul.

The chronological limits of this study are set by the questions it has posed and need little explanation: both iron age and early Roman Gaul bear on the question, as do the cultural history of the late Republic and the early empire in general. It was tempting to pursue the study of Gallo-Roman civilization further in time to the late empire, despite the immense extension to this work that that would have entailed. But the focus of the study remains the process by which Gauls became Romans, and subsequent developments – among them the decline of cities, Christianization and the redefinition of Romans in opposition to new barbarians – belong to another story or stories, although the cost is that some issues, language change for example, receive less full attention than they might have had. At all events, the cultural history of late antique Gaul deserves more than a coda to a book on the early empire. Instead I have left Gaul at the end of the third century, when the Gallic Panegyricists could at least conjure up the image of a civilization founded in the age of Caesar and Augustus. Most of the book concerns the first and second centuries AD, the period within which Gallo-Roman culture was first created and then generalized.

This book has grown from a doctoral thesis written in Cambridge in the late 1980s. It is a pleasure once again to thank Ian Hodder, Keith Hopkins and Sander van der Leeuw who shared in its supervision, and most of all Peter Garnsey, who has seen the whole project through from beginning to end. I could not have hoped for better guides and teachers. Collectively I wish also to thank all those who shared the exciting experience of graduate study in Cambridge in that period, both in the Faculty of Classics and the Department of Archaeology. I was fortunate in having Andrew Wallace-Hadrill and Dick Whittaker as my doctoral examiners, whose comments gave me much to think about and have led to substantial refinements in the arguments. Many others have been generous with advice and help. Numerous French archaeologists generously welcomed me as a student, rather than a practitioner, of cultural imperialism. I owe particular debts to Christian Goudineau and Olivier Buchsenschutz who started me on the right path, and to Jean-Louis Cadoux, my colleague in field survey in Picardy, from whom I have learned much about Gallo–Roman archaeology. Throughout the long gestation of thesis and book, a number of colleagues have (not always knowingly) offered argument and inspiration at critical stages, among them John Collis, Michael Crawford, John Drinkwater, Chris Gosden, Colin Haselgrove, J. D. Hill, Fergus Millar, Martin Millett, Daphne Nash, Simon Price, Nicholas Purcell and Ian Ralston. I am also extremely grateful to Chris Gosden, Martin Millett, Simon Price and Andrew Wallace-Hadrill, who all commented on sections of the penultimate draft, and especially to Peter Garnsey, who read it in its entirety. Pauline Hire has been the most patient as well as the most helpful of editors. Tamar Hodos left the text much clearer than she found it and saved me from many errors and inconsistencies. The work was been supported by a number of institutions including the British Academy, the CNRS, the Laboratoire d'Archéologie of the Ecole Normale Supérieure, and my two Cambridge colleges, Trinity and Christ's. The actual writing of this book took place while I was a Fellow of first Magdalen and then Brasenose Colleges in Oxford. I am grateful to both institutions for support and sabbatical leave, and to my colleagues at Oxford in Ancient History and in Archaeology. It is impossible to say how much I owe to all those named and to others too numerous to name.

Other debts too are immeasurable. My mother, my brother and my late father, to whose memory this book is dedicated, gave limitless love and support, as has Johanna Weeks, who has cheerfully born the brunt of the enthusiasms and frustrations of a decade, and our daughter Maud, who arrived just in time to cheer me through the final revisions. My thanks to all.

Abbreviations

AFEAF	Association française pour l'étude de l'âge du fer
AJA	*American Journal of Archaeology*
AJAH	*American Journal of Ancient History*
AJPh	*American Journal of Philology*
ALB	Annales Littéraires de l'Université de Besançon
Annales ESC	*Annales. Économies, Sociétés, Civilisations*
ANRW	*Aufstieg und Niedergang der römischen Welt*
ArchPrehLev	*Archivo de Prehistoria Levantina*
ARW	*Archiv für Religionswissenschaft*
ASA	Association of Social Anthropologists
BAR	British Archaeological Reports
BASP	*Bulletin of the American Society of Papyrologists*
BCH	*Bulletin de correspondance hellénique*
BEFAR	Bibliothèque des écoles françaises d'Athènes et de Rome
BJ	*Bonner Jahrbücher*
BRGK	*Bericht der Römisch-Germanischen Kommission des Deutschen Archäologischen Instituts*
CAH	*The Cambridge Ancient History*
CBA	Council of British Archaeology
CEFR	Collection de l'école française de Rome
CIL	*Corpus Inscriptionum Latinarum*
CPh	*Classical Philology*
CQ	*Classical Quarterly*
CLPA	*Cahiers Ligures de Préhistoire et Archéologie*
CSSH	*Comparative Studies in Society and History*
DAF	Documents d'Archéologie Française
DHA	*Dialogues d'Histoire Ancienne*
HSCP	*Harvard Studies in Classical Philology*
ILGN	*Inscriptions Latines de la Gaule Narbonnaise*
ILN	*Inscriptions Latines de Narbonnaise*
ILS	*Inscriptiones Latinae Selectae*

ILTG	*Inscriptions Latines des Trois Gaules*
JRA	*Journal of Roman Archaeology*
JRS	*Journal of Roman Studies*
MAAR	Memoirs of the American Academy in Rome
MEFRA	*Mélanges de l'école française de Rome, antiquité*
MHA	*Memorias de Historia Antigua*
OJA	*Oxford Journal of Archaeology*
PBSR	*Papers of the British School at Rome*
PCPhS	*Proceedings of the Cambridge Philological Society*
RA	*Revue Archéologique*
RAC	*Revue Archéologique du Centre*
RAE	*Revue Archéologique de l'Est et du Centre-Est*
RAN	*Revue Archéologique de Narbonnaise*
RAO	*Revue Archéologique de l'Ouest*
RCFRActa	*Res Cretariae Romanae Fautorum, Acta*
REA	*Revue des Études Anciennes*
REL	*Revue des Études Latines*
RIG	*Recueil des Inscriptions Gauloises*
RSI	*Rivista Storica Italiana*
SAR	*Scottish Archaeological Review*
TZ	*Trierer Zeitschrift*
ZPE	*Zeitschrift für Papyrologie und Epigrafik*

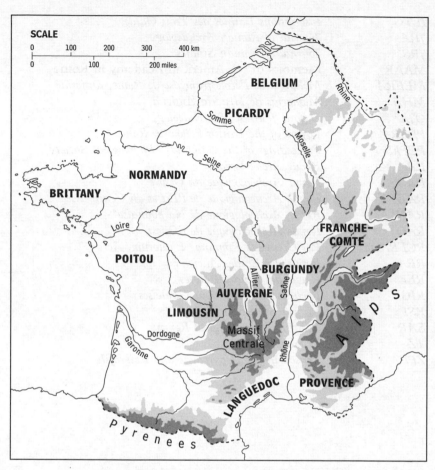

Map 1   Modern regions and river names

0   100   200   300   400 km

0   100   200 miles

GERMANIA
INFERIOR

B E L G I C A

L U G D U N E N S I S

GERMANIA
SUPERIOR

ALPES GRAIAE
ET POENINAE

ALPES
COTTIAE

A Q U I T A N I A

ALPES
MARITIMAE

N A R B O N E N S I S

Map 2   Provincial boundaries c. AD 100

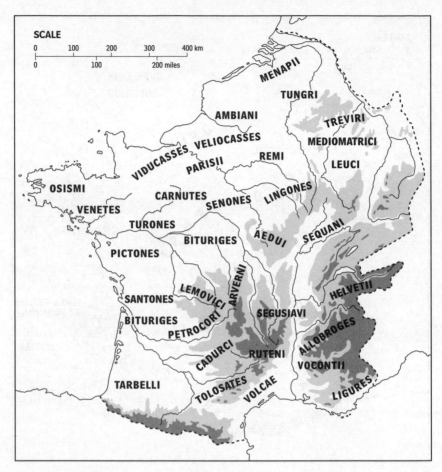

Map 3 Major peoples of Roman Gaul

I On Romanization

I The civilizing process

At some point in the late 290s AD, an orator from the town of Autun in present day Burgundy made a speech before an imperial governor, perhaps the Prefect of the province of Lugdunensis I.[1] The orator, Eumenius, was a powerful and wealthy citizen of the community of the Aedui, whose capital Autun was, and had recently returned from serving as Magister Memoriae at the court of Constantius Chlorus, one of the two Caesars, or junior emperors, who assisted the Augusti, who at that time ruled the Roman empire. Constantius had set in hand the restoration of Autun, which had been sacked a generation before during a Roman civil war; the work had already begun, and Eumenius had been entrusted by the Caesar with the task of instructing the Aeduan youth of Autun in the liberal arts, which meant above all in oratory. Now, in his speech, he sought the Caesar's permission to dedicate his considerable salary to the physical restoration of the Scholae Maenianae, the celebrated schools of Autun. Recalling Constantius' past services to the city, and both the ancient and recent services of the Aedui to Rome, Eumenius sought permission to perform an act of euergetism, of civic munificence, that would at the same time express his loyalty to his imperial patron, his civic patriotism, his adherence to the highest cultural ideals of the empire and his pre-eminence among his own people.

For the historian of Rome, the incident recalls a hundred others throughout the empire, just as the ruined monuments that still distinguish Autun from the average Burgundian municipality evoke ruins from all over what was once the Roman world. The Scholae Maenianae are gone, but Autun still boasts a classical theatre, long stretches of her Roman city walls, including two gates, and the remains of a huge suburban temple. Likewise, the tombstones and statues, the glass and

---

1 Eumenius' *Oratio pro instaurandis scholis*, numbered 9 (4) in Mynors' OCT edition of the *Panegyrici Latini*, 9 (5) in Galletier's Budé. For the uncertainties about the exact place, date and addressee of the speech, see Nixon and Rodgers (1994, 145–50).

I

pottery vessels, and the personal ornaments and utensils displayed in the Musée Rolin resemble the Roman period collections of hundreds of local museums from Scotland to North Africa, Spain to Turkey. For us, the discovery of these familiar ruins and objects in a small French town is a reminder of a vanished age when the civilizations of this huge area came closer together than they have done ever since. But a second- or third-century visitor from another part of the empire would have gained the opposite impression, of a civilization grander and more ex- tensive than had existed ever before. Eumenius' own grandfather had, as it happens, been born in Athens, and had lived in Rome before coming to Autun. On his arrival in Autun, he would have felt immedi- ately at home, not just because the architecture and crockery were similar to that to which he was accustomed, but also because he would have found himself among people who shared his tastes and values, from a common diet to common ideas about the importance of educa- tion and of civic responsibility. Life in Autun was not always rosy, of course, although Eumenius' grandfather liked it well enough to settle there. The monuments and panegyrics which are our main source of knowledge about Roman Autun conceal, in part by design, the char- acteristic tensions of any early imperial city. The emperor had fixed Eumenius' huge salary but had commanded that it be paid by the Aedui, so that the orator's generosity consisted of redirecting public funds to his chosen project. The fact that he sought the support of the governor and of Constantius suggests that the scheme had its critics, whether jealous rivals or those who knew how easily grandiose building projects could involve communities in debt and heavy maintenance expenses.[2] Nor were emperors as constant in their patronage as the Aedui might have desired. The political prominence of the Aedui in the early first century AD and again under Constantius and his son Con- stantine was evident in Autun's two names, Augustodunum for the first emperor, and Flavia Aeduorum for Constantius' new dynasty, as well as in its monuments, but at other periods they commanded less influ- ence and enjoyed less prosperity.[3] But the rise and fall of the fortunes of

2 On euergetism: Veyne (1976), reviewed by Garnsey in *JRS* 81 (1991) 164–8. For tensions between cities and their would-be benefactors: Pliny *Epistulae* 10.81–2; Dio Chrysostom *Orationes* 47, 48 on Prusa; Rogers (1991a) on Oenoanda; and Johnston (1985) on their expression in Roman law.

3 Political prominence in the first century derived from an early Aeduan alliance with Rome (Caesar *de Bello Gallico* passim). The first priest of Rome and Augustus at Lyon was an Aeduan (Livy *Epitomae* 139), as were the first senators from the Three Gauls (Tacitus *Annales* 11.25), and a school for the children of Gallic aristocrats existed at Autun under Tiberius (Tacitus *Annales* 3.43). On Autun's monuments: Bedon *et al.* (1988) vol. II, 70–3 with bibliography, and Rebourg (1991). Evidence for the later period of prominence is almost entirely confined to four of the speeches collected in

individual cities too was a classical trope. The story of Autun, like its monuments or domestic bric-a-brac, might be paralleled in any province of the Roman empire.

How should we understand the growth of this common civilization throughout the area ruled by the Roman emperors? Aeduan commentators were aware that their culture had a history.[4] But their portrayal of their own past bears little resemblance to the iron age society, known as the late La Tène, that archaeologists have uncovered in excavating sites like the old Aeduan hillfort of Bibracte on Mont Beuvray, twenty kilometres from Autun on the edge of the remote Morvan.[5] Aeduan images of their past were thoroughly classical in character. 'What people in all the world can claim to precede the Aedui in their love of the Roman name?' asked one of Eumenius' successors, speaking before the emperor Constantine, and went on to recall how the Aedui alone among the wild and barbaric peoples of Gaul had been addressed by the Roman senate as brothers of the Roman people. In contrast to other cities and peoples – Saguntum, Massilia, the Mamertines and even Ilium – whose alliances and claims to kinship were self-interested and imaginary, the Aedui alone had shown themselves worthy of a title which expressed the reciprocity of love and parity of honour which existed between them and the Roman people. When that honour aroused the jealousy of their neighbours, an Aeduan chief then visited Rome, and, leaning on his shield as he addressed the senate, invited Caesar into Gaul. By this action and by sharing in the burdens of the conquest of Gaul, the Aedui had brought all the land enclosed by the Rhine, the Pyrenees, the Atlantic and the Alps into the empire. 'So, uniting all the peoples of the Celts and the Belgae together into one common peace, the Aedui had joined to the Romans those whom they had detached from the barbarians'.[6] The myth of the Aedui as Rome's partners in freeing Gaul

the *Panegyrici Latini*, Mynors 5 (8), 6 (7), 8 (5), 9 (4), suggesting that the Aedui were able to capitalize on their unsuccessful support for Claudius II Gothicus against the Gallic emperors, and the desire of Constantius and his successors to establish a power-base in the West. Periods of decline are less well documented, but cf. Buckley (1981) on the late third century. By the mid-fourth century, the schools of Autun were eclipsed by those of Trier (Haarhoff 1920, 48), and at least two Aeduan towns, Auxerre and Chalon, were independent (Février et al. 1980, 114–15).

4 For further discussion, see Woolf (1996b).
5 Bertin and Guillaumet (1987) and Goudineau and Peyre (1993) provide brief general guides to the site and the history of research on it, principally the extensive excavations conducted by Bulliot and then Déchelette between 1867 and 1907, largely published in the *Mémoires de la Société Éduenne*. Interim reports on the current programme of research on the site are published in *RAE* 38 (1987) 285–300, 40 (1989) 205–28, 42 (1991) 271–98 and 44 (1993) 311–63.
6 *Panegyrici Latini* Mynors 5 (VIII), 2–3. Braund (1980) suggests one possible explanation for the *fraternitas* of the Aedui.

from barbarism, like the rhetorical medium in which it was expressed, reflects the extent to which third-century Gauls subscribed to the values of Roman civilization, but tells us little about how that civilization came into existence in Gaul. Civilized values seemed, to the Gallic orators, unproblematically superior to what had gone before, just as they were superior to the values of those other barbarians who remained outside the empire, and who had recently invaded Gaul, when the emperor's attention was distracted.

The founding fathers of the modern study of the Roman world held rather similar views about civilization and the barbarians. 'Our civilization' wrote Haverfield, 'seems firmly set in many lands; our task is rather to spread it further and develop its good qualities than to defend its life. If war destroys it in one continent, it has other homes. But the Roman Empire was the civilized world; the safety of Rome was the safety of all civilization. Outside roared the wild chaos of barbarism'.[7] Mommsen, too, had written of 'the Latin-Greek civilizing process in the form of perfecting the constitution of the urban community and the gradual bringing of the barbarian, or at any rate alien, elements into this circle', and compared the civilization and national prosperity of the Antonine age favourably with that of his own day.[8] Classical civilization played an even more important role in contemporary French histories of Roman Gaul. Fustel de Coulanges wrote that 'it was less Rome than civilization itself which won over the Gauls . . . Being Roman, for them, was not a matter of obeying a foreign master so much as of sharing in the most cultivated and noble manners, arts, studies, labours and pleasures known to humanity', and argued that Roman institutions enabled the Gauls, who were in any case of the same race as the Greeks and Romans, to develop a latent potential for civilization. The alternative to Roman rule was German rule, which would have condemned the Gauls and France to centuries more of barbarism.[9] Camille Jullian, whose influence over Gallo-Roman studies paralleled Haverfield's over Roman Britain, wrote that the Gauls were intelligent enough to recognize the charms of the South, and that they were members of European civilization, even if new arrivals.[10] Behind these late nineteenth- and early

7 Haverfield (1912, 10), although if Haverfield subscribed to a similar notion of civilization and barbarism, he was careful to distinguish British and Roman imperialism in other respects, for which see Freeman (1996). Hingley (1996) sets Haverfield's views in wider literary and historical contexts, but perhaps underplays the extent to which Haverfield differed from popular beliefs about the closeness of British and Roman imperialism.
8 Mommsen (1886, 4) 'die Durchführung der lateinisch-griechischen Civilisirung' in the (1885) German original. On his influence over Haverfield, see Freeman (1997).
9 De Coulanges (1891, 134–9). The nationalist agenda is evident.
10 Jullian (1908–26) vol. VI, 531–8.

twentieth-century accounts can be detected two premises: first, a belief that not all races had an equal potential to participate in civilization; and second, a faith in the absolute validity of the values of European culture, seen as the heir to the civilization of the classical world. Both ideas were part of the legacy of European imperialism: neither are widely held today among cultural historians.[11]

Writing cultural history takes on a special character if the historian believes in the universal validity of one particular set of cultural values. It is perfectly possible to write cultural histories from that standpoint, but they tend to become either appraisals of alien cultures, or else genealogies of the historian's own civilization. The criticism applies equally to Eumenius of Autun and to Francis Haverfield. Cultural relativists, on the other hand, start from the premise that all cultural systems are equally valid. Roman civilization was no better, in other words, than the culture of late La Tène Gaul, but simply different, and we cannot explain cultural change in terms of intelligent savages recognizing the superiority of classical civilization.[12] Cultural relativism too is open to objections, and not just from the adherents of particular absolutist value systems,[13] but in the absence of a satisfactory definition of civilization, it seems to offer the best working hypothesis available. In this instance, it has the additional advantage that it promotes a critical stance to Roman claims to cultural superiority, and to European claims to be their heirs.[14] For better or worse, modern accounts of Roman culture have moved further and further away from the absolutist positions represented by de Coulanges and Haverfield, but the change has been a gradual one and the central concept deployed by Roman cultural historians today remains the term coined by that generation, Romanization.

Over the century since Mommsen, Jullian and Haverfield laid the foundations of the archaeology and history of the Roman West, Romanization has become a major preoccupation, perhaps *the* major preoccupation,

11 Blázquez (1989), citing earlier discussions of the relationship between Romanization and nineteenth-century imperialism; Millett (1990a, xv); Freeman (1993) and (1997) show how the agenda for research on this issue was set in this period. The studies cited also show the period of their composition in other ways, for example in the stress on institutions, and on the treatment of the Germans by the French writers.

12 But compare Knapp (1977, 144) on the Romanization of Spain: 'The more advanced towns saw the need to adjust to Roman ways in order to co-exist with the conquerors. The less developed peoples quite naturally took Roman forms as models when they sought to develop their communal life.'

13 For example, it is often objected that cultural relativism cannot in its nature claim to be a more valid philosophy than any other, and that it is as intimately related to conditions of political and cultural pluralism as more absolutist approaches are to imperial and totalitarian regimes.

14 Herrin (1987, 295–306) shows how Islam, Byzantium and Western Europe have equal, if contrasting, claims to be considered the heirs of Rome.

of their successors. Thousands of studies have employed the concept of Romanization to organize accounts of the cultures of the western Roman provinces. Ancient historians have used literary and epigraphic evidence to chart the spread of Roman-style institutions, names, language and citizenship, while archaeologists have identified styles of architecture, metalwork and ceramic that distinguish Roman sites from those of the pre-Roman period, and Romanized from less Romanized provincials. On the basis of these studies, an approximate ranking in terms of Romanization is produced: the West is seen as more Romanized than the East; the Mediterranean world more Romanized than temperate Europe, southern Gaul more Romanized than northern Gaul, Italy more Romanized than the provinces, and cities more Romanized than the countryside.[15] That distribution may then be related to other variables – the political history of the region, the nature of pre-conquest societies, veteran colonization, the presence of the army, proximity to roads or river systems – to produce an explanation for the level of Romanization. The methodology has not altered much from that used by Mommsen.[16] The careful mapping of the phenomena collectively taken to provide indices of Romanization has been very valuable as a first stage in exploring Roman culture, especially when it has been put on a solid, quantitative basis, although it is noticeable that more attention has been directed towards distributions in space than in time, perhaps in part because of the difficulties in dating inscriptions and other artefacts.[17]

But if a careful mapping of Roman provincial culture is a useful, and perhaps even an essential preliminary to understanding it, the same cannot be said for expressing the results in terms of contours of Romanization. Even detached from the notion of a civilizing process, it is easy for the study of Romanization to become an appraisal of provincial cultures, measured against the standards of supposedly pure Roman culture. 'Roman' components of provincial culture are then privileged at the expense of indigenous ones, which are dismissed as residual.[18] Nor are the results of such an analysis worth having: 'Let us not conclude by pronouncing a judgement that will in some way evaluate the Romanization of Vaison (very, quite, moderately or only a little Romanized) . . . Suppose we were to compile some artificial list

15 For more precise exercises in mapping the distribution of culture, see Price (1984, 78–100) on Asia Minor and Wallace-Hadrill (1990a) on Pompeii.
16 Mommsen (1886, 86, 102).
17 Ward-Perkins (1970) is an exception to the rule, pointing out how little impact Rome seems to have made on provincial cultures in the Republican period. See also Millett (1990b, 39–40), Woolf (1995).
18 Bénabou (1976a, 16–19) provides a very clear analysis of the problem, although his solution is open to criticism.

of bogus "Roman traits" and imaginary "Celtic survivals", and then tried to add up or balance out all the disparate data – there is no *atrium*, but there were *aediles*, there was no *duumvir*, but the toilets are similar to those at *Timgad* – we would end up playing a misleading intellectual game with no real meaning or interest.'[19] Besides, there was no standard Roman civilization against which provincial cultures might be measured. The city of Rome was a cultural melting pot and Italy experienced similar changes to the provinces.[20] Nor did Romanization culminate in cultural uniformity throughout the empire. Eumenius' grandfather would not have felt culturally disorientated in Autun, but he would have been perfectly aware of its differences from Athens or Rome, and regional variations are apparent to archaeologists in every sphere of material culture. Contrasts between capital and provinces, East and West, rich and poor, city and countryside are themselves a major feature of Roman imperial culture. Romanization may have been 'the process by which the inhabitants come to be, and to think of themselves as, Romans', but there was more than one kind of Roman, and studies of provincial culture need to account for the cultural diversity, as well as the unity, of the empire.[21]

Romanization has often been used as an umbrella term to conceal a multitude of separate processes. Some regard that as a major drawback of the concept, others see it as its most attractive feature.[22] Romanization has no explanatory potential, because it was not an active force, the course of which can be traced through a variety of indices, and the level of which can be measured. But used descriptively, Romanization is a convenient shorthand for the series of cultural changes that created an imperial civilization, within which both differences and similarities came to form a coherent pattern.

II Cultural change

Becoming Roman was a slow process. An Aeduan who had fought alongside Caesar in his youth would have had to have lived to a ripe old

---

19 Goudineau (1979, 312–13).
20 On Romanization in Italy in general: Crawford (1981), Salmon (1982, 153–6), Wallace-Hadrill (1990a). On the constant renegotiation of what 'Roman' meant in cultural terms, cf. Barratt (1997), Woolf (1997).
21 The definition is from Harris (1971, 147). On diversity and unity, see Woolf (1992a), reviewing Blagg and Millett (1990).
22 Goudineau (1979, 312): 'sous ce vocable de "romanisation" se dissimulaient foule de canevas trop commodes, de schémas trop simples, de concepts plus ou moins confus'; Mócsy (1970, 7): 'da er [der Terminus] demnach auch sehr dehnbar ist, werden geschichtliche Prozesse, die doch verdienten, eingehender untersucht zu werden, einfach unter seinem Sammelbegriff zusammengefasst und daher verhüllt.'

age to have seen the foundation of Augustodunum. His childhood would
have been spent in an iron age farmstead, or perhaps in one of the
defended hilltop sites that appeared in Gaul in the last decades before
the conquest. Those sites, usually called *oppida* by archaeologists of the
late La Tène, were the nearest thing that iron age Europe ever got to
towns, and at a pinch Caesar could occasionally refer to them as *urbes*
if he wanted to stress his achievements, but they were probably little
more than clusters of houses and compounds gathered together behind
huge earthworks.[23] Whether he lived on an isolated farm or in a hillfort,
our Aeduan would have been brought up in a house built out of posts,
wattle and daub, and the only goods of Roman manufacture he would
have been likely to have seen would have been the pottery vessels called
amphorae in which Mediterranean wine was imported. Caesar's description of Gallic society probably applied as closely to the Aedui as to any
group.[24] Nobles and druids ruled over a commons, whose lot was hardly
better than that of slaves. The power of the warrior nobles derived from
their birth, their wealth, the number of clients they could protect and
muster, and their reputation among their peers. The druids' influence
derived from their possession of arcane knowledge, their monopoly of
cult and their authority to settle disputes. But those disputes divided
the society that Caesar described at every level, and the power of any
noble family was anything but secure and entrenched. Archaeology
adds to this picture an impression of the growing scale of that power
over the last three centuries BC, expressed in steady agricultural expansion, in the construction of more and more massive timber and earth
ramparts, and in the production of iron tools and weapons in unparal-
leled quantities.[25] It is difficult to detect archaeological traces of the
elites described by Caesar, whether because their status was maintained
in ways which left no trace, like the magnificent sacrifices and funerals,
and distributions of food, wine and coins described by classical sources,[26]
or because their power was expressed in communal projects, such as warfare or the construction of the huge, elaborate fortifications of the *oppida*.
But the rich burials that are attested from some areas reinforce the

23 On late La Tène settlements, see chapter 4 below.
24 Caesar *de Bello Gallico* 6.11–19. On the need to distinguish his account carefully from
   those refering to the Gauls of earlier time (or of different areas), see Nash (1976a).
   On the problems of reconstructing late La Tène society from a combination of
   Caesarian ethnography and archaeological evidence, see Ralston (1988), Haselgrove
   (1988) and Woolf (1993d), dissenting from the views of Crumley (1974) and Nash
   (1976b), (1978a), (1978b), (1981). On the reliability of Caesar, cf. Stevens (1952),
   Rambaud (1966), Collins (1972) and especially Buchsenschutz and Ralston (1986).
25 Woolf (1993c).
26 E.g. Caesar *de Bello Gallico* 6.15–19, Strabo *Geographia* 4.2.3, Athenaeus *Deipnosophistai*
   4.150–4. For discussion and interpretation of these customs, see Daubigney (1979).

impression created by the literary evidence of the magnitude and pre-
cariousness of the power that might be amassed by able individuals.[27]

That way of life came to a sudden end with Caesar's conquest of
Gaul. The sequence of events that followed was complex, and varied
considerably from region to region, but among the Aedui, a new city
began to be built within a few years of the conquest, on the site of the
oppidum of Bibracte.[28] One of the chief objects of the current excavations on Mont Beuvray is to discover the precise relationship of this city
to its late La Tène predecessor, which it replaced around the end of the
last century BC as well as to the new town of Augustodunum some
twenty kilometres away. Despite the enormous amount of archaeological research conducted both on Mont Beuvray and at Autun, severe
problems of chronology make it difficult to trace this evolution in detail,[29] but some contrasts stand out. Both iron age Bibracte and Roman
Autun were originally enclosed by very extensive defences, probably
serving more symbolic than practical defensive functions in both cases.
The late La Tène inner rampart of Bibracte was five kilometres long
– a larger outer circuit has only just been discovered – enclosing some
135 hectares with a ditch and a wall made of earth heaped over a timber
frame, held together with iron nails a foot long, and finished off with a
stone facing and an elaborate gatehouse of the type known as a *Zangentor*.
The defences as a whole closely resemble those found on fortified sites
throughout late la Tène Europe.[30] Some parts of this were demolished
and the ditch filled at some time after the conquest, but over most
of its length the rampart survives today. The Augustan circuit wall of
Augustodunum was six kilometres and enclosed about 200 hectares,

27 E.g. Metzler *et al.* (1991) especially 158–74. See also Ferdière and Villard (1993).
   Burials on this scale are not known from every region of Gaul, but it is not safe to
   assume that powerful individuals were only present in some areas. Much of the literary
   evidence for their activity concerns the Auvergne, where no rich graves of the second
   iron age have so far been found comparable to those of the north east or the Berry.
   Chances of recovery and the existence of a variety of alternative means of establishing
   status probably both played a part. For surveys of late La Tène burial practices, see
   Collis (1977) and more recently Cliquet *et al.* (1993).
28 Goudineau and Peyre (1993).
29 Duval *et al.* (1990) discuss the problems of the chronology of the late La Tène period
   in France. The situation is a little better for the succeeding period, known as Gallo-
   romaine précosé, as it is possible to date sites on the basis of the ceramics used in
   military camps known to have been occupied for short periods. But as Wightman
   (1977) and Goudineau (1989, 95–118) make clear, many problems remain. On the
   difficulties posed by coinage as a basis of chronology before the middle of the first
   century AD, see Nash (1978c). In addition, the earliest phases of many Gallo-Roman
   towns have been largely obliterated, either by the more substantial buildings constructed from the middle of the first century AD, or by later building (Février *et al.*
   1980, 53–66).
30 Collis and Ralston (1976), Ralston (1981).

but it was very different to the defences of Bibracte. Built of stone, it had more than fifty towers and was entered via monumental stone gates. We know next to nothing of the internal organization of Bibracte in the late La Tène period, but if it resembled other *oppida* of the same period, we might expect post-built structures in compounds and an absence of monumental architecture.[31] After the conquest, houses began to be constructed on Bibracte, that employed Roman materials like masonry and tile and resembled Mediterranean houses in their design, but whereas in Augustodunum the houses were arranged in blocks marked out by an orthogonal street plan, articulated in Italian fashion on two axial streets, the *cardo* and the *decumanus*, the houses on Roman Bibracte were more haphazardly arranged. Differences in relief provide part of the explanation: although the site of Autun is not level, Bibracte is on a mountain top. But topography cannot explain all the contrasts between the two cities. From the first Augustodunum had a forum, a theatre and an amphitheatre, and temples and a school, too, by the middle of the first century AD, whereas Bibracte had at most a temple complex with perhaps some sort of forum, although uncertainty surrounds the nature and chronology of the earliest structures on the site of the Gallo-Roman temple. Mont Beuvray has produced no public inscriptions, while Autun has produced over 150, admittedly over a much longer period of occupation. Connected to this is a difference in burial rite: at Autun, as at most Roman cities, the dead were buried in cemeteries outside the city's sacred limits, while at Bibracte there are burials within the inhabited area, often in the remains of imported wine *amphorae*.[32]

Iron age Bibracte became a Roman city and then was supplanted by the Augustan new town within a single lifetime (just), but the cultural changes involved were complex. Roman Bibracte epitomizes the problems facing attempts to understand these changes: we know enough to be sure that Romanization was more complex than simply the rejection of one cultural system in preference for another one, but the chronological problems posed by the archaeology make it very difficult to disentangle the changes in detail, and it is not immediately obvious why change proceeded in some areas rather than others. Why, for example, was domestic architecture transformed, but no town planning or public building undertaken? Why did the Aedui adopt the Roman taste for wine, but not Roman taboos about disposal of the dead? For enlightenment on these complexities, it is natural to turn to those anthropologists and archaeologists who have made special studies of cultural change.

31 Cf. Woolf (1993b), Collis (1984), Audouze and Buchsenschutz (1988).
32 Laubenheimer (1991, 23–5) provides a map, but cautions that many *amphorae* may be mis-classified as funerary deposits.

Anthropologists and archaeologists use the concept of culture as a way of making sense of the diversity of human societies that cannot be expressed simply in terms of biological variation. It is a finer tool than the concept of civilization, because it allows societies to be compared in other respects than simply in terms of their relative moral worth, or in terms of how developed, advanced, or complex they are supposed to be. But since describing a way of life is a more complicated process than deciding how civilized a group is, it is very difficult to define culture in a way acceptable to all of those who use it professionally,[33] definitions differing according to the sources and methods used and the preoccupations of the analyst. Since for present purposes a loose definition is most useful, I shall define Roman culture as the range of objects, beliefs and practices that were characteristic of people who considered themselves to be, and were widely acknowledged as, Roman. Roman culture thus includes characteristic styles of pottery, building materials and costume; particular beliefs about the dead, tastes in beverages, and notions about education; customs such as baking bread instead of making porridge, building stone monuments instead of earthworks, and competing with one's neighbours through Latin declamations, rather than on the battlefield. Yet the definition must be even more complex than this, since Roman culture was not static and its composition was never a matter of consensus. Over the centuries in which the identity 'Roman' was felt to be important, ways of eating, ways of dealing with the dead, styles of education and so forth underwent many transformations. Porridge was replaced by bread as the staple in the second century BC, and inhumation by cremation and then again by inhumation. Often the acceptance as 'Roman' (or at least as not 'un-Roman') of some new style or practice – marble statues, silk clothes, homosexuality – entailed debate and conflict. Becoming Roman was not a matter of acquiring a ready-made cultural package, then, so much as joining the insiders' debate about what that package did or ought to consist of at that particular time.[34]

Most cultural analysis attempts to understand particular cultural traits by relating them to other features of that society. Practices that might seem strange when taken in isolation appear meaningful when seen 'in context'. For example, the presence of weapons in some iron age burials makes more sense when related to the martial virtues associated with the late La Tène elite, to the importance of funerals, to the nature of sanctuary deposits, to the extent to which individuals had to win and

33 For contrasting views, cf. Geertz (1973), Leach (1976), Sahlins (1976).
34 Barratt (1997) for some suggestive thoughts on this subject.

earn status, and to the high level of conflict within and between iron age communities. Even if we cannot ever completely enter into the thought world of iron age Gaul, we can at least see how some practices were related to each other in systematic and repetitive ways, even if we do not know how far Gauls were conscious of it, beyond a vague sensation that each element in some way 'made sense' or 'fitted'. Anthropologists have made various attempts to describe this patterned nature of culture, writing of cultural or symbolic systems, folk models or mental structures, and comparing culture to language.[35] Recently attention has moved from culture as a system to the creative cultural activity of individuals.[36] Culture must be shared for it can have any meaning at all, and the fact that it is shared makes it a powerful medium for communication,[37] but what is shared is a set of associations or conventions, not rules, and individuals are free to conform, ignore or even change those conventions. For example, wearing the Roman *toga* had a specific set of associations, evoking adulthood, citizenship, or peace according to context, and not wearing a *toga* was a conventional sign of mourning. On the other hand, a failure to wear a *toga* might also be taken as a sign that one was a barbarian or hopelessly currupted by *luxuria*. Failure to conform might therefore signify ignorance, but equally it might be taken as a wilful neglect of propriety. If cultural expertise is *savoir faire*, then the cultural expert is not someone who never gives offence, but rather is like the archetypical English gentleman who never gives offence unintentionally.

But culture is more than just a tool. Although culture may be used strategically, to achieve particular ends, it also influences the nature of those ends.[38] Eumenius' speech provides a good example. Mastery of Roman oratorical culture provided him with a medium to communicate with Constantius, and perhaps to persuade him. His education provided him with wide resources ranging from historical references to stylistic devices, together with the ability to select from them and deploy them in a way he knew would appeal both to his fellow Aeduan citizens and to the Caesar. But his very desires – to monumentalize

---

35 E.g. Geertz (1973), Basso and Selby (1976) for cultural and symbolic systems; Holy and Stuchlik (1980) for folk models; Lévi-Strauss (1963) for mental structures. The analogy with language is important in all work deriving from the French structuralist school, e.g. Lévi-Strauss (1963), Leach (1976) and in a different way in Ardener (1971), but cf. Connerton (1989) for an important critique.

36 E.g. Sperber (1975), Bourdieu (1977), Giddens (1984). Ortner (1984) provides a clear account of recent trends in this direction.

37 Smith (1966), Leach (1976).

38 Sahlins (1976) makes this important point in a critique of utilitarian and especially Marxist theories of culture.

Autun, to support education and to win favour among the Aedui and at court – were a product of Eumenius' cultural identity. Mastery of Roman culture gave him the means to achieve his ambitions, but also played a part in determining what those ambitions were. Likewise, the selection of one pottery vessel rather than another, might be made to express a discriminating taste, or to accompany new styles of food preparation or serving, but like education, that pottery might also come to represent an object of desire for its own sake.[39] Two conclusions can be drawn. First, culture has a degree of autonomy, and does not simply respond to other social forces. Second, the practices, beliefs and things out of which culture is comprised are interconnected to the extent that it is not always easy to pick and choose, to select what is strategically useful while rejecting other elements outright. The things and ideas that we term Gallo-Roman culture were somehow bound up into a package. Jullian provided what is still the fullest characterization of this cultural package in a two-volume excursus inserted into the narrative of his *Histoire de la Gaule*.[40] Volume five dealt with 'état matériel', taken to comprise population, urbanism, settlement, agriculture and land use, production, exchange and the distribution of wealth, while volume six covered 'état moral', treating religion, language, education, art, family life and social relations, before concluding with a study of local and regional diversity and an assessment of the impact of Rome on Gaul. For Jullian, the interconnectedness of 'la civilisation gallo-romaine' derived from the unity of the civilizing process, as manifested in every sphere of life. It is less easy for cultural anthropologists to explain how it is that cultures cohere, and how that interconnectedness affects processes of cultural change.

Much energy has been devoted to attempting to explain cultural change. If culture were just a tool, cultural change might be explicable simply as an adaptive strategy. Naturally, cultures are constrained or influenced by their historical contexts, and since most comprise a range of symbols and principles, change often takes the form of a shift in their relative importance.[41] Many anthropologists have thus treated cultural

39 On the strategic use of material culture, see Hodder (1982), (1989), Miller (1982), (1985), and for the closely related debate on the uses of style, see Conkey and Hastorf (1990).
40 Volumes 5 and 6, together entitled *La civilisation gallo-romaine*, were both published in 1920. The scope of this account has never been rivalled, not even by Grenier's (1931–60) account of Gallo-Roman archaeology, volumes 1, 3 and 4 of which concentrate on military and urban structures and monuments. Volume 2, *l'Archéologie du sol*, is the least comprehensive and is largely devoted to roads and other means of communications.
41 Leach (1954) is the classic description of alternative models of society co-existing in the same culture. Salzman (1980) shows the strategic utility of this feature of culture.

change as a product of contacts and exchanges between different cultures. This approach has some drawbacks. Although it is true that the beliefs and artefacts of a culture are to some degree associated in a systematic way, it is misleading to think that watertight cultures exist in such a definite sense that they, rather than individuals and communities, can be treated as the primary units of analysis.[42] The stability of cultures tends thus to be overstressed when the real problem is not why do some cultures change, but rather why, given the cultural creativity of humans, do other cultures appear to have remained relatively fixed for long periods of time. It is also easy to underestimate the capacity of communities to appropriate new goods and invest them with new values. The adoption of tea drinking in Europe is a good example of how an item may be detached from one cultural system and incorporated into a new one.[43]

But with these caveats, investigations carried out by anthropologists into what has often been termed acculturation,[44] provide many insights and have already inspired a number of studies of Roman provincial cultures.[45] Studies of acculturation focus on interactions between different cultures, and seek to identify the mechanisms through which components of one culture are incorporated into another, directing attention to the personnel and institutions involved, the nature of the contacts, the items transferred, factors which accelerate or retard the process and those features of cultures that make them particularly receptive or resistant to change. For example, some studies have shown that new artefacts are often incorporated into existing ways of life long before new ideas or customs.[46] The Roman wine amphorae found at iron age

42 See Hodder (1978) for a critique of the culture-historical paradigm in archaeology.
43 For this example, and discussion of many relevant issues, see Sahlins (1988).
44 On acculturation, Bee (1974) chapter 4 and Wachtel (1974) provide the clearest accounts. Bohannon and Plog (1967) collect key essays which illustrate the development of the idea. For earlier formulations, see Redfield et al. (1936) and Broom et al. (1954). Like many approaches adopted by archaeologists from neighbouring disciplines, acculturation is no longer a major focus of research among anthropologists, although some of the issues involved continue to attract attention, for example in studies of ethnicity, tradition and symbolism.
45 Brandt and Slofstra (1983), Blagg and King (1984), Barrett et al. (1989), Blagg and Millett (1990), Wood and Queiroga (1992) collect various papers largely on the north-west provinces and many of them drawing on these approaches. Bartel (1980), Dyson (1985) and several of the contributors to Miller and Steffen (1977) make suggestive use of modern analogies for the Roman experience. On Romanization and acculturation in general, see Slofstra (1983), Bartel (1985), Okun (1989a, 10–27). Many of the earliest of these studies were more suggestive and programmatic than substantive, but important insights have emerged from more recent work (Woolf 1992a). The best application to France is probably Haselgrove (1990a).
46 Renfrew (1975) for the original distinction, van der Leeuw (1983) on more specialized application of information processing to the archaeological study of acculturation.

French sites provide a fair example of goods that were widely used, but in social settings far removed from that of wine drinking in Italian society.[47] Other studies have emphasized the key roles played by cultural brokers, whether they are traditional authorities or more marginal figures whose prominence is due primarily to their position as mediators.[48] It has also been shown how the nature of the societies in contact affects cultural change. Colonial powers are often known to locals only through a contact culture – military, missionary or settler, for example – which often represents only a selective view of metropolitan society or even aspects of it that only exist as ideals back home.[49] The nature of the indigenous society also plays a part in determining the end-product of these changes, retarding or accelerating change, or in determining which areas of culture are most affected.[50] There is, however, a tendency for such studies to focus on cultural homogenization, sometimes seen as inevitable, rather than on the creation of difference.[51] Many of the earliest studies of acculturation treated the impact of colonialism on non-European societies, and this may have led to an overemphasis on cultural change as imitation, but it is important to remember that even in the context of imperialism, alternative responses are possible, such as the rejection of elements identified as alien or the appropriation of alien symbols by investing them with new meanings.[52] Arguably, when contacts

47 Fitzpatrick (1989), Woolf (1993c), cf. the thoughtful comments of Willis (1994) on the appropriation of Roman imports into Britain.
48 Curtin (1984, 1–59) discusses the variety of mechanisms which exchange between different cultures may be managed. On cultural brokers and other mediators, see Wolf (1956), Fallers (1955), Silverman (1965) and Löffler (1971). Cultural brokers may also be examples of 'marginal men', individuals whose power derives from their contact with the outside, rather than is threatened by it: Geertz (1960), Firth (1965), Press (1969). Various forms of collusion and competition between the partners in these exchanges are attested, just as cultural change can strengthen or weaken existing regimes of power.
49 See Foster (1960) for the notion of contact culture. The idea of frontier societies reproducing the ideals of the metropole is exemplified by several papers in Bohannon and Plog (1967) and is a theme of Kopytoff (1987).
50 For the concept, see Broom et al. (1954). Steward (1951) suggests different ways in which the distinction between areas of culture that change and those that do not can be viewed. For the application of this idea in the Roman North West, cf. Blagg and Millett (1990), Millett (1990a).
51 This focus of interest has led some archaeologists to postulate that interaction, broadly defined, generally leads to cultural convergence, e.g. Renfrew (1973), Renfrew and Cherry (1986). Compare Kopytoff's (1987, 10) definition of an ecumene, a culture area, as 'a region of persistant cultural interaction and exchange.' While interaction of one kind or another has been a necessary pre-condition of cultural convergence where it has occurred, other outcomes are possible since some forms of interaction, for example competition for scarce resources, can lead individuals to emphasize cultural difference and boundaries. Hodder (1978), (1982), drawing on Barth (1969), notes examples of interaction leading to cultural divergence in conditions of ethnic or social conflict.
52 Cf. Clifford and Marcus (1986) and Stewart and Shaw (1994). The similarities between the discourse of modernization and that of civilizing are evident.

become intense enough, the only strategy not available is to ignore similarities and differences between cultures.

Understanding cultural change requires a more sophisticated notion of how cultures are organized than is used in most studies of acculturation. Links between the different components of a culture derive in part from the everyday connections between ideals, practice and things already discussed. For instance, the characteristic forms of Roman tableware are partly influenced by Roman diet, and the construction of public bath-houses in towns relates to conceptions of cleanliness, ideals of municipal benefaction and the adoption of new public and social rituals. But at another level, some items seem more central to a cultural system than others. Goods, it seems, can more easily be transferred than can information, so architecture was easier for the inhabitants of Roman Bibracte to adopt than the ways in which Romans in Italy would have inhabited and used those houses. Even among beliefs, some seem to be more central than others. One factor which does seem to preserve the integrity of a cultural system is a strong self-description, often supported by ideological and institutional controls. For example, one of the most conservative cultures studied by anthropologists is that of the Amish, whose self-identity is backed up by religion, a rigid patriarchal social structure and strong social sanctions against non-conformers.[53] Other cultural systems are also characterized by self-definitions that equate their own culture with Culture and local values with Truth.[54] The notion of Civilization, as opposed to barbarism or savagery, is another example of such a belief, and the Roman version of this ideal, *humanitas*, was a central component of Roman culture under the early empire.

III   An imperial civilization

Eumenius' speech in Autun marks, in some senses, the end of Gallo-Roman civilization at least as it was characterized by Jullian. Constantius Chlorus' son, Constantine the Great, by converting to Christianity, added a new component to Roman cultural style that would eventually transform the cultural system that had grown and developed in the western empire over the first three centuries AD. Like all historical watersheds, that division is a little arbitrary and not at all clear cut. Fourth- and fifth-century Gaul even experienced an expansion of classical culture.

53 Hostetler (1964).
54 On ancient ethnocentrism, cf. Lattimore's (1962, 487) comparison of the Greek notion of the *oikoumene* with the Roman idea of *orbis terrarum* and the Chinese concept of *T'ien Hsia*.

The career of Ausonius of Bordeaux illustrates how education continued to be widely, perhaps even more widely, available in the fourth
century, and how the proximity of Caesars and full emperors both on
the Rhine frontier and in northern Italy opened up unprecedented
opportunities to the aristocracies of fourth-century Gaul.[55] If the towns
did not recover their second-century magnificence, some of the villas
of the fourth century were more splendid than ever. Even in the fifth
and sixth centuries, the works of Sidonius Apollinaris and Venantius
Fortunatus show how classical culture of a sort might persist under
barbarian kings.[56] Nevertheless, something had changed with the Christianization of the empire, marked by the appearance, alongside the continuing classical tradition of late antique Gaul, of religious texts, the
works of men like Salvian of Marseilles, Faustus of Riez, Caesarius of
Arles and Gregory of Tours.

The growth of Christian culture differed from the growth of Roman
imperial culture in important ways. It had grown up within the empire,
but had already spread beyond it before the conversion of Constantine,
and continued not to be limited by the boundaries of imperial power.
Christianity's independence of the empire was most graphically illustrated when it survived the latter's collapse to become the most important integrating force of early mediaeval western Europe. Christianity's
power in this period did not derive from a centralized ecclesiastical
organization. Nothing of the sort had existed before Constantine, and
in the West the papacy only achieved the status of a European power
in the eleventh century, mirroring the political growth of secular lords.
The success of Christianity is the classic illustration, then, of the autonomy of culture. Its history contrasts sharply with that of Roman imperial
culture. Classical culture flourished in Gaul as long as the empire did,
and then only subsisted as long as barbarian kings attempted to run their
states on Roman lines.[57]

Culture and imperialism have been related in many different ways. It
is easy to forget, if only the Roman empire and the modern world are
considered, that cultural systems do not always grow in the context of
conquest, and are not always the result of subject peoples imitating
their new masters. Christianity provides one counter-example, but there
are others. Sanskritization comprised a series of social and religious
changes that were not consistently linked with political conquest, and

55 Matthews (1975, 56–87).
56 On fifth-century Gaul as an age of transition, see Matthews (1975, 307–51), Van Dam
    (1985), Drinkwater and Elton (1992). On Sidonius, see Stevens (1933), Harries (1994).
    On the end of classical culture in this period, see Haarhoff (1920) and Wood (1990).
57 Heather (1994).

Hellenization advanced in some areas without conquest or colonization, although Greek settlement, the conquests of Alexander and the Roman empire also played a part.[58] Even when conquest did provide the stimulus to cultural change, the conqueror's culture has not always been the dominant one, as is illustrated by the influence of Hellenistic culture on the Romans as they extended their power over the Greek world. Equally, although the expansion of Han culture was promoted by both conquest and colonization, when China was conquered first by the Mongols and later by the Manchus, they, too, were Sinicized. It was a peculiarity of Roman imperial culture that it was so closely linked to the fact of empire that it never extended beyond the limits of the territory under Roman political and military control. Individual items of Roman manufacture, to be sure, were imported by some neighbouring societies, but often put to very different uses by them,[59] and there is no sense that groups outside the empire developed a fascination with the totality of Roman culture that compares to Roman or Lycian fascination with Hellenism, let alone came to think of themselves as Roman. Understanding the nature of this linkage between empire and culture is the key to understanding the processes usually termed Romanization.

One feature of this linkage was the role played by Roman culture in bringing together the local elites of the empire into a unified ruling class. The process of admitting the leaders of conquered groups into the inner circle of the Roman elite had begun during the conquest of Italy, and Brunt has linked the extension of citizenship under the empire to efforts made by conquered elites to acquire Roman culture through imitation, so that their 'political assimilation corresponded to a cultural assimilation'.[60] Emulation in order to assimilate may have been one important means by which the culture of the empire was created, but Roman culture was not simply an elite culture, any more than imperial society was clearly divided into elite and commons. Literature,

58 Momigliano (1975) on Hellenization. On cultural change in the ancient world in general, cf. the conference papers published in *Rayonnement . . .* (1965), Pippidi (1976) and *Modes de Contacts . . .* (1983).

59 This distinction, and the notion of 'Romanization before the conquest' is discussed in full in chapter 7 below.

60 Brunt (1976, 169) provides the clearest study of this aspect of the process, and the best brief introduction to Romanization as a whole, although he makes it clear that his analysis is confined to local elites. Compare Gellner's (1983, 8–18) thesis that 'agroliterate' states were normally organized in this way, with a unified high culture and laterally separated low cultures, to Brunt's (1976, 165) idea that lower class groups in the Roman provinces remained divided by 'the persistence of old jealousies and rivalries,' although it is not clear that that the elites of neighbouring cities such as Vienne and Lyon, Pompeii and Nuceria, or Prusa and Nicodemia, did not share in the fierce rivalry felt by their citizenries. Cf. also the ideas of Galtung applied to the Roman world by Kunow (1990) and Alcock (1993, 18–19).

language, domestic architecture and tableware did not combine to mark a single divide across Gallo-Roman society. Cultures of exclusion operated at many levels of Roman society, from snobbery over grammar and pronunciation among the senatorial elite on down, and we might expect imperial culture to reflect this cultural differentiation as much as any cultural unity. It is also important to understand, if the adoption of Roman culture was a unifying process, why its progress was so uneven between different areas. One approach is to regard limited cultural change as an indication that one area or group had had less contact with Romans than others.[61] Variations in contact certainly played a part. Within the Roman West as a whole there is a clear contrast between Mediterranean regions, like Narbonensis, with Roman colonists and higher levels of urbanization which usually conform culturally fairly closely to Italian models, and more isolated inland areas, like central France, where cultural change is less evident. But varying levels of contact cannot explain the limited extent of cultural change throughout the Greek East, an area with long and intensive contacts with Romans and which was anything but isolated under the empire, while Judaism has long been seen as an important factor in determining the complex cultural map of the Roman Near East.[62] The experience of the East illustrates the drawbacks of viewing Roman culture as essentially a side effect of Roman power. Greek remained, after all, the language of power in the East, and Roman culture in the West cannot be understood without some explanation being offered for the success of Latin over other languages and Roman over other cultures.

One approach which does take the power of other cultures seriously is the idea that Roman culture is the product of a tension between Romanization and Resistance to it.[63] Roman provincial cultures, like that of Roman Gaul, comprised amalgams of elements derived from both pre-Roman, as well as Roman, traditions. Proponents of this approach argue that it is just as important to take account of the locally

61 Hence Brunt (1976) argues that greater concentrations of troops in the West accounted for higher levels of Romanization there than in the East, although when troops were billetted in major eastern cities the results were not always greater cultural assimilation (Isaac 1990, 268–82), while Roman colonies in the East were eventually hellenized (Millar 1990). On the Roman East, cf. also Macready and Thompson (1987). MacMullen (1984a), in a useful general discussion, also argues that Rome's subjects chose to imitate their rulers wherever and whenever they were able to do so.
62 Brunt (1976), Millar (1987).
63 Bénabou's (1976a) study of Africa, summarized in Bénabou (1976b), is the most sophisticated statement of this position, although it is implicit in many of the contributions to Pippidi (1976). Curchin (1991, 180–90) and Keay (1992) use, but do not discuss, the concept in relation to Spain. Garnsey (1978) provides a critique of Bénabou's thesis.

derived components of provincial cultures, as of those that are recognizably alien in origin. Just as the survival of Judaism does not indicate that the Jews were isolated from contact with Roman culture, so the survival of elements of pre-Roman culture in Gaul might indicate a conscious decision not to replace some aspect of pre-Roman culture. Elements derived from the late La Tène are not necessarily the result of an inability rather than of an unwillingness to change (although in some cases they might be), nor is the combination of new and old in Gallo-Roman culture necessarily the result of a failure to civilize on the part of the conquerors. All these points are valid as a critique of the concept of Romanization. But the solution adopted is to regard any 'failure' to adopt Roman culture whenever possible as resistance on the cultural plane, just as rebellion was resistance on the military plane.[64] In fact, the relationship proposed here between culture and power is far too simplistic. For a start, it is difficult to assess the cultural significance of artefacts like the hundreds of altars dedicated in the early third century AD in two shrines on either side of the southernmost mouth of the Rhine.[65] The altars were set up by local traders working the channel crossing and were inscribed in Latin, with the usual epigraphic conventions of the period, but to a local goddess, Nehalennia. The form of the cult suggests Romanization, the name of the goddess implies resistance, but the reason that the altars were set up was not to signal a particular view of the legitimacy of Roman rule, established in the area some three centuries earlier, but to thank the goddess for her protection during the dangerous sea voyages between Germany and Britain. The complex cultural genealogy of these altars tells us little about the working of Gallo-Roman culture in the third century AD, and their dedicators may have been quite unaware of it. After all, 'Roman' culture itself drew on Greek, Etruscan and other Italian roots, and the iron age cultures of Gaul had included elements drawn from Britain, Germany and Spain as well as from contacts with Mediterranean societies.

Even at an earlier period, the relationship between the adoption of Roman culture and the acceptance of Roman rule was not as simple as the dichotomy of Romanization and Resistance might suggest. It is very

64 Bénabou (1976b, 368) writes that 'le terme de résistance n'a valeur ici que de concept unificateur', a device to promote a unified view of the culture of Roman Africa, instead of marginalizing 'non-Roman' elements. But in practice his analysis sets military and cultural 'resistance' on the same level and treats all 'traditional' elements as signs of resistance. The implication that adoption of Roman culture indicates political assimilation has much in common with the view of Brunt (1976) and others that Roman culture operated, as it were ideologically, to underwrite the solidarity of the imperial ruling classes.

65 Hondius-Crone (1955), Stuart (1971) summarized in Hassall (1978).

difficult to divide Gauls into pro-Roman and anti-Roman camps in any period after Caesar's Gallic War, let alone to compare their political views with their cultural preferences,[66] but the series of rebellions against Roman rule in the mid-first century AD, seem to have been led largely by Gauls who were not only Roman citizens, many of them even second and third generation citizens, but who had also held positions of responsibility in the imperial administration. Tacitus describes how the revolt of AD 21 was led by Julius Florus and Julius Sacrovir, both noblemen descended from men enfranchized for their good services to Rome. Although a number of tribes were involved, the revolt began among the Treveri and the Aedui, arguably those tribes which had undergone the greatest cultural change since the conquest.[67] The instigator of the revolt of AD 68 which brought Nero down was Julius Vindex, said to be the descendant of Aquitanian nobility, but also a second generation Roman senator and the governor of a Gallic province.[68] The uprising was partly that of a Roman governor against a despotic emperor, but both the nature of the support he mustered and the character of the hostile reaction he incited from the Rhine legions suggest the revolt was understood as a Gallo-Roman conflict by at least some participants on both sides.[69] The possibility of freeing Gaul from the empire was certainly canvassed in the chaos following Nero's death, and again the leaders of both sides carried the *nomen* Julius, indicating that they or more usually their ancestors had been granted citizenship during Caesar's Gallic War or in the reign of Augustus.[70] Whatever the situation in other provinces, military resistance in Gaul was not linked to a rejection of Roman culture. It has even been suggested that a common factor in a number of early imperial revolts throughout the empire may have been the stresses and strains set up by too rapid cultural and social change.[71] Whether or not that is the case, the idea of

66 Wightman (1976a) makes the attempt, but in the absence of detailed historical accounts there is a danger of circularity in trying to infer political views from material culture.
67 Tacitus *Annales* 40–7. On the Gallic revolts, see Grenier (1936), Syme (1958, 458–63), Christopherson (1968). On the Treveri, see Clarke (1965) and especially Wightman (1970).
68 Chilver (1957), Brunt (1959), Hainsworth (1962), Wightman (1976a) on the events.
69 Dyson (1975, 158–61) and Matthews (1975, 350) capture the complex nature of the revolt.
70 Drinkwater (1978) on the Gallic Julii. On the Batavian revolt and the notion of a separatist *imperium Galliarum*, see Tacitus *Histories* 4.12–37, 54–79, 5.14–26, with Brunt (1960). Tacitus *Hist.* 4.55 relates that the leaders of the revolt claimed ancestry from pre-conquest royalty or nobility and in one case from Julius Caesar. It is more certain that many were rich, had citizenship and held military commands.
71 Dyson (1971) with (1975). Corbier (1988) probably overstresses the importance of taxation as an immediate cause of revolt. A study of Roman descriptions of revolt is probably needed before any firm conclusions can be drawn from the literary evidence.

cultural resistance needs rethinking. The predicament of first-century Gallo-Roman aristocrats like Gaius Julius Vindex was that their power depended on their position as mediators between Gauls and Romans, and so in a sense they needed to present themselves as the friends of both.[72] Their 'resistance' to the threat to their power posed by Rome, had been to use Roman culture against the Romans, to win power in the new order. The worst situation they feared was one in which they were forced to choose whether to be Gauls or Romans. If the commons wanted to revolt badly enough, it could find alternative leaders, like the mysterious Mariccus, a Boian commoner who took advantage of the civil war of AD 68–9 to proclaim himself a god and champion of Gaul, until the Aeduan aristocracy called in Vitellius' troops to help them suppress the revolt.[73] The dilemma is best documented at the other end of the empire, but in the same period, by the case of Josephus, a hellenized Jew caught between Romans and Zealots in the Jewish War. Much of his writing, in particular the account of the war and his auto-biography, is the product of his struggle to keep faith with both Judaism and Hellenism and to remain loyal both to Rome and to his people. Josephus shows that it is even too simplistic to try to present provincial nobles as bent on retaining power under whatever cultural guise was necessary. Gallo-Roman nobles may well have felt as Gallic and as Roman as Josephus felt Jewish and Greek, while provincial elites everywhere must have been torn between loyalty to their rulers and responsibility to their people. The tensions between Gallic and Roman culture existed at this level, in the dilemmas of individuals caught in the middle, rather than in the clash of civilizing policies and opposition to them.[74]

More fundamentally, Resistance may be an inappropriate concept because the notion of Romanization itself is fundamentally flawed as an heuristic tool. The critique of studies of Romanization that has led some scholars to make use of the notion of Resistance correctly identified a series of biases and omissions in accounts of the creation of an imperial culture in the Latin West, but grouping together the missing

---

72 For a very clear analysis of a similar predicament, cf. Fallers (1955).

73 Tacitus *Hist.* 2.61.

74 The issue has become entangled with the question of whether or not the Romans had a deliberate policy of 'Romanizing' their subjects. Bénabou (1976b) argues that this was the case, but for strong objections, see Brunt (1976), Garnsey (1978), Blagg and Millett (1990), arguing for emulation as the main motor. The approach adopted here is to reject the opposition of compulsion and choice, *pace* MacMullen (1984a), and instead to explore the roles played by Romans, Gauls and those who were in some sense both, in constructing Gallo-Roman culture. For further discussion of the issue of agency, see chapter 3 below.

elements under the heading Resistance only serves to entrench further the concept of Romanization. Understanding the relationship between Roman power and Roman culture involves developing a more nuanced picture of power in Roman Gaul, one that admits the power of Nehalennia and the dilemma of a mediating aristocracy in time of revolt. Conflicts existed not just between Romans and Gauls, but also between and within Gallo-Roman tribes and their elites. Eumenius' attempt to confound his enemies among the Aedui by invoking imperial aid to restore the premier school of Latin rhetoric in Gaul illustrates how far the relationship between culture and power had changed in the course of the principate. Exploring that process is the subject of this book.

2 Roman power and the Gauls

I Imperialisms, modern and ancient

Power is a slippery concept. A generation before Julius Caesar's conquest of the North, Vercingetorix' father was ejected by the Arverni for aiming at supreme power, and at about the same time the Aedui and the Sequani contested for supreme power in Gaul.[1] We know little about how these conflicts were conducted or even what form supreme power or hegemony would have taken in this period. Roman rule, however, changed both in the methods of competition and in the prizes that could be won by it. This too was an aspect of Roman cultural style in Gaul. Gauls were not passive objects of Roman rule, but had been implicated by Rome in new configurations of power, new complexes of domination. In so far as a power structure existed it was constituted by the regular forms these contests took.[2]

The career of Titus Sennius Solemnis illustrates the nature of this power structure.[3] The inscription through which we know this third-century Gallo-Roman aristocrat originally formed part of a typical honorific monument, a statue set up in AD 238 in a public area of his home city, by decree of the senate of the free community of the Viducasses,

1 Caesar *de Bello Gallico* 7.4; 6.12.
2 Giddens (1984) offers one way of conceptualizing how social structure can emerge through the routinization of human actions. The idea seems close to Abrams' (1978, 31) useful notion of a complex of domination, defined as 'an ongoing and at least loosely integrated struggle to constitute and elaborate power'. Societies, in other words, may be thought of as more or less stable battlegrounds and the balance of forces at any time constitutes social power. That dynamic conception of social power may also be related to Foucault's emphasis on the creative and productive aspects of power, and rejection of the notion of power as something that may be possessed and that acts primarily to prevent action. Naturally there are also marked differences in the ways these authorities treat power, society and culture, but I shall not enter into those debates except to signal my (eclectic) understanding of the term to denote the dynamic and productive aspect of a social configuration. The expansion of Roman power over Gaul thus denotes the creation of a society / a complex of domination / a social configuration in which and by which power is organized in a Roman way.
3 Pflaum (1948) on *CIL* XIII 3162.

24

who lived around Caen in modern Normandy, after Solemnis had been voted the honour by the Council of the Three Gallic Provinces. The decree and the vote were commemorated on the main inscription on the marble statue base, which also enumerated Solemnis' impressive series of offices and priesthoods held among the Viducasses and at the Council, and his benefactions to both. Alongside these civic and provincial offices and acts of euergetism less formal distinctions were also noted. Solemnis had become the client and friend of two governors of the province, whose letters, commemorating the services he had performed for them, were inscribed on either side of the statue base. Solemnis deserved their favour. As high priest at the Altar of Rome and Augustus at Lyon he had headed off an attempt by some members of the Council of the Three Gauls to impeach one of them, Tiberius Claudius Paulinus, who had gone on to become a governor in Britain and commander of the Sixth Legion based at York: the inscription records the promise he made Solemnis to give him a post on his staff, the salary for which he sent in advance along with other presents. The second letter was from Paulinus' successor as governor of Lugdunensis, Aedinius Julianus, who had been in post at the time when Solemnis exercized his influence over the Council on Paulinus' behalf. Solemnis' action had really paid dividends in this case since Julianus had gone on to become Praetorian Prefect. Seizing his opportunity, Solemnis had visited Julianus in Rome and obtained from him a letter of recommendation to the current governor, this letter being the second document inscribed on the statue base.

By the early third century competitions for power and influence in Gaul had become part of wider contests. Few were as successful as Solemnis: the patronage of a Praetorian Prefect was second only to the patronage dispensed by emperors and their relatives, and whether or not through his influence, Solemnis also achieved a military post in Africa. Solemnis' career also gives us a feel for the texture of Roman power in the provinces. On the one hand power was entrenched in the rational-legal structures of cities and empire, with the councils and magistracies appropriate to each level from the duovirate of the Viducasses up to the praetorian prefecture. But alongside the formal system ran a patrimonial system articulated by patronage and the exchange of favours. Both systems could be admitted (and indeed boasted of) and they interlocked, so that together the empire of cities and the empire of friends constituted Roman power in the provinces.[4] A cultural history of Gaul

4 Saller (1982) for these two forms of social organization, discussed in Weberian terms. Veyne (1976, 411–15) couches his notion of 'le double fonctionnement de la société

depends on some understanding of how this configuration of power was created. Put more concretely, it is important to know the stages by which the world of Vercingetorix's father was transformed into the world of Titus Sennius Solemnis. The aim of this chapter is to chart the changing geography of Roman power in Gaul.

The expansion of configurations of power of this kind is usually termed imperialism. The Roman term *imperium* is probably better translated as 'power' than as 'empire',[5] and many of the connotations now evoked by the term 'imperialism' are inappropriate in a Roman context. But much may be gained by comparing the expansion of Rome with other imperialisms, so long as the immense differences between the Roman world and that of the nineteenth and twentieth centuries are borne in mind.[6] Modern imperialisms provided one context within which ethnographers first began to catalogue and describe systematically the peoples they regarded as primitives, and later the development of anthropology was enabled and sponsored by colonial administrations, resulting in a series of studies of the impact of imperial rule on societies very different to those of Europe and the West.[7] Perhaps the most striking impression to be gained from those studies is that there is no single or uniform experience of imperialism. At one extreme, some societies experienced extreme dislocation. Customary rights to use and inhabit land were often converted into property rights, and sometimes vested in only a few individuals within that society, or in outsiders, thus converting tribesmen into peasants and traditional leaders into land-lords and/or the agents of the state. The imposition of taxation and the economic activities of entrepreneurs or simply monetarization have caused hardship and debt, and even where economic change has opened up new opportunities for some individuals, their new found wealth can be as disruptive as new found poverty. Individual members of the same society have often fared very differently, with the result that integration into a wider world has gone hand in hand with the disintegration of

romaine' in terms of the interplay of citizenship and friendship. Cf. also Murray (1991, 12) for an historical perspective of this characteristic of Roman society. Herman (1987), Millar (1983) and a number of the contributions to Wallace-Hadrill (1989a) explore ways in which the two systems could come into conflict.
5 Lintott (1980), Richardson (1991), showing the relatively late emergence of a territorial sense of the term.
6 Brunt (1965) provides a model analysis of this type.
7 No distinction is made here between different periods of modern imperialism, between military and political expansion and the growth of the world economy, nor between 'external' imperialism and the extension of the power of nation states within 'their own' territories. Although those distinctions would be vital in any systematic comparison of ancient and modern imperialisms, in this context at issue is the general effects of incorporation in wider systems of local societies and their members.

communities. On the other hand, not all societies have fallen to pieces upon incorporation into larger entities. Many groups seem actually to thrive within a new imperial context, making use of educational and economic opportunities to increase their standard of living and political entitlements without sacrificing what they valued most in the process. Without suggesting for a moment that imperialism should be regarded as benign, it is clear that not all subjects of empires have suffered equivalent fates. Key variables have included both the diversity of imperialisms and considerable contrasts between the societies incorporated. British and French imperialisms in Africa were very different, but equally British Africa also differed enormously from British India. At a more detailed level, a number of factors seem to have been important. The attitude of representatives of the imperial power to their subjects, the nature of the demands they made on them and the institutions they used to govern them all have influenced the impact of incorporation, while on the side of the subjects of empire the variables seem even more complex, ranging from patterns of land tenure and family structure to religion and the ways in which cultural identity was defined. Other factors might be mentioned – racism, disease, sexual politics – but the point is made. The experience of modern imperialism has been very diverse, and the significant variables complex and numerous.

Unfortunately we know little or nothing about some of what must have been key variables in Roman Gaul. The Gallic family, Gallic land tenure and customary law are matters for speculation. Even the most basic questions about iron age societies are matters of dispute – we do not know for certain whether or not Gallic polities are better described as states or as tribes, whether the Gauls had a concept of property or an hereditary aristocracy before they became part of an empire which took all these for granted. As a result, attempts to reconstruct the Gallic experience of Roman imperialism by detailed analogy with the Scottish Highlands after Enclosure, with Canadian Indians in contact with European trading companies, or with non-European societies drawn into monetary economies can never be more than suggestive.[8] But if detailed correspondences cannot be securely established, may more general resemblances be discerned? One popular approach has been to apply generalizing theories of imperialism developed for the modern world to the Roman empire, and in the case of Gaul a number of studies have been cast in the terminology of centre and periphery and based more or less closely on Immanuel Wallerstein's account of the expansion of

8 Hodder (1979), van der Leeuw (1983), Slofstra (1983), Wells (1974), Buchsenschutz and Ralston (1987).

Europe in the pre-modern and modern periods.[9] Wallerstein's work, which chronicled the rise of a global division of labour powered first by mercantilism and then by industrial capitalism, remains controversial among modern historians, and he himself limited its applicability to the modern (capitalist) period, before which he regarded 'world empires' as the main means by which extensive configurations of power were organized. Nevertheless, attempts have been made recently to show similar processes at work within Roman imperialism, despite the enormous differences between the economy of the Roman empire and that of modern Europe.[10] Roman expansion is not convincingly explained, however, as driven by a search for raw materials, cheap labour or new markets, and the distribution of Mediterranean goods in Gaul does not conform very closely to the patterning predicted by centre-periphery theory.[11] Modern historians have criticized world systems theories for economic determinism, for not providing an explanation of the diversity of imperialism and for not allowing the nature of 'peripheral' societies any historical significance. Much the same criticisms apply to centre and periphery accounts of Roman imperialism in Gaul.

Perhaps a safer course is to abandon the search for close analogies, but to bear these questions in mind when focusing on the peculiar features of the Gallic experience of being incorporated into a broader entity. Naturally it will be easier to characterize Roman imperialism than iron age Gallic societies, but Rome is not the only imperial power to be better documented than its victims.[12] Some very general expectations do emerge out of the anthropology of imperialism. It has been suggested, for example, that processes of incorporation force societies to adopt a more specialized role in the larger whole, and to develop mediating institutions between local communities and the centre of power.[13] It is also striking that empires impose not one but a variety of constraints on the societies they dominate, and that the different pace of these impositions means that there is no single moment of incorporation. Empires in any case are themselves changed in the course of their growth, giving rise to new tensions. Finally, the ideology of empire often leads rulers to treat different subjects in different ways. All these themes will recur in what follows.

9 E.g. Hingley (1982), Haselgrove (1987a), Nash (1987), Cunliffe (1988). For full bibliography and discussion, see Woolf (1992a), especially 351 note 5.
10 The issue is discussed more fully in Woolf (1990a). Cf. Millett (1990b) for similar points.
11 Woolf (1993c), drawing on Tchernia (1983), (1986), and Fitzpatrick (1989) *pace* Clemente (1974), Nash (1987), Cunliffe (1988).
12 Wolf (1982).   13 Wolf (1956).

II   Warfare and peace

Roman imperialism in Gaul is simply one fragment of the broader
history of the Roman conquest of the West, and it exemplifies all the
major themes of that history.[14] Republican interest in the area was
sporadic and often consequential on other campaigns – defensive actions against invading Carthaginians and Germans, wars of conquest in
Spain and police actions against the Ligurians of the Alps[15] – or else it
was driven by domestic political agendas.[16] Equally, the tools of imperialism were the usual ones of the period;[17] alliances were made, notably
with Marseilles, and were supplemented by the occasional major campaign and the construction of a road from Italy to Spain. But here, as
elsewhere, the republic found it difficult to limit her attention (and that
of her generals) to the coastal plains of the Mediterranean and following the wars of the 120s against the Arverni and Allobroges and the
invasion of the Cimbri and Teutones which rapidly followed them,
Rome's sphere of influence was extended up the lower Rhône valley
to Savoy and part way across the Gallic isthmus to Toulouse, forts
and garrisons were established, a colony was founded at Narbonne and
(perhaps a little later) a governor installed.[18] The result was a growing
awareness at Rome of events and groups in the interior of the continent,[19] and it was probably no surprise when Julius Caesar, in search of
an opportunity for conquests to rival those of Pompey, seized on one of
these reports to begin eight years of campaigning which eventually took
him as far as the Rhine and southern Britain. Subsequent campaigns
conducted by Caesar, Augustus and their lieutenants also conformed to
general patterns of Roman imperialism, as did the slower consolidation
in the latter part of Augustus' reign, and the eventual virtual atrophy of
the Roman advance along what was to become the German frontier.

But a bare narration of campaigns provides a poor account of the
extension of Roman power within Gaul. The aim of the pages that

14 Goudineau (1978) is the best account of the conquest of the South. Cf. also Dyson
   (1985, 126–73), Rivet (1988, 27–111) and most recently Hermon (1993) and Soricelli
   (1995). On non-Mediterranean Gaul, cf. Drinkwater (1983, 5–71). For Republican
   imperialism, cf. Badian (1968), Veyne (1975), Brunt (1978), Harris (1979) with North
   (1981) and more recently Harris (1984) and Rich (1993).
15 Ebel (1976), Dyson (1985).
16 Cf. Hermon (1993), stressing both competition between dynasts and the land question.
17 On the development of Roman infrastructure in the period, cf. Richardson (1976),
   Purcell (1990).
18 It is possible that governors began to be sent out regularly from the 120s, but Badian
   (1966) argues for a later date and Ebel (1976), less convincingly, for an earlier one.
19 Nash (1976a) on Poseidonius' activities and influence in this period. Cicero ad Att
   1.19; 1.20; 2.1 (all written in 60 BC) display at least an attempt to keep track of events
   in the interior.

follow is to pick out some of the main themes of that process, and to draw attention to three in particular: the sudden change in the nature of Roman goals and methods at the end of the last century BC (and its consequences for the Gauls); the ways in which Gallic energies and resources were harnessed to the new imperial configuration of power; and the mediating roles adopted by a remodelled Gallic elite in the course of these events.

Warfare nevertheless provides a good starting point. Roman historical tradition represented the growth of Roman power in terms of a series of victorious campaigns, alternating with periods of relative calm. Achievements (*res gestae*) of this kind were recorded in both the public tradition and that of the families of the successful generals, and were memorialized in speeches, on monuments like the trophy set up by Pompey to record his conquest of the Pyrennees, in the *Fasti Triumphales*, the public and authorized list of triumphs, and in written histories. In the pluralist political environment of the republic it was possible to claim that previous conquests had been left incomplete, but with the rise of the dynasts and an ideology of progressive expansion, Roman wars came to be seen as irreversible stages in the pacification of the world. The provinces, once conquered, were regarded as pacified, and major disturbances within them became if not unthinkable at least inadmissable.[20]

Yet fighting did continue. One way Romans dealt with this was to represent renewed warfare as revolts of limited significance. That tactic was pursued whenever possible.[21] We have only scattered references to fighting in Transalpina after the great campaigns of the 120s which culminated in two triumphs, but it is clear that it continued up until the eve of Caesar's command.[22] Caesar himself represented the final stage of his campaigns as the suppression of a revolt, although he had never campaigned against most of the tribes involved,[23] and despite his claim to have conquered Gaul already by 52 BC and to have restored order

---

20 Woolf (1993a).
21 Woolf (1993a). Cf. Thompson (1952) for a parallel case. Only in the most extreme cases were setbacks admitted, and then the blame was fixed on the commander, as happened when three legions and a province were lost in AD 9. A determined attempt was made to fix the blame for this on P. Quinctilius Varus (Velleius 2.117–8; Suetonius *Aug.* 23; Florus II.31–3; Dio 56.19). See Wells (1972, 238–9).
22 The historical record is patchy but notes conflicts in 107 and 106 in connection with the Cimbric migrations; campaigns against the Salluvii in 90; a triumph in 81 over 'Celtiberia ac Gallia'; campaigns fought by Flaccus, Manlius, Pompey and Fonteius in the 70s and major campaigns against the Allobroges in 66 and 61. See Goudineau (1978, 689–91) and Dyson (1985, 162–70) for details.
23 Caesar *de Bello Gallico* 7.43–4, 54, 59–63. On the propagandist nature of Caesar's *de Bello Gallico*, Cf. Stevens (1952), Rambaud (1966), Brunt (1978).

before he left again in 50, fighting certainly continued well into Augustus' reign.[24] Augustus reinforced his claims to have completed the conquest by returning Narbonensis to the Roman people in 22 BC – the public provinces generally being regarded as peaceful and not needing large garrisons, unlike those retained under the emperor's direct control – and by advancing the legions from the interior provinces to the Rhine in 15 BC. Yet sporadic fighting continued to occur.[25] The best example of an emperor playing down military conflicts in Gaul is provided by Tiberius' response to the major disturbances of AD 21. Although the revolt involved some of the most important Gallic communities, Tiberius made no official statement about it until he could also announce its suppression, refused to visit the area in person, and declined the offer of an *ovatio* to mark the Roman success.[26] The final detailed record of disturbances in Gaul is Tacitus' account in the *Histories* of the events of AD 68–70. His narrative portrays Roman rule in Gaul as a delicately balanced economy of power. As soon as it was disturbed by civil war, the Gauls are revealed not as disempowered and pacific subjects bereft of their leaders and protectors, but as dynamic participants who might be recruited to one of several possible new orders. But Tacitus' account represents itself as subversive of the official version, as revelatory of the secret life of empire and of the chaos lurking beneath the surface of the principate. Once an imperial order was re-established, subversive conflict in the provinces disappears, at least from sight. Nevertheless, a growing catalogue of substantial military installations shows that Roman troops continued to be stationed within the Gallic provinces. Most impressive are the remains of a stone-built legionary fortress at Mirebeau near Dijon, surrounded by *canabae* and all the other equipment of a

24 Campaigns against the Bellovaci in 47–6; campaigns by Hirtius suggested by local coinages struck in his name, for which see Scheers (1977) nos. 153 and 162; campaigns in 39–38 in both Aquitaine and the Rhineland; again in the Rhineland in 29; in Aquitaine in 28; and Gallic campaigns in 19 and 16. Wightman (1974), (1977) and (1978a) discuss the literary and archaeological evidence, accepting Ritterling's (1906) view that the six legions or so in the interior were probably most engaged in the North-East and in the South-West, but argue for a dispersed occupying force, some within iron age fortifications, others on sites that later developed into towns or fortresses. On the difficulties in identifying Caesarian and Augustan military sites, cf. the Colloque de Dijon (1974) and *Travaux militaires* (1978), especially on Arlaines and Mirebeau. Rivet's (1980) argument that Romano-British place names with -dunum and -durum might indicate the locations of Roman forts may also be relevant in the Gallic provinces.

25 Dio 54.4 for the return of Narbonensis. Unrest is also mentioned in 13–12 BC (Dio 54.32, Livy *Epit.* 139) and implied by Drusus' activities there, while the Allobroges were a source of concern in AD 9 (Velleius 2.120–1).

26 Tacitus *Annales* 3.40–47 representing it as a case of Tiberius' lack of candour, but Velleius' contemporary account (2. 129–33) is more favourable to Tiberius. On the revolts, see ch.1 note 64 above.

contemporary Rhineland camp. It was apparently occupied from the late first century AD well into the second century. Other camps are also known from periods when literary sources represent Gaul as an 'unarmed province'.[27] The continued presence of military personnel within the Gauls is unsurprising in view of their activities in other provinces,[28] but is passed over by literary accounts informed by official representations of *pax et imperium*. The point is not that the Gauls were not conquered and pacified – they were repeatedly – but rather that the establishment of a Roman order (*pax*) in Gaul was a longer process than Romans liked to admit, and one punctuated by reversals – breakdowns in relations followed by the temporary return of the legions, as happened in AD 21 – followed by sometimes lengthy periods of military occupation. Even when few troops were actually based in the Gallic interior, the German legions constituted an ever present threat that – as the suppression of Vindex's revolt demonstrated – might be mobilized as quickly against provincials as against enemies beyond the frontier.

The deliberate distortion of the historical record makes it difficult to trace the expansion of Roman power in detail, but some general conclusions may be drawn. First of all, it is clear that incorporation into the Roman empire was a traumatic process, and that that trauma was not restricted to the years immediately following Caesar's campaigns but recurred from the 20s BC on as Augustus, Agrippa and Drusus conducted the first censuses and put into place the administrative framework of the Gallic provinces, right up until the early years of Tiberius' reign. These outbreaks of violence might be viewed as interruptions in the building of an imperial system of power in the Gallic provinces, but they also contributed to the building process, providing some Gauls with the chance to prove their loyalty to Rome, and Rome with the chance to demonstrate the benefits of collaboration and the new discipline of empire. It is difficult to judge how quickly those lessons were learnt, but even allowing for the dominance of the imperial narrative, nothing on the scale of the war of AD 21 seems to have occurred in the second century, and the Severan civil war stirred up nothing like the *imperium Galliarum* of 69–70. Reports of banditry in Gaul are presumably

27 Tacitus *Histories* 1.16 for the label *provincia inermis* describing the state of affairs in AD 68, cf. Josephus *Bellum Judaicum* 2.372–3. On Mirebeau: Goguey (1978) and Goguey and Reddé (1995); on Arlaines: Reddé (1985); on Aulnay-de-Saintonge: Tassaux and Tassaux (1983–4). On other sites: Agache (1978) 207–50, Reddé (1989). Le Bohec (1993) resumes the latest evidence.

28 On Judaea: Isaac (1990), 54–160. On Britain: Hurst (1988), showing the presence of a garrison at Gloucester as late as the second century AD, and Bowman and Thomas (1991) on the *de facto* dispersal throughout the provinces of centurions stationed in principle on Hadrian's Wall. On Spain: Le Roux (1982). Literary sources such as Apuleius' *Metamorphoses*, the *Acts of the Apostles* or Petronius' *Satyricon* frequently represent soldiers as ubiquitous within the empire.

understated,[29] but it is difficult to resist the conclusion that after the middle of the first century AD, Gallic violence only escaped Roman control in exceptional circumstances. Even the brief Gallic Empire of the late third century is best seen not as a secession from Roman control so much as a set of local expedients that made use of the systems of dominance established in the formative period, to marshal provincial wealth and support and Rhineland troops alike to defend Roman civilization in the region.

The emergence of this order can be viewed as an increase in the capacity of Roman power to prevent 'rebellions', but it can also be seen in terms of Rome's success in harnessing the energies of the Gauls to the imperial project. The role played in this process by a new Gallic aristocracy was mentioned briefly at the end of the preceding chapter. Not all Gallic leaders had chosen to side with Rome, and those who had not had been purged and replaced with Roman adherents, presumably often the leaders of allied contingents during the Gallic and Triumviral campaigns, rewarded for their loyalty with lands and positions of power.[30] But if the conquest was accompanied by major redistributions of wealth and power within the Gallic élites, in social terms there was no radical break with the pre-conquest leadership (except in so far as Druidism was concerned) and many of the same expressions of status, such as rich burials, continued. The new aristocracy also enjoyed, however, power and status derived from their position as mediators between Romans and the mass of Gauls. From the new regime they gained legal privilege, perhaps a title to landed wealth and an affirmation of the hereditary principle, and most of all support from above that emancipated them a little from the need to pander to the masses. Their position was partly a reward for past loyalty, but they also served Rome in helping harness the energy of the Gauls to Roman ends, both by ensuring peace at home and by raising troops to serve Rome's interests abroad. Gauls had served as mercenaries during the Punic Wars and were levied from Transalpine communities after its conquest. It was probably as a reward for service in Spain and in the conquest of the Pyrenees that Pompey enfranchised a number of Aquitanian Gauls: some Gauls bore his name generations afterwards.[31]

29 Two outbreaks of violence are reported in this way. Herodian 1.10 describes the banditry associated with Maternus and his deserters in Gaul in 185–7; Drinkwater (1984) discusses the third century *bacaudae*.
30 Drinkwater (1978) is fundamental on this process.
31 For Gauls as mercenaries in the Hellenistic period, see Griffith (1935, 252–4), Nash (1985), although the origins of particular groups are not always clear; Gauls from Mediterranean France served during the Punic Wars, For which see Polyb. 3.41, 3.50, Livy 21.29; others were levied from Transalpina (Cicero *pro Fonteio* 13, Dio 36.37); Aquitanian Pompeii: DeWitt (1940), Badian (1958) 309–21, Ebel (1976) 86–7.

Caesar used Gallic cavalry from the Province as well as from allied states during his campaigns in the interior, and Gallic cavalry and Gallic communities were drawn into the civil wars at the end of the Republic.[32] The earliest stages of this may be indicated by a group of widely distributed late Celtic coinages in silver and bronze, which may have been used to pay Gallic troops in the 50s and 40s BC,[33] and local troops and militias continue to be mentioned occasionally throughout the first century AD.[34] To begin with these troops fought within native units raised and commanded by individual aristocrats like the *ala Indiana* raised by Julius Indus, but then tribal regiments like the *ala Vocontiorum* were formed, and finally semi-regular auxiliary units supporting regular citizen units recruited from colonies and Latin *municipia* in Narbonensis.[35] This pattern of change indicates an intensification and, formalization of Roman control, as treaties with communities were replaced by arrangements with aristocrats and finally, through recruitment and the levy, with individual Gauls of much lower status. That sequence may stand as a paradigm for the process by which Roman power extended down into, as well as over, Gallic societies.

III   Friendship and politics

Titus Sennius Solemnis, with whose career this chapter began, was distinguished both by his friendships and by the offices he had held. Like most Gallo-Roman aristocrats who had reached a high enough position to attract honorific statues, he glossed over the minor posts he had held in his community, but he had become *duovir*, the highest office among the Viducasses of Caen, four times and had probably held

32 For Gallic cavalry serving with Crassus in Syria in 53 BC, see Plut. *Crass.* 25; with Caesar in Gaul, see Caesar *de Bello Gallico* 2.5, 7.65 and *passim*); involved in civil wars, see Cicero *ad Att.* 9.13, *ad Fam.* 10.8, 10.21, 10.32, Appian *Bellum Civile* 2.49, Caesar *Bellum Civile* 3.59.

33 Wightman (1977) discusses the possibility. The best candidates for Roman-sponsored coins are the Hirtius issues (n. 17 above) and the coins marked TOGIRIX (Dayet 1962, Colbert de Beaulieu 1962). On the coinage of the period in general, see Nash (1978c).

34 See Brunt (1975) on policy towards disarming troops. On Gallic troops in the first century AD, see Livy *Epit.* 141, Tacitus *Annales* 3.42, *Histories* 1.67.

35 Cf. in general Drinkwater (1978). For troops supplied by allies, see Caesar *de Bello Gallico* 1.15, 2.24, 5.7, 6.5, 7.65, 8.11; with tribal commanders, see Caesar *Bellum Civile* 3.59, Cicero *ad Fam.* 10.21, cf. Holder (1980, 109–23). See Reddé (1985) on the *ala Vocontiorum* and Gechter (1990) on German auxiliaries. On the developed recruitment system, see Brunt (1974). See Forni (1953, 164–5, 174, 180–2) on the developing role of first Narbonensis and then the Germanies as suppliers of legionary recruits, and Mann (1983, 25–30) on the predominance of Gallic recruits in the Rhine legions.

a string of lesser magistracies in the *pagi*, the constituent districts of the tribe, and perhaps served in other financial or administrative posts as a *quaestor* or *actor publicus*, an *aedilis* or maybe a *praefectus annonae*.[36] He had also held at least one local priesthood, but the really important one was the priesthood of Rome and Augustus held at the Altar at Lyon. Each year, every community in the Three Gauls (and after a while in Narbonensis too) sent delegates to the Council where a *sacerdos* was elected to officiate at a ceremony of the imperial cult on behalf of all the Gauls. The priesthood was the culmination of a Gallo-Roman aristocrat's career but other chances for distinction existed. There were lesser posts at the Council, an aristocrat might be elected *patronus* of a *collegium*, or become a *curator* of one of the associations of resident Roman citizens which existed in many communities and had a central organization based at Lyon. Solemnis also served in an equestrian military post, and from Claudius' reign a senatorial career was open to aristocrats from the Three Gauls, as it already was to those from Narbonensis, although in practice few of them seem to have exercised this option, if indeed it was really available to them.[37] But careers like Solemnis', with the municipal benefactions that went with them – Solemnis had given gladiatorial games and built a bathhouse for his people – and underwritten by friendships with others engaged in the same pursuits, were the essence of civilized aristocratic life. Like military recruitment, the political system may also be seen as operating to harness Gallic energies and extend Roman power, and its evolution may be traced in much the same way. Friendships and treaties with whole communities gave way, in a fairly short period, to a system in which relationships between empire and city and ruler and subject were more formally specified, and were supplemented by networks of patronage. Both in the empire of cities and the empire of friends, it was men like Solemnis who occupied the key mediating positions and were rewarded accordingly.

By Solemnis' day, the early third century, Gaul was formally structured by territorial provinces, each comprising a number of communities, the statuses, rights and obligations of which were legally defined. The origins of that system in Gaul are very unclear. Transalpine Gaul may have been formally established following the wars of the 120s BC, although much earlier and much later dates have recently been proposed, and it is equally uncertain precisely when the areas conquered

36 Drinkwater (1979a) on the complexities of local careers.
37 Burnand (1982), Syme (1986) and Eck (1991) for recent discussions. The impact of these processes on Gallic societies is a theme of Burnand (1990a) and (1990b), although the meagreness of detailed information makes precision impossible.

by Caesar were organized systematically.[38] The problem is only partly one of poor information. The Republican empire had little infrastructure, preferring to harness the power of subordinate groups through friendships and alliances, and set up the minimum administrative machinery necessary to ensure security in the areas under its control, and only then where there were no pre-existing political structures that might be used. Besides, during the last century of the Republic, the empire was expanding faster than ever before or after and was periodically convulsed by vicious civil wars.[39] That combination of minimal government and political instability meant that whatever political settlements were established before Augustus were unsystematic and liable to frequent revision.

For the same reasons, there was a wide diversity in the relationships between Republican Rome and various communities in the South. Treaties are mentioned in accounts of the earliest Roman activities in Gaul, often as the justification for military action, and treaty-making probably preceded and accompanied most campaigns in this period,[40] operating to accentuate existing cultural, linguistic and political contrasts between the tribes of the south.[41] Growing Roman interest in the region

38 The precise nature and periodization of Roman domination of Transalpine Gaul is a theme of Hermon (1993). On Gallia Comata, Balsdon (1939, 171) argues that Cicero *de prov. cons.* 28 refers to a commission of ten legates to organize the province, but it is not certain that other kinds of *legati* might not be meant, as in *ad fam.* 1.7.10. See Wightman (1974) on the situation in general between Caesar and Augustus. Dio 53.22 implies that little had been done since the Caesarian conquest.

39 See Lintott (1980) on Republican provincial organization and Galsterer (1986, 16) for triumviral confusion.

40 Livy 43.5, 44,14 and Appian *Celtica* 13 record comparable treaties with groups north of the Alps. Ebel (1976) discusses the tradition of a longstanding relationship between Rome and Marseilles, but cf. Richardson in *JRS* 69 (1979) 156–61 for some doubts. Polyb. 33.8–11 cites such a treaty as the reason for the campaigns of 154 BC against the Ligurians. On relations with the Aedui, see Braund (1980). Florus 1.37 cites an alliance with the Aedui as one justification for the campaigns against the Arverni and Allobroges in 123 BC. An alliance with the Tolosates before 106 is implied by Dio 27.90 and the award of the title of Friend to a Nitiobrogian king in the same area (Caesar *de Bello Gallico* 7.31) may be contemporary as may a similar grant to the grandfather of one of Caesar's allied commanders, a Gaul named Piso (*de Bello Gallico* 4.12). The Sequani handed over a Teuton chief in 102 (Plutarch *Marius* 24), which may have been the occasion for king Catamantaloedis being saluted as Friend (Caesar *de Bello Gallico* 1.3). Other alliances were probably made in the 60s in the context of the war scare recorded by Cicero (*ad Att.* 1.19; 1.20; 2.1). Ariovistus was recognized as a Friend at this time (Appian *Celtica* 16, Dio 38.44), and in 56 BC Cicero refered to treaties with the Cenomanni, the Insubres, the Helvetii and the Iapudes among other Gauls, not all of whom need have been Italians (*pro Balbo* 32). Some of the states listed as *foederati* or *liberi* in the mid-first century AD by Pliny *NH* 4.17–19 may also have won this status before or during the Gallic wars, although in some cases, like that of the Treveri, a previous grant had been revoked (cf. Clarke (1965), Wightman (1970, 39)), and new ones may have been made.

41 Barruol (1969) on the south east.

is marked by the embassies that came to Rome from groups both inside and outside the Province in the 60s, and by Caesar's claim that all of Gaul had been a Roman sphere of influence since the 120s.[42] Rome's policy was perhaps never seriously constrained by these relationships, but her Gallic allies played essential roles as providers of information, troops, supplies and increasingly of tribute.[43] But growing interest in Gaul did not immediately lead to any rationalization of Roman relations with the Gauls. Even when generals like Domitius, Pompey or Caesar had the opportunity to impose administrative uniformity they chose instead to reward friends and punish enemies by differentiating them. Traces of these grants remain in the administrative geography of the provinces as described by Pliny the Elder in the first century AD, who lists Roman colonies, Latin *oppida, fora* and an allied state in Narbonensis and free states, allied states and ordinary *civitates* in the north.[44] Although the titles remained important as marks of status, they were mostly administrative fossils by the imperial period, relics of the looser patrimonial organization of the Republic and of the deliberate favouritism of Republican generals. The Volcae Arecomici, one of the larger of the groups occupying territory west of the Rhône, provide an example of how precarious these arrangements had been.[45] According to one recent reconstruction, Pompey first deprived them of land which he assigned to Marseille, Caesar subsequently granted the Latin right to all communities in Transalpina, and finally a Latin colony was founded at the Volcan capital of Nîmes to which twenty-four other communities were later attributed. Under Augustus, the colony acquired the title Augusta, a set of town walls and a very early series of monuments that may have included an *Augusteum*, a shrine to the imperial cult. An impressive number of equites and senators originated in Nîmes, indicating the continued prosperity of the Volcae throughout the principate. Other communities did less well. After Marseille picked the wrong side in the civil war between Caesar and Pompey it was deprived of its own colonies.

That civil war marked the beginning of an intensification of Roman intervention. Roman colonization provides one measure of this change.

42 Embassies in the 60s: Sallust *Catilina* 40–45; Caesar *de Bello Gallico* 1.31. A sphere of influence: *de Bello Gallico* 1.45. Stevens (1980) goes perhaps a little far beyond the evidence. For Caesar's account as a source of Roman attitudes, see Brunt (1978).

43 E.g. Caesar *de Bello Gallico* 1.16; 1,40; 2.5; 6.12; Velleius 2.39.1–2; Suetonius *Iul.* 25.1; Dio 40.43; Eutropius 6.17.3.

44 Pliny *NH* 3.4, discussed by Goudineau (1980, 92–3). On northern Gaul, see Pliny *NH* 4.17–19.

45 See Goudineau (1976), Christol and Goudineau (1987) for what follows, admitting the speculative nature of the enquiry. The key passages are Caesar *Bellum Civile* 1.35; Pliny *NH* 3.4: On the possible *Augusteum*, see Gros (1984).

The first colony established in Gaul was Narbo, founded shortly after the campaigns of the 120s BC. Like its predecessors in Gallic northern Italy it seems to have been accompanied by centuriation, the marking out and division of land for the colonists, in a grid aligned on the Via Domitia.[46] But, although some lesser settlements were created – forts, *fora* and Pompey's settlement at Lugdunum Convenarum – the province evoked in Cicero's *pro Fonteio* contained only islands of urbanism.[47] Citizen colonization only resumed on a large scale when first Caesar and then Augustus needed land to settle the veterans of triumviral armies. The exact chronology is controversial, and it is not always easy to distinguish veteran colonies from existing settlements granted the title, but in the course of just one generation, veterans were settled at Narbonne, Arles, Béziers, Orange, Fréjus, probably Nyon, Augst and Lyon, and possibly Valence and Vienne.[48] Further veteran colonies were later founded at Cologne under Claudius, possibly at Avenches under Vespasian and at Xanten under Trajan. The scale of the disruption caused was considerable: lands were confiscated or subjected to compulsory purchase before being centuriated and redistributed to colonists and, in some cases at least, the locals were restricted to poorer territory in the vicinity. Caesar's dictatorship and the first half of Augustus' reign transformed the administrative map of southern Gaul: the veteran foundations together with centres like Nîmes and Vaison among the Vocontii, formed the basis of a province of cities within which non-urban communities had little place. What little evidence there is for the political institutions of indigenous communities supports the notion that their constitutions were formed in the Caesarian and Augustan periods rather than before.[49]

It does seem that this period witnessed a marked rationalization of Roman rule, in the sense of the promotion of systematic and formal structures of power at the expense of more arbitrary patrimonialism.[50] The shift can be seen in the global measures undertaken by Caesar and especially Augustus, although in many respects they continued to act like Republican dynasts, as the case of Nîmes shows. Caesar extended

46 On Narbo and southern Gaul, see Chouquer *et al.* (1983), Clavel-Lévêque (1983b). On centuriation in general, see Clavel-Lévêque (1983a).
47 Cicero's account is in this instance confirmed by archaeological evidence, cf. chapter 5 below.
48 Brunt (1971, 588–9), Goudineau (1980a, 88–91). On Lyon: Goudineau (1989). Suetonius *Tib.* 4 records the foundation of colonies between 46 and 44 BC. *Res Gestae* 16, Dio 54.23 records Augustus' foundations in 14 BC allegedly on purchased land.
49 Goudineau (1975).
50 Nicolet (1988) for the Augustan apogee of this process, although its genesis can be traced further back to the global settlements of dynasts like Pompey and Caesar, cf. Purcell's review in *JRS* 80 (1990) 178–182, or in some respects even earlier, cf. Veyne (1976, 411–15).

the Latin right to the Republican province as a whole and created a series of communities constituted as Latin *coloniae*, with Roman magistrates (*quattuoviri*) and orders of *decuriones*. Augustus held a *census* in 27 BC and 'reorganized the lives and constitutions of the Gauls', northern as well as southern, holding a *conventus* at Narbo to settle disputes.[51] When Augustus visited again in 16–13 BC his activities fall more into the pattern of piecemeal intervention, the remedying of the abuses of tax collectors, the foundation of colonies, and his activities as a whole are glossed as spending money on some, extracting it from others and the giving and taking away of freedom and constitutions. But a second census was conducted in 12 BC by Drusus, who also set up the Altar at Lyon and the cult organization surrounding it.[52] Much remains obscure, for example the date at which northern Gaul was divided into the three provinces of Lugdunensis, Aquitania and Belgica and the means by which those areas were administered between the Caesarian war and 27 BC. But it is clear that the period from about 46 to 12 BC was characterized both by continued patrimonial interventions and also by a series of rationalizations. Subsequent emperors continued this pattern. Patrimonial interventions included grants of autonomy to a number of communities and the creation of a new province in Aquitania[53], but there were also occasional rationalizations, for example the Flavian creation of two German provinces to separate the military zone from the civilian Gallic provinces, and the establishment of a network of procuratorial posts throughout Gaul, although the details and chronologies of these developments are difficult to reconstruct.[54] But the broad lines of the imperial system were defined in the Augustan age.

One striking contrast with the Republican system was the extent to which Roman power now involved individual Gauls as well as communities, just as recruitment of individuals had replaced the use of tribal retinues to assist Roman armies. Individuals were recruited through both the patrimonial and the more formal aspects of the Roman system. Caesar and Augustus had harnessed the energies of Gallic leaders to their causes through friendship, and men like Solemnis remained important to Roman governors. But institutions like the Latin *municipia*, provincial communities, the laws and political life of which were based

---

51 Dio 53.22. Livy *Epit.* 134 for the *census* and the *conventus*.
52 Dio 54.21 for fiscal corruption in 16 BC with Bénabou (1967); Dio 54.23 for colonization in 15 BC; Dio 54.25 for his activities in general; on Drusus in 12 BC, Dio 54.32 and Livy *Epit.* 138–9 linked in both cases to unrest in the region.
53 Goudineau (1980a, 110–17) on civic promotions; on Novempopulania, see *CIL* XIII 412 and most recently Bost and Fabre (1988).
54 On the administrative structure of the three Gauls, see Drinkwater (1983, 93–118), on Narbonensis, see Pflaum (1978). The best general guide is now Jacques and Scheid (1990).

closely on Roman models, and the provincial cult organizations also
provided routes into the system, while censuses, taxation and the
Roman law that came with Roman citizenship taught new Gauls new
ways of behaving. The means by which citizenship itself was spread also
underwent a transformation as grants made by Republican generals
were replaced, under Caesar and Augustus, by more formal institutions
for its dissemination, for example its automatic grant to anyone who
had held a magistracy in a Latin community or served in the irregular
battalions known as *auxilia*. Most prominent among the new Romans
were the Gallic aristocracies. At the Altar, priests won prestige for their
tribes but also excelled as pre-eminent members of the new society of
the *primores Galliarum*, 'leaders of the Gallic provinces'. At Lyon and in
their communities they competed to patronize the new *collegia* and to
build monuments. Acts of euergetism and honorific statues displayed
their personal wealth and achievements. We can identify some members of the first generation of Gallo-Roman aristocrats. C. Iulius Vercondaridubnus was the first priest at the Altar and an Aeduan of the
generation who abandoned Roman Bibracte for Augustodunum. A family
from Saintes in Aquitaine produced a priest of the Altar a generation
later in AD 19, C. Iulius Rufus, who celebrated by constructing an
amphitheatre at Lyon and an arch and bridge in his home town on
which he declared his descent from C. Iulius Otuaneunos, the son of
G. Iulius Gedomo, the son of Epotsorovidos.[55] After Claudius, the
wealthiest nobles in the three northern (Comatan) provinces could stand
for election to the senate. Only a few are known to have done so, but
Narbonensian senators, and *equites* from all the Gallic provinces are well
attested.[56] Gallic nobles were certainly pre-eminent within the Gallic
provinces, in their own communities and outside them, and since the
emperors chose not to rule through an expatriate colonial civil service,
Roman power in Gaul was from the start most often the power of Gauls
over Gauls.

IV   Wealth

Power was desirable in itself, and conquest brought political rewards, as
well as the satisfaction of furthering an end that was divinely ordained
and socially sanctioned. But the wealth of Gaul was certainly coveted
by generals, by emperors and by other powerful individuals.[57] A full

55 *CIL* XIII 1036, *ILTG* 217.   56 Eck (1991).
57 On the economic dimensions of Roman imperialism, see Brunt (1978), Harris (1979)
    and the papers collected in *Ktema* 8 (1983), and on the broad economic interests of
    the elite, Finley (1976), D'Arms (1981).

account of the economy of Roman Gaul is beyond the scope of this study,[58] but a consideration of the economic dimensions of the extension of Roman power in the region contributes to an understanding of the changing pressures on indigenous societies, the means by which their local resources were harnessed to new ends, and the basis of the power of the new aristocracies.

Certainly Gaul was wealthy. The economies of southern Gaul were broadly similar to those of regions like coastal Spain where familiar Mediterranean crops were cultivated for local consumption by populations inhabiting hilltop villages.[59] Extracting a surplus from those communities and channelling it to more distant markets would be relatively simple, and some gains in productivity might be hoped for from peace and from the introduction of new crops and technologies. Continental Gaul presented both greater potential and greater problems. Romans rightly regarded temperate Europe as rich and fertile compared to the arid Mediterranean basin. The steady economic growth experienced by late iron age societies has already been noted. But inter-tribal warfare and the difficulties of communications within the continent meant that growth had mostly taken place at a local scale: harnessing that productive potential to satisfy the desires of distant consumers would be more difficult.[60]

By far the most information available concerns the changing impact of the Roman state on Gallic wealth. Republican wars imposed a double burden on the Gauls, compelling allies to provide supplies and subjecting enemies to plunder and the confiscation of land. Raising supplies from allies was so regular a practice that it is rarely recorded, but grain was being sent from Transalpina to Spain in the 70s BC, and Caesar frequently received supplies from his Gallic allies. Foraging while on campaign seems only to have been used when absolutely necessary, as during his British expedition.[61] Even after the imposition of regular tribute on the Gauls, extra demands were generated by major imperial

58 For surveys of the economic history of the Gauls, see Grenier (1937), drawing largely on Jullian (1908–26), and the important suggestions of Kneißl (1988).
59 Py (1990b) on southern settlements, with the papers gathered in Bats et al. (1992).
60 Drinkwater (1979b) and Duncan-Jones (1981) take different views on how successfully this wealth was harnessed by municipal aristocrats engaged in euergetism, cf. also De Kisch (1979). Fulford (1992) presents a pessimistic view of the contribution of European production to the imperial economy. See Kneißl (1988) for the contrast between the pace of economic development in the south and in the north.
61 See Richardson (1976, 149–51) on the ad hoc measures by which grain was acquired by armies in Spain in the second century BC. Cicero pro Fonteio 13 describes Narbonensis supplying Spain in the 70s. Examples of Caesar being supplied by allies are in de Bello Gallico 1.16; 1.40, and foraging in Britain at 4.31, 5.17. See in general Labisch (1975), especially 50–62.

expeditions, like Germanicus' campaigns across the Rhine and Trajan's Dacian War.[62] The extraction of booty imposed more dramatic strains, associated as it was with military defeat, and in those Gallic societies where the display, religious dedication or redistribution of wealth were important means by which status was constructed, the removal of huge quantities of bullion must have had a very disruptive effect. Stories of the plunder to be had from Gaul circulated from the time of the earliest Roman campaigns in the south.[63] Caesar refers to booty rarely in his own account of his conquests, but the wealth he gained from it was fabled.[64] These stories receive some support from the dramatic improvement of Caesar's personal finances, from deep debt to extreme wealth, and from the collapse of the precious metal content of Gallic coinages over the course of the war.[65]

The confiscation of land has a special significance since it entailed control not just of wealth but of the basis of its production. The redistribution of territory between the Volcae and Marseille has already been discussed, and other land was given to individual Gauls,[66] or found its way into Roman hands. Information for the Republican period is sketchy, but some land was centuriated and allocated to the colonists of Narbonne,[67] and by the early first century BC some estates were owned by both private citizens and Italian municipalities.[68] Cicero, in a speech made in 81 BC in defence of P. Quinctius, described Roman estate owners and their agents resident in southern Gaul and doing business in Narbo. Quinctius himself owned several estates including a stock ranch, held in

62 Tacitus *Ann.* 2.5, *RMR* no. 63.
63 Dyson (1970) on Caepio and the gold of Tolosa; cf. Florus 1.37, Appian *Celtica* 14.
64 Suetonius *Div.Iul.* 54 claims the quantity of gold brought back to Rome depressed its value against silver by a third (cf. Polybius 34.10, quoted in Strabo 4.6.12, for a similar story set in an earlier period). Caesar's gains are also mentioned by Appian *Bellum Civile* 2.17. 41; Orosius 6.121; Velleius 2.56. Hirtius *de Bello Gallico* 8.4 mentions gifts by Caesar to his troops in lieu of booty at a rate of 200 HS per legionary and 1000 HS for each centurion.
65 On Caesar and debt, see Frederiksen (1966, 130). On Gallic precious metal coinages, see Haslegrove (1984a), providing an excellent illustration of the general processes described in Crawford (1985). Nash (1978c) charts the subsequent disappearance of Celtic coinage and its replacement by Roman coin.
66 Caesar *Bellum Civile* 3.59 on two Allobrogian brothers rewarded by Caesar for their service in the Gallic wars with offices 'agrosque in Gallia ex hostibus captos praemiaque rei pecuniariae magna'.
67 Appian *Bellum Civile* 1.29 describes a *popularis* proposal to redistribute Gallic land recaptured from the Teutones to Roman settlers, but it is difficult to associate this with any known colonial foundation, and the project was probably aborted on the fall of Saturninus. Cf. Hermon (1993) on possible connections between wars in the south and *popularis* politics.
68 See Cicero *pro Fonteio* 13 for confiscations. For municipal holdings, see Cicero *ad Fam.* 13.7, 13.11, cf. Varro *Res Rustica* III.12.1–3.

partnership, and was also engaged in slave trading. A similar range of business activities is described in the *pro Fonteio* delivered a decade later. The origins of these estates, which were certainly much bigger than colonial allotments,[69] are obscure, but they most likely originated from sales of captured territory, which then circulated like any other property through inheritance and purchase. Further confiscations accompanied the colonization of the Triumviral and Augustan periods. Nothing similar is attested for Gallia Comata at any period. The little centuriation that has been certainly established there may show Roman styles of land ownership rather than actual transfers of property,[70] and such redistribution of property as did take place may have been largely in favour of Caesar's partisans and at the expense of his enemies.[71] Apart from a few accounts of first century emperors confiscating and selling off the property of selected Gallic notables there is no evidence for significant disruption of patterns of land-holding of the sort that occurred in the south,[72] and changes in this region may have affected the nature of landholding more than the identity of the landholders.[73] The reasons for this contrast in the treatment of different parts of Gaul are obscure.[74] What is very clear, however, is the timing of these economic dislocations. The impact of successive confiscations in the Republican should not be underestimated, but the period of fastest and most disruptive change throughout Gaul was the second half of the last century BC.

That same period was also marked by a shift from irregular exactions to regular taxation as Rome transformed herself from a conquest state to a tributary empire. This process may be compared to the formalization of political structures in the same period. Republican imperialism had extracted large profits at irregular intervals, but at the cost

69 Cicero refered to them as *saltus* and Quinctius used an *eques Romanus* to administer them in his absence.
70 Chouquer and Favory (1980), Clavel-Lévêque (1983a).
71 Drinkwater (1978) for this suggestion.
72 Confiscations of property: Suetonius *Tib* 49, *Gaius* 39 cf. Dio 59.21–2. A procurator of imperial estates in Belgica and the Germanies is attested by *CIL* XIII 1807, for which see Pflaum (1960–1, 1051–8). No certain imperial estates have been located in the Gauls, although they are known in Germany, for which see Crawford (1976).
73 For various reconstructions of the impact of markets in land and produce and of Roman fiscal, legal and tenurial systems, cf. e.g. Clavel-Lévêque (1975) for a Marxist interpretation; Slofstra (1983) on the shift from tribesmen to peasants; Wightman (1978b) on tenants and slaves, with elements of continuity; and Stevens (1970) and Whittaker (1980) arguing for substantial continuity. Some of these studies deal with only southern Gaul or Comata. The evidence is abundant from neither region.
74 Romans may have believed these areas too difficult to exploit, although that view coheres badly with the perception of Gaul as very fertile. Possibly the south was preferred for veteran colonization because of its Mediterranean climate, or because it was believed to be more peaceful. The phenomenon is perhaps best considered in relation to Rome's use of her non-Mediterranean empire in general.

of weakening and destabilizing provincial communities, which then became unwilling or unable to resist the aggression of their neighbours, or else renewed armed conflict with Rome. No Jugurtha or Mithridates arose on the borders of Transalpine Gaul, but the province shared in generalized solutions that culminated in the development of a tax system, comprising property and poll taxes based on censuses which from Augustus' time on were held at fairly regular intervals in Gaul,[75] supplemented by various forms of indirect taxation.[76] Roman public finances could naturally not establish this closer relationship with local economies without transforming the latter. Although much tax probably continued to be raised in kind, taken together with the demands of Gauls for products not yet available locally, it may have stimulated some monetization.[77] Equally, the requirement imposed on Gallic elites to supervise collection of the sums specified by the census will have transformed their economic behaviour. Finally, taxation and the desire for imports may have provided the context for indebtedness. Loans to provincial communities and grandees are not as well attested for Gaul as for other western provinces, but debt is frequently mentioned as a cause of unrest.[78] If some Gauls were forced to sell their property to raise money to pay taxes, buy foreign goods or repay loans, these tensions will also have led to capital transfer. Repeated adjustments were made to the level of taxation from Augustus on, partly no doubt in the context of the regular redistribution of privileges and penalties in accordance with virtue and favour, partly perhaps to adjust tax burdens to the highest sustainable level that would not prompt unrest.[79] Whatever

75 Jacques (1977), with Brunt (1990, 532–3). Suetonius *Div.Iul.* suggests a Caesarian precursor of this system, but the impact of the Augustan *census* must have been a much more dramatic change, cf. Grenier (1937, 498–503). On taxation in general, see Brunt (1981).

76 France (1993) for the probable Augustan origins of one of the most important indirect taxes, the *quadragesima Galliarum*, a 2.5 per cent tax on goods entering or leaving the Gallic provinces.

77 Howgego (1992) for the monetized nature of the Roman economy. For the debate of taxation in kind versus taxation in cash, see Hopkins (1980), Duncan-Jones (1990, 187–98), Brunt (1990, 531–2). Howgego (1994, 16–20) casts some doubt on the role postulated for taxation in stimulating the circulation of coin.

78 Debt and unrest: Tacitus *Ann.* 3.40 (Florus and Sacrovir), cf. Dio 54.36 on the Dalmatians and 62.2 on Boudicca. Corbier (1988) discusses the connection. For other factors, see Dyson (1971), (1975). For money lending among the Helvetii, see Suetonius *Vesp.* 1 and van Berchem (1978).

79 On capital transfer, Freyburg (1988) is very suggestive, but the paucity of quantifiable data makes it difficult to assess the scale of the phenomenon. For adjustments in the fiscal system, see Dio 54, 21, 25 (Augustus); Tacitus *Hist.* 1.51, 4.57; Plutarch *Galba* 16; Suetonius *Vesp* 16 (civil war) and in general Corbier (1988).

the intents and results of these measures, the more emperors intervened in the economic life of the Gallic provinces, the more economic life was drawn into Roman patterns.

It is more difficult to assess the impact on Gaul of the economic activities of private individuals. The extension of first military power and then of the fiscal system opened up opportunities for Roman entrepreneurs of various statuses, among them soldiers and colonists, ranchers and slavers like Quinctius, bankers and tax farmers like Vespasian's father, and of course traders. Behind many of the more humble figures we may suspect the presence of the Roman aristocracy, who were also perhaps major creditors and landlords, but in Gaul at least they are mostly invisible. Trade has received the most attention, due to its archaeological visibility and its significance for the world-systems analyses already discussed. The appearance of Italian wine amphorae first at southern Gaulish sites and then in the interior has been documented in detail.[80] Classical texts mention traders operating in several parts of Gaul, some in the wake of military activity, some in areas not yet under Roman control.[81] The latter at least seem to be engaged in low-capital /high-risk ventures on the penumbra of the Roman economy, but we know little of them, and despite Strabo's mention of several entrepots, nothing like the Augustan trading post on the Magdalensberg in Noricum has ever been excavated in Gaul.[82] Traders are well attested in early Roman Gaul, and dealt with a much wider range of commodities than in the pre-conquest period.[83] These *mercatores* and *nautae* may well have represented the interests of wealthier Romans although it is equally possible that some were small independent traders. The individuals who represented themselves in later inscriptions as *negotiatores* seem

80 On the south, Clemente (1974) is superceded by Goudineau (1983a) with Bats (1986). On the interior, see Tchernia (1983), Fitzpatrick (1985). Middleton (1983) alone regards imports as supplied to Roman garrisons. Fitzpatrick (1989) and Woolf (1993c) argue that the role of these exchanges in transforming local societies has been overestimated. Roman (1983) and Cunliffe (1988, 80–104) offer general accounts.

81 Strabo 4.2.1 (from Polybius); Diodoros 5.26 (from Poseidonius) on trade beyond the frontier. Cicero *pro Fonteio* discusses at length a tax Fonteius was accused of having imposed on wine exporters. Caesar makes frequent mentions of traders, e.g. Cicero *de Bello Gallico* 1.1, 1.39, 2.15, although some may have been in Gaul to organize his commissariat and/or buy up booty; see Buchsenschutz and Ralston (1986) on the circumstances in which Caesar mentions them.

82 Strabo 4.16; 12; 14; 4.2.3; 4.3.3, although it is unclear at what date these operated. On the Magdalensberg, see Egger (1961), Obermayer (1971), Collis (1984, 145–6).

83 Some of the relevant epigraphy is discussed by Hassall (1978), Middleton (1979), Krier (1981) and Wierschowski (1995). See West (1935) for the range of goods exchanged, although the documentation is very out of date. See Jacobsen (1995) for a good discussion of the new character of trade.

mostly to be Gauls and perhaps men of rather lower status than men like Solemnis.[84]

Eventually, as a taste for Roman goods developed, there were new opportunities for stonemasons, architects, sculptors and potters, many from north Italy, others from Spain.[85] That movement, responding to patterns of consumption and values already learned, will have been less disruptive for indigenous societies, even if to begin with it may have contributed to drawing wealth out of Gaul and encouraging Gallo-Roman landowners first to raise their productivity and then to develop local production wherever possible.[86] The point of this discussion is not, however, to trace economic growth in Gaul, which would require discussion of the economic significance of Gallic urbanism[87] and the development of trade with neighbouring regions.[88] There is little sign that private enterprises subjected indigenous societies to anything like the same stresses and strains as were created first by war, and then by land confiscation in the south and the imposition of systematic taxation, with the consequences that entailed, throughout Gaul.

The extension of Roman power, in all its forms, over Gaul was a complex process and one experienced in different ways from one community to another. Political favour, colonies and garrisons were all distributed unevenly across the Gallic provinces and there were winners and losers among tribes as well as among individuals as the empire of cities and friends was brought into being. That granted, the rhythm of change in all these spheres and in most regions was rather similar: one particularly disruptive period, beginning just before Augustus' victory at Actium and petering out by the end of his reign, affected all Gaul. At that point the configuration of power that encompassed the Roman empire, imperial society and a new economy was transformed and expanded downwards *into* Gallic societies, upsetting the old order and

---

84 A few *seviri Augustales* are known, many with commercial links. Inscriptions recording *seviri* are much more common in Narbonensis than in Comata, for which see Duthoy (1976) .

85 Ward-Perkins (1970), Wierschowski (1995). The spread of *terra sigillata* production from Arezzo and Pisa to Lyon (initially to supply the Rhenish armies) is discussed in chapter 7.

86 See Woolf (1992b) for a sketch of the process in the empire as a whole. Laubenheimer (1985) illustrates developments in Gaul with a study of the development of the wine production in Narbonensis.

87 Grenier's (1937, 509–62) view of the productivity of Gallic cities now needs to be modified in the light of the arguments of Goudineau (1980b, 365–81).

88 See *ILS* 6987 for Narbonensian grain supplied to Rome. For the Atlantic trade, see *AE* 1922.116 and Chastagnol (1981); for the North Sea, see Stuart (1971) and Hassall (1978).

forcing the creation of new mediating institutions through which the energies and resources of the Gauls were harnessed to new ends. The process might be compared to the demolition of street upon street of old houses, materials from which were used to create a towerblock to house the former inhabitants in a new style. Destructive and disruptive though this process was, some Gauls did well out of it. One group in particular stands out, a new aristocracy created out of the rubble of the old, but with greater authority, status, wealth and security than their grandfathers had ever had. That group was to take the lead in building Roman Gaul.

3   The civilizing ethos

I   The Gauls observed

The greater part of the Roman empire was conquered in the last generation of the free Republic and the reign of the first princeps. The rapidity of Roman expansion in that period, along with the new intensity in the encounter with Hellenism that it entailed, prompted many Romans to reconsider conventional wisdoms about their place in the world. From those reflections emerged new conceptions of Rome's past and Rome's destiny and new ideas about Roman identity, Roman virtue and Roman civilization. One of these new ideas has special relevance for this study: a growing consciousness that Romans were destined by the gods to conquer, rule and civilize the world.[1]

Recent attempts to explain the diversity of modern colonialisms and imperialisms have led historians to examine the attitudes and ideals with which each power approached empire – among them notions of race and class, religion and sexuality, civility and nature, history and progress – and the ways in which consensuses and debates about these issues affected, and were in turn affected by, the imperial project. Unless the historian's aim is simply to condemn past imperialists by modern standards, understanding empire necessitates some consideration of these issues, perhaps even some empathetic efforts. It follows that some attempt must be made to discover how Romans understood the expansion of *imperium Romanum* and the cultural processes that accompanied it, particularly since that consciousness of an imperial vocation and a civilizing process exercized an influence not only on those who conquered and established the empire, but eventually also on those Gauls who came to share that vocation. The subject is enormous, but it is possible to

---

1 Brunt (1978) on Roman ideas of empire in the last century BC, picking up from Harris (1979, 117–30). For an earlier period, see North (1993). The change is perhaps best characterized as the emergence of a new, global perspective. If Roman wars had, individually, been favoured by the gods, now Roman conquest as a whole was sanctioned by them. Nicolet (1988) (with Purcell's review in *JRS* 80 (1990) 178–82 on the chronology of change) and Richardson (1991) chart different aspects of this shift of consciousness of empire.

sketch the outlines of Roman thinking on these issues, and to suggest ways in which it played a part in shaping the Roman civilization of Gaul.

A convenient starting point is the way Romans regarded the Gauls at the time of the conquest. Roman military expeditions themselves generated a great deal of new information. Ethnographic and geographical knowledge acquired during the wars of the 120s, for example, provided much material for Poseidonius when he visited the region, probably in the 90s BC, and his published work was an important source for later writers including Diodoros, Strabo and (much later) Athenaeus.[2] Roman generals and emperors promoted enquiries, perhaps only partly for immediate strategic purposes. Caesar's questioning of merchants about Britain prior to his first invasion served tactical ends (even if his account of how little he learnt from them emphasized that he was about to invade The Unknown), but Polybius also records a Scipio questioning men from Marseille and Narbonne about Britain.[3] New information provides only a partial explanation for the new images of Gaul produced in this period. There were also deliberate attempts to impose an imperial order on the Gauls, either by asserting a new Roman organization of peoples and places, or by associating Roman achievements with a supposedly natural order.[4] Domitius' construction of a new road along the old Herculean way into Spain and the centuriations associated with the colonization of southern Gaul are examples of the imposition of a new order, while the naturalization of Roman conquests is represented by the trophies established by Fabius Maximus at the confluence of the Isar and the Rhône, by Pompey at the Mediterranean terminal of the Pyrenees and of Augustus at la Turbie, which announced the conquest of the Alps 'from the upper to the lower sea'.[5] Geography thus served to map Roman achievements onto the shape of the world and Roman history onto world history.

But as fast as Roman generals declared the conquest of the world complete and asserted definitive descriptions of it, like Agrippa's map, in which their own achievements were inscribed, the new knowledge created by Roman conquest and Roman rule prompted fresh intellectual efforts to make sense of the world. It is what is implicit in these accounts, rather than what is explicitly presented in the propaganda

2 On Poseidonius' Celtic ethnography, Nash (1976a) supercedes Tierney (1960). Momigliano (1975, 60–3) emphasises the importance of Rome in promoting Greek ethnographic investigation of the Celts. For the date of Poseidonius' visit to the west, see Kidd (1988, vol. II (i), 16–17).
3 Caesar de Bello Gallico 4.20; Strabo 4.2.1 quoting Polybius. On imperially sponsored explorations, see Nicolet (1988, 97–101, and 103–31 on Agrippa).
4 Nicolet (1988) especially 48–61.
5 Strabo 4.1.11 Fabius Maximus; 4.1.3 for Pompey's trophies; Pliny NH 3.20 for Augustus'.

of Roman generals, that is the best source for wider understandings of the impact of empire. Strabo's *Geography*, written in the tradition of Hellenistic science and in the immediate aftermath of the Augustan conquests, is the fullest and most revealing example.[6] But a similar perspective emerges from the short Latin *Geography* of Pomponius Mela, produced a few decades later. Although the elder Pliny's *Natural History* is a very different work, drawing eclectically on Stoicism, other philosophical schools and on traditional Roman moral discourse to produce an holistic account of the world and of man's place in it, unified by preoccupations that were ethical and religious as much as scientific,[7] it also reflects views common among two generations of Roman administrators and writers, of whose works it is in part a synthesis.[8] All these writers also made use of earlier histories and ethnographies, of the propaganda of Roman generals, of administrative documents, itineraries and, no doubt, also of the accounts of soldiers, prisoners-of-war, exiles and traders. But it is the shape they imposed on their accounts, their criteria of relevance and interest and their occasional comments that reveal the attitudes of the period of composition.

Strabo's *Geography* presents itself as a scientific account of the entire world, but its organization displays the extent to which that world is Rome-centred. After two books of prolegomena, the material is ordered province by province. Beyond the provinces, Strabo focuses on Rome's relations with her neighbours, while within them the history of Roman expansion and its (beneficial) effects form a leitmotif. Thus his account of the Gauls in book 4 deals in turn with Narbonensis, Aquitania, Lugdunensis, Belgica and then (outside the empire) Britain and the other Atlantic islands and finally the Alps. Mela's account of the world and the geography that comprises books 3–6 of the Elder Pliny's *Natural History* are much briefer but are organized along the same lines. The exact sequence of the three geographies varies, yet in each case the administrative geography of the empire joins the three classical continents with the inner and outer seas as the structuring principles of the world. This Romano-centrism is also evident in the natural rationales claimed for various Roman provincial boundaries, in the correlations between the extent of Roman knowledge and the extent of Roman power, and in the role accorded to Roman rule in civilizing the Gauls and in realizing their potential for prosperity.

Take, as an instance, the major distinction that all three accounts draw between Narbonensis and the three provinces of the interior.

---

6 Nicolet (1988, 93–4). On the literary tradition, cf. most recently Romm (1992).
7 Beagon (1992), Wallace-Hadrill (1990b).   8 Beagon (1992, 5–9).

Mela and Pliny actually adopt arrangements of material that lead them to consider Narbonensis along with its neighbouring Mediterranean provinces, and to discuss the other three, non-mediterranean Gauls elsewhere along with the rest of northern Europe. Strabo does not divide his account in this way, but he makes the distinction equally clear, describing Gaul as a rectangle stretching between the inner seas and the Ocean, bounded to the west by the Pyrenees and to the East by the Rhine with the southern part divided off from the north by the 'natural' boundary of the Cevennes. Narbonensis produces Italian-style fruits – olives, figs and vines – but while Outer Gaul is fertile in grains, nuts and livestock, it has only recently begun to be farmed productively. Mela also stresses the division of Gaul into two (by the Cevennes and lake Leman), and the superior wealth and agriculture of the south, and the productivity of the north in terms of grain and livestock, but not for crops sensitive to the cold. Pliny describes Narbonensis as separated from the rest of Gaul by the Cevennes and the Jura and writes that in terms of its agriculture, the *dignitas* (worth) of its men and its *mores* (customs) and of its wealth it is more like Italy than a province.[9] To be sure, real differences in climate did exist in Gaul as they do in modern France. But the division between north and south is only one possible axis of differentiation: contrasts might also be drawn, for example, between the temperate Atlantic west and the more continental climate of eastern France, between upland areas like Brittany and the Massif Central and lowlands like the Paris basin. The exclusion of Aquitaine from the warm, productive south gives the game away: the boundaries of Narbonensis were inherited from the historically fortuitous boundaries of the Republican province, and this attribution to it of climatic, ethnographic and geographic unity is an ideological naturalization of a contingent political order.

The contrast in the treatment of southern and northern Gaul also reflects the very different extent to which Roman power had penetrated the two areas. Most noticeable is the disparity in the amount of information about each area, and its detail and precision. Strabo's account of Narbonensis is almost as long as his account of the other three provinces put together. It names a very large number of places, many of them linked by detailed itineraries, and several of the communities are described in some detail. His account of Marseille, for example, discusses the topography and cults of the city, its constitution, history and long relations with Rome, and he also discusses the detailed topography of the Plaine de la Crau, the mouths of the Rhône and the coastal

9 Strabo 4.1.1–2, Pliny *NH* 3.4, Mela 2.5, 3.2.

plain. Each major centre – Vienne, Narbonne, Toulouse – has its story
and each story is an episode in Roman history. By contrast his ignorance of the north is profound. His impression of the shape of Gaul is
so vague that, like Caesar, he seems unaware of the very existence of
the Armorican peninsula. At times his account becomes a mere list of
peoples, interspersed with mentions of *emporia* and mines and the occasional anecdote about Caesar's campaigns. The ethnography is also much
more general. While in the south, his stories refer to particular places
and peoples, in the north Strabo describes the habits of 'the Gallic
people as a whole'. Much of his information about them is no longer
valid, as he is aware, in fact being drawn from Polybius, Poseidonius
and Caesar, who visited the Gauls 'before they were enslaved by the
Romans'.[10] Mela and Pliny are a little better informed, but their accounts
of the north are still very brief. The overall impression is that Romans
conceived of Gaul as comprising a southern province, like Italy, with
cities and a long history intermeshed with the history of the Greek and
Roman world, backing onto mountains beyond which stretched a vast
hinterland, only vaguely comprehended, a territory that was fertile and
populous but wild and uncultivated . . . until recent times, that is.

In fact, Strabo's account repeatedly draws contrasts between the pre-
conquest period characterized by life in villages, warfare and barbaric
language, and life under Rome, when war has been replaced by peace
and farming, and urbanization and the use of Latin have taken root.[11]
He attributes the prosperity of 'outer Celtica' more to the size of the
population than to its energy, 'since the women are good at bearing and
raising children, but the men are fighters rather than farmers: now,
however, they have been compelled to lay down their weapons and to
farm'.[12] The barbarians who inhabited the hinterland of Marseille became progressively more peaceful 'turning their attention from warfare
to civilized life (*politeia*) and farming, on account of the dominance of
the Romans'.[13] The Allobroges 'used to wage war with many thousands
of men, now, however, they farm the plains and valleys of the Alps,
some of them living in villages but the most important of them live in
Vienne, a city which they have made into the capital of their people,
although it was once a village'.[14] The Volcae Arecomici 'are no longer
barbarians, since most of them have been converted to Roman standards

10 Strabo 4.4.2. A characteristically Strabonian device, used elsewhere in his *Geography*,
   making clear that his world is not passively Romano-centric so much as recently given
   a centre by Rome.
11 Clavel-Lévêque (1974) for the oppositions. Thollard (1987) and Kremer (1994, 304–
   15) for more detailed treatments of the same theme.
12 *Geography* 4.1.2.   13 *Geography* 4.1.5.   14 *Geography* 4.1.11.

of language and lifestyle, and some of civic life too'.[15] No individual people outside Narbonensis wins similar accolades, but even there Strabo represents Rome as having worked a transformation. The Gallic race as a whole is addicted to war. 'Now, however, they are all at peace, since they have been enslaved and live according to the commands of their captors, the Romans.' In fact, he states that his ethnography is based on their former lifestyle and on the contemporary habits of the Germans, and he interrupts his account of their institutions again to reassert that 'now for the most part they follow the commands of the Romans'.[16] Strabo does not envisage these changes as the sudden exchange of one condition for another – the process may take time and be incomplete at the time of writing. But the civilizing of the barbarians under Roman rule provides a unifying historical theme of the *Geography*.

The idea that Roman rule and contact with Rome had beneficial effects of this kind recurs in other texts. Mela relates how the worst barbarity of the Gauls of the interior, human sacrifice, had now been abolished,[17] and he also mentions that Narbonensis used to be called Gallia Braccata, 'trousered Gaul', (as opposed to Gallic Togata, the term used at the time for Gallic Italy). By Caesar's day, however, the southern province was favourably contrasted with the barbarism of Gallia Comata, 'long-haired Gaul'. Caesar's *Gallic War* also alludes to the spread of civilization among the Gauls as a result of Roman influence. The Belgae are the most powerful people of the Gauls 'as they are furthest from the culture and civilization of the province (*Narbonensis*), and as merchants visit them less often, importing the kind of goods that lead to effeminacy'. Similarly the Ubii are the most civilised of the Germans because their territory touches the Rhine and so they are visited by merchants and have become used to Gallic *mores*.[18]

All these accounts make or assume a close connection between the spread of civilization and the advent of prosperity in Gaul. The association of settled agriculture with civilization and the attribution to barbarians of a nomadic existence, depending on hunting or livestock alone, was a classical trope,[19] and so the association of farming with peace and Roman rule in Strabo's account comes as no surprise. Strabo's work in general has sometimes been thought to be informed by wider economic interests.[20] Among the relevant passages in his description of the Gauls

15 *Geography* 4.1.12.   16 *Geography* 4.4.2–3.   17 Mela 3.2.
18 On the Belgae: Caesar *de bello Gallico* 1.1 'a cultu atque humanitate provinciae longissime absunt', on the Ubii: *de bello Gallico* 4.3.
19 Shaw (1982), cf. Polybius 2.14–35 on the Gauls of northern Italy; Caesar *de bello Gallico* 4.1, Tacitus *Germania* 26 on the Germans; Strabo 4.5.2 on the Britons.
20 Most recently Nicolet (1988, 93).

are the remarks on the fertility of the land, the lists of *emporia* in the interior, the mentions of transit duties and of mineral wealth, agricultural produce, exports and imports, and the passages where he discusses the providential organization of the Gallic river systems and the trade that is carried by them. But his interest in the wealth of the Gauls is echoed in a number of other sources.[21] Rome's power is presented as effecting a realization of this potential, by turning warriors into farmers and by enabling exchanges of goods between regions, 'especially now that they have laid aside the weapons of war and begun to cultivate the land seriously and organize civilized lifestyles for themselves'.[22]

The perspective that emerges from all these accounts of the Gauls is an imperial one. Gaul is a Roman artefact, organized by Roman power as much as by nature, and its history is part of the history of Rome. The power of Rome has not only civilized the Gauls but has provided the optimal conditions for them to achieve their full potential, moral (*bioi*), political (*politeia*) and economic. The ideological importance of these views is all the greater because they are not presented in the course of explicit discussions of Roman imperialism. These vaguely formulated and probably widely held beliefs can be contrasted with the highly crafted rhetorical set pieces in which Tacitus several times confronted the material advantages offered by the *pax Romana* with the loss of liberty it entails.[23] Yet even Tacitus' famous description of how the Britons, imitating Roman lifestyles, mistook slavery for civilization, presupposes these more everyday understandings that moulded Roman responses to the Romanization of Gaul.

II   Roman civilization

What the Belgae lacked, and what the Britons mistook slavery for, was *humanitas*. Like the term 'civilization', by which it is usually translated, it stood for and organized a whole complex of ideas, some descriptive, others prescriptive and all contributing to a definition of self. Like 'civilization' and the concepts that have largely replaced it since Haverfield's day – culture and education, development and modernity[24] – the idea

21 Cf. Velleius 2.39 for an appreciation of the tax revenue of the Gauls in the same period; Josephus *BJ* 2.364 on the prosperity of the Gauls under Roman rule. More generally, see Drinkwater (1979b), Duncan-Jones (1981).
22 *Geography* 4.1.14.
23 See Beagon (1992, 14–15) for a similar point contrasting the elder Pliny with Seneca. Among many Tacitean treatments of the theme, cf. *Histories* 4.64, 73–4 and especially *Agricola* 21.
24 On the articulation of ideas of culture and power relations in contemporary European society, see Bourdieu (1984).

of *humanitas* underwrote and was sustained by a particular configuration of power, and it reflected an understanding of the world and of history that was inextricably linked to the fact of Roman imperialism. *Humanitas* encapsulated what it meant to be Roman, and understanding it is central to an understanding of how a Roman identity was acquired in Gaul.

The precise content of the term is difficult to define.[25] One approach is to see it as articulating a series of other Roman concepts, such as *benevolentia, observantia, mansuetudo* and *facilitas*[26] or *severitas, dignitas,* and *gravitas*,[27] (relating respectively to one's proper attitude towards others and to one's personal qualities) and so connected with concepts like *religio, fides* and *mores*, the basic building blocks out of which Roman society was held to be constructed. Another approach is to look at the Greek concepts to which it was related, *philanthrôpia* and *paideia*. The first term relates to a general regard for human worth, something like our idea of 'common humanity', a guiding principle in human relations which the Stoics developed to prescribe the concern of a master for a slave and of rulers for their subjects. The second term, *paideia*, is more like our notion of 'Culture', the intellectual property of an educated and cultivated person, particularly in this case of a well-born male Greek. The combination of these two qualities more or less, but not exactly, reflected the content of *humanitas*, which might be translated by either Greek word depending on the context.[28] The origins and development of the Roman term, and the extent to which it was influenced by Greek philosophical concepts, is controversial and unlikely to be resolved because of the paucity of evidence earlier than the writings of Cicero.[29] But it is clear that by the late first century BC *humanitas* had been formulated as a thoroughly Roman concept, embodying concepts of culture and conduct that were regarded by Romans as the hallmarks of the aristocracy in particular, yet also appropriate for mankind in general. *Humanitas* thus distinguished an elite as cultivated, enlightened, humane and so fitted to rule and lead by example, but it also encapsulated a set of ideals to which all men might aspire.

25 For attempts see s.v. *humanitas* in *TLL* and Heinemann in *RE* supp. 5, col. 304 and Veyne's (1993) perceptive but idiosyncratic treatment.
26 Gordon (1990, 235).   27 Schadewalt (1973).
28 Aulus Gellius *NA* 13.27 debates which Greek term more accurately reflects the Roman meaning.
29 Ferrary (1988: 344–94) for scepticism about the significance of the middle second century BC, the period when Schadewalt (1973) locates the crucial interaction of Hellenistic philosophy and Roman concepts. On the mid-first century BC, (the age of Varro and Cicero) as a formative period in general, see Rawson (1985) and Beard (1986).

The centrality of this concept to Roman imperial culture is evident from the ways in which it may be seen to have operated. First, there is an ideological naturalization, the representation of a sectional and contingent value system as a set of beliefs with universal validity grounded in the very nature of man.[30] The term *humanitas*, cognate with *homo*, the Latin term for a human being, emphasizes this point. Second, there is the relationship to Roman power, the formulation of *humanitas* as a qualification for rule, and, in so far as Roman rule propagated it, a legitimation of it.[31] Third, *humanitas* provided a description of Roman culture which also operated to define it and bind it together. Symbolic systems or cultures may be envisaged as complexes of values and ideals which are more or less tightly bound together into a package. Loosely structured systems may be particularly vulnerable to change through the substitution of new components for old, or through a reordering of existing elements. Concepts like 'civilization', *humanitas* or *paideia*, by providing detailed descriptions and definitions of a cultural system and sometimes of the differences between those who adhere to it and those who do not, operate to bind cultural systems into more coherent and resilient wholes. What Gauls thought of their own culture remains a mystery. Druidism may have provided alternative descriptions of Gaulish culture, but the Gauls were unable to mobilize them to the same extent as were (to different degrees) Greeks, Jews and Egyptians, perhaps because all of those cultures had won some limited recognition from their Roman conquerors. It is in this sense that *humanitas* can be seen as a central component of Roman culture. It is unclear how long the concept had played this pivotal role: in early Rome it might have provided a cultural focus for a community that considered itself ethnically diverse and was not distinguished from its neighbours by language or material culture.[32] But in the form in which we know most about it, *humanitas* is a product of reflections prompted by the expansion of Roman power.

Particularly important was the sense of historical progress provided by the idea of the dissemination of *humanitas*. Cicero once tried to give some idea of the antiquity of a cultic association called the *coitio Lupercorum* by claiming that it antedated both *humanitas* and law, while Vitruvius conceived of the *initia humanitatis* as the beginning of history, and described how before discovering the arts and sciences, *artes* and

---

30 On naturalization, see Giddens (1979, 193–6).
31 See Erskine (1990, 192–200) on the application of these ideas to Roman rule in the second century BC, cf. also Strasburger (1965) and Momigliano (1975, 31–6). See Gordon (1990, 237) on the legitimizing role of *humanitas*, although in the nature of the concept only the already civilized would properly appreciate this aspect of Roman rule, as opposed to benefits like peace and prosperity.
32 Herescu (1960) and Schadewalt (1973) both argue for a very early origin.

disciplinae, men had lived in the open like savages.[33] That state of nature was presented as part of the common history of mankind in these accounts. *Humanitas* was believed to have been invented only once, however, and although Latin authors sometimes seem slightly reluctant to admit it, its discovery was always attributed to the Greeks.[34] But if the Greeks had invented *humanitas* and disseminated it to some of the barbarians,[35] it was through Roman agency that it was now spreading throughout the world. Pliny the Elder eulogized Italy as:

a land nourished by all, and yet parent of all lands, chosen by the power of the gods to make even heaven more splendid, to gather together the scattered realms and to soften their customs and unite the discordant wild tongues of so many peoples into a common speech so they might understand each other, and to give civilization to mankind (*humanitatem homini*), in short to become the homeland of every people in the entire world.[36]

This passage is one of the few explicit accounts of the civilizing power of Rome in Latin literature, although it can be set alongside the words put into Jupiter's mouth by Virgil: 'remember Roman, these are your skills: to rule over peoples, to impose morality (*morem*), to spare your subjects and to conquer the proud'.[37] It can also be compared to the vision of the transformative power of Rome that emerges from the accounts of Gaul produced by Caesar, Strabo and others. Roman rule is presented as providing the conditions for human beings to realize their potential fully, by becoming civilized, and so truly human. This ideal of civilization is at odds with our notion of civilization as somehow unnatural, but makes perfect sense in terms of much ancient philosophical thought. Roman expansion could thus be understood as the means by which the potential of the world and the entire human race might be fulfilled. Earlier justifications of imperialism had been based on the idea that each war was individually righteous, a *bellum iustum*, but the notion of Rome as the propagator of *humanitas* provided a sanction for the entire process of world conquest.

The concept of *humanitas* served another ideological end. By representing Greek culture as the first stages of a universal process, Romans

33 Cicero *pro Caelio* 26, Vitruvius *de Architectura* book 2, pref. 5, and 1.6.
34 Cicero *ad Quintum fratrem* 1.1.27–8; Pliny *Epistles* 8.24 bracketing the discovery with that of writing (*litterae*) and agriculture (*fruges*). Balsdon (1979, 63–4) on *humanitas* as a quality of both Greeks and Romans. Suetonius *De Grammaticis et Rhetoribus* 1–3, although he does not use the term *humanitas*, presents a similar account of Rome's emergence from barbarism through the study of the liberal arts, for which see Kaster (1995, xliii–xlv).
35 E.g. Vitruvius *de Architectura* 2.8.12.   36 Pliny *NH* 3.39.
37 Virgil *Aeneid* 6.851–3, cf. Vitruvius *de Architectura* book 9 pref. 2. on the establishment of *humanitatis morem* by educated men as one of the prerequisites of secure civic life.

could counter the exclusive claims of *paideia* or hellenism. Greeks may have invented civilization but Rome was destined to bring the process to fruition. The development of the notion of *humanitas* can be seen as part of the Roman response to the cultural anxieties generated by the encounter with Greek culture over the last two centuries BC.[38] Romans might appreciate Greeks for their past achievements, but need no longer feel culturally inferior. From their new position of cultural security they might even condemn present-day Greeks as degenerate, no longer living up to their former achievements, and making excessive uses of nature that went beyond the more appropriate *mores* implicit in *humanitas*.[39] Roman experiences of Greek culture had profound consequences for western peoples like the Gauls. On the one hand, the appropriation of the Greek ideal of civilization, albeit in a modified form, opened up a gap between Romans and others. Cicero, in a letter to his brother Quintus, contrasted rule over the Greeks, 'that people to whom *humanitas* is said to have first come and also by whom it was transmitted to others,' with rule over 'Africans, Spaniards or Gauls, wild and barbarous peoples'.[40] By inheriting civilization, in other words, Rome had inherited the barbarian.[41]

Roman writers were also concerned, however, with disengaging civilization and barbarism from their connections with Greek identity. Cicero contrasted Greek and Roman definitions of civilization in the *de Republica* in a passage where Scipio asks Laelius whether or not Romulus ruled over barbarians. The answer depended, he replied, on whether one defined barbarism, as the Greeks did, in term of language (*lingua*) or, as Laelius would prefer, in terms of customs (*mores*).[42] Equally, a definition of civilization in terms of culture (rather than language or descent) opened up the possibility of barbarians becoming civilized by learning civilized behaviour (*mores*). Greeks conceptualized barbarians as the antithesis of Hellenes, not merely those who spoke Greek and behaved like Greeks, but a people descended from a common stock.[43] Barbarians were unproblematically inferior to them, natural slaves and morally underdeveloped. The distinction could be, and was, elaborated in numerous ways. Romans adopted much of this definition of barbarism – strange

---

38 On these responses, cf. Rawson (1985), Beard (1986), Wallace-Hadrill (1988).
39 Edwards (1993, 92–7), Wallace-Hadrill (1990b). That view of the Greeks provides part of the explanation for Romans' lack of concern to civilize them, as opposed to restrain them from decadence, cf. Woolf (1994b).
40 Cicero *ad Quintum fratrem* 1.1.27.
41 Momigliano (1975, 47) on the role of Polybius and Poseidonius in this process.
42 Cicero *de Republica* 1.58.
43 Hall (1989) for the best treatment of Greek self-definition through elaborating the idea of barbarism. Hartog (1988) explores similar themes through Herodotos' text.

languages, bizarre behaviour and moral inferiority – but there were crucial differences.[44] For a start, common descent was no longer an issue. Common descent had provided one of the main obstacles to Hellenization. It was not enough to behave like a Greek and speak Greek but a Greek genealogy was also required, hence the importance of foundation myths and the frequent assertions of (fictive) kinship by formerly barbarian cities in the Hellenistic and Roman East.[45] Civilization, on the other hand, was more easily acquired. It was also, unlike descent, a matter of degree, hence Caesar's discussion of the relative degrees of *humanitas* possessed by different Gallic and German groups. Greeks thus distinguished themselves from barbarians in terms of a barrier, clear-cut and difficult to cross, while Romans conceived of a continuum along which it was relatively easy to progress. That dichotomy of viewpoint is not straightforward, of course. Many found themselves struggling uneasily between the two positions, as did Strabo, who represented Roman rule in the West as a civilizing force, yet was unhappy with Eratosthenes' suggestion that Romans and Carthaginians might be appropriately considered civilized on account of their political institutions and urban lifestyles.[46] Nor does the continued fascination with Greek culture at Rome suggest that all Romans were wholly confident that Roman civilization was on a par with Greek. But in common usage, the disengaging of civilization from ethnicity was a commonplace among Roman writers.

Romans could not define themselves purely in contradistinction to barbarians, since not all civilized men were Romans. Civilization remained a necessary but not a sufficient precondition of full integration. To become a Roman one also had to be enfranchised, received, that is, into the political and religious community of the *populus Romanus*.[47] But culture remained an important criterion. *Humanitas* in its highest form was represented by a series of intellectual and moral accomplishments and qualities that, in a Western context, were the exclusive property of a narrow elite of Roman citizens. Yet *humanitas* was also quintessentially human, the fulfillment of the potential of the *genus humanum*. Barbarism in its lowest form was the absence of these qualities, and as a result barbarians were imperfect humans, part way to

---

44 Haarhoff (1938, 51–2), Christ (1959), Saddington (1961), Herescu (1961), Dauge (1981, 514–20) for discussion.
45 On foundation myths, see Bickerman (1952); on fictive kinships, see Robert (1977), Spawforth and Walker (1986).
46 Strabo *Geography* 1.4.9.
47 Gautier (1981) for contrasts between Roman and Greek ideas of citizenship. Greek political membership was much less closely linked to cultural and religious identity.

beasts.[48] The moral qualities attributed to them, both in casual comments and in the ethnographies, were bestial.[49] Barbarians were *feroces*, wild like beasts. Their *feritas* was exhibited both in warlike, irrational behaviour and they were also marked out by strange styles of clothing, eating habits and their language. They lacked, in other words, both the general moral qualities of human beings and the culture that defined the Roman elite. Eventually *humanitas* was transformed into a characteristic of imperial civilization, opposed to a barbarism increasingly conceptualized as confined beyond the moral frontiers of the empire.[50]

Elaboration and literary subversion of these ideas were always possible. Barbarians might be represented as free from the corruption of civilization; individual Romans might be presented as behaving barbarously, and barbarians might even be attributed alternative wisdom, like the Druids, portrayed not only as savages who indulged in human sacrifice, but also as natural philosophers who taught the transmigration of souls.[51] But these rhetorical games and intellectual speculations depended for their effect on more common Roman understandings of *humanitas* and barbarism, understandings that were little discussed precisely because they were so widely accepted.

III   The costs of barbarism, the rewards of civilization

That vision of Rome's civilizing vocation had practical consequences, through its impact on the ways Roman rulers exercised their power. Romans discriminated positively as well as negatively – in favour of civilization as well as against barbarism – and Gauls learned from the experience of this discipline.

The Romans arrived in Gaul with their prejudices already formed. The Gallic invasion of Italy and the sack of Rome were central episodes

---

48 Wiedemann (1986, 189–92) for this analysis.
49 On the difference between stereotypes in ethnographies and in other writings, cf. Sherwin-White (1967, 25) and Balsdon (1979, 60). Dauge (1981) is the fullest account of Roman ideas of barbarism, but although he gathers much useful material and makes many valuable observations, his account forces Roman ideas into an over-schematic series of oppositions.
50 Brunt (1978, 185–91) on Republican ideas and Christ (1959) on the transition to empire. Alföldi (1952) and Miller and Savage (1977) discuss the moral valency of the frontier. But Cato's attempted prosecution of Caesar for his treatment of the Usipetes and Tencteri (Appian *Celtica* 18) illustrates how *humanitas* might also be used to assert the rights of 'lesser peoples'.
51 For inversions, see Tacitus *Agricola* 21, *Germania* 19; for barbarous Romans, cf. Dauge (1981, 554–60), Wiedemann (1986), Hall (1989, 201–23); for traditions about the Druids, see Piggott (1968, 91–103).

in the much mythologized history of the early Republic, and Gauls had become objects of imperialist discourse in the course of the Roman conquest of northern Italy in the third and early second century BC.[52] Their strange lifestyle, their mobility, their ferocity and unpredictable behaviour, their greed for gold and their terrifying physical appearance had already been described by Roman observers, and by Greeks for whom they evoked in addition the tribes that had sacked Delphi before occupying the Anatolian plateau and terrorizing the surrounding Greek cities. At Rome a human sacrifice, of two Gauls and two Greeks, was carried out at moments of national crisis.[53] The term *terror Gallicus* is a modern coinage, but the fear of the Gauls persisted at Rome and a store of treasure was laid aside to meet the costs of any further Gallic threat until Caesar emptied it (claiming to have removed forever the Gallic threat) to fund his war against Pompey.[54] Classical writers connected the Gauls north of the Alps with those already encountered in Italy and in the Greek East. Livy recorded a 'sacred spring' legend according to which the sons of the Gallic king Ambigatus divided between them Gaul proper, the lands to the east and Italy.[55] North Italian Gauls were believed to have received reinforcements from their Transalpine 'cousins', and Gauls from both areas had sided with Hannibal against Rome. Appian's history of Rome's *Celtic Wars* began with the Gallic invasion of Italy and continued up to Caesar's campaigns.

Those prejudices and anxieties were frequently mobilized to serve political ends. The process can be illustrated from a number of other late Republican authors, including Livy and Caesar.[56] Perhaps the best example is Cicero's speech *pro Fonteio*, written in defence of a governor of Transalpina, against the usual cocktail of charges levelled against Republican pro-magistrates.[57] Cicero's speech mingles emotional appeals to Roman prejudice with more sophisticated arguments based on

52 Purcell (1990) for discussion of some aspects of the relationship between the conquest and comprehension of Gallia Cisalpina. Cf. Momigliano (1975, 65–7).
53 E.g. Livy 23.57.6 in the aftermath of Cannae, cf. most recently Briquel (1981) with full bibliography.
54 Appian *Bellum Civile* 2.41 for Caesar's action. Cf. the clause preserved in the Caesarian colonial charter of Urso in Spain, permitting a levy in time of Gallic invasion *FIRA* I² 21, ch. 62. I owe the observation that the term *terror gallicus* does not occur in Latin literature to Dr. J. Williams.
55 Livy 5.34–5. Cf. the belief, refuted by Poseidonius (Strabo 4.1.13), that the gold of Toulouse was part of the plunder of Delphi.
56 Kremer (1994) for a very full study, distinguishing and relating popular prejudice to the specific rhetorical-cum-political aims of a number of texts. Philosophical and literary contexts might also be invoked.
57 The speech is fragmentary and the exact nature of the charges is unclear, but Brunt (1961) provides a general account of charges of maladministration. On Cicero's portrayal of Gauls in the speech, cf. de la Ville de Mirmont (1904).

the barbarism of the Gauls and their supposed long standing enmity towards Rome. So he alleges that the prosecution 'defends the treasury of the Ruteni more diligently than that of Rome, and prefers unknown witnesses to familiar ones, foreigners to citizens, and believes it can establish the crime more securely on the basis of the passion of barbarians (*lubidine barbarorum*) than on the written accounts of our countrymen (*hominum nostrorum*)'.[58] The theme of ancient enmity is brought out in his description of Transalpina as consisting 'of men and states who, to say nothing of ancient history, have either fought fierce and lengthy wars against the Roman people within living memory, or have only recently been subdued by our generals, recently defeated in war, recently commemorated in triumphs and on monuments, only recently deprived of their lands and cities by the senate'.[59] Cicero even casts doubt on the capacity of the Gauls, to give testimony: 'does Indutiomarus even understand what it means to give evidence? . . . Indeed, do you think such nations are influenced by the oaths they have to swear, or by fear of the immortal gods when they are giving evidence?' and he goes on to elaborate the theme of the impiety of the Gauls, exemplified by the sacks of Delphi and of Rome, and by human sacrifice.[60] The Gauls have a blood feud with the Roman people, Cicero alleges, which provides him with an opportunity to recall the wars of the 120s and of Marius in southern Gaul.[61] The final chapters of the speech employ the metaphor of a Gallic war. Fonteius is under attack by 'savage and unbearable barbarism', his opponents are 'enemies' (*hostes*) but Marseille has come to his aid.[62] Alongside these arguments the speech is peppered with casual jibes. The Gauls drink to excess and their ambassadors wander proudly and confidently around the forum, clad in cloaks and trousers (*sagatos bracatosque*), and uttering who knows what threats in their ferocious and barbaric tongue (*barbaro atque immani terrore verborum*).[63] Elements of this characterization are familiar from numerous other classical texts, Greek and Roman.[64] The rhetoric of the *pro Fonteio* does not necessarily reflect Cicero's personal opinions, indeed later in his career he was forced to depend precisely on Allobrogian testimony for the crucial evidence of Catiline's conspiracy. But this speech provides an example of how Roman notions of civilization might form the basis of discrimination.

58 *pro Fonteio* 4.   59 *pro Fonteio* 12.   60 *pro Fonteio* 28–31.   61 *pro Fonteio* 33–36.
62 *pro Fonteio* 44–9.   63 *pro Fonteio* 9 (drinking), 19 (enemies), 33 (in the forum).
64 E.g. impiety: Lucan *Pharsalia* 3.402–5, Mela 3.18, Tacitus *Hist.* 4.54; drunkenness: Livy 5.33, Diodorus 5.26, 5.28, Athenaeus 4.151–2, Ammianus 15.12; costume: Cicero *ad fam.* 9.15, Suetonius *Div. Iul.* 76, 80 (both referring to the senators Caesar drew from Gallic Italy), cf. Strabo 3.2.15, 3.4.20 for *togatus* as short-hand for 'civilized'.

Indutiomarus' lack of *humanitas* was a double disability. Firstly, it implied a lack of that education and cultivation that made those who possessed it the elite of the human race as well as of the Roman state. That deficiency was manifested in his lack of rhetorical competence. Mastery of *humanitas* in that sense enabled men like Cicero to achieve upward social mobility through education, and could still ensure power in Gaul centuries later, as is shown by the careers of Eumenius of Autun and Ausonius of Bordeaux.[65] Without a similar cultural competence, Indutiomarus was unable to persuade.[66] But the second disability engendered by the lack of *humanitas* was even more serious. Because *humanitas* denoted possession of those qualities that made human society possible, the absence of it made normal social relationships impossible. The empire of friends which Solemnis infiltrated so successfully depended on the construction of trust, *fides*, between individuals. Roman *amicitiae* entailed *officia* and required *pietas*, qualities that only *humanitas* guaranteed.[67] Access to the patrimonial structures of the empire, in other words, was denied to barbarians. The rationale can also be understood in anthropological terms. The characterization of the barbarian as irrational, unpredictable and so untrustworthy derived in part from a lack of fit between cultural categories, analogous to the non-translatability of key concepts from one language to another.[68] Behaviour that seemed consistent and thus comprehensible in Gallic terms was inconsistent and unnerving to Romans. Only when Gauls acquired cultural competence in Roman standards could these misunderstandings be avoided, and only when they were avoided could Gauls be depended on by Romans. Romans needed to trust Gauls, because of the patrimonial means by which the empire was run. But they were bound to discriminate in favour of those Gauls who appeared dependable and trustworthy, with whom they could communicate easily and who at least seemed to share their values, in short Gauls who exhibited *humanitas*.

Culture could thus offer Gauls a chance to enter the empire of friends. What of the empire of cities? That aspect of the empire can be thought of as a complex hierarchy of privileges and statuses, communal as well as individual, which had acquired a more systematic form in the processes of rationalization of the Augustan period. The key question then

65 For later examples from Gaul, cf. Hopkins (1961) and more generally on social mobility (1965).
66 *pro Fonteio* 29.
67 See Saller (1982, 7–39) on the ideological connotations of these terms, pointing out (8) that for Romans *officia* and connected terms were more central to the descriptions of the relationship than *fides*. See Eisenstadt and Roniger (1984) for patronage as the construction of trust in society.
68 Chapman (1982), drawing on the editorial introduction to Ardener (1971).

is how far was cultural capital convertible into privileged places in that hierarchy? The best documented case is the debate that took place in the senate during Claudius' reign on whether or not to allow Comatan Gauls to stand for senatorial office. The consequences of the decision in favour were not momentous – hardly any senators from the Three Gauls are known[69] – but the account of the arguments employed on either side given by Tacitus, and by an inscription recording the emperor's speech in favour, provide some indications about what was regarded as a sufficient entitlement for admission into the innermost circle of the community of the Romans.[70]

Claudius argued for the admission of the Gauls on three grounds: that it was ancient Roman tradition to admit foreigners into the Roman state, a tradition Augustus and Tiberius had endorsed when they admitted Italians into the senate; that there were already senators and knights from Vienne, a Roman colony and the capital of the Allobroges, who had proved their worth; and that after Caesar's conquest of Comatan Gaul its inhabitants had displayed unshakeable loyalty and service (*immobilem fidem obsequiumque*) in the conquest of Germany. That argument evokes the progressive civilizing of the Gauls and argues that their behaviour now shows that their former *feritas* has been replaced by a capacity to enter into civilized relationships. Tacitus reworks this speech in several ways; he condenses and polishes it and he generalizes the argument a little to reflect the concerns of his own day about the decline of Italy and to echo contemporary Greek portrayals of Rome as the latest in a sequence of empires, comparing Roman openness to the exclusiveness of Athens and Sparta.[71] But essentially he preserves Claudius' main argument, that Rome had always welcomed deserving foreigners and that following Caesar's conquest, Comatan Gaul had experienced a long, loyal peace (*continua inde ac fida pax*) in the course of which Gauls had acquired *mores* and *artes* and intermarried with Romans. The opposing arguments, in addition to assertions of Italy's capacity to supply her own senate, echo the *pro Fonteio*, recalling the wars against Caesar and the sack of Rome. A secondary motif of both speeches in Tacitus is the wealth of the Gauls, for Claudius a potential to be realized, but for his opponents a threat to impoverished Italian nobles. It is clear that *humanitas* was only one of a number of factors that influenced the

---

69 Syme (1958, 461–2), Sherwin-White (1967, 52–61), Burnand (1982), Eck (1991).
70 Tacitus *Ann.* 11.23–4, *ILS* 212.
71 Griffin (1982) compares the two arguments, with further bibliography. For concern about Italy in the empire in Trajan's day, see Woolf (1990b, 220–7). To the parallels gathered by Griffin (1982, 410) for the comparison of Rome to earlier empires, add Aelius Aristides *Oration* 26. 22, 43–67.

distribution of privileges within the empire. More pragmatically, the sectional interests of Italian senators and the wealth of the Gauls were at stake. Emperors may have been aware of the dangers of allowing a politically disenfranchised but economically powerful alternative elite to develop.[72] Yet the argument is still conducted in principled terms of whether or not the Gauls had shaken off their well established past *feritas* and acquired *humanitas*, expressed through peaceful behaviour and faithful service to Rome.

That debate was not an isolated case. Gallic communities might also have hoped to acquire new civic statuses. Under the empire, most such grants were made as personal gifts (*beneficia*) of the emperors, often formally in response to petitions.[73] Our knowledge of the criteria employed to assess the relative merits of applications is limited by the scarcity of accounts of failed petitions, and by uncertainty about the kind of expectations and preliminary enquiries that led some communities to petition and others to decide that they had no chance of success. Claims might be based on the antiquity of a city, on its cultural prestige or on the basis of services rendered. The granting of colonial status to several Gallic communities, and the acquisition by others of the privileged status of free or allied communities,[74] were no doubt often rewards for more concrete services, since many such grants, like tax concessions, were redistributed during the civil wars of AD 69.[75] Yet *humanitas* also seems to have provided a basis for such claims.

Perhaps the best example is offered by the spread of the Latin right. The nature of *Latinitas* underwent a series of transformations, the details of which are not always clear. Originally the term Latin denoted the member of one of a group of communities around Rome with whom the Romans shared language, some cults and perhaps for a time admitted kinship, in recognition of which they enjoyed some rights at Rome normally reserved for citizens. During the conquest of Italy the term came to be used for a variety of halfway positions between being a foreigner (*peregrinus*) and being a Roman citizen. From the end of the Republic, virtually all Latins, with the exception of one category of freedman, held that status by virtue of being members of provincial communities which had been granted the Latin right. No ancient source explicitly asserts that grants of *Latinitas* reflected imperial recognition of the level of civilization attained by provincials, indeed the only motives

---

72 Hopkins (1983, 184–93) on the reproduction of the senate.
73 Millar (1977, 275–6).
74 Wolff (1976), Drinkwater (1979a, 89–90) for lists.
75 Plutarch *Galba* 18.1–2, Tacitus *Hist.* 1.53, 1.78, 3.55, although many of these grants were rescinded by Vespasian: Suetonius *Vesp.* 8.

explicitly recorded for particular grants are to reward past services or secure future loyalty.[76] But a number of pieces of evidence are extremely suggestive that the Latin right was normally considered as appropriate for areas which had progressed some way along the path to *humanitas*.[77] Strabo wrote of the Turdetanoi of Baetica, one of the Iberian groups he considered as *togati*, that they had so completely adapted their lifestyles to Roman models that they no longer even remembered their own language, and 'most of them have become Latins, and have received Roman colonists, so that they are almost entirely Romans themselves'.[78] Latin status here seems to fit into Strabo's general impression of a gradual civilizing process consequent on Roman rule. Moreover the rate at which the Latin right was extended throughout the West seems to echo classical impressions of the relative rate of the spread of *humanitas* in various provinces. Caesar began the process when, following his enfranchisement of Cisalpina, which completed the extension of Roman citizenship to all free inhabitants of the Italian peninsula, he extended the Latin right to Sicily, and to at least some communities in Narbonensis.[79] Some Aquitanian communities had been granted the Latin right by the time of Strabo's account (hence probably under Augustus or Tiberius) and in the course of the first century AD at least some Comatan communities also received it,[80] although there is no certain evidence for a bloc grant of *Latinitas* to all Gallic communities, like those made by Nero to the Maritime Alps and by Vespasian

76 Suetonius *Aug.* 47, Tacitus *Histories* 3.55, to which Pliny *Natural History* 3.3.30 should be added following Fear (1996, 145).
77 For similar views, see Sherwin-White (1973, 249), Brunt (1976), Millar (1977, 401). Against this view, cf. Fear (1996, 131–47), arguing that grants of *Latinitas* were always simply *beneficia* bestowed in return for past or expected services. While it is undeniable that grants of *Latinitas* (as of citizenship) were occasionally used for that purpose, it does not follow that that was regarded as the normal justification of the grant. Long term loyalty (*fides*) was in any case central to conceptions of *humanitas* as the Claudian debate on Comatan entry to the senate shows. That debate provides a plausible model of how particular decisions about *Latinitas* might have been reached in the light of a number of considerations. From an empire-wide (as opposed to Spanish) perspective the spread of the Latin right does seem to correlate fairly well with the spread of other Roman institutions and customs.
78 Strabo 3.2.15.
79 Transpadanes enfranchised: Suetonius *Div.Iul.* 8; Latin rights for Sicily: Cicero *ad Atticum* 14.12; on Narbonensis, see Goudineau (1976), Rivet (1988, 75), and on Nîmes, see Strabo 4.1.12.
80 Strabo 4.2.2 on the Auscii and the Convenae in Aquitainia. Maurin (1978, 155–9) and Chastagnol (1995, 181–90) provide the best accounts of the Latin right in Gaul. For slightly different accounts which have not won complete acceptance, see Galsterer-Kröll (1973) and Wolff (1976), but it should be admitted that the paucity of Gallic epigraphy together with uncertainties about the relationship of *Latinitas* to particular political forms, such as *coloniae* and *municipia*, makes a definitive account very difficult.

to Spain.[81] Eventually, Latin communities are attested in most of the western provinces from Africa to Noricum, but are completely absent from the Greek East.

Latinitas was no doubt valued for the prestige it conferred on provincial communities, but it also offered a series of more tangible benefits. Members of Latin communities were bound by their own laws and had their own political institutions, modelled in practice on those of Rome. But one of the most important privileges incorporated in the Latin right was that the magistrates, or more rarely all the town councillors, of Latin communities acquired Roman citizenship. Latin communities thus operated 'automatically' to disseminate Roman citizenship among provincial elites.[82] Latins also had the right of *commercium*, the ability to enter into contracts with Roman citizens, a valuable privilege for traders. In this, and in other respects, Latins had access to Roman law, even if Roman law was in practice probably often interpreted in the light of local traditions.[83] Practically and in symbolic terms, then, Latins were privileged among Rome's subjects.

The utility of *humanitas* was patent. Its possession offered access to the patronage networks that articulated the empire and might even provide an entitlement to more formal privileges. Exposed to such institutionalized discrimination in favour of the civilized, it would not have been surprising if provincial aristocrats had sought to cultivate themselves for purely pragmatic and material reasons. Yet the ambitions and desires of men like Eumenius and Solemnis do not encourage us to believe that Roman culture was adopted only as a strategy, and that the Gauls retained a place within themselves where their core values were untouched. The civilizing process did not simply offer rewards, then, but also had the power to enchant and beguile, indeed neither conquerors not conquered were immune to its charms.

IV   The seductions of civilization

The Roman way had doubtless many attractions for the rich, besides whatever political rewards it offered. Country mansions and rich town

81 Alps: Tacitus *Ann.* 15.32, Spain: Pliny *NH* 3.30. It is possible, of course, that a similar grant to Gaul, made perhaps in the mid-first century AD, is simply not attested, as argued by Jullian (1908–26) vol. IV, 246, and more recently Goudineau (1980b, 318–19) and Chastagnol (1995, 184–6).
82 For various views of Latin communities and the Latin right, cf. Sherwin-White (1973, 360–75), Millar (1977, 401–7), Humbert (1981), Alföldy (1986), Chastagnol (1995, 73–112). The discovery of the municipal law of the Latin community of Irni (Gonzalez 1986) has clarified the relationship between the communal status and its consequences for individuals. The best summary of these issues is Jacques and Scheid (1990, 232–8).
83 Galsterer (1986).

houses offered sensual comforts, warmth in winter and the luxuries of bathing, to which we might add the softness of new fabrics, the glitter of Roman jewellery and the gastronomic splendours of the Roman table. But for the moment I wish to consider other attractions, the means by which Gauls came to be persuaded that civilization was not only a prudential choice, but also a good thing in its own right. The best starting point is to see how the same conceptions worked in the minds of the Romans to form their ideals of how they ought and might civilize their subjects.

One way of framing the question is to ask what obligations *humanitas* placed on a Roman governor of a western province. *Humanitas* consisted of a series of qualities, but in so far as it corresponded to *philanthropia* as well as *paideia* it also provided a guide to conduct and behaviour, and in particular to the proper exercise of power over one's inferiors.[84] Hence Cicero's injunction to his brother that 'if fate had given you authority over Africans or Spaniards or Gauls, wild and barbarous nations, you would still owe it to your *humanitas* to be concerned about their comforts, their needs and their safety'.[85] That ideology was still in place a century and a half later when Pliny the Younger produced an epistulary and autobiographical representation of an aristocratic lifestyle ruled by *humanitas*, and the literary, political and ethical sensibilities and behaviour that characterized it. The last book of Pliny's letters provides us with a representation of how *humanitas* is to be manifested in the government of an eastern province. The partnership between the humane aristocrat and an emperor who was presented as a paragon of *humanitas*,[86] is shown working for the benefit of the provincials to restrain the expensive excesses of the Greek cities and improve their quality of life through a judicious combination of discipline and generosity (*indulgentia*). Unfortunately, Pliny offers no similar account of the government of a western province, although his forensic patronage of the Baetici in their prosecution of two Roman governors suggests he would have agreed with Cicero's views on the obligations imposed by *humanitas* on the governor of barbarians.[87]

The closest analogy is a very different text, Tacitus' *Agricola*, part biography, part ethnography and part political pamphlet, but which can

---

84 Strasburger (1965), Ferrary. (1988, 511–16), Erskine (1990, 192–200).
85 *ad Quintum fratrem* 1.1.27, discussed by Ferrary (1988, 511–16).
86 *Panegyricus* 2.7. For the stability of the ideology, compare *Epistles* 8.24 with Cicero's first letter to his brother.
87 On the Baetican prosecutions, see *Epp.* 3.4; 3.9; 6.29; 7.33. Pliny quotes Thrasea Paetus in 6.29, listing among those forensic cases that an orator should take on '*causas destitutas*', cases no one else would take on, because they most of all display one's *constantia agentis* and *humanitas*.

also be read, like the tenth book of Pliny's letters, as a construction of the ideal governor. But while Pliny represents Bithynia as just another sphere within which aristocratic *humanitas* can be exercized, Tacitus presents Britain as the moral antipodes of Rome, the utmost ends of the earth and hence the only place where aristocrats can, under a bad emperor, enjoy even the most limited freedom (*libertas*). In contrast to the harmonious picture of Roman rule presented by Pliny, Tacitus' monograph explores a constant tension between aristocratic virtue and the limits imposed on it by the tyrannical principate of Domitian. So Tacitus adheres to the traditional and official equations of Roman *imperium* with *pax* and *humanitas* but glosses them as equivalent to rape, slaughter and pillage, and to devastation and slavery.[88] The tone of Tacitus' description of Agricola's activities between campaigning seasons, related in the much discussed twenty-first chapter,[89] is thus very different from that of comparable statements in Pliny the Younger, or indeed in the works of the latter's uncle or of Virgil. The passage in question runs as follows:

The following winter was devoted to projects of the most admirable sort. By private encouragement he set about persuading men who were scattered, un-cultured and thus easily aroused to warfare, to become peaceable and accus-tomed to the pleasures offered by leisure. In public, he assisted them to build temples, *fora* and residences, praising those who were quick to follow his advice and criticizing those who were slow. A competition for honour thus took the place of compulsion. He went on to give the sons of the nobility a proper education and praised the Britons' intellect above the diligence of the Gauls, so that he aroused an enthusiasm for rhetoric among a people who had recently spurned the Latin language. As a result our national dress, the *toga*, was held in honour and adopted everywhere, and by stages they were led on to the more acceptable vices, public arcades, bathhouses and the sophistication of banquets. In their inexperience they took this for *humanitas* when in fact it was a part of their slavery.

What Tacitus has produced is an ironical reworking of the *humanitas* theme, which preserves a number of the standard elements but under-mines them by interweaving the components of another trope, that of the decline of Roman morality. So the Britons are described, like Strabo's pre-Roman Allobroges, as living scattered and they are uncultivated and warlike. Again like Strabo's barbarians, under Roman influence they begin to adopt an urban lifestyle and to live according to civilized

---

88 *Agr.* 30: '*auferre trucidare rapere falsis nominibus imperium, atque ubi solitudinem faciunt pacem appellant*'; *Agr.* 21: '*idque apud imperitos humanitas vocabatur, cum pars servitutis esset*'.

89 Bénabou (1976b, 369–70), Garnsey (1978, 252–3) and Ogilvie and Richmond's (1967) edition *ad loc.* for differing views.

constitutions, and they learn Latin and wear the *toga*. But Tacitus sets this familiar story to the equally familiar but very different music of Roman decadence: the Britons are won over by the pleasures offered by leisure, and by the attractions of vices – baths, banquets – and finally slavery, that loss of freedom which is more evident at Rome than anywhere else. This tension between the optimistic and harmonious vision of Rome's destiny and the anxiety that Romans have already begun to go beyond *humanitas* into the excesses of luxury to which the Greeks have already fallen victim, already present in the Elder Pliny, finds an acute expression in the *Agricola*. The central character's dilemma is that he constantly strives to exemplify the traditional virtues of a Roman aristocrat, but his efforts are repeatedly subverted by the moral and political decadence of Domitianic Rome. Agricola's life story is not a series of accomplishments, *res gestae*, so much as things nearly accomplished but in the end wasted: 'Britain subjugated and at once thrown away'.[90] So in this passage, Agricola's conduct is not an attempt to weaken the Britons by guile, but a part of his exemplification of the ideal governor, frustrated as ever by Roman decadence. The *Agricola* thus can be taken as evidence for a set of ideas about the role of a governor of barbarians, even if Tacitus' subversive reworking of that theme is original, rhetorical and unrepresentative.

Agricola civilized his Britons in a variety of ways. Most evident is his use of his power to exercize the discrimination his *humanitas* enables him to make, encouraging the Britons with praise as well as criticism until they compete for his approval. The symbols Tacitus chooses to represent civilization are interesting: the temples and *fora* are quintessential public buildings, located at the centre of a Roman city, the setting for the political and religious activity that binds the community together and to Rome. The *domus* are the urban residences of the nobles, whose sons by learning *liberales artes* and *eloquentia* acquire that elite literary culture that is the other meaning of *humanitas*. The least clear part of the passage is the distinction Tacitus makes between private encouragement and public assistance. Agricola used words to civilize, private conversations and public speeches, but did he offer more substantial help in the form of money or help in kind? The passage is inconclusive but active help was not always out of the question. Trajan was prepared to contemplate providing skilled engineers for building projects in Bithynia and more rarely funds might be provided.[91] On the

90 Tacitus *Hist.* 1.2.
91 Skilled personel: *Epp.* 10.41–2; 61–2; funded imperially: MacMullen (1959) but more often from local sources, cf. Duncan-Jones (1990, 174–84). On building in Gaul, see Frézouls (1984).

whole, however, there is little evidence for substantial imperial investment of funds in the civilizing process, and local resources supplemented by private loans were probably more important. The governor's
role was probably more to promote and guide the efforts of locals to
civilize themselves and perhaps also to provide models for their civilizing projects. But governors did exercize a more active civilizing role in
two spheres, by establishing civil communities of the kind within which
they believed man's potential was best realized and by encouraging the
education of the best of the provincials. Through participation in civil
societies and through education, provincials were to have the opportunity to acquire the humane sensibilities that Pliny described in his *Letters*.

Roman generals everywhere are regularly described as setting up and
'correcting' political institutions and laws.[92] Corbulo followed up pun-
itive campaigns in Germany in AD 47 by giving the Frisians 'a senate,
magistrates and laws'.[93] The verb used, *imponere*, recalls the Virgilian
injunction (put into the mouth of Jupiter) to Romans to *imponere mores*
as part of their obligation as rulers. Varus is described as engaging in
similar activity in Germany in AD 9: 'cities were being founded, the
barbarians were beginning to adapt their lifestyle to that of the Romans
and were setting up markets and peaceful assemblies'. Varus' mistake
was allegedly to have rushed the process of change and to have underestimated the extent to which 'they had not forgotten their ancestral
habits and indigenous customs, nor had they forgotten their independent existence and the power that comes from arms'.[94] At one level all
this activity can be seen as a pragmatic policy, the establishment of auto-
nomous communities in areas where they had not previously existed, so
that they could take on the burdens of organizing taxation and the levy,
and of maintaining public order. But it is important to situate political
institutions in the context of the connections Strabo repeatedly makes
between new *politeiai*, political systems or constitutions, and new *bioi*,[95]
lifestyles, or of the links Cicero made between *humanitas* and law.[96]

The best illustrations of this ideology are the charters issued to provincial communities in the Latin West.[97] None survive from Gaul and it
is unsafe to assume that the constitutions of Gallic communities corresponded in detail to those outlined in the Flavian municipal laws found

92 For examples from the East, see Woolf (1994b, 122–5).   93 Tacitus *Ann.* 11.18–19.
94 Dio 56.18.1–3.   95 Strabo 4.1.5; 4.1.12; cf. Dio 54.25 on Augustus.
96 To the connection made between the two in *pro Caelio* 26 should be added the *pro
rege Deiotaro* 12, where Castor's cruel and immoderate *inhumanitas* and barbarism is
said to threaten the *iura* of the city and its moral life.
97 Gonzalez (1986) for the fullest edition of the municipal law, with the analysis of it by
Galsterer (1988) and Fear (1996, 152–69).

in Spain. Nevertheless there were Caesarian colonies in the south which must have had similar charters to that of the Caesarian colony of Urso and it seems *a priori* likely that the Latin *coloniae* of Narbonensis and the *coloniae* of the north were provided with similar charters. What is immediately striking about the Spanish charters is the detail in which they provide a blueprint for 'civilized' life: procedures for elections, assemblies and meetings of *decuriones*, regulations on the conduct of magistracies, on the management of public finances, on relations with other communities and the basis of a judicial system. Much more is included than is necessary to ensure that these communities met the minimal demands – tax and security – made on it by the empire. Concretely these charters had implications not just for politics in the narrow sense but also for property, marriage and legal custom, and – despite imperial protestations that vested interests would not be affected, and that the *municipes* were subject to their own laws – the charters introduced Roman-style political institutions, and were based on and referred back to the Roman *ius civile*. The charters thus represent new *politeiai*, which required dramatic changes of *bioi*, and must have been one of the main means by which Romans could impose new *mores* (culture, manners, behaviour, morality). Naturally these ideals were probably never completely adhered too. Many communities were too small to need or sustain even the 'minimal civil society' envisaged by legislators, and many provisions were probably ignored or interpreted in local terms.[98] But these laws were published and might be appealed to by the knowledgeable in disputes and they presented local elites with a brief guide to how to govern their communities in a humane manner. Political practice and political culture could not have been separated from political theory, especially since knowledge of that theory and conformity to those rules would give an advantage to political actors.

The same lesson, and others, were also to be learned in the schools set up for the children of the elite all over the West. Education featured prominently in Agricola's programme, and here it is clear that his was not an isolated initative. Tacitus mentions that the rebel Sacrovir briefly captured Autun in AD 23 in order to take hostage 'the most well-born youth of the (Three) Gauls who were there receiving a proper education (*liberalibus studiis*)' and Suetonius mentions what may have been a similar school for German youths.[99] Agricola himself had been educated in Marseille for a while.[100] Strabo describes the southern Gauls as

98 Galsterer (1986).   99 Tacitus *Ann.* 3.43; Suetonius *Caligula* 45.
100 Tacitus *Agricola* 4.

being inspired by the educated lifestyle of Roman Marseille to hire teachers, both privately and publicly, and a number of inscriptions record the activities of teachers in the major Gallic towns.[101] The region is occasionally mentioned (like Africa and Spain) as a source of orators, the most famous being Favorinus of Arles,[102] Gallic oratory is alluded to by Juvenal,[103] and all but one of the speakers in Tacitus' *Dialogus de Oratoribus* are Gauls, as Tacitus himself may have been. Certainly Gaul does not rival either Spain or Africa as a source of Latin writers in the first three centuries AD, and Pliny professes himself amazed that there are bookshops in Lyon.[104] But that comment, like Juvenal's remarks on Gauls teaching Britons rhetoric or the occasional claims of Latin poets to be read in distant parts, depends for its effect on a perception of Gaul as unlettered and is poor evidence for actual practice. In fact, education in Gaul, as generally in the West, followed the pattern outlined in the works of Quintilian and the Elder Seneca, beginning with the study of language and proceeding to that of rhetoric. Although training in philosophy was available, for example in Marseille, rhetorical training dominated education in the West. Language was taught through intense reading of the Latin classics, among them Virgil, Cicero and Livy, and the same texts also contributed to the teaching of rhetoric, along with practice speeches on themes drawn partly from Roman history. These exercises exposed students to Roman conceptions of their exemplary past and their glorious future, and to implicit definitions of virtue and civilization, in short they provided a guide to the imperial and humane vocation of the Roman elite. For a society in which social mobility was high by pre-modern standards, education played a central role in the social reproduction of the ruling classes.[105] For the Gauls it offered a guide to entering that elite.

Lessons learned from Virgil provided the children of the Gallic elite with the means of communicating with their Roman rulers, and of impressing them with their possession of humane literary sensibilities and an appreciation of the moral universe of the empire. Rhetoric, the art of persuasion, was naturally of immense value for that class which

101 Strabo 4.1.5. Marrou (1965, 428) lists epigraphic evidence for teachers at Narbonne, Marseille, Arles, Vienne in Narbonensis and Lyon, Autun, Besançon, Limoges, Reims, Avenches, Trier and Cologne in the Three Gauls.
102 Marrou (1965, 422–30) remains the best survey of education in the western provinces, stressing both Rome's 'oeuvre éducatrice' and its social limits, cf. Haarhoff (1920, 33–8), although some of his Gallic orators are in fact clearly Cisalpini, cf. now Kaster (1995) on the individual orators. On Favorinus and the cultural milieu from which he emerged, cf. Gleason (1995, 3–5).
103 *Satires* 7.148 and 15.111. 104 *Ep.* 9.11.
105 Kaster (1988) discusses this for a later period. On its significance in western provincial cultures, cf. Woolf (1996b).

mediated between Gallic communities and the empire and for those individuals who wished to penetrate the empire of friends. But the Roman cultural myths acquired in the course of this education had other attractions, and were themselves persuasive. Roman senses of their own past included their rise through virtue and consequent divine favour from a small heterogeneous community to rulers of the world. That myth did not define Romans as a descent group like the Greeks nor a chosen people like the Jews but as a community that had grown by recruiting others to its values, loyalties, customs and cults. Educated Gauls, in other words, knew the history of Rome's acceptance of loyal subjects long before Claudius' oration on the subject was inscribed and published at Lyon. That myth offered an account of the Gauls' past – as barbarians – and hope for the future as civilizers. If they had been barbaric they were not predestined to remain so, indeed the recognition of their former barbarism provided some sort of explanation for their conquest by Rome. This new history of Gaul is that understood in Eumenius' speech. Equally, acceptance of Roman myths of civilization offered the Gallo-Roman aristocracies a place in the future, a place they were quick to take as the Gallic participation in the conquest, garrisoning and civilizing of Britain and Germany makes clear. *Humanitas* also provided Gallo-Roman aristocrats with a title to rule over their less educated subordinates. No longer barbarians, they acquired a sensitivity to the cultural deficiencies of their subjects, so education provided a means of conceptualizing and expressing the economic and political gulfs that had opened up within Gallic societies as a result of incorporation into the empire. The success of those who did adopt Roman culture will have made the Roman myths learned at school seem all the more persuasive. The motivations of individuals are always difficult to disentangle, and it is probably pointless to attempt to disentangle cultural action designed as a conscious strategy for self advancement from that prompted from a deep internalization of elite Roman values, but there is a clear convergence between the pragmatic interests of new Gallo-Roman aristocrats and the civilizing ethos of the empire's ruling classes.

What this argument amounts to is a claim that Roman conceptions of civilization operated ideologically, offering beliefs that convinced because they made sense of experience and cohered with the interests of the new aristocracies that emerged in the formative period of Gallo-Roman culture. Like most dominant ideologies it was probably more convincing to ruler than to ruled, but it was none the less sincerely held for all that. Just as the real-life Agricola and his colleagues subscribed to the civilizing ethos, so those they civilized acquired a similar vocation and became civilizers themselves. It is thus pointless to ask whether Rome civilized the Gauls or whether they civilized themselves. The educated elite of the empire joined together in the civilizing mission, sharing an identity that was Roman, humane and aristocratic.

A graphic illustration of the extent to which Gauls internalized the civilizing ethos is offered by a monumental arch constructed in the Sequanian capital of Besançon at the point where the great road from Italy and the south entered the city.[106] The arch draws on a tradition of triumphal monuments that in Gaul can be traced back to a series of municipal arches set up in the *coloniae* and major cities of Narbonensis and neighbouring regions during the reigns of Augustus and Tiberius and to the trophies set up to mark the conquest of the Alps and the Pyrenees.[107] Those arches, themselves part of a broader Roman tradition, were later imitated further north, for example at Cologne. Celebrations of the *pax Romana*, they were decorated in representations of Roman troops and subject barbarians, images of emperors and deities, and symbols of the peace achieved by Roman arms. The images are stereotypical, drawing on Pergamene models for the defeated Gaul, and a standard repertoire of Roman public art. It is only possible to guess at how they were understood by veteran colonists, and by the generation of Roman citizens and of Gauls that saw them when they were first set up. But the images they present illustrate the civilizing ethos, making them visual counterparts of the classical school texts through which Gauls learned the new history of civilization. Possibly images of this sort, like those on coin, reinforced those lessons. The Besançon arch, however, is later and different in important respects. To begin with, it was produced by local craftsmen. That much is clear from the style of the sculpture which closely resembles that of funerary and religious monuments produced in north-east Gaul at this period, and from the peculiarly local versions of classical myths and deities. It has, however, the standard images of soldiers and weapons, victories and garlands and of course captives, and within the arch depictions of Roman soldiers fighting generic Easterners (presumably recording victories in the Parthian war) faced scenes of similiar battles against Westerners. Although the inscription has not survived, it is likely that the arch is to be dated to the reign of Marcus Aurelius, who campaigned both in Sequania (in the early 170's) and in the East, and in any case the arch is Antonine or

106 Walter (1986) for what follows.
107 Silberberg-Pierce (1986) on the southern monuments. Examples are known from St Bertrand-de-Comminges, Toulouse, Béziers, Narbonne, Nîmes, Avignon, Orange, Carpentras, St Rémy, Arles, Marseille, Fréjus, Vienne, Aosta, Susa. Walter (1993) discusses the representations of barbarians on surviving examples.

(less likely on stylistic grounds) Severan. Above the apex of the arch and surrounding it, however, is a representation of Jupiter with a thunderbolt scattering a crowd of giants whose human bodies taper into serpent bodies. The image of the gigantomachy, representing order defeating chaos and civilization routing barbarism, is an ancient theme of classical art, but the representation is wholly local and best known in north-east Gaul and Germany on the Jupiter columns with which the arch has other affinities.[108] The mythological programme of the arch as a whole has been interpreted as representing *virtus* and *pietas* as rewarded by *felicitas* (prosperity), and *impietas* as resulting in misfortune.[109] Whether or not that formulation is accepted it is clear that the arch of Besançon represents a blend of local and imperial images of Roman virtue sustaining the moral order. Gallic adherence to that order and acceptance of the Roman myth of civilization could hardly be better attested.

108 Bauchhenß and Noelke (1981) for a corpus and discussion.
109 Walter (1986, 384–423).

4 Mapping cultural change

I Gallo-Romans in their own words

Gallo-Roman civilization was not built in a day. Nor were all parts of Gaul, nor all sectors of Gallic societies equally affected by the civilizing process. The aim of this chapter is to map out – in broad lines – the cultural geography of Roman Gaul, the rhythms and timing of change, and its social distribution. The picture that emerges will be elaborated and nuanced later, but this outline is sufficient to make clear the over-riding importance of Roman power in explaining the emergent patterning of Gallo-Roman culture.[1] Gallic culture was transformed at the points of most intense contact between Romans and Gauls. The period of maximum change corresponded to the period when Roman power over Gaul was suddenly intensified. The social groups most effected were those in closest contact with the various representatives of the imperial state. All this is exactly as might have been expected in view of the relationships that have been established between Roman imperialism and cultural change in Gaul.

Mapping cultural change is not easy. Ideally a wide range of variables would be considered, each well dated and provenanced and socially unambiguous, but the result would be a book in its own right and very difficult to construct from the state of the evidence for Roman Gaul.[2] Instead, a single category of evidence – epigraphy – will be used here to establish a provisional outline of the cultural geography of Roman Gaul. Inscriptions are a convenient medium for several reasons. To begin with, bronze and stone inscriptions in Latin represent the traces of a wide range of Roman cultural practices, funerary, cultic and political, among others, and record the spread of Roman names and statuses, institutions and the Latin language in the provinces. Secondly, the systematic fashion in which they have been catalogued and studied

---

1 On the shift in the broad patterning of cultural differences from the iron age to the Roman period, see Woolf (1997).
2 For a brilliant study of this kind in a much more recent period, see Weber (1979).

since the nineteenth century makes them accessible source material.[3] Finally, they are quantifiable and relatively easy to date and provenance, at least approximately. For all these reasons, inscriptions have often been used as an 'index of Romanization'.[4]

But if the rise of an 'epigraphic habit' in the provinces is correctly seen as a sign of the adoption of a variety of Roman practices,[5] it does not necessarily follow that inscriptions were set up in order to assert a Roman identity.[6] The majority of Latin inscriptions were set up in the second and third centuries AD, when an individual's place in the Roman social order was indistinguishable from his or her place in the social order in general, and when the cultural boundary between Gaul and Roman was no longer so clear cut. It has also been suggested that the spread of the epigraphic habit is largely a product of the spread of citizenship, reflecting the importance Romans invested in an heir's duty of commemoration.[7] But the concern to name individuals and to locate them in a network of social relationships and in the social order extends well beyond the funerary sphere, and it is more useful to see inscriptions as attempts to assert identities, sometimes defined more in relational terms, sometimes more in terms of their achieved or ascribed status, against a background of social mobility.[8] Latin inscriptions in Gaul thus provide evidence for the adoption of Roman cultural practices and for the spread of Roman social structures, but were not designed or understood by contemporaries primarily as symbols of Roman identity.

Consider, for example, this honorific inscription, set up at the sanctuary of the imperial cult at Lyon.[9]

Q. IVLIO . SEVERINO
SEQVANO . OMNIB
HONORIBVS . IN
TER . SVOS . FVNCTO
PATRONO . SPLENDI
DISSIMI . CORPORIS
Ñ . RHODANICOR . ET

---

3 Latin inscriptions from the Gauls are collected in *CIL* xii (Narbonensis) and xiii (the Three Gauls and Two Germanies), with their supplements. The former is also supplemented by *ILGN* and now by the first volumes of *ILN*, and the latter by *ILTG*, and, for the German provinces, by surveys in *BRGK* 17 (1927) 1–107; 27 (1937) 15–134; 40 (1959) 120–229; and 58 (1977) 447–604.
4 E.g. Mócsy (1970, 199–212), Wightman (1985, 162–77), Nicols (1987), Cepas (1989, 54–8).
5 See MacMullen (1982) for 'the epigraphic habit'. On the significance of different media of inscription, cf. Veyne (1983) and Williamson (1987a).
6 E.g. Wightman (1984, 71).   7 Meyer (1990).
8 See Woolf (1996a) for elaboration of this argument.   9 *CIL* xiii.1695.

ARAR . CVI . OB . INNOC
MORVM . ORDO . CIVI
TATIS . SVAE . BIS . STATVAS
DECREVIT . INQVISITO
RI . GALLIARVM . TRES
PROVINCIAE . GALL

(In honour of Quintus Julius Severinus, the Sequanian, who had performed all the offices among his own people and was patron of the magnificent guild of the shippers of the Rhône and the Saône, and was twice decreed statues by the council of his own state on account of his integrity. The three Gallic provinces voted this in his honour on the occasion of his holding the post of Inquisitor of the Gauls.)

The translation conceals the highly formulaic nature of the original, with its plethora of abbreviations such as Q. for Quintus and N with a bar to stand for Nautarum, and its reliance on stock phrases like *omnib(us) honoribus inter suos* to signify a full career among the Sequani, probably consisting of two or three minor posts followed by a quaetorship or aedileship and finally the duumvirate.[10] The document, in other words, is a text for insiders to read, only fully comprehensible to those with the requisite cultural expertise, which involved much more than a knowledge of Latin. Inscriptions like this one acquired their full significance only in relation to other inscriptions of the same kind. Although it was set up by the Council of the Three Gauls, the inscription was probably paid for by Severinus and he certainly must have selected the content. The text can thus be also read as a form of self-representation. On the one hand it asserts Severinus' individual accomplishments and identity, on the other it constitutes a claim to a place in an existing order, identifying Severinus in terms of his local citizenship, the offices he had held and honours he had received among the Sequani. The patronage of the guild of shippers may also reflect activity within his own community, since the Saône ran through Sequanian territory, and since it is mentioned between the record of his local career and that of his local honours. The final post, the *inquisitor Galliarum* is one of the offices of the imperial cult organization at Lyon, a post of very high status which marks Severinus' arrival on the same international stage as Titus Sennius Solemnis.[11]

We may infer more about Severinus from the inscription. His name, for example, shows him to be a Roman citizen, while the *nomen* Julius suggests his family was enfranchised under Caesar or Augustus. The institutions and honours mentioned – civic magistracies, the patronage of guilds, the award of statues, honorific decrees by town councils and

10 Drinkwater (1979a).   11 See Audin *et al.* (1954) for the cult organization.

the provincial *concilium* – are thoroughly Roman in character. But what Severinus chose to stress in his self-representation was not so much his Roman citizenship, but his *honores* first among the Sequani, and second in Gaul as a whole. There may well have been contexts in which he was intensely conscious of his identity as a Roman and keen to distinguish himself from non-citizens and barbarians, but his self-representation at Lyon takes the Romanness of Roman Gaul for granted, and his implied rivals are not non-Romans but other Sequani and aristocrats from other Gallo-Roman communities, who claim such a splendid place in the order of things.

A little lower in the social hierarchy is the subject of a long funerary inscription from Autun.[12]

> Q. SECVND
> QVIGONIS
> CIVIS . TREVERI
> IIIIIVIR AVGVS
> TALIS IN AEDVIS
> CONSISTENTIS
> OMNIB . HONO
> RIB . INTER EOS
> FVNCT . QVIGO
> NI . SECVNDVS
> ET . HIBERNALIS
> LIBERTI . ET HE
> RED PATRONO
> OPTIMO SVB AS
> CIA DEDICAVERAT
> L . D . EX D . O

(In memory of Quintus Secundus Quigo, a Treveran citizen and *sevir Augustalis* resident among the Aedui, who had performed all the offices among them. Secundus and Hibernalis his ex-slaves and heirs set this up *sub ascia*, to Quigo, the best of patrons in a place assigned by decree of the town council.)

The web of relationships asserted here is more complex, combining Quigo's relationship to his adoptive community, in which he had played an active role, with that of his relationship to the two ex-slave slaves he had made his heirs. He was quite probably an ex-slave himself to judge from his holding the priesthood of Augustus.[13] As in the case of Severinus,

---

12 *CIL* XIII.2669.
13 A slight puzzle is that, although an *incola* and a *libertus*, Quigo seems to have been able to enjoy a municipal career among the Aedui yet was also a *sevir Augustalis*, usually thought to have been reserved for those debarred membership of the *ordo*. It is conceivable that the explanation lies in the difference between Trier's colonial constitution (if it was there that he held the sevirate) and the allied status of the

however, the identity that is stressed is local rather than Roman, even if the relationships and offices, like the form of the inscription itself, are themselves thoroughly Roman.

Most surviving inscriptions are short epitaphs and votives, rather than long honorific or dedicatory inscriptions, and most were set up by more humble dedicators. But no rigid divide can be drawn between humble and grand epigraphies. The inscribing classes included many more than simply the *decuriones* and *seviri Augustales* of the cities, but many fewer than the total population, and so indicate how Roman power and Roman culture operated well beyond whatever narrow group we might designate as 'the provincial elite'. To some extent the creation of these intermediate classes was itself a consequence of Roman rule, since there is little evidence for them in the iron age, and illustrates the operation within Gaul of social processes well attested elsewhere in the empire, in particular urbanization, manumission and the growth of trade. The extent of the epigraphic habit in Gaul demonstrates that cultural change was not confined to a narrow section of society. Its limits, on the other hand, are underlined by the paucity of the epigraphic record in Gaul compared to other provinces and to Italy (Fig. 4.1). If the average number of inscriptions surviving per 100 hectares is calculated, none of the Comatan provinces or lower Germany registers above 2, upper Germany is just under 5 and Narbonensis is just over 6. For comparison, Italy averages just over 13 (within which *regio* I has an average of 55 inscriptions per 100 ha.) and Africa Proconsularis an average of over 12. Of the western provinces, inscriptions are thinner on the ground only in inland Spain, Britain, Raetia and Mauretania Tingitana.[14] There is no reason to think that the survival rate of Gallic inscriptions is any lower than in other provinces. Stone was everywhere recut and reused, was buried, crumbled and shattered and occasionally melted down. It seems difficult, then, to explain these inter-regional contrasts except in terms of differences in the total number of inscriptions ever set up, especially since they seem to correspond at least in part to relative levels of urbanism.[15] That low level of epigraphic culture needs to be kept in mind throughout all that follows.

Aedui. Alternatively, this and some other problematic cases might suggest that the nature and function of the sevirate needs to be re-thought.

14 Harris (1989, 266–8) gives the figures, calculated on the basis of *CIL* totals. Values for the Italian *regiones* range from 2–55, the median is 11.5 and the mean 13.2: Duncan-Jones (1982, 339).

15 On the survival rates of inscriptions, see Duncan-Jones (1982, 360–2) and Mann (1985); on the correlation with urbanism in Italy, see Jongman (1988, 67–70), although the suggestion of a link to population seems less secure.

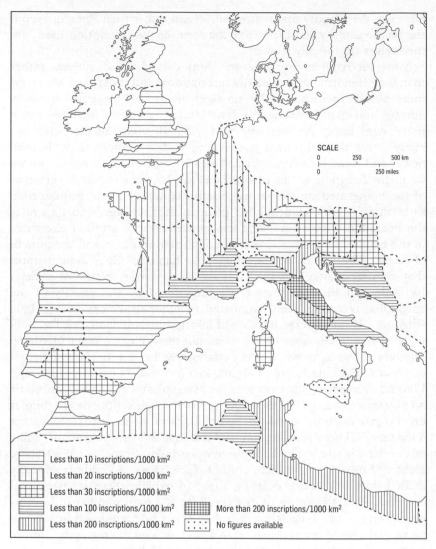

Fig. 4.1   Epigraphic density in the western provinces

II   Cultural geography

Inscriptions provide one means of mapping cultural geography. The concept of a cultural geography is a convenient shorthand for the answer to questions like which parts of Gaul experienced the most change? And which regions were most involved in Roman cultural practices? It also provides the basis for asking how these patterns relate to other phenomena that can be mapped in space, such as the distribution of troops or colonists, the road network and river systems of Gaul and other aspects of its physical geography. Mapping the distribution of culture can be done at different scales, empire-wide, provincial, or within individual *civitates*. At the largest scale, epigraphic density indicates differences between the Gallic provinces and their neighbours (Fig. 4.1). But within the Gauls and Germanies the differences recorded by this method are slight: Narbonensis with a value of 6.1 inscriptions/ 100 ha stands out in sharp contrast to Aquitania and Lugdunensis, each with values of 1.1. Belgica and lower Germany both give values of 1.9, and Upper Germany occupies an intermediate position with 4.8.[16] But large differences within these provinces are concealed, particularly in the case of Lugdunensis which extended from the political hub of the Gauls to its Armorican periphery.

An alternative technique is to compare the absolute numbers of inscriptions known from particular locations. One advantage is that this method better reflects the actual distribution of inscriptions, not evenly dispersed throughout the landscape but concentrated in clusters such as cemeteries, sanctuaries or the public buildings of town centres.[17] The main disadvantage is that since so few inscriptions are known from most sites in Gaul, the totals may be distorted by their post-Roman histories. The late antique construction of circuit walls, in which many earlier inscriptions were re-used and thereby preserved, can make a considerable difference to the totals surviving, as can the activities of local *érudits* who, since the seventeenth century, in some towns systematically collected or recorded many inscribed stones. A secondary difficulty concerns the different Roman-period histories of Gallo-Roman cities, particularly from the third century AD on, when, while most cities shrank in size, a few, like Bordeaux, Arles and Trier, attained a new prominence.[18] The problem is rendered less serious by the generalized rise and decline of the epigraphic habit, which means that the majority of Gallic inscriptions were produced in the late second and early third centuries,[19] nevertheless some of those cities which remained prominent for longer are disproportionately represented in these totals. For these

16 Harris (1989, 266–8).   17 Corbier (1987) discusses the urban setting.
18 See Février (1980, 399–421) on the different fates of different towns after the third century. Both Arles and Trier were briefly imperial capitals. See Jullian (1908–26) VI, 299–527 on the diversity already present among the Gallo-Roman cities of the early empire. Kneißl (1988, 245–7) compares the situation in the south, where epigraphy began and tailed off early, with the slower take-off and decline in the north, attributing this pattern to contrasting patterns of economic growth. Christol (1995, 164–5) shows this is truer of colonies than other centres.
19 Mrozek (1973), (1988).

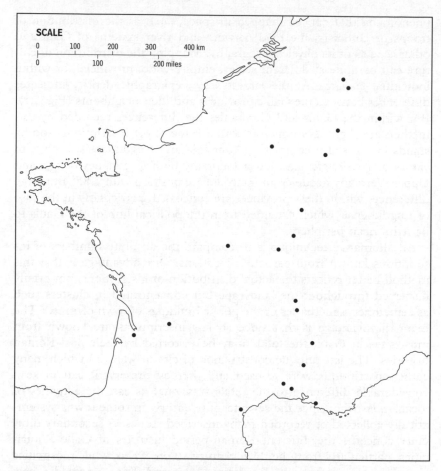

Fig. 4.2   Clusters of at least 100 inscriptions

reasons, the total number of inscriptions deriving from individual centres cannot be used to rank order Gallo-Roman cities at any particular period. The significance of these results, then, lies not in individual cases, but in what emerges about general patterns within the Gallic provinces.

The results of plotting concentrations of inscriptions in the Gauls and Germanies are presented cartographically (Figs. 4.2–4.5).[20] The

20 This survey is based on a count of the lapidary inscriptions (excluding milestones) in *CIL* XII and XIII, with their supplements, but without taking account of inscriptions published later in *ILGN* (1929), *ILTG* (1963), *ILN* (1985), in the survey in *BRGK* (1977), or in the annual notices in *AE*. In order to assess the extent to which inclusion of these supplements would have altered the results one of the supplements, *ILTG*, was examined. This volume collects additions and revision to *CIL* XIII's coverage of

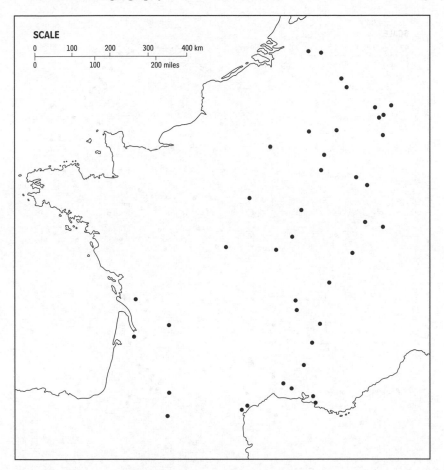

Fig. 4.3   Clusters of at least 50 inscriptions

first observation to make is that the size of the concentrations varies considerably, and that the ranking is strongly primate, in other words there are a few sites with very large totals and a large number with fairly small ones, but there are relatively few medium size concentrations

Comatan Gaul (although not of the two Germanies) for the period 1916–1963. The new texts, again excluding milestones, total 373, representing an increase of about 7 per cent and are fairly evenly distributed although St Bertrand-de-Comminges had 57 new texts, constituting an increase of 70 per cent, which illustrates the effect of chance finds on these low totals. The new *ILN* volume on Fréjus lists 207 lapidary inscriptions where *ILGN* in 1929 recorded only 122, including *instrumentum domesticum*. In view of the difficulties of compensating for the variations between regions in the extent to which *CIL* has been revised, it was decided to use *CIL* totals in this survey, but to register this caveat.

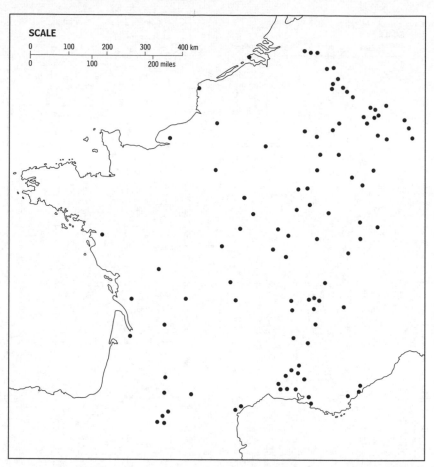

Fig. 4.4   Clusters of at least 20 inscriptions

(Fig. 4.5). Two cities have produced over a thousand inscriptions, ten have produced over 200, twenty over 100 and about one hundred over 20. The significance of this is difficult to gauge. One factor may be the activities of collectors in areas where inscriptions were relatively common, the collectors assembling large collections in some French provincial towns. Another may be exponential growth within epigraphic environments, where a lively epigraphic culture encouraged dedication. But the order in which the towns appear seems to correspond fairly well with their political, military and economic pre-eminence in the early empire, insofar as it can be assessed by other criteria.[21] The 'top ten' are, in order of precedence, Narbonne, Nîmes, Lyon, Mainz, Trier,

21 See Wightman (1985, 163–4) for a similar assessment.

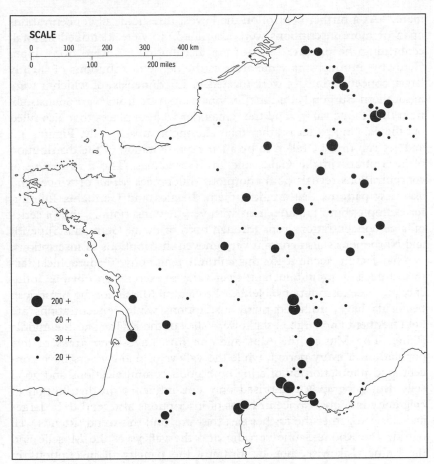

SCALE

| 0 | 100 | 200 | 300 | 400 km |
| 0 | | 100 | | 200 miles |

200 +

60 +

30 +

20 +

Fig. 4.5   Clusters of inscriptions

Bordeaux, Arles, Cologne, Vienne and Langres, all of them large cities located on one or more major routes, most of them heavily monument-alized, and several of them centres of provincial administration. The relative numbers of inscriptions are not too badly affected, then, by post-depositional factors and the primate distribution reflects a feature of Gallo-Roman urbanism as a whole.

As an attempt to illustrate both the distribution of concentrations and their relative size, figures 4.2, 4.3 and 4.4 show the distribution of concentrations of 100 or more, 50 or more and 20 or more inscriptions respectively. As a control against the effect of the thresholds selected, figure 4.5 shows on a single map the same series divided at a different set of thresholds, 200 or more, 60 or more, 30 or more and 20 or more.[22] As a further control on the lowest threshold, all concentrations of 12 or more inscriptions were examined. 40 were identified in total, confirming the primate form of the distribution. 15 were from upper Germany, in much the same areas as the dense distributions of slightly larger concentrations, 5 were located in Lugdunensis, of which 4 were in southern Burgundy and the Lyonnaise, 7 were from Narbonensis, all from the Rhône valley, and the remainder were in places that also filled out the existing pattern rather than altering it substantially. Figures 4.4 and 4.5 can thus be taken to be a fair representation of the distribution of inscriptions in the Gauls and the Germanies. The distribution of concentrations reveals both enormous differences *within* provinces and also new patterns that straddle them. Belgica and Germania Inferior, for example, both include areas with very few inscriptions, but a series of large concentrations runs through both of them. Germania Superior and Narbonensis also contain very uneven distributions of inscriptions.

What factors account for this cultural geography? Geographical factors, especially mountains and river valleys, exercise an obvious influence on these distributions. Neither the Central Massif nor the Armorican peninsula have produced many inscriptions while concentrations are both frequent and large in the lower valley of the Rhône and the middle Rhine. The Massif, the Alps and the Jura have been areas of low population in every period, while the valleys of major rivers have concentrated population by offering both good communications and good soils. But geography comprised only one influence on distribution of epigraphy in Gaul. Concentrations of inscriptions also tend to be larger and closer together the further east they are, and this trend extends well outside the Rhône-Saône corridor and the valleys of the Moselle and the Rhine. Likewise, outside Brittany the paucity of inscriptions in Atlantic France, the Loire valley, and much of the Paris basin cannot be explained in terms of poor soils or low populations.

A second major factor seems to have been the Roman communications system. If the map of major Roman roads in Gaul and Germany (Fig. 4.6) is compared to the distribution of inscriptions it becomes clear that towns like Langres, which were situated at key points on the road network, have produced many more inscriptions than similar towns which were less well connected. Naturally the roads responded to geographical constraints and were integrated with the river systems of Gaul, following valleys, connecting urban centres spaced along them and

22 For a further comparison, cf. the map in Goudineau (1980a, 49), using thresholds of 1000+, 500+, 250+, 100+ and 50+. Among the minor differences are the omission of Langres from his map, no doubt accidentally, and slightly different totals for some towns such as Marseille.

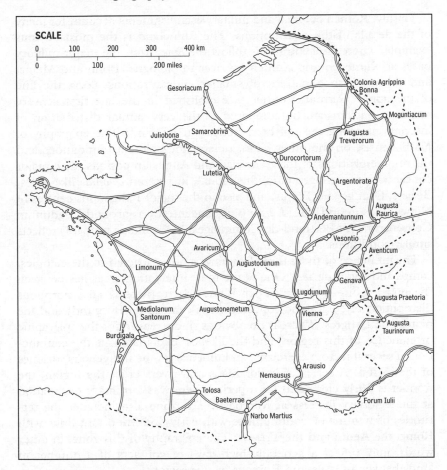

Fig. 4.6   Major roads

providing links between them. But the Agrippan road system was not the only possible enhancement of the 'natural' patterns of communications. The choice of Lyon as the fulcrum of the network was to some extent arbitrary, and the general plan of the road system was arguably partly a result of the inadequacy of Roman knowledge of Gallic geography and partly designed to meet the military demands of the projected conquests of Britain and Germany.[23] As such the road system represents a man-made contribution to the cultural geography of the Gauls.

23 See Drinkwater (1976) on the location of Lyon, and Goudineau (1996, 464–9) on the
    relation between the picture of Gaul presented by Strabo and the Augustan provincial
    organization and road system.

Thirdly, Roman colonial and military establishments account for many of the details of the distributions. The Rhineland is the most obvious example, where concentrations follow the *limes* from the major military bases at Nijmegen and Xanten up river to Cologne, Bonn and Mainz, and thence form a pattern of smaller concentrations along the line of the upper German frontier as established in the late first century AD. That pattern can be compared to the very similar distribution of inscriptions along the northern frontier in Britain.[24] The epigraphy of Narbonensis, on the other hand, reflects the colonial foundations and the re-organizations of the Caesarian and Augustan periods, with major concentrations at Narbonne, the capital, in veteran *coloniae* like Arles, Béziers, Orange and Fréjus, and also in the major indigenous centres of Nîmes, Vaison and Die. A group of concentrations around Lugdunum Convenarum (St Bertrand-de-Comminges) in Aquitania probably reflects similar conditions.

The influence of these three factors was not restricted to the colonies, camps and roadside *vici*. One of the most interesting areas lies between the upper Loire and the upper Rhine where there is an amorphous distribution of epigraphic concentrations centred on Burgundy and the plateau de Langres. There is no obvious single reason for the epigraphic prominence of this region, and the likeliest explanation is the conjunction of several factors exercizing an influence on the indigenous societies of the region. A series of major roads and rivers cross the region, the frontier is fairly close and for a period there was a military occupation at the legionary fortress at Mirebeau. The zone also includes the territories of two major communities with early and important links with Rome, the Aedui and the Treveri. The epigraphy of this zone, in other words, may reflect a generally high level of contacts of a number of kinds between Gauls and Romans in this region.

It is much more difficult to discern the cultural geography of the Gauls on a smaller scale. A recent study of the distribution of inscriptions within the province of Belgica divided the epigraphy by community, and within each community distinguished those inscriptions located in the capital from those found in the hinterland.[25] Some broad patterns emerged, such as the greater number of inscriptions known from the east of the province, perhaps relating to the proximity of the army, and the contrast between large communities like the Treveri, the Remi and the Mediomatrici, whose capitals produced more than 300 inscriptions

---

24 Some 87 per cent of Romano-British epigraphy is in the militarized zones (Mann 1985, 205), where it may be an almost entirely military phenomenon: Biró (1975, 32 and 46 with maps).
25 Wightman (1985, 162–8), building on Wightman (1984).

each, and the much smaller communities of the north-west where the capitals had 50 or fewer. More generally inscriptions are most common around cities, large *vici* and communications routes: among the Treveri, the Remi and the Mediomatrici, the capitals usually provide more than half the inscriptions and rural sites less than a quarter.[26] Further south, among the Aedui 46.5 per cent of extant inscriptions were found in the capital and a further 17.6 per cent in four *vici*, and among the Senones 49.7 per cent came from the capital and another 31 per cent from two large *vici*.[27]

Analysis of this sort cannot be safely pushed much further in Gaul, where the low absolute numbers of inscriptions mean further division of the epigraphy has little statistical significance. It is unclear how far contrasts between individual towns and their rural hinterlands or between the relative totals of votives and epitaphs known from a particular community reflect the original patterns of dedication and how far they have been distorted by the chance of discovery and preservation. The broad outlines of the cultural geography of the Gauls are, however, clear enough as is the influence of geography, roads and Roman establishments, most of all provincial and *civitas* capitals but also some of the larger *vici*. The correlation between areas where contacts between Romans and Gauls were frequent and intense and those places where Roman cultural practices were most enthusiastically adopted seems well established.

III   The rhythm of change

Virtually no Latin inscriptions of the Republican period are known from Gaul. A milestone of the Via Domitia is the earliest example, Pompey's trophy at the Pyrenees bore an inscription and it is probable that some of the earliest inscriptions from Narbonne should be dated to the mid-first century BC or even earlier.[28] But outside the epigraphic island represented by the Republican colony and its territory, Latin epigraphy was scarce in the south even in Caesar's day and was nonexistent in the north until the reign of Augustus.[29] Writing, on the other hand, was already in use by various iron age communities in both

---

26 Wightman (1984, 72). The Leuci are an exception to this pattern, but the high proportion of rural inscriptions may be related to the high proportion of votives known from this *civitas*.

27 Figures from the tribe by tribe surveys in Bérard and Le Bohec (1992).

28 See Christol (1995, 174–80) on the basis of *formulae* similiar to better dated examples from Rome.

29 Barruol (1976, 402).

Mediterranean and continental Gaul.[30] From the fifth century BC a number of societies around the western Mediterranean had adapted the alphabetic scripts used by Greeks, Carthaginians and Etruscans. Excavations in north-west Spain and southern France have recovered several texts in the languages of these visitors, including letters and documents relating to commercial transactions, and writing was also used by all three groups for religious dedications and treaties. Documents of this kind and the various scripts in which they were written provided the models for Iberian, Celtiberian, Celtic and north-Italian literacies, but few long texts survive in these languages, the vast majority being graffiti and coin legends.

One of the most striking features of this epigraphy is its regional diversity.[31] West of the Hérault, Iberian texts appear on *oppida* from the fourth century BC. In this respect, as in others, the culture of the Languedoc is an extension of that of Cataluña and the script used was originally based on Punic models. Inland around Toulouse a modified version was in use a century or so later, while at roughly the same time some coinages from the lower Rhône valley used a script based on that originally created by Celtic speakers in north-Italy on an Etruscan model. Late in the third century BC or early in the second, groups east of the Rhône adapted the Greek script used in Marseilles and its colonies to write a Celtic language, producing the so-called Gallo-Greek inscriptions. Greek script was also used in the upper Rhône valley and Burgundy from the early first century BC.[32] Most of the texts in question are short graffiti on potsherds, often simply a name, but longer inscriptions were possible and may simply not have survived. Much writing must have been on perishable materials, like the Helvetian tablets described by Caesar,[33] while coin legends suggest that many late iron age groups who have left no graffiti made use of scripts derived from Greek, Etruscan or Latin models.[34] Others probably never used writing, although the evidence is so scarce that arguments from silence are risky.

30 A corpus of Celtic language inscriptions from Gaul, *RIG,* is in the course of preparation and Untermann (1980) provides a corpus of Iberian texts from southern France. Untermann (1969), Lejeune (1983), Bats (1988a) and Lambert (1992) provide overviews of the development of these literacies. A number of papers relevant to pre-Roman writing in Mediterranean France are collected in *RAN* 21 (1988).
31 See Woolf (1994a) for what follows with full bibliography and documentation.
32 See Woolf (1994a) for a chronology based on recent excavations.
33 *de Bello Gallico* 1.29. For other classical testimony, cf. Diodoros 5.28 on letters written to the dead and thrown on funeral pyres, perhaps deriving from a Poseidonian account and so referring to the south; Strabo 4.1.5 on Gauls learning to write contracts from the Massiliots; Caesar *de Bello Gallico* 6.14 on the use of Greek writing for public and private *rationes* of all business except for religious lore.
34 Allen (1980, 180) with comments by Moberg (1987).

The overall impression is that writing spread in a piecemeal fashion, adopted by community after community, over a long period of time. At any rate, the process was a discontinuous one. Some non-literate communities co-existed for generations with literate neighbours without adopting the alphabet, and when writing was adopted it might be based on a variety of models and put to a variety of uses.[35] That pattern of cultural change is very different from the processes that are the subject of this book, that is cultural change in the context of imperialism by a people with a strong sense of the difference between civilization and barbarism. Cultural change was a matter of choice in both cases. But the consequences either of adopting or not adopting writing were relatively minor in iron age Europe, while the freedom to adapt it to meet local needs was relatively unconstrained. Power in iron age Europe was locally or at the most regionally circumscribed.[36] The kinds of cultural change that might take place within that sort of social and political environment were quite distinct from those that accompanied Roman expansion.

The appearance of Latin epigraphy marks not merely a change in language but the adoption of new cultural practices that were wholly Roman in nature. It also coincides, as far as the precise chronology can be ascertained, with the end of the Gallo-Greek and Iberian epigraphies of the south.[37] Latin written in Latin script became the dominant form of epigraphy throughout Gaul, and although pre-Roman languages continued to be spoken as late as the fourth or fifth centuries AD, almost nothing was written in them.[38] Once this new cultural system was established a distinction evolved between a language of writing, which in its spoken form was also the language of power and education, and a vernacular spoken by the majority of the population but rarely written. The situation might be compared to that of many mediaeval or modern colonial societies. Between the two (or more) languages, mediating devices must have existed, some forms of bilingualism among the elite and their principal agents and servants, translators and scribes and perhaps one or more pidgins and more or less formal education systems. The details of those accommodations are difficult to reconstruct.

---

35 Bats (1988a) is the most sophisticated discussion of these issues.
36 Woolf (1994a). For further discussion, see Woolf (1997).
37 See Untermann (1992) for the shift in epigraphic practice, although it cannot be assumed that this marked the end of spoken Iberian and Celtic languages in the region. Christol (1995) discusses the origins of Latin epigraphy.
38 On the complex question of vernacular languages in the provinces, cf. Brunt (1976, 170–2), Harris (1989, 175–90) and the papers collected in Neumann and Untermann (1980) and in ANRW II.29.2 (1983). Much depends on the interpretation of a small amount of late and ambiguous literary testimony.

Little is known of the extent of bilingualism, nothing of the means by which Latin was learnt by those outside the local aristocracies, nothing even of what language was spoken by aristocratic women, or in the towns by those who had themselves commemorated with funeral reliefs that bore Latin epitaphs. Comparative evidence indicates only the variety of possibilities and confirms that the language used in public writing is a poor guide to the language of speech. But the fact of a change in the written language is undeniable.

The manner in which this new Latin epigraphy was created is worth considering further. First, its appearance is strikingly different from the way in which the use of writing had spread within Gaul up to that point. Latin inscriptions appeared suddenly and previous systems were replaced virtually immediately. Public epigraphy begins, outside Narbonne, in the early 20s of the first century BC, both in the new veteran colonies and in native centres like Nîmes.[39] The Iberian and Gallo-Greek scripts disappeared altogether and all subsequent texts use Latin script, the vast majority to write Latin. This sudden replacement can be contrasted with the piecemeal process by which iron age communities adopted and adapted writing systems for their own purposes. The importance of Roman power as a context for the change is clear. Second, the cultural practices associated with Latin epigraphy began to be disseminated throughout Gaul during the reign of Augustus. The time lag between the conquest of the south and Caesar's campaigns in the north seems to have had little impact on the rhythm of change.

Even the non-Latin epigraphy of the post-conquest period was produced in relation to a culture in which Latin was the language of writing. A small number of texts do exist written in a Celtic language but in Latin script, and are hence termed Gallo-Latin.[40] Less than twenty monumental inscriptions survive and there are also between one hundred and two hundred graffiti and a handful of longer texts. The stone inscriptions are funerary monuments and religious dedications to non-classical deities, but they do not continue indigenous traditions – there was no monumental writing in the late iron age – and they are occasionally found associated with Latin texts.[41] Most are distributed in

---

39 Christol (1995, 169–172).
40 *RIG* II.1 collects the monumental Gallo-Latin inscriptions with the exception of the calendars published in *RIG* III. Although some of the longer Gallo-Latin texts have been published, for most of the graffiti and the other *instrumentum RIG* II.2 is awaited. The Gallo-Latin graffiti are said to be three to four times as numerous as Gallo-Greek ones.
41 *RIG* II.1 L8 is on a statue of an anthropomorphic deity which also bears a Latin dedication to Mercury and Augustus, L14 is on a pillar also inscribed with a dedication by the *nautae* of Paris to Tiberius. The texts are not, however, properly bilingual.

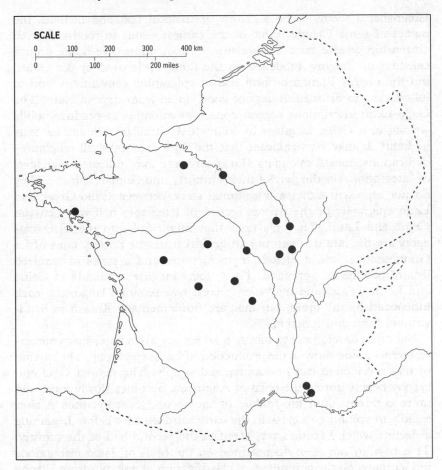

Fig. 4.7   Gallo-Latin inscriptions on stone

an arc around the Massif Central, only partly coinciding with the distribution of Gallo-Greek graffiti[42] in Burgundy and the Berry, and well outside the areas where Latin epigraphy proper was to be commonest (Fig. 4.7). Those considerations, plus the use of the Latin script, suggest that the texts were written in response to or at least in the knowledge of Latin epigraphy. The longer texts also indicate an awareness of Roman styles of writing. One late first century AD example found at Larzac is a curse tablet[43] and another lead tablet deposited in a sacred spring at

42 L4 and L5 from Genouilly (Cher) were associated with a lapidary Gallo-Greek inscription (*RIG* I. G225) and both Gallo-Greek and Gallo-Latin texts occur at Alesia. *RIG* II.1 emphasizes a general lack of fit.
43 Lejeune (1985).

Chamalières seems to be a charm or magical text and includes the names of some Claudii, some of the earliest Gauls to receive Roman citizenship or else their descendants.[44] Most impressive is the bronze calendar of Coligny, modelled on the lunar cycle used by the Gauls, but thoroughly Roman in form and in epigraphic conventions, and in its concern to distinguish days of good omen from days of bad.[45] The Gallo-Latin inscriptions suggest conscious attempts to produce public writing in a Celtic language by individuals familiar with similar texts in Latin. It may be significant that the uses are nearly all religious – dedications, curses, calendars. But in any case they indicate a high level of integration, on the part of their authors, into Roman culture. They do not represent either a transitional stage between Gallo-Greek and Latin epigraphy or the written record of languages half way between Celtic and Latin. The only texts that might fall into the latter cat-egory are the late first century AD graffiti from the pottery kilns of La Graufesenque, which include memos, notes and a series of itemized lists of batches of pots fired. Those texts include a mixture of Celtic and Latin words, and may even record two separate languages, each influenced by the other, but they are fundamentally Roman in hand-writing, form and function.[46]

But those developments, mostly first century AD in date, are in numer-ical terms a side show to the production of Latin epigraphy. The rhythm of that production can be summarized simply. Throughout Gaul epi-graphy begins during the reign of Augustus, becomes slowly more and more common until the middle of the second century when it rises rapidly in volume to a peak in the early third century before beginning a decline which becomes very steep in the second half of the century. That rhythm can been documented on the basis of dated inscriptions in Germany, on the chronological classification of epitaphs from Vienne and Lyon, and seems to be echoed in the chronology of uninscribed as well as inscribed funerary reliefs from Saintes and Bordeaux.[47] The

44 Lejeune and Marichal (1976–7).   45 *RIG* III.
46 See Marichal (1988) for the texts. On their language, he writes (57) that no clear distinction can be drawn between Celtic and Latin texts and that in general 'il convient, je crois, de considérer tous les bordereaux comme des textes en "latin vulgaire" sur un substrat gaulois plus ou moins apparent'. He does not, however, discuss Meid's (1983) contention that these and other Gallo-Latin texts represent a popular fusion between the two languages.
47 Wightman (1985, 163) on the German and Belgican material, concluding that most inscriptions in the Germanies were produced between 140 and 260 AD and that two-thirds of Belgican inscriptions were produced in the same period. For the epitaphs of Lyon, cf. Audin and Burnand (1959), although some of their dating criteria might be doubted, particularly the assumption of no overlap between successive styles of com-memoration, and hence the rejection of Hatt's (1951) chronology for the *cippi*. That

Latin epigraphy of Gaul thus reflects two processes, first the sudden discontinuity with pre-Augustan practices and second the slower generalization of epigraphic culture. This chronological patterning was not unique to Gaul. Numerous lists of dated Latin inscriptions throughout the West display similar trends, although variations between provinces and between categories of inscriptions certainly existed.[48] The pattern largely reflects changes in modes of commemoration since the majority of inscriptions are epitaphs,[49] and the apparent closeness of fit between uninscribed reliefs and inscriptions in Gaul confirms this impression. But other categories of inscription were also important, for example votives. The sudden appearance and subsequent dissemination of epigraphic culture thus represents the spread of a whole series of Roman cultural practices through Gaul.[50]

Epigraphy is not the only medium to exhibit this chronological patterning. As will become clear, a wide range of innovations and changes, from architecture to civic organization and from ceramic style to cults, exhibits the same pattern of a formative period of dramatic change, located around the turn of the millennia, followed by a more gradual pattern of generalization and diversification that lasted centuries. The implications are enormous. Because the Romanization of Narbonensis began no earlier than the Caesarian and Augustan periods,[51] cultural

error probably accounts for the unusually large number of epitaphs assigned to the period AD 70–115, some of which were almost certainly earlier. Burnand (1961) used the same criteria to date the much smaller sample from Vienne. Burnand (1992) proposes some revisions to the dating criteria. On Saintes, see Maurin (1978, 124–60) and on the reliefs from Bordeaux, see Braemer (1959, 17). Most Gallic cities have produced too few epitaphs for surveys like Audin and Burnand's to be significant.

48 See Mrozeck (1973), (1988) for the tables, but MacMullen (1982, 245) rightly points out that Mrozeck's explanation of decline in terms of the third century crisis is inadequate. For variations, Duncan-Jones (1982, 351) contrasts inscriptions dated by imperial reign from Italy and Africa, and (1990, 60–7) shows a steady production of building inscriptions.

49 Meyer (1990), stressing commemoration. Saller and Shaw (1984) estimate that about 70 per cent of extant Latin inscriptions are funerary. When figures for Gaul exist, they conform to these empire-wide patterns, e.g. Wightman (1984), Bérard and Le Bohec (1992).

50 For the epigraphic habit as the sign of the expansion of a new social order, see Woolf (1996a).

51 Ward-Perkins (1970), Février (1973), Goudineau (1975), Gros (1976), Barruol (1976, 399–400). The issue is complicated by the debates about the extent of the cultural influence of Marseille and its colonies in the south, but in terms of script and architecture at least, cultural borrowings from the Greeks seem limited to the area east of the Rhône. The issue is, however, controversial, cf. most recently Bats et al., eds. (1992, 263–379). Gros (1992, 369–79) argues that Rome was so Hellenized that it is impossible to distinguish Greek and Roman contributions to southern Gaulish culture, but both Goudineau (1983a) and Bats (1992) argue convincingly that it is possible to trace a complex and evolving pattern of contacts between southern Gaul and a series of other cultures.

change cannot be explained as an automatic response to conquest, nor as a response that followed conquest after a regular period of delay.[52] Other areas of the empire also show major cultural discontinuities in the late first century BC, irrespective of the date at which they were conquered. Turdetania in southern Spain, for example, was conquered a century and a half before Narbonensis but follows a very similar pattern of cultural change.[53] It is traditional to explain this in terms of local factors that retarded cultural change, the resistance of local elites in Spain for instance, or the influence of Massiliot Greek culture in southern France. But it is more economical to posit a single explanation in terms of a link between cultural change and the wholesale redefinition of Roman culture in the Augustan period.[54]

IV   The inscribing classes in Gaul

Who set up inscriptions in Gaul?[55] The epigraphy of Narbonne, which has provided the largest number of inscriptions of any Gallic city, provides a convenient starting point. The colony was the oldest in Gaul, founded in the late second century BC, refounded in 45 BC, and apart from its administrative prominence, it was located at the junction of two major communications routes, the coastal road from Italy to Spain and the Gallic isthmus, the shortest route between the Mediterranean and the Atlantic, through the lowlands between the Pyrennees and the Central Massif. Narbonne, with over a thousand surviving inscriptions, shows intense epigraphic activity compared to most Gallic cities. The inhabited area of Amiens, for example, was almost twice as big, yet it has produced less than thirty inscriptions. The inscribed and inscribing classes are thus likely to have been as broad in Narbonne as anywhere in Gaul. Of the 1800 or so individuals named in Narbonne's epigraphy, it is possible to establish the status of just over a thousand, about a

52 Dyson (1971) attempts to establish a regular sequence linking conquest, cultural change and revolts, but the chronology and causation of revolts are too complex to fit a simple formula.
53 Keay (1992), and for urban monuments in Baetica as a whole, Fear (1996, 170–226).
54 Millett (1990b, 40), following the observations of Ward-Perkins (1970), and Woolf (1995).
55 On the social extent of the epigraphic habit in general, see Saller and Shaw (1984, 128), Morris (1992, 164–6). The case of Gaul is a good indication, however, that the 'take-up' of the practice varied widely from place to place and that studies based on early imperial central Italy can at best provide a standard of comparison for provincial epigraphies.

third of whom were freeborn citizens of the colony, the remainder being freedmen.[56] Both groups were very diverse. The freeborn included traders, soldiers and veterans, some of whose Celtic names occasionally suggest recent enfranchisement, and also decurions and magistrates, some descendants of the original colonists, often mentioned in honorific inscriptions recording acts of euergetism and public honours. The freedmen also spanned a great social range, from rich public benefactors and priests of the imperial cult to civic functionaries, small craftsmen and shopkeepers.

Despite this range, the people recorded on surviving inscriptions cannot be considered a representative sample of the population of the city. Some groups are noticeably under-represented. Only 15 slaves are recorded as opposed to 763 ex-slaves and there is hardly any sign of freeborn citizens of humbler status except those engaged in commerce or the army, although the less wealthy descendants of the colonists, immigrants and the freeborn descendants of ex-slaves must have had some place in the society of Narbonne. It is possible, of course, that some of those whose status we cannot identify fall into these categories, but even if all 800 were slaves and freeborn *coloni*, the proportion of ex-slaves would still be implausible as a reflection of Narbonne's society. Even allowing for the low survival rate of inscriptions it seems likely that only a proportion of the population can ever have set up or have been commemorated by inscriptions. Estimates of the populations of ancient cities are notoriously difficult, and figures suggested for Narbonne have varied by a factor of ten. The most recent tentative estimate of about 35,000 in the second century AD seems a little high.[57] But even if the city had a mean population of 10,000 over the first three centuries AD, the survival rate of inscriptions would have to be very low indeed if everyone had received an epitaph, and higher population estimates entail still lower survival rates. A very tentative estimate suggests

56 See Gayraud (1981, 461–76) for analysis of statuses, estimating that, of known individuals, at least 16.5 per cent (305) were freeborn citizens of the colony, up to 3.9 per cent (72) were *incolae*, up to 42.5 per cent (763) were ex-slaves and just under 1 per cent (15) were slaves. The remaining third were presumably not identifiable.

57 Gayraud (1981, 476–8) estimates 35,000 in the second century, calculated on the basis of an occupied area of 100 hectares and a density of 350 people per hectare. The latter figure seems much too high. Goudineau (1980b, 309–10) suggests 150/ha as the maximum plausible density of population in Gallic towns. Gayraud is also influenced by recent estimates of peak populations of about 20,000 for Bordeaux and Toulouse, which he rightly expects to have smaller populations than Narbonne. It may be that all these estimates should be scaled down and that a figure of 10,000–15,000 would be preferable for Narbonne.

between twenty and thirty per cent of the population may have been commemorated.[58] That figure may well conceal changes as the epigraphic habit spread, with perhaps a slightly higher percentage being commemorated in the late second and early third centuries. The conclusion that epigraphy spread beyond the elite but remained a minority practice conforms with the impression of social range communicated by the status of the commemorators. Beyond the various political, social and economic elites of the city, such as *decuriones* and *seviri Augustales*, commemoration by epitaph was also practised by soldiers and freedmen, traders and artisans, but not on the whole by slaves, the freeborn *plebs* or the peasantry.

It is important not to conceive of this pattern simply as the extension of the epigraphic habit 'down the social scale'. In terms of political status, the poorest freeborn citizen was formally superior to the richest *sevir*, and some small landowners, many probably descended from colonist stock, must have despised urban craftsmen of libertine status or descent, although it was characteristic of Roman imperial society that such issues of status were contested. Equally, although considerations of expense partly account for the under-representation of some groups – slaves and the poorest of the freeborn *plebs*, for example – it cannot explain the over-representation of freedmen or the under-representation of landowners of modest means. Locating cultural change means not so much charting a 'trickle-down effect' of elite culture through a single social or economic hierarchy as exploring a complex series of linked social milieux. The epigraphy of the elite of the colony is easy to account for as a part of wider patterns of elite culture imported from Italy along with political and social competition,[59] and notions of status underwritten by Roman law, and, from 45 BC at least, by a colonial charter similar to the near-contemporary one from Urso in Spain. The prominence of ex-slaves in the colony's epigraphy, however, needs a slightly different explanation. Freedmen are in fact over-represented in epigraphy all over the Latin West, partly perhaps because their experience of servitude and subsequent upward social mobility had made them especially sensitive to issues of status. But freedmen may be more prominent than the freeborn because of their continuing close contacts with the colony's elite, whether as rich *seviri* and participants in the cult of

58 Assuming four generations per century, the total number of inhabitants would have been 120,000, giving a survival rate of under 1 per cent if everyone had received an epitaph. If survival rates were in fact about 5 per cent, as Duncan-Jones (1982, app. 13) suggests for the empire as a whole, we arrive at a figure of about 20 per cent of all deceased received epitaphs. If the population estimates are still a little high, that figure might rise to 30 per cent or so. These figures only provide orders of magnitude.

59 Christol (1995).

the *numen Augusti* or simply as clients operating small concerns partly owned by their patrons. The culture of ex-slaves, in other words, might be more closely modelled on that of their ex-masters, than on that of the free-born plebs. The epigraphy of veterans and soldiers may have derived from quite a different source, given the prevalence of funerary epigraphy in the military societies of the Rhineland. Soldiers everywhere set up inscriptions, in practices that were perhaps more straightforwardly emulative of those whose higher status was guaranteed by the social hierarchy defined by military rank. The distinctions between all these epigraphies should not be drawn too rigidly. They were similar, each deriving ultimately from a common source, the funerary epigraphy of the elite of the city of Rome, and cross-fertilization between epigraphies may also have occurred. But it is worth remembering that between the colonial elite and their dependants on the one hand, and the veterans returning from the Rhineland on the other, were large segments of the population of Narbonne who rarely featured in its epigraphy, and that the spread of the epigraphic habit there was complex.

Other Gallo-Roman cities varied enormously in the scale and nature of their epigraphies. Differences in size, population and survival rates account for only a part of this variation, and it seems likely that the size of those groups practising funerary commemoration with Latin epitaphs was very variable. The epigraphy of Lyon was naturally similar to that of Narbonne, both in quantity and in composition. Over a thousand individuals are known; decurions, magistrates and *seviri* are relatively well attested, as are freedmen in general, but although the *corpora* of traders, builders, wood carriers and textile workers appear prominently on the honorific inscriptions set up to their elite patrons, the freeborn population of the city is otherwise under-represented and slaves are rarely mentioned.[60] Vienne and Béziers are similar on a smaller scale, with notables, *seviri* and other freedmen prominent, slaves (except municipal and imperial slaves) and other freeborn almost absent, at least as far as those whose status is recorded are concerned.[61] Soldiers crop up now and again as in Narbonne.

Beyond Mediterranean Gaul and the Rhône valley the numbers of inscriptions drop dramatically, and much faster than urban populations. Paris, for example, with a population of between 5,000 and 8,000 inhabitants has produced less than 50 inscriptions, again with elite individuals, soldiers and traders predominating.[62] Saintes, about twice Paris' size in the second century, has produced only about twice as

60 Wuilleumier (1953, 43–56), Audin (1986, 66–83).
61 Pelletier (1982, 225–52) on Vienne; Clavel (1970, 577–604) on Béziers.
62 Duval (1961, 249, 250–64).

many inscriptions. The elite predominate there, many with imperial names that indicate early grants of citizenship, and there are few freedmen.[63] Most northern cities have produced so few epitaphs that it is impossible to characterize the inscribing population, and even in cities like Bordeaux, where inscriptions are relatively numerous, uninscribed figured reliefs are much more common than epitaphs.[64] Only 30 or so funerary epitaphs are known from the whole of Armorica and most tombs there must have been marked either with perishable wooden boards or not at all.[65] Possible variations in survival rates must always be borne in mind, but it seems impossible to escape the conclusion of many of the studies of individual cities that the epigraphic habit was much less firmly rooted in some areas than others.[66] As an indication, the ratio of surviving inscriptions to probable population was close to 1:10 in cities like Narbonne and Lyon, but nearer 1:100 in Paris and Amiens. If the estimate that 20–30 per cent of the population of the southern capital were commemorated with Latin epitaphs was correct, the implication is that epigraphy was a very rare practice indeed in the cities of northern and western Gaul.

The social range of epigraphy did not remain constant over time. The rhythm of change outlined above – a gradually accelerating increase in the number of inscriptions over the first century and early second centuries, peaking in the early third century before a rapid decline – suggests some change in the kind of people who set up inscriptions in Gaul. The inscribing classes expanded from originally colonists and immigrants, such as imperial slaves and soldiers, spreading early to local elites and finally including their dependants and connections. The process is difficult to trace in detail but some evidence may be mustered in support. Funerary reliefs, whether or not inscribed, illustrate the dissemination and diversification of Roman burial customs. Sculpted reliefs first appeared in Narbonensis and Germany, and spread gradually, over the first century AD, along the major roads and via the main military and administrative centres before becoming generalized in the second and third centuries AD.[67] There is a clear correlation between Roman military and political activity and the early spread of the custom, but after the end of the first century regional traditions developed, most famously around Bordeaux and in the north-east. The independence of these regional traditions is illustrated by the quantitative

63 Maurin (1978, 161–5).
64 See Etienne (1962, 160–3) on inscriptions, and Braemer (1959) on figured reliefs.
65 Galliou (1989, 28–30).   66 E.g. Raepsaet-Charlier (1995) on the cities of Belgica.
67 Hatt (1951, 157–163). Braemer (1959) shows Bordelais funerary reliefs peak in precisely the same period as epigraphy, from the mid-second century to the mid-third; cf. Wightman (1985, 177) on Belgica.

decline of sculpture in the south at the same time. Funerary sculpture had ceased, in other words, to be an expression of Roman culture and came instead to reflect a series of local customs with distinctive characteristics and trajectories of development. In some areas, reliefs often depict the deceased associated with tools suggesting their crafts, or depicted in scenes modelled on local constructions of everyday life. These tools and activities evoke an urban milieu and suggest a non-aristocratic but reasonably affluent clientele.

The names recorded on epitaphs provide a second example. To begin with they are overwhelmingly Roman in form with the *tria nomina*, like Quintus Julius Severinus, characteristic of citizens or Latins, but over the first three centuries the proportion of Celtic or Germanic elements, often with only two- or one-part names, increases in the towns, while Roman names begin to appear in the countryside. The process can be documented, with variations and occasional exceptions, all over Gaul.[68] At first sight this looks like Romanization in reverse, and has been taken to imply an influx of countryfolk into the towns in the second century AD. But when the onomastic shift is set in the context of the spread of the epigraphic habit its significance is rather different. The practice of setting up inscriptions, particularly funerary ones, seems to have extended (in the towns at least) beyond the elite to groups without Roman citizenship and Roman style names, while Roman names began to catch on in the countryside for the first time. The observation that in the second century groups might adopt a Roman funerary practice without wishing to adopt Roman names, suggests that the process may have had more to do with imitating the culture of the local elite than with asserting or claiming a Roman identity.

What conclusions can be drawn from this mapping of cultural change in Gaul? First, the geography of cultural change. Colonies and garrisons were important points of contact, accounting for the marked differences between the Roman cultures of the south and of the Rhineland from those of the rest of Gaul. But a special role was also played by cities with strong military and commercial presences and most of all by the various provincial capitals. Lyon, where a key military and commercial route node coincided with the Council of the Three Gauls and the Altar and the largest Roman administrative establishment north of the Alps, was in a class of its own. Narbonne, a major veteran colony, a

---

68 Hatt (1951, 23–42) is the original study, but investigations of the relative incidences of Celtic, Latin and also Greek names have been included in most subsequent studies of individual Gallo-Roman cities. The most dramatic example is Béziers where the number of individuals recording themselves with a single name jumped from 2.25 per cent of names in the first century to 15.65 per cent in the second and third, cf. Clavel (1970, 580). On the issue as a whole, see most recently Le Glay (1977), Raepsaet-Charlier (1995).

governor's residence and, from at least the mid-first century AD, the provincial centre of the imperial cult, occupied a somewhat analogous position in the south.[69] At these privileged points in the new imperial order new habits were most easily learnt and displays of cultural expertise were most effective. Second, the timing of change. The distinction between the relative absence of cultural change in the Republican province, and the speed with which it occurred throughout Gaul following the rationalizations of the Caesarian and Augustan periods, highlights the significance of the new institutions and ideologies of empire that appeared in that formative period. The slower patterns of cultural change that can also be traced echoed the gradual extension of Roman society, as Gallic nobles became Romans and exercised their own civilized discrimination over the rest of Gallo-Roman society. Third, the identity of those drawn most quickly into imperial society. Most prominent are the new aristocracies of Gaul, whose contacts with Romans were the most intense and most frequent, through military service and administrative office with all the patronal relationships that those activities involved. Their education too, would have contributed to their socialization, as they came to realize that the disparity between Gallic and Roman practice concerned them most acutely, since *humanitas* was a property of social class as well as of ethnic affiliation, and even in Rome and in Italy, artisans, the urban plebs and especially country dwellers were thought to exhibit *humanitas* very imperfectly.[70] Learning to be Roman, for this group, meant learning the virtues and *mores* appropriate to their place in the empire of cities and the empire of friends. Yet other groups were also important, in particular those who had passed through those other two great socializing institutions of Roman society, the army and the slave *familia*. One way to envisage this process is in terms of the extension of Roman power in Gaul, conceived of as the expansion of a complex configuration of power, evoking cultural change as a response or resistance that traced the contours of the new hegemonic relations it established. Those new relations included not only the initial social distance between conqueror and conquered, but also the distances established between Gallo-Roman elites and their subordinates, between town-dwellers and countryfolk, and soldiers and civilians.[71] Less abstractly,

69 On Lyon, see Wuilleumier (1953), Audin (1965); on Narbonne, see Gayraud (1981). On their pre-eminence at the beginning of the first century AD, see Strabo *Geography* 4.3.2

70 Ramage (1973, 67–70, 124).

71 Cf. Kemp (1994, 110): 'Resistances can be understood as tracing hegemonic power relations ... since power and resistance are reciprocally related; they bring about and pervade each other. There is therefore no space independent of power for resistance to occur in.' On the contours of Roman hegemonic relations in Gaul, see Woolf (1997).

we might conceptualize the process as the expansion of Roman society through the recruitment of Gauls to various roles and positions in the social order. That society reproduced itself through rituals and customs, the traces of many of which are to be found in Latin inscriptions. Even the blanks on the epigraphic map reveal the contours of this new social world, marking the lower and more marginal positions to which most Gauls were relegated by Roman power. Epigraphy traces not the limits of Roman power, culture or society, then, but its shape in Gaul.

I   A world of villages

Barbarism might be defined in negative terms as an absence of civilized qualities. Among the many respects in which Gauls might be found lacking by the discriminating gaze of their new rulers was that they did not live in cities. The city was conceived of as a community of citizens united by laws and the worship of the gods, the natural environment of men, in other words that in which they could best realize their moral potential. Beyond the civilized world of cities, the classical writers described men living in villages, scattered through the countryside, or else as nomads, wanderers with no fixed abode eating raw flesh like animals, drinking only milk.[1] The spread of civilization could thus be traced in the foundation of cities. The public monuments of a city were the physical expression of its *politeia* and the high culture of the elite might be termed *urbanitas*, a term that came to embrace refinement, taste and literary style.[2] Even in their suburban and rural *villae*, the elites of the early empire created little islands of urban culture, residences marked out as urban by architecture and domesticated gardens, by the comforts with which they were equipped, baths, mosaics and wall paintings depicting idealized rural vistas, and slave staffs. Those excluded by the ideal of *urbanitas* were the uneducated of the town as well as of the country, and like *humanitas*, the ideal operated as a class marker.

Urbanization has been widely treated by moderns, too, as a central component of the changes encompassed in the term Romanization,[3] especially perhaps because the phenomenon provides a link between the political culture discernible through epigraphy – magistrates, priesthoods, councils, decrees, euergetism – and the monumental remains uncovered by archaeologists. Prehistorians have been less content to accept Roman

1 See Shaw (1982) for the theme.
2 Ramage (1973), with Wallace-Hadrill (1991, 244–9). Cf. Fear (1996, 6–13).
3 E.g. Gagé (1964, 153–4): 'romaniser c'est municipaliser en même temps qu'urbaniser: c'est à dire habituer les populations locales aux cadres politiques de la vie romaine...' discussed and expanded by Mackie (1990).

claims that urbanism was absent from iron age Gaul. Up to a point, the debate on whether or not there were towns in late prehistoric Europe turns on issues of definition (although not all definitions of urbanism are equally good). It is undeniable, however, that Roman conquest resulted in enormous changes in settlement patterns, in architecture and in the lifestyles lived in the major settlements. Whether or not we choose to regard the largest settlements of late prehistoric Gaul as urban, Gallo-Roman cities were the result of an alien model imposed over a relatively short period.[4] The study of how Gaul was urbanized thus provides an opportunity to examine central issues in the cultural transformation of the region: the chronology of change, the parts played by various groups in the process and the extent to which Roman ideas of civilization had been adopted by the Gauls. The nature of the Gallo-Roman urbanism that emerged is also revealing, showing how Roman power operated to create new cultural differences *within* Gaul, and how classical models were transformed when transplanted into a new environment.

The late prehistoric landscapes encountered by the Romans in Gaul were very diverse,[5] and regional settlement patterns reflected that diversity. Discussions inevitably concentrate on the largest settlement sites of any region. The majority of these sites in late Iron Age France were hillforts, termed *oppida* both in the south and the north although they were very different in size, form and origin and perhaps also in the services they provided. Although many of the same questions are posed about both continental and Mediterranean *oppida* – in particular the extent to which either category can be termed urban, and the influence of classical models on each – the marked differences between them mean it makes sense to consider them separately.

The settlement patterns of southern Gaul had been laid down in the seventh and sixth centuries BC, the period when the transition from bronze to iron coincided with an increase in contacts between local populations and Greek, Etruscan and Punic visitors.[6] The characteristic form

4 On Gallo-Roman urbanism in general, see most recently Février *et al.* (1980), Drinkwater (1985), and Bedon *et al.* (1988), synthesizing a vast body of recent research. The importance of secondary urban centres as well as the *coloniae* and *civitas* capitals has emerged from a series of conferences, especially Chevallier (1976), *Villes et agglomérations* (1992) and Petit *et al.* (1994a), and some exemplary regional studies, in particular Mangin *et al.* (1986) and Bénard *et al.* (1994).

5 See Braudel (1988) vol. 1 for an insightful, if sometimes impressionistic, view of the diversity of France and its influence over settlement.

6 See Bats (1992) and Arcelin (1992a) for the development of these settlements and the relationship between their development and contact with traders and colonists. Py (1990a) is the most complete study of the development of these communities in one region. For an overview, see Goudineau in Février *et al.* (1980) 140–193, now supplemened by reports on a number of these sites in Dedet and Fiches (1985), and Py (1990b).

adopted was a small fortified site typically perched on the edge of one
of the small plains that shelter the best agricultural territory in the
south. By the second century BC these southern *oppida* varied considerably in shape and location, in the kinds of structures they contained,
and in the extent and manner in which they were planned. Some had
long histories of occupation, others were recent sites, the construction
of which had been accompanied by the abandonment of neighbouring
settlements. Most sites were very small, usually about one hectare in
size and very rarely over five, so they provided shelter for at most a few
hundred individuals. Both ramparts and the simple single or double
roomed houses within them were built out of dry-stone walls, the style
and construction of which developed over time. The larger sites were
equipped with gates and towers, housed storage facilities and had adjacent cemeteries, but monuments, public spaces and religious structures
were comparatively rare.

Alongside this broad similarity there was considerable diversity. Lattes
near Montpellier is a lowland coastal village founded in the sixth century BC and continuing in occupation until the middle empire.[7] Other
such sites probably existed but attention has been focused hitherto on
the hilltop sites. There were also marked regional differences. In the
Languedoc, the major sites tend to be a little larger and often – for
example Ensérune, Cayla de Mailhac, Montlaurès and Ruscino – had
been occupied continuously since the beginning of the iron age. These
sites, associated with Iberian graffiti, form part of a regional group that
extends into Cataluña to sites like Ullastret. Further east in the Var the
settlements were a little smaller and slightly more mobile. Our understanding of the Rhône valley is made more difficult because a number
of important sites – such as Nîmes – lie under Roman and modern
towns, and our information derives from important recent work on
secondary centres, in particular Castels à Nages and Ambrusson. But
some sites in this area were large with complex ramparts with towers,
and a few, like Nîmes, Ambrusson and Vaison, extended down onto
the surrounding plains at the end of the iron age. Finally there are a
group of sites such as St Blaise and Entremont, in the vicinity of Marseille, the influence of which may be reflected in the style of fortifications, in their division into upper and lower towns, and in the appearance
of public spaces, monumental structures and figure sculpture. Attempts
to represent sites like Entremont, let alone Ensérune near Béziers, as
local imitations of Greek colonies have certainly gone too far, but equally
it is difficult to explain the existence at late second century BC Glanum

7 See Garcia (1990) for a survey.

of houses, built on hellenistic lines with interior courtyards and classical decoration, without reference to cultural borrowing of the same kind that led to the adoption of Greek script to write a Celtic language in the same area at about the same time.[8]

The largest southern *oppida* clearly shared some features with classical cities. Some at least were 'extensive, organized settlements',[9] within which houses were densely packed and often organized into blocks divided by narrow streets. On some sites there is a close relationship between the position of the rampart and the organization of space, and those closest to the territory of Marseille exhibited even more morphological complexity. Most sites, however, were little more than villages with no signs of monumentality or urban planning, and there is little sense of a differentiated settlement hierarchy through which activities and functions were distributed across the landscape. From this perspective it may be preferable to classify most southern *oppida* as nucleated but non-urban settlements, like the fortified hill villages of modern day central and southern Italy, inhabited largely by peasants working and living off the neighbouring plains. Against this background of village societies, the Hellenized centres of the south-east, and the larger sites of the lower Rhône valley and the Languedoc-Catalan coastal plain, stand out as islands of nascent urbanism.

The major late iron age settlements of the Gallic interior were rather different. The architecture of non-mediterranean Gaul in the second century BC was constructed of wattle, daub and thatch, and fortifications enclosed much greater areas with massive earthen ramparts often laced with timber.[10] Yet over most of temperate France hillforts were only one part of a wider repertoire of settlement types and, except in some upland areas, periods in which hillforts were constructed and used alternated with much longer periods when settlement was dispersed in the lowlands in scattered farms or open, unfortified villages,[11] an oscillation that can be traced back to the Neolithic and forward to the Middle Ages. Local sequences varied but in most regions there were two major periods of hillfort building during the iron age, one at the end of the late Hallstatt, in the late sixth and early fifth centuries

---

8   See Treziny (1992) for a recent, balanced view.
9   Py (1990a, 133), 'habitats étendus et structurés' beginning his argument (133–9) in favour of urbanism in the late iron age. For earlier discussions, see Fiches (1979), Goudineau in Février *et al.* (1980, 162–70).
10 Collis (1984), Buchsenshutz (1981), Audouze and Buchsenschutz (1989) provide the best accounts of settlement in late iron age Europe. For non-mediterranean France in particular, see Buchsenschutz (1984), Ralston (1992).
11 Collis and Ralston (1976).

BC, and the other in the late La Tène period, immediately before the Gallic War. This oscillation between fortified and open settlement was superimposed over another trend, one of a marked growth in the material and human resources of late prehistoric societies. While Mediterranean Gaul seems in some respects to have been stagnating economically in the late iron age,[12] in the interior there was expansion onto new soils, new crops were being introduced and iron tools became more and more common.[13] Other symptoms of this growth are the increasing power of Gallic polities and the staggering scale of late La Tène fortifications. Few of the southern *oppida* were larger than 5 ha in area but the smallest of the northern ones covered at least 20 ha while the largest enclosed hundreds of hectares. These fortifications appeared at the very end of the iron age in most parts of France.[14] While Mont Beuvray may have been occupied in the late second century BC, in most parts of northern Gaul the abandonment of lowland sites and the fortification of neighbouring hilltops dates to around 80–70 BC.

The late La Tène *oppida* resembled in many respects the largest of the open settlements that preceded them. Both types of site were effectively collections of farmsteads within compounds, sometimes apparently organized along wide streets, and iron working and other craft activity are well attested on both kinds of site. Aside from their fortifications and size nothing distinguished the northern *oppida* from other forms of late La Tène settlement. Arguably the most important features of late iron age centres are shared by both open settlements and fortified ones, and it is a mistake to concentrate on the exceptional constructions of the generation before Caesar's conquest rather than on the more enduring structures of iron age Gaul. Composed as they were of compounds, rather than the densely packed cabins that filled the southern *oppida*, the largest settlements of continental Europe were much less densely occupied and despite their much greater extent they may not have sheltered much larger populations, since only limited areas within the largest sites were ever occupied. Precise details are difficult to establish since many Gallic *oppida* experienced a period of post-conquest occupation, which has obscured the much less durable remains of iron age habitation.[15] But it is clear that regional differences existed

---

12 One of the main conclusions of Py (1990a) for the region around Nîmes, although more studies are needed to confirm the picture for other regions.
13 Champion *et al.* (1984, 304–5), Audouze and Buchsenschutz (1989, 196–213), Haselgrove (1990b, 250–2).
14 Buchsenschutz and Colin (1990).
15 Collis (1984, 105–36), Audouze and Buchsenschutz (1991, 233).

in design and in the extent to which particular communities invested in a number of small fortifications or in a single large one.[16]

Inevitably the issue of urbanism has been discussed in relation to these settlements, just as it has in the south.[17] But the settlement archaeology of these regions has in fact revealed contrasting patterns. The case for urbanism in the south depends on an evolutionary model, villages that become more and more regularly planned, perhaps under external influences, until they have converged on classical models of a dense fortified settlement built in stone and with a developing monumentality. At best these developments occurred only in a few parts of the south. In the north, however, the proposed model is of crisis or catastrophe, the sudden concentration of a dispersed pattern of settlement into centres that become, almost at once, urban.[18] There is no question in the north of a differentiated settlement hierarchy with the *oppida* at the summit, there is little sign of specialized quarters within the *oppida*, they performed no functions (except defence) that had not been performed by the larger villages before them. The case for urbanism in inland Gaul before the Roman conquest seems much weaker than for the south. The complexity of continental iron age societies should not be underestimated, as their growth and prosperity indicates. But the means by which prosperity was achieved were quite unlike those employed in the Mediterranean basin. Large, self-sufficient villages, supplemented in some regions by large farms, were the primary means by which agricultural and craft production were organized in much of the Gallic interior. Tribal affiliations were wider, and not based on the city.

North and south, then, Gaul was a world of villages. Against that backdrop stand out a few more complex and perhaps urban centres in several parts of the Mediterranean coastal plain, and the huge if sparsely populated fortifications that appeared in the north on the eve of the conquest. Roman writers were certainly capable of interpreting such centres as urban when it suited them, for example to enhance their victories or to provide the nucleus for a new city, and equally they were capable of treating them as the typical habitations of barbarians, villages or 'forts' (the literal meaning of *oppida*). But in terms of their

16 Ralston (1988), Woolf (1993b) discuss this aspect of regional variation. For regional groups in general, see Collis (1984, 191–227), Audouze and Buchsenschutz (1988, 313–16). On the south-west, see now Boudet (1987, 214–16).
17 See Woolf (1993b) for what follows in more detail.
18 Collis (1984, 65–85) endorsed for France by Audouze and Buchsenschutz (1988, 307–11), Haselgrove (1990b).

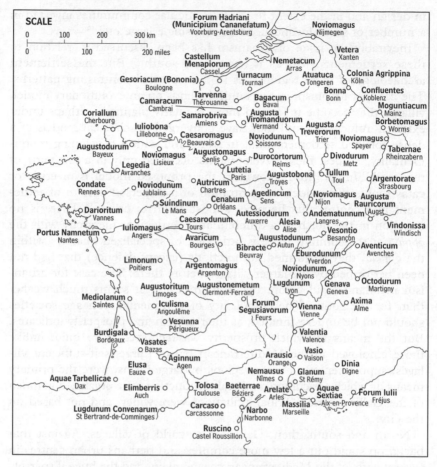

Fig. 5.1 Major cities of Gaul and Germany

morphology, the functions they performed for the surrounding territory and their degree of integration into supra-local networks, very few settlements stand comparison with the cities of the Mediterranean world.

II   The creation of Gallo-Roman cities

Two hundred years after Caesar's invasion of the interior, all of Gaul had been provided with an urban network that seems thoroughly Roman, both in its component parts and in the ways they fitted together. The construction of the new cities is the subject of this section, the nature and working of that urban network the subject of the next.

To be sure each city had its own history. The La Tène *oppidum* on Mont Beuvray was transformed gradually into an early Gallo-Roman town and was then replaced by a new city on a green field site twenty miles away at Autun, where an orthogonal street grid, circuit walls and civic monuments might be constructed from scratch. At Nîmes, one tower of the iron age settlement formed the core of a Roman monument, but most of the vast Augustan city lay below it on the plain around an iron age sanctuary rededicated to the imperial cult. Roman Narbonne had an iron age predecessor, but two colonial foundations completely remodelled the site, and other southern colonies, like Orange, were laid out in a single imperial moment. At Tongres, Xanten and Nijmegen in Belgica, cities were built on sites previously occupied by Roman military bases and indigenous settlements.[19] This diversity cannot easily be resolved into two or three 'modes of urbanization', but some general trends can be discerned in the urbanization of Gaul.

It is helpful to begin by distinguishing several components of city building. First there are the changes of site, both new foundations and shifts down onto neighbouring plains; second there is the organization of urban space, including, but not restricted to, the impositions of street grids; third there is the provision of monuments; and fourth the construction of domestic housing on Roman lines and in Roman materials. The relative chronology and importance to the city builders of each of these components is suggestive both of the aims of city building and the difficulties faced by those who built them. Two initial problems should be noted. Recent archaeological work has greatly increased our understanding of these processes, but their chronology can rarely be fixed closer than to a decade.[20] Information is also scanty about the earliest phases of urbanization, before cities built in timber, wattle and daub began to be rebuilt in stone from the mid-first century AD.[21] The possibility that

---

19 On Mont Beuvray, see ch. 1 above, and, in its latest form, Colin *et al.* (1995); on Nîmes, see Goudineau and Rebourg (1991, 35–43); on Narbonne, see ch. 3 above. For patterns of urbanization in Belgica, see Walthew (1982), Mertens (1985), Wightman (1985, 49–50, 75–80), Bloemers (1990) and the papers collected in *Les Villes de la Gaule Belgique* . . . (1984).

20 Duval *et al.* (1990). Current chronologies are very dependant on the presence of imported artefacts the chronology of which has been established in other areas. Associated difficulties include uncertainty about the time lags between regional sequences created by the slow spread of objects like the Nauheim fibula, Dressel amphorae, *terra sigillata* or Roman coins; risks of circularities in dating these artefacts; and the small number of historically dated contexts such as the destructions of Carthage and Entremont and some short-lived military camps on the Rhine. Despite painstaking work on all aspects of the problem the smallest margin of error possible is at least a decade and the possibility remains that some sequences may be up to twenty years out.

21 See Lasfargues (1985) on the earliest wooden structures. On the first cities built in stone, see Drinkwater (1985, 52), Goudineau (1991a, 7–9).

Gaul was hardly urbanized until this date, however, can be rejected on several grounds. First there is the gap in the settlement record to fill between the abandonment of the hillforts in the last quarter of the last century BC and the first Gallo-Roman monuments; second a number of recent excavations have uncovered traces of very early timber structures on the sites of Roman cities;[22] finally even on sites like Lyon and the southern colonies, where early foundations are attested by historical evidence, there is frequently a gap of up to thirty years before the first archaeological traces of the city.[23] Accepting these caveats, however, a provisional outline of the urbanization of Gaul can be constructed.

First the sites of the new cities. Most common were local shifts like those undergone by Nîmes, Vienne, Levroux or Ambrusson, which simply moved their centres of gravity down to the plain. Not all sites did shift, and at Bourges and Paris the *oppida* lie directly underneath the Roman and mediaeval cities. Shifts over longer distances reflected the increased importance of supra-regional communications under imperial rule, but they were comparatively rare. Perhaps more common were redistributions of functions and prominences between settlements within a regional system, since Roman rule entailed a greater level of functional specialization between settlements. The issue exposes the weaknesses of posing the question in terms of continuity or change of occupation at individual sites. The shift in location of settlement at Nîmes was accompanied by a huge expansion of the site and by the subordination to the city of two dozen other settlements. Likewise the iron age village of Feurs, in the Forez, provided the nucleus for a concentration of population, while others in the vicinity were abandoned.[24] The process is best described as a reconfiguration of the settlement pattern as a whole. The chronology of those changes might be complex. Vaison-la-Romaine seems to have relocated down to the plain gradually, over the last half of the last century BC, rather than in a single movement.[25] In the Aisne valley in the same period there were successive occupations of major lowland settlements at Condé-sur-Sippe and Villeneuve St Germain, of the hillfort at Pommiers, and of the Augustan city of Soissons.[26] Both there and in the Auvergne, where a series of middle-late La Tène open settlements were replaced first by three late La Tène hillforts and then by the Roman city of Clermont Ferrand,[27] it

22 E.g. the excavations of 'Ma Maison' at Saintes, for which see (Maurin 1988); and of St Romain-en-Gal, for which see Laroche and Savay-Guerraz (1984).
23 Desbat (1990). Cf. Goudineau (1989) on Lyon, Rebourg (1991) on Autun.
24 Vaginay and Guichard (1988).   25 Goudineau (1979, 196–203).
26 Haselgrove (1990b, 252–5), stressing the chronological complexities. Compare the neighbouring sequences at Reims and Vieux-Reims.
27 Collis (1984, 78–82), Sauget and Sauget (1985).

seems likely that there were overlaps in the occupations of 'successive' sites. Settlement shifts are more striking in northern France than in the south. Such movements were facilitated there by the structures out of which northern settlements were constructed: post-built houses with straw roofs and wattle and daub walls would need to be renewed every generation or so, and thus represented a smaller investment of energy than dry-stone structures. The creation of a Roman settlement pattern represented not just a shift in sites but also a shift to a less mobile form of settlement.

The complexity and variability of these shifts excludes the possibility that hillforts were abandoned in response to an imperial ruling or policy.[28] The co-existence of hillforts with the new towns in the early Gallo-Roman period strengthens this impression.[29] It seems better to see these relocations in the context of the long oscillation of temperate European settlements between hill and plain, and of the civilizing aspirations of the elites who decided on them, organized them and paid the considerable costs of relocation. The chronology is complex. The majority of non-mediterranean *oppida* were constructed around 80–70 BC and some continued to be built for some years after the conquest before being abandoned in the last decades of the century.[30] A number of new foundations appeared between 30 and 20 BC,[31] but the Roman pattern was not fully established in the north-east for another fifty years.[32] Even then, some minor towns, like Alesia, continued to occupy hill sites. Their monumental equipments show this did not reflect a rejection of Roman urban models, and perhaps indicates a reluctance of local elites to fund relocation from sites than were not too inaccessible except when it concerned the capitals of the new tribal states. Settlements moved less in the south. Lowland sites like Glanum and Lattes naturally continued in the same locations, and some hill sites, including Ensérune, were occupied well into the first century AD. But hillforts were no longer constructed after

28 Vespasian's letter to Sabora in Spain (*CIL* II 1423) sanctions a shift down to the plain but does not require it.
29 Colin *et al.* (1995).
30 Collis (1984, 49–50), Audouze and Buchsenshutz (1989, 318), Haselgrove (1990b, 252–5), Ralston (1992, 110–12). Exceptions abound, however, including Mont Beuvray, occupied in the second century BC and abandoned very late, possibly in the early first century AD, possibly because their unusually early adoption of Roman building styles made Aeduan nobles reluctant to relocate despite the disadvantages of the site. Likewise the hillfort on the plateau de Merdogne in the Auvergne was constructed in the middle of the last century BC and continued to be occupied until the mid-first century AD (Sauget and Sauget 1985).
31 See Maurin (1988, 14) for Saintes. See Chevallier (1985), Goudineau and Rebourg (1991) for collections of regional surveys.
32 Mertens (1985), Frézouls (1991).

the middle of the last century BC, and abandonment or more usually a partial or complete shift down to the plains characterized the last decades of the millenium.[33] As in the north, the fates of individual settlements depended to a large degree on how well integrated they were into wider patterns, in particular into the road network. Ambrusson benefited from its location on the Via Domitia to expand onto the surrounding plain in the late second century BC, and the fortified hilltop was abandoned a few generations later.[34] It is striking that southern and temperate Gaul experienced changes in their very different settlement patterns at much the same time. Iron age patterns in both zones were disrupted around 70 BC, the early Roman landscapes began to emerge c. 30–20 BC, the transition continued in many areas until about AD 50 and was complete everywhere by about AD 70–80. The process illustrates the commitment of the Gallo-Roman elites of the formative period to change.

Second the organization of urban space.[35] The plans of Gallo-Roman cities (like the architecture of their public buildings) were initially modelled on those of north Italian cities.[36] The city of Rome offered models for individual buildings,[37] but was neither accessible enough nor topographically typical enough to serve as a model for the design of Gallic towns. Caesarian and Augustan *coloniae* offered other accessible images of urbanism, but were themselves strongly influenced by Italian models.[38] The most obvious and often discussed feature of the planning of northern Italian cities is the grid-plan, laid out with geometric regularity in Turin, Aosta and Piacenza. Civic space, roads, walls, the forum and its monuments might all be made to conform to a perfect order, itself an expression of religious and political ideology.[39] That pattern was in practice often tailored to suit local conditions, and both in Cisalpina and in

33 Fiches and Nin (1985). Py (1990a, 210–46) is the most detailed study of the development of southern Gallic communities in this period, arguing for little change in indigenous lifetyles or material culture until c. 70 BC and then an acceleration in change from c. 25 BC.
34 Fiches (1986, 117–24).
35 For other studies using changes in urban space to investigate cultural change in the ancient world, cf. Kennedy (1985), Cormack (1990), Bowman (1992).
36 On public buildings, see Ward-Perkins (1970); on plans, see Pinon (1988, 15–18), von Hesberg (1991). Note however the importance of central Italian models for private houses, e.g. Goudineau (1979, 239–48) on Vaison. Early peristyle houses are also known from St Romain-en-Gal and Mont Beuvray.
37 Bedon et al. (1988, vol. 1, 418–25) for some suggestions.
38 Goudineau and Rebourg (1991), with essays on Nîmes, Vienne, Lyons and Autun; see Colin (1987) on Augustan circuit walls.
39 See Purcell (1990) on these issues. On the connection between Roman religious ideas and the layout of town, see (with care) Rykwert (1976).

transalpine Gaul irregularities and extensions were created to accommodate local topography, strategic conditions, pre-existing roads and subsequent growth. It was the very flexibility of the grid that allowed it to become a characteristic component of Roman urbanism. Yet other structuring principles existed: the exclusion of burials from the inhabited area, for example; the location of temples either at the centre of the town, often around the forum, or at its edge in suburban sanctuaries; and patterns of residence, still poorly understood, but apparently consisting not of rich, middle and lower class districts but of larger houses (*domus*) distributed in choice locations around the town, often on major routes, and surrounded by smaller houses and shops.[40] Manufacture, as opposed to retail trade, seems to have been pushed to the margins of the town, partly for practical reasons, but also perhaps to remove it from the most public zones of the city, its thoroughfares, monuments and open spaces.[41] If towns mould and reflect cultural practices and habits, zoning is in some ways a more significant expression of the Roman styles of urbanism than is the grid plan.

The grandest Gallo-Roman cities eventually came to exhibit most of these patterns of spatial organization,[42] but the evolution was a long, slow one from diverse starting points in the late iron age. On the iron age settlements of the interior the predominant pattern was a uniform occupation by huts and paddocks, interspersed by unoccupied areas, with agricultural and craft activities taking place in all areas indiscriminately.[43] Interestingly the same seems to be true of the earliest levels of Gallo-Roman towns. At Saintes, artisanal activities are mixed with domestic occupation across the entire site until AD 30–40, and at Autun craft activities do not become excluded from the civic centre until c. AD 70.[44] The southern *oppida* exhibited more internal differentiation in their final stages, but even Entremont was organized very differently from a Roman town.

The first indication of a new conception of urban space emerges in most cases not with the imposition of a grid, but with the construction of the first civic monuments, often forum complexes. Many iron age sites were of course topographically unsuitable for orthogonal planning – Glanum was in a gorge while Mont Beuvray, Ruscino, Amboise and other *oppida* were on hilltops – nevertheless the precocious construction

40 See Wallace-Hadrill (1991) for this pattern at Pompeii, and Perring (1991) on the northern provinces.
41 For this vision of public space, see MacDonald (1986).
42 See Goudineau (1980b, 261–72) on organization in general. Frere (1977) and Pinon (1988) focus mainly on grid plans.
43 Wells (1987), (1993), Woolf (1993b).   44 Maurin (1991, 54), Rebourg (1991, 106).

of Roman-style houses and monuments on these and other sites indicates the adoption of some Roman notions of space not embodied in the
street-grid. Glanum, for example, was given a new monumental centre
between 30 and 20 BC with the construction of two Italianate temples
and a forum complex.[45] The much cited plan of Mont Beuvray tells us
nothing about the organization of space in late iron age hillforts, but
it does show how Gauls could build a Roman city without a grid. A
forum complex with temples was constructed on the highest plateau of
the mountain, grand noble residences occupied the ridges of the hills
(as in Rome itself), while smaller residences and artisan workshop quarters occupied the lower slopes and the outermost edges of the city.

Planning of this type was common to all categories of Gallo-Roman
towns, the secondary centres as well as the tribal capitals and colonies.
The best known Gallo-Roman example of a minor town is Alesia, in
north-east Burgundy.[46] Traces of a wooden temple and open space
have been dated to the period 60–30 BC, although the construction of
the first proper forum complex dates to AD 20–30. Alesia follows in
other respects, too, much of the same chronological development as the
larger cities of the area. In the first century AD the wooden forum and
portico were rebuilt in stone, and a theatre and a *basilica* had been
added by the beginning of the second century. This monumental quarter was clearly separated from an artisan quarter and from the larger
residences. The houses were arranged on streets and into blocks (*insulae*),
but the plan was dictated not by a grid but by the relief. Alesia seems to
reflect a common pattern among the minor towns of Gaul, both in
southern examples like Ambrusson and in other northern towns such
as Mandeure, Mâlain and Antigny. They display a sense of space that
diverges from that of late iron age *oppida* but which lacks the regular
grid-plans of the *civitas* capitals and *coloniae*. Monumental complexes
including *fora*, temples and sometimes *basilicae* were common in the
larger minor towns, as in the capitals.[47] But whereas in the capitals the
grid-plans often determined the location of monuments, in smaller settlements, like Les Bolards, the monuments themselves, together with
the major roads, dictated the organization of urban space. The contrasts between major and minor towns can be exaggerated. The earliest
monuments at Saintes preceded the laying out of the grid,[48] and grid

45 Roth Congès (1992a, 49–55).
46 Le Gall (1980), Mangin (1981), Bernard and Mangin (1985).
47 Broise (1976), Mangin (1983), Mangin and Tassaux (1992, 462).
48 See Bedon *et al.* (1988, 5–42) on the general pattern. For monuments preceding the
    street plan, see Maurin (1988, 38–44) on growth of Saintes, and Vaginay and Guichard
    (1988, 191–2) on Feurs.

plans might in any case be adapted to accommodate major routes and structures, as at Amiens.[49] Finally some secondary towns do show some influence of orthogonal planning. Part of Mandeure was laid out on orthogonal lines, but the roads nearest the river curved to accommodate it, and the principal monuments were not aligned on the grid. There is no sharp distinction in other words, but an emphasis on orthogonality, as opposed to linearity, is much less pronounced in minor towns than it is in the case of the capitals.[50]

The grid plans of the *coloniae* and *civitas* capitals do mark one important contrast with lesser centres. The laying out of a grid across an entire city implies a single moment of foundation or re-foundation, with an impact on existing property rights and structures, and a cost in resources and manpower that can only be guessed at.[51] In *coloniae* like Orange, that single moment of foundation reflects the power of the conqueror to dispose of property without any constraint. The settlement of veterans involved the eviction of locals and the redivision of rural space as well as the laying out of the colony with its monuments aligned on a grid plan inserted into the road network. But the majority of planned towns in Roman Gaul were not veteran colonies, nor were they created in the immediate aftermath of conquest. The plans of Autun and Nîmes, for example, both privileged indigenous communities, laid out at the earliest in the first decade AD, might be linked to other contemporary displays of power over space – the redrawing of provincial and communal boundaries, the census, the laying out of the road system – seen by some as characteristic expressions of Augustus' imperial style.[52] But in Aquitaine, the grid-plans of the *civitas* capitals were probably not all in place until the 30s AD and a number of cities in north-east Gaul did not receive them until the mid-first century AD, sometime on sites that had almost certainly been occupied for a generation, such as Bavai.[53] In cases like Amiens and Trier, the timing of these later re-orderings of space might be connected with the end of a military occupation of the site, although it is often difficult to disentangle such relationships; sites well placed on major communication routes were attractive for military garrisons and civil settlements alike, and military

49 Bayard and Massy (1983), with useful general discussion of grids.
50 Mangin (1983, 43–4), Drinkwater (1985, 53–4) for discussion.
51 Goudineau (1980b, 267–8).
52 Nicolet (1988), but see Goudineau and Rebourg (1991) on the limitations of Augustan urbanism in Gaul.
53 On Aquitania, see Garmy (1992, 226) following Colin (1987). On the north, see Bayard and Massy (1983, 209–10), synthesizing reports from the Colloque de Saint-Riquier, published in the *Révue Archéologique de Picardie* 3–4 (1984). On the significance of this period for the urbanization of Belgica, see Wightman (1985, 75–80).

garrisons might sometimes be located to control indigenous centres. But these exceptions aside, it remains likely that in most cases grid-plans were the result of a collective decision by the rulers of a Gallo-Roman community to create a new capital city for themselves on the model of the *coloniae* and other imperial foundations. The enormous costs, social as well as financial, of demolition and reconstruction and of the redistribution of land, must provide a large part of the explanation for the rarity of grid-plans outside the *civitas* capitals. Their meaning is clear. The immense gridded areas of northern capitals in particular represented a pledge of future urbanism. In many cases, Carhaix for example, that pledge was never redeemed. The cities remained empty of monuments and houses alike, and the outlying *insulae* defined by the grids remained as huge vacant lots. But at the moment when they were laid out, the grids of the new cities were signs of the urban aspirations of the elites of the formative period.

Third the monuments themselves. Perhaps the best way of conveying some idea of the range of monuments that a Gallo-Roman city might accumulate is to consider Saint-Bertrand-de-Comminges, ancient Lugdunum Convenarum, one of the only Gallic *civitas* capitals that does not lie beneath a modern town.[54] The city was founded by Pompey in the late 70s BC, but there is no archaeological trace of urban structures until 30–20 BC when a temple and its precinct, probably devoted to the cult of Rome and Augustus, were built in the centre of the town. This was just the first component of a developing civic complex, which by c. AD 20 included a *forum*, one or more other temples, a *macellum* (the monumental market place) and public baths. A theatre was added at some point in the early first century AD, and the second half of the century saw rebuilding of the baths on a grander scale and elaboration of the *macellum*. Similar refurbishments took place in the second century, when a large portico was constructed south of the *macellum*, and a second set of baths was built in the north of the town, probably associated with a sanctuary complex. It is likely that an amphitheatre and aqueduct were also constructed in the late first or early second century AD. Even when rebuilding followed fires, it was usually carried out on a larger scale than before and using more expensive materials.

St Bertrand illustrates some general features of urban monumentality in Gaul. To begin with, Roman styles of monumentalization cannot be attested anywhere before about 30 BC, neither in new foundations like Narbonne and St Bertrand nor on indigenous sites. *Oppida* had their own monumentality, of course, in their ramparts, furnished with towers

---

54 May (1986) and Guyon (1991), with further bibliography.

in the south and huge gatehouses in the north. The enigmatic cult structures of Entremont and Ensérune can indeed usefully be considered as monumental, as can the Hellenistic structures at Glanum. But, with the possible exception of the last example, these monuments would not have been recognizable to a Roman eye as signs of an urban civilization. Monumental civic centres in the Roman style, of which the *forum* with its surrounding temples and *basilicae* was a central element, did not appear until 30–20 BC, or even later in some parts of northern Gaul.[55] It is likely, however, that even in areas where stone built *fora* appeared late, they were preceded by timber constructions organized around a cleared space. The earliest monuments often celebrated the imperial house, not just in altars and temples to Rome and Augustus, but also commemorations of Gaius and Lucius Caesar (at Glanum, Trier and Reims), images of Tiberius and his sons (on the arch at Saintes), of Tiberius alone (on the Pilier des Nautes at Paris), of Livia and Augustus (at Vienne), of Agrippina the Elder (at Avenches) and many other examples. To these monuments may perhaps be compared the imperial elements of the names given to many of the new cities, titles like Augusta, Augustodunum, Augustomagus, Augustonemetum, Augustobona, Augustoritum, Augustodurum, Caesaromagus, Caesarodunum, Juliomagus and Juliobona,[56] and also the marked prominence of imperial dedications among the earliest Gallic epigraphy.[57] This phenomenon is not limited to Gaul, and implies no 'special relationship' between the Julio-Claudian house and the Gauls,[58] but it is very characteristic of the earliest stage of Gallo-Roman urbanism.

The sequence in which the various monuments were constructed varied, but some general patterns hold good for most cities.[59] Where the smaller cities have been studied in detail, the chronology of their development mirrors that of the *civitas* capitals, although in general

55 For the recognition of the significance of the later part of this period, usually identified as the reigns of Tiberius and Claudius, see Grenier (1936), de Laet (1966), Garmy (1992). For recent assessments of the importance of the 'Augustan' period, see Goudineau (1991a, 7–9), Aupert and Sablayrolles (1992, 284–5).

56 See Goudineau (1980b, 99) for a map and Frézouls (1991, 109) for discussion. The significance of similar place-names in Britain is discussed by Rivet (1980).

57 Wightman (1984).

58 *pace* Drinkwater (1983, 20–2, 35), who rightly emphasizes the care taken by Augustus and his immediate successors to establish personal links with the Gauls, especially through frequent personal visits. Similar policies were, however, pursued elsewhere, for example in Asia, Syria and Judaea, and any 'special relationship' can only have existed in the minds of Rome's Gallic partisans. Many Julio-Claudian visits to Gaul were in any case intended to maintain their much more vital relationships with the Rhine armies, for which see Campbell (1984).

59 Bedon *et al.* (1988) vol. 1 for a good introduction to the various styles of monument characteristic of Gallo-Roman cities.

monuments were scarce in all but the largest secondary centres.[60] Theatres were among the earliest amenities provided after the *forum* complex at the centre.[61] The first theatres were constructed in the *coloniae*, but most indigenous centres acquired them in the course of the first century AD, even if they were subsequently modified or refitted, stone replacing wooden structures and further embellishments being added later. Well over a hundred examples are known from all over Gaul, the vast majority built in the second half of the first century and the first half of the second century AD. Theatres were common in all categories of towns (as at rural sanctuaries) in central and northern Gaul, while in Narbonensis and Aquitaine south of the Garonne they were rare outside the *civitas* capitals. They might be constructed in town centres, as at Orange, but more frequently were at the edge of towns, often associated with suburban sanctuaries. Specific local architectural variants have been identified including the Gallic theatre-cum-amphitheatre.[62] Theatres, then, were regarded as an indispensable adjunct of a Roman-style city and the entertainments that took place within them were an indispensable part of civic life. Amphitheatres were rarer, almost unknown outside *civitas* capitals, perhaps owing to their greater cost and/or because *spectacula* were often provided by civic magistrates during their year of office. If a town had both an amphitheatre and a theatre, the theatre was usually earlier, but only the most prominent towns had both.[63] Almost no amphitheatres are known to have existed before the mid-first century and most were constructed in the last quarter of the first and in the second century AD. The other main category of monuments consists of public baths and fountains and the aqueducts that supplied them, again appearing from the middle of the first century AD.

If most Gallo-Roman cities first acquired monumental centres around the turn of the millenium, and gradually furnished themselves with other amenities through the first century AD, they continued to repair, embellish, replace and add to their monumental equipment up until the

---

60 On the chronology, see Aupert and Sablayrolles (1992); on Aquitaine, see Petit *et al.* (1994b). For the rarity of monuments in most small towns, see Bénard *et al.* (1994, 219–22) and Petit *et al.* (1994a, 283–90).

61 Goudineau (1980b, 288–9), Dumasy and Fincker (1992) for maps and lists. See Doreau *et al.* (1982) for a recently excavated example. Landes (1989) provides the best introduction, including a convenient Atlas.

62 See Bouley (1983) on theatres and sanctuaries in the north.

63 Antibes, Arles, Avenches, Autun, Béziers, Fréjus, Lyon, Narbonne, Nîmes, Paris, Toulouse, Valence and possibly St Bertrand, Saintes and Limoges. Although the list of monuments is very incomplete, and more cities may well turn out to have had both, the prominence in this list of *coloniae* and 'favoured cities' such as Autun, Nîmes and Saintes is evident. For a discussion of chronology and typology, see Golvin (1988).

late second or early third century AD.[64] The monumentalization of Gallo-Roman cities was a slow process, depending as it did on the availability of skilled craftsmen and architects, on adequate supplies of building stone and manpower, and on the resources of the local elite members who funded most projects.[65] But the desire to monumentalize was clearly widespread from the turn of the millenium until the late second century AD when the pace of monumentalization seems to have slackened in some areas. The building boom of the late first and early second centuries simply reflected the delays necessitated by financial and technical constraints, and the existence of very early timber monuments like the 'proto-forum' of Amiens attests early attempts to construct Roman-style civic centres in whatever materials were available.[66] The public building of the first and early second centuries demonstrates a continued adherence to that set of values.

Finally domestic architecture.[67] The construction of aristocratic *domus* out of *opus caementicum* with mosaic floors and tiled roofs was not generalized in Gaul until the late first century AD, but new architectures which developed much earlier may be distinguished from both their iron age predecessors and contemporary Italian models. Stone was already in widespread use in the south, but changes in design have been detected in some of the *oppida* at the end of the last century BC, and the earliest Roman structures of Nîmes and Narbonne used adobe, daub and unfired bricks. Meanwhile in the north, La Tène post-built architecture gave way to new styles of construction employing timber and earth, occasionally dried into daub, and half-timbering on stone socles. These techniques did not disappear when masonry construction and tiles became more widely available. Perhaps the most striking innovation in domestic architecture is the appearance of large residences among the smaller timber and earth structures inhabited by the majority of the population. That distinction contrasts markedly with the relatively undifferentiated residences of iron age settlements. *Domus* were constructed at Vaison, St Romain-en-Gal and Ambrusson in the early first century AD, but they are rare in the *civitas* capitals of non-Mediterranean Gaul

---

64 Bedon *et al.* (1988, vol. 1, 418–25) for a representative list of dated monuments.
65 Bedon (1984) on the slow development of stone-quarrying in Gaul, Frézouls (1984) for epigraphic documentation of urban building funded by Gallo-Roman aristocrats. Tardy (1989, 15–30) for Augustan column capitals from Saintes that suggest the employment of specialist craftsmen in the first decades AD.
66 See Bayard and Massy (1983, 74–5) for the 'proto-forum'.
67 Research on domestic achitecture has lagged behind that on monuments, cf. Goudineau (1980b, 296–307), Blagg (1990, 203–4), although important recent excavations at Limoges, Saintes, Vaison and St Romain-en-Gal have helped clarify the picture. In general, see Lasfargues (1985), Balmelle (1992).

until the second half of that century.[68] Once constructed, however, the houses were luxurious, extending over several thousand square metres, built of masonry or half-timbered, and they were equipped with peristyle courtyards, wall paintings and occasionally mosaic floors. The construction of these grand houses was roughly contemporary with that of theatres and bath houses. An earlier generation had lived in wattle and daub houses scattered throughout newly planned but sparsely populated cities, with a few half-timbered monuments arranged around a recently cleared public space in the centre, and perhaps a single stone-built temple of the imperial cult. Introducing a report of an excavation that has revealed as much as any of this earliest phase of Gallo-Roman urbanism, its editor remarked on 'the slow stages in the Romanization of a population who had doubtless been gathered in from the surrounding countryside to form the new urban community'.[69] The slowness of those processes is clear in every part of Gaul. The first shifts away from the *oppida* took place around 30 BC, but the new settlements did not acquire a Roman style plan for a generation and then had to wait another generation for the first stone-built civic monuments and aristocratic monuments to be built. That building process then took forty or fifty years in most regions. Apart from a few lucky recipients of imperial patronage, few Gallo-Roman cities had a full complement of monuments and noble residences much before the end of the first century AD. At the origin of this enduring vocation for urbanism, however, was a moment of inspiration, the point at which a new set of cultural channels were established.

Why did the Gallo-Roman aristocracies build these cities, in particular the immense grid-planned *civitas* capitals with their grand monuments and public spaces? By the second century AD, elaboration and rebuilding might simply be a sign of conformity to cultural patterns widespread in the empire and more importantly well established by previous generations in Gaul. It is the moment of origins that poses the real problem, that formative period when communities were willing to abandon ancestral sites, found capitals from scratch, gather their dependents together from their scattered residences and spend immense sums on foreign architects and craftsmen, and on building materials

68 Goudineau (1979), Fiches (1986), Balmelle (1992, 343). The large house in the Parc aux Chevaux, Mont Beuvray, was constructed in masonry before 20 BC (*RAE* 42.2, 1991, 286–98). Amiens follows a more regular pattern in the north with *opus caementicum* replacing timber in the mid-first century AD and wall painting becoming common in the Flavian period (Bayard and Massy 1983, 114–26). For other regions, cf. the surveys in Lasfargues (1985).

69 See Maurin (1988, 5–6) on Saintes.

that were not yet easy to come by. Their committment is all the more evident from their willingness to construct public monuments before devoting these resources to their own residences. Various pragmatic or strategic considerations might be advanced. City building will have pleased those governors who, like Tacitus' idealized Agricola, encouraged the construction of temples, *fora* and *domus*. Romans would certainly approve these developments, and might reward those individuals and communities who implemented them. A second rationale might be the desire of the new elites to impress their own subordinates and legitimize the ascendancy Rome had granted them within their own societies. Gauls, after all, were the usual spectators of city building and the main beneficiaries of *spectacula* that took place in the new theatres and amphitheatres, as of the public baths and the distributions at civic festivals. The new elites were in need of some such legitimatory devices since Roman rule had ended some pre-conquest practices, such as inter-tribal warfare, through which iron age chiefs had won prestige and power, and since the social distance between ruler and ruled in the Gallo-Roman communities was so much greater than before. Roman euergetistical monumentalization may have provided a technology that was much in demand in the immediate post-conquest period in the north. Thirdly, perhaps the construction of new cities was valued (as at Rome) as a means of providing employment for Gauls of lower status, a beneficial act then on the part of the new ruling classes.

Yet it may also be that the first generation of truly Gallo-Roman aristocrats embraced the urbanizing project for reasons that were not wholly pragmatic or strategic, but rather because the city was so central to the vision of civilization they had embraced. A flavour of this vision can be gained from a passage of Virgil's *Aeneid*. Fleeing the collapse of their own (pre-conquest) society, Aeneas and his followers are driven ashore on the African coast where they encounter other refugees from the eastern Mediterranean, this time from Tyre, who are engaged at that very moment in the foundation of Carthage. Rendered temporarily invisible by Venus, the Trojans observe the foundation of the city that is to be Rome's great rival, and see the Tyrians busy building gates and laying out streets, where there had once been only primitive huts, planning a circuit wall and fortifying the citadel in stone, marking out on the ground the location of future buildings and also selecting laws, magistrates and a senate. Meanwhile some excavated the harbour, others dug out the foundations of a theatre, while yet others cut huge columns for its stage. At the centre of the city was the site of a huge temple to Juno, the city's patroness, richly and elaborately decorated with bronze doors on which were depicted scenes from the Trojan War, already receding into a legendary heroic past. These images finally reassure Aeneas that they have arrived among civilized people capable of praise, pity and sympathy, a moral society.[70] As the epic continues, Aeneas is to be cruelly disappointed: Carthage is a civilization, but it is the wrong one, and his destiny is to go on to found an alternative. But the scene does present a pattern for planting civilization in a barbarous land.[71]

That image may be compared to Strabo's account of the civilizing of the Allobroges, once warlike and living in villages, now peaceable farmers whose nobility inhabit the city of Vienne.[72] Virgil portrays the origins of civilization in the post-heroic era as a process that encompasses the monumentalization of the city, the making of laws (iura), together with those constitutional arrangements which Strabo summed up in the term politeia, and the development of an humane sensibility. The complex and evolving inter-relationship between the physical, political and ethical nature of the classical city could be traced back much further and much more widely exemplified. But this passage is important for two reasons. Not only does it represent an expression drawn from precisely that formative period in which the first recognizably Roman cities were created in Gaul, but it was also a uniquely influential expression, since the Aeneid was the basis of the education of the new Gallo-Roman elite. We may imagine the sons of the Gallic aristocracy gathered in Autun in the early decades of the first century AD to learn their Latin from this text, while a model city was literally being built around them. Leaving their lessons to wander through the still-empty street grid that framed the building sites where the monuments of Augustodunum rose around them, would it be surprising if they too had come to share Aeneas' mission?

III   The Gallo-Roman urban system

The cities of Gaul were built because the richest and most influential citizens of Gallic communities learned to associate civic life with civilization. That conclusion emerges if we focus on urbanization in the terms in which it was perceived by Romans and Gallo-Romans. A different

---

70 Virgil Aeneid 1. 421–63.
71 Virgil Aeneid 1. 339. Compare the images of wilderness evoked in Aeneid 8. 347–50 during Aeneas' visit to the futute site of Rome (and the contrast between the ekphrasis of the shield there which looks forward to Rome's future, unlike that of the temple doors in book 1 which look back to the Trojan past).
72 Strabo Geography 4.1.11, cf. Tacitus Agricola 21.

but complementary perspective allows Gallo-Roman urbanism to be set in a wider context, that of the modern geographer's conception of urbanization as a process by which settlements become differentiated. Likewise Romanization may be thought of in terms of the creation of structured systems of differences, rather than in terms of processes of assimilation, acculturation or cultural convergence. The origins of Gallo-Roman cities, as of Gallo-Roman culture in general, may thus be approached by asking how and why Roman power created this differentiation.

Central place theory and urban network analysis are concepts devised to investigate aspects of urbanism that cannot be studied through the concentrated examination of individual towns, the histories of which inevitably reflect chance and local conditions.[73] Central place theory treats towns as the higher ranking elements within hierarchically ordered settlement patterns, by means of which activities are ordered and distributed within a landscape. Settlements may then be classified and ordered in terms of the services they provide to the population of a region, for example by creating a regional hierarchy of markets, or of places where various specialists can be found. A hierarchy of central places displays certain regularities in spatial patterning, so that roughly equivalent settlements are separated by roughly equivalent travel times.[74] Urban network analysis, on the other hand, starts from the place of cities within supra-regional systems and considers settlement hierarchies as means by which those systems penetrate peripheral regions and rural areas, for example to gain access to their resources through taxation.[75] The distinction between bottom-up approaches to urbanism like central place theory and top-down approaches like network analysis re-enacts on a larger scale debates familiar to historians over whether cities exploit the countryside, or whether they pay their way by enriching rural existence. A false compromise is to treat all cities and urban systems simply as neutral organizers. It is more accurate to admit that both cities and urban networks vary in the extent to which they contribute to the servicing or the exploitation of populations, and that their development often exhibits a tension between the desires and interests of locals and

73 Hohenberg and Lees (1985, 47–73) for a brief introduction. The approach has also been applied to the earliest urban origins, cf. Skinner (1977), Clarke (1979, 435–43). On the need to appreciate cities in terms of wider systems, see Wheatley (1972). De Vries (1984) is a classic demonstration of the strengths of this approach.
74 See Grant (1986) on central place theory applied to archaeological and historical cases. On marketing systems, see Skinner (1964) and on analysis of regional systems in general, see Smith (1976), especially the editor's introduction to volume I, 2–63.
75 For examples, see Rozman (1973), (1976), Abu Lughod (1989).

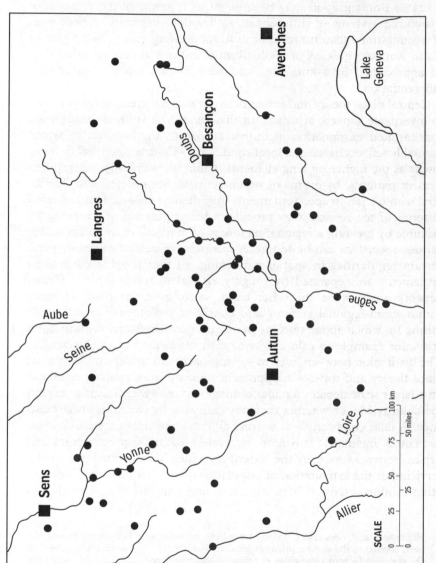

Fig. 5.2 The urban network of Burgundy and the Franche-Comté

those of outsiders.[76] Urban hierarchies reflect spatially extensive systems of power, and are one way in which those complexes of power become entrenched.[77]

The nature of the urban system that developed in Gaul in the early Roman period is perhaps best exemplified by considering one of the more intensively studied regions. Attempts to document and analyze all the elements of Gallo-Roman landscapes are currently being pioneered by French archaeologists, but in a few regions a reasonably complete record of all settlements larger than isolated farms does exist. One of the best studied areas in this respect is the Franche-Comté, a modern French region comprising the *départments* of Jura, Haute-Saône, Doubs and the Territoire de Belfort, extending from the Saône northeast to the Belfort Gap along the north-west flank of the Jura and to the south-east of the plateau de Langres.[78] The centre of this area based around the valley of the Doubs corresponds very roughly with the territory of the Sequani, one of the more powerful peoples of eastern Gaul in the late iron age. Their main centre, Besançon, is the only *civitas* capital within this area but at least twenty-one other nucleated settlements existed between the mid-first and the mid-second century AD. Of these, Mandeure alone was a substantial town equipped with a street grid, a forum and other monuments including a theatre and a number of fairly luxurious private houses. Three others possessed some form of a gridded street plan, but most were organized along a single main axis. About one in four had public baths and three had market places but there is little evidence from most of them for *fora* or other monumental structures. Almost half, however, have produced evidence for zoning (*quartiers specialisés*) and a third have produced evidence of private residences with mosaics, wall painting and hypocausts. On the basis of their probable

76 On the consumer city/exploiter city debate, see most recently Whittaker (1990), with full bibliography, and Leveau (1983a), with Goudineau's response, all three arguing largely from Gallic evidence. For other recent contributions, cf. Engels (1990) (with caution), Osborne (1991) and Wallace-Hadrill (1991). The debate has been bedevilled by confusions between Weberian ideal-types and taxonomic categories and by imprecision in the use of terms such as exploitation and parasitism, see Wrigley (1978) for a clear analysis. It may be preferable to follow Abrams' (1978) argument that towns on no account should be treated as social actors, but are better considered in relation to larger 'complexes of domination', 'as moments in a process of usurpation and defence, consolidation, appropriation and resistance' (31) and to conclude with Whittaker (1990, 117) that 'the interesting economic questions about manufacture or exploitation and redistribution of wealth, whether between rich and poor or between province and empire, are unrelated to the internal divisions between town and country.'

77 Giddens (1984, 130–2).

78 Mangin, Jacquet and Jacob (1986), updated in Mangin (1994). Broadly similar results have emerged from a similar survey of the settlement pattern of the Côte d'Or, for which see Bénard *et al.* (1994).

occupied areas and the remains of private and public architecture, some five or so sites might form a third level in the local hierarchy, perhaps as small towns, but it would be a mistake to detach them too sharply from the other nucleated settlements. Although it is convenient to describe the sites in the the top third of the hierarchy as small towns or second-ary urban centres, it is important to remember both the differences within that category, especially between Mandeure and the others, and also the steady continuum of differentiation from small town to small village. The major secondary centres tend to be located on the major Roman roads of the region, in particular on the route to Lyon, but the relief also exercised a major influence, nucleated settlements being dis-tributed along the valley bottoms, even when these do not coincide with major Roman routes. On the whole, the lower the settlements' ranks, the closer they are to one another, suggesting that they served smaller areas: the mean distance between them is less than 20 km, although Besançon monopolized an area almost 50 km in diameter.

It would be convenient if the settlement patterns of the Franche-Comté could be generalized to the whole of Gaul, but in fact there were considerable variations between regions. Within the province of Aquitania, a clear contrast can be seen between the region south of the Garonne, where small towns are virtually unknown, and the area between the Garonne and the Loire, where secondary centres are com-mon especially in the Atlantic west, and along and around the valley of the Loire.[79] Several factors contributed to this pattern. Physical relief exercised an important influence: few urban centres are known on the Massif Central, but they cluster around the edges of it, especially to the north and east in Poitou, the Berry and the basins of the Allier and upper Loire. The contrast between areas north and south of the Garonne is only one of a series of contrasts that may be drawn between these regions: theatres of any sort, for example, are rare south of the river although they are particularly common in both rural and urban locations in west-central France,[80] and the area retained some sense of identity which eventually was recognized in the creation of a separate province of Novempopulania.[81] In some of these respects, and in others, like the use of the Iberian language, the southern sector resembled parts of Narbonensis, where secondary urban centres were also rare, and it may be that administrative boundaries truncated geographical and ethnic divisions. The success of secondary urban centres may also be related to *civitas* size. Because the *civitates* of southern Aquitaine tended to be

79 Mangin and Tassaux (1992).   80 Dumasy and Fincker (1992).
81 Bost and Fabre (1988).

much smaller than those of the north, they were quite close together, and it may be that secondary centres arose in the larger *civitates* to provide services to areas remote from the capitals.[82] Secondary urban centres are known in moderately sized northern *civitates*, but it appears that they were neither as common nor as urbanized as those of areas like the Côte d'Or or Poitou.[83] Narbonensis too had a dense network of secondary centres, similar in many respects to that of Italy.[84] It increasingly seems that only part of the distribution of urban centres may be explained as a function of geographical constraints and transport factors. Some areas of Gaul, in other words, were less urbanized than others.

It is worth contrasting these urban systems with those of the late iron age. Once again it is easiest to do this by examining one well-studied area in detail. The Berry is a geographically diverse region across which the rivers Cher, Indre, Allier and Creuse drain off the Massif into the middle Loire which forms its northern limit.[85] Fortified settlements appeared in the region in the second quarter of the last century BC, to judge from the best known example, Levroux, which was preceded by an open settlement on a slightly different site. The settlement at Bourges which features in Caesar's narrative is almost unknown archaeologically, but of the thirty to forty late La Tène sites in the region, a dozen or so others were probably fortified sites enclosing between 2 and 30 ha, about half of which enclosing areas of 15–30 ha. Riverine locations are common, possibly because of their defensive potential, but otherwise the distribution of sites seems fairly uniform, with some slight differences in site density possibly being related to variations in the

82 The distribution of secondary urban centres in Roman. Britain has been much discussed since Hodder and Hassall's (1971) demonstration that the spacing of walled settlements is not random within southern Britain, cf. Hodder (1972), (1975), Millett (1986). Similar studies are not possible in Gaul, where, in some regions at least, most nucleated settlements were not walled until the third, fourth or possibly even the fifth centuries AD (Maurin (1992)), and it has in any case been doubted whether walls are a good criterion of urbanism even in Britain (Hingley (1989) 114; Millett (1990a) 150–1) where more nuanced definitions are now in use, cf. Burnham (1986), (1987), Burnham and Wacher (1990). Nevertheless, it remains clear that some of the postulates of central place theory are satisfied by Romano-British settlement patterns, and it would perhaps be surprising if the same were not true for Roman Gaul.
83 See Mangin and Tassaux (1992, 477–8) for tentative conclusions along these lines, conclusions broadly supported by the regional surveys gathered in Petit *et al.* (1994a).
84 See Leveau (1994) for a thoughtful survey.
85 On the Berry in the late La Tène, see Buchsenschutz (1981), Buchsenschutz and Ralston (1981), Buchsenschutz (1988), with full bibliography. On the Roman period, see Leday (1980), Mangin and Tassaux (1992) and Dumasy-Mathieu (1994). The area occupied by the Bituriges is generally held to have corresponded to that of the pre-revolutionary diocese of Bourges, approximately equivalent to the modern *départments* of Indre and Cher together with the western half of the *départment* of the Allier.

productivity of different terrains. Aside from those locational factors, however, little overall patterning is evident and the various attempts that have been made to order these *oppida* into settlement hierarchies appropriate to early states remain extremely speculative.[86] For the Roman period around twenty nucleated sites apart from Bourges have been identified. About half of them succeeded late La Tène *oppida* on the same or adjacent sites. A group of these latter sites display some urban features and one of them, Argenton, received an impressive complement of monuments, including a theatre that was rebuilt during the second century, that is compared to that of Mandeure. As in the Franche-Comté, secondary urban centres flourished best at some distance from the capital, and sites on the road network developed at the expense of others. The nucleated sites of the Roman Berry varied considerably in function, from the spa town of Bourbon, to scattered settlements around monumental centres like Baugy, to settlements with no monuments, which sheltered populations engaged in diverse economic activities and simple roadside settlements. At present there are no Biturigan examples of the economically specialized settlements known from elsewhere in Gaul, such as miners' and potters' villages, although it is possible that some of the rural sanctuaries common in the Berry may have sheltered small populations of attendants.[87] Although the Berry did not experience major settlement shifts, then, there was a moderate increase in settlement nucleation and a redistribution of population to the benefit of the emergent higher-order central places, and crucially settlements came to differ from one another much more than had been the case in the late La Tène.

Settlement differentiation is one aspect of the process by which the incorporation of small communities into wider social systems leads previously self-sufficient units to become more specialized and hence interdependent.[88] In Gaul, it occurred not only within *civitates* but also at a provincial level, and it is possible to produce various rankings of Gallic cities on the basis of criteria such as formal status (e.g. *coloniae, civitates liberae* or *vici*); degree of monumentalization, surface area, number of known equestrian and senatorial citizens, or size of extant epigraphy.[89] No absolute hierarchy existed, but it is clear that differentiation of various sorts was occurring among Gallic cities and also that on most

86 Crumley (1974), Nash (1978a), (1978b); cf. Buchsenschutz and Ralston (1981) and Ralston (1992, 154–61) for critical overviews.
87 Mangin and Tassaux (1992).
88 Wolf (1956). For a study of these effects within another Roman province, see Alcock (1993).
89 For attempts, cf. Pounds (1969, 149) on the basis of size, Goudineau (1980b, 387), combining several criteria.

criteria the major cities of Narbonensis outranked all northern ones bar Lyon, Autun and the capitals of the Comatan provinces. Equally, on some criteria the capitals of the smaller Belgic and Armorican communities might well be ranked below larger secondary centres like Alesia, Mandeure and Argenton.

If urbanization is thought of as settlement differentiation, we may pose the question of the origins of Gallic cities in the form, How did Roman power draw up an urban hierarchy out of the relatively undifferentiated settlement patterns of the late iron age? It helps to consider separately the various ways in which Roman power was manifested over the Gauls. First there was the military power of Rome. The foundation of military *coloniae* is the most obvious way in which military power created cities, and garrisons might also promote the growth of civil settlements. But more influential in the long term may have been the road systems built in association with these military sites. The continued success of Ambrusson, for example, relative to that of other secondary centres attributed to Nîmes, may be explained in terms of its location on the Via Domitia, and the Agrippan road system explains in part the early prominence of Saintes and the continuing importance of Lyon.[90] New routes became strategically important as the German frontier was created and elaborated and then again after the Claudian invasion of Britain. Towns located on the new thoroughfares to the Rhine and the Channel, like Langres and Amiens respectively, benefited accordingly.[91]

Second, there is the differentiation produced by the Roman administrative hierarchy. At the head were Lyon and Narbonne, with the imperial cult and provincial councils; then the other seats of Roman governors and procurators; and then the capitals of the *civitates*, to which Rome delegated most of the administration of Gaul.[92] In addition there was an internal administrative hierarchy within some of the larger *civitates*, based on some of the second rank centres, which were governed by junior magistrates.[93] The public buildings uncovered at sites like Alesia,

90 See Goudineau (1980a) on these issues. The dating of the Agrippan system's construction is unclear in Strabo 4.6.11 but a number of scholars have recently favoured an early date in connection with Agrippa's governorship of Gaul from 39 BC. Cf. Drinkwater (1983, 123), Roddaz (1984, 66), Goudineau (1991a).
91 On the importance of military roads in explaining the relative success of urban settlements in other provinces, cf. Burghardt (1979), Burnham (1986). For Gaul, see Drinkwater (1983, 130–5). For similar factors influencing the growth of smaller settlements, see Petit et al. (1994a, 241–8).
92 See Drinkwater (1983, 95–8) for the debates over which Comatan cities housed Roman officials. The system was probably not static.
93 Wightman (1976b), Drinkwater (1979a). Broise (1976) discusses urban features of these settlements. Until recently the term *vicus* has been applied to many of these secondary centres (e.g. Chevallier 1976) but the imprecision of the Latin term and the

Argenton and Mandeure might be interpreted in various ways. Some of these complexes might be the relics of abandoned capitals like Bibracte. But others, like Argenton, remained prominent from the late iron age through into at least the second century AD. It is possible the council of some Gallic communities could be convened at more than one centre within the *civitas*, although permanent structures like *fora* and *diribitoria* (voting booths) were hardly necessary for council meetings. But other evidence suggests that local loyalties, often based around pre-Roman centres, remained important within some of the larger *civitates*. Luxurious residences have been found in some secondary centres and a small number were granted autonomy in the course of the first three centuries AD. Possibly the civic buildings of these areas reflect the persistence of local elites, and the sub-*civitas* magistracies were devices designed (sometimes unsuccessfully) to integrate them into larger wholes.

Roman rule also stimulated urbanization in less direct ways. Peace and taxation created conditions in which economic specialization could develop. Bordeaux, for example, was at the terminus of a major road and was probably the residence of a provincial governor for a time, but it also owed a part of its prominence to its role in the Atlantic trading system that developed under the empire. Similar considerations may have contributed to the growth of Narbonne and the cities of the Rhône valley, including Lyon and Vienne, where huge warehouses have been recently excavated. Inscriptions recording the presence in numerous communities of Treveran citizens suggest that Trier, too, grew by exploiting its commercial connections as well as its administrative ones.[94] It is difficult to assess the relative contributions of economic, military and administrative networks since all exploited the same combination of natural communications, like navigable rivers, and man-made facilities, such as ports and roads.

Trade certainly played less of a part in the growth of Gallo-Roman cities than it did in the development of their mediaeval French successors,[95] yet economic factors should not be excluded altogether. The small towns provide some of the clearest indications of the complexity of the genesis of Gallo-Roman urbanism. While some were local civic centres, others specialized in craft production and yet others provided religious services. The presence of soldiers stimulated settlement growth

fact that its archaeological usage was departing from its original sense, owing to the diversity of secondary towns and other nucleated settlements, has led to its abandonment in favour of *agglomération secondaire*, encompassing all sites between *villae* and *civitas* capitals. In juridical terms, however, those secondary centres with administrative functions would probably have been termed *vici* and are described as such on Gallic epigraphy (Jacques 1991).

94 Krier (1981).   95 Goudineau (1980b, 365–81), Jones (1987).

in some areas, especially in the Germanies, while other towns arose along the major roads, and yet others developed to take advantage of natural resources, for instance clay, stone and thermal springs. Many secondary centres grew to satisfy a growing demand, local and occasionally supra-local, for manufactures.[96] Part of that demand may have been ultimately created by Roman exactions,[97] but much of it was generated by new tastes as these spread through Gallic society.

Finally there is the differentiation generated by the uneven take-up of the civilizing project by different Gallic elites, who in some areas played an important part in the growth and monumentalization of the larger secondary centres.[98] Paradoxically, the importance of the newly acquired cultural vocation to urbanize is evident from the unevenness of its success. If the differentiation of settlements in Gaul had been purely a consequence of the application of uniform administrative structures by Rome we might expect that the growth of towns should be broadly comparable between regions, even if within them towns located on major trunk roads would do better than others. In fact, secondary urban centres developed much more fully in some regions than in others. Compared to the Franche-Comté and Burgundy, for example, the north-west is much less urbanized, although it experienced similar fiscal pressures and had a similar administrative network imposed on it.[99] The civic complexes built at some minor towns in the centre and east demonstrate an urbanism beyond that prompted by Roman demands, and the extent to which local elites had internalized Roman cultural ideals.

IV   The limits of urbanism

How urban was the Roman civilization of Gaul? Modern-day visitors to the remains of Nîmes or Trier, of Vaison-la-Romaine or Autun could easily gain the impression that Roman Gaul was an urban civilization.

96 Mangin (1985), Whittaker (1990).   97 Hopkins (1978).
98 The responsibility of the Gallo-Roman elite for the urbanization of the secondary centres is clear from the epigraphy found at the latter, cf. Wightman (1976b) and Picard (1975), although Picard's notion of *conciliabula* has not found general acceptance, cf. Aeberhardt (1985) and Jacques (1991). Desbordes (1985) pointed out that many supposedly isolated monumental complexes have turned out on examination to be surrounded by less visible residences. These inscriptions, the monumentalization of the larger secondary centres and their chronology, which is much the same as that of the *civitas* capitals, indicate that in Gaul at least it is not helpful to distinguish artificial, administrative, public towns from more economically vibrant small productive centres appearing later at the boundaries of tribal territories where the power of local aristocrats was weakest, as has been suggested for Roman Britain by Millett (1986), (1990a, 143–51), but see Burnham (1994, 231) for some doubts.
99 Mangin and Tassaux (1992, 477–8).

In a way this is no accident, since the first monuments were designed to draw the eye towards aspirations to civilization and away from the surrounding houses built in dry-stone walling or out of wood and earth.

We might imagine the progress of a Roman visitor, perhaps one of the provincial governors conducting the assizes, moving out from his capital along Roman roads that would lead him straight into the *fora* of the *civitas* capitals. If he dined in a private residence it would have been in an elaborate town house, equipped with mosaic floors, painted walls, tiled roofs and hypocausts, or else in one of the luxurious sub-urban *villae* around the capital. If he ate Gallic food off Gallic tableware (and he may well have been served Mediterranean produce off imported silver) his attention would have been focused on a civilized style of its consumption, not the barbarous context of its production. The next day he would continue his journey along Roman roads towards another capital, where the performance would be repeated. Even if the visitor were a simple grandee from a neighbouring *civitas*, his eye would be guided in a similar fashion to the civilized faces of local culture. The urban network operated as a frame that guided the discriminating gaze of the Roman rulers (and Romanizing Gauls) when they looked at Gaul. The stratagem might seem transparent, but in a sense there was nothing so Roman as judging a culture by its cities. Romans expected the countryside – any countryside – to display less *urbanitas*, to be more beastly and wild than the town. The Gallo-Roman subterfuge operated by exploiting the elision, encompassed in the ideals of *humanitas* and *urbanitas*, between Roman values and elite culture, by presenting those Gauls deficient in those qualities as peasants rather than barbarians.

Viewing Gaul only through its cities, Romans can have had little notion that the difference between the cities of Gaul and those of Italy was so much greater than the difference between their respective countrysides. Only when campaigning against Gallic rebels might Romans be surprised and horrified by the other face of the Gauls. Gauls, too, may have been taken in by the charade. Few can ever have seen Italy, and those who did saw an equally partial picture. The urban network provided channels through which Gauls and Romans might deceive each other and themselves. We, on the other hand, should not be so deceived. In fact, even by the standards of the ancient world, Gaul was under-urbanized. Few Gauls lived in the cities or even near them, and as a result few can have had much contact with them. Roman cities in Gaul were thus islands of civilization scattered over a world of villages that in its operation, although not in its appearance, strongly resembled the iron age world it had replaced.

The first stage in establishing this picture is to attempt an estimate of the proportion of the population that lived in urban settlements. The practical difficulties of such estimates are enormous, of course, since reliable figures exist neither for the total population of the Gallic provinces nor for that of individual towns, and in any case the distinction between small town and large village is necessarily arbitrary, the more so since in conditions of low urbanization settlement differentiation is at a minimum. Nevertheless, it is possible to use a variety of estimates to arrive at an order of magnitude which at least allows comparison with other provinces.

A good starting point is to calculate the total number who lived in towns in Gaul. In addition to the hundred odd *civitas* capitals it is important to include some but not all of the secondary centres. Adequate surveys have not yet been conducted for all regions, but in those areas where nucleated settlements have been found the number in each territory, which in terms of size, architecture and function might be thought urban, varies from nil to half a dozen.[100] An average of three or four secondary towns for each capital seems a reasonable estimate, and so a high estimate produces a figure of around 100 capitals and 400 other urban centres. Population estimates for individual cities have included 35,000 for Lyon, 25,000–30,000 for Vienne, 20,000–25,000 for Bordeaux and Toulouse and 6,000–9,000 for Paris, but not all these figures are plausible.[101] Of the various means used to calculate ancient urban populations, only an extrapolation from occupied area is possible in Gaul, with all the hazards this entails.[102] A crucial figure is thus the number of inhabitants per hectare. A combination of comparative evidence and examination of house plans and urban density in the few residential quarters that have been excavated, such as that at St Romain-en-Gal, suggests that any figure over 150 inhabitants per hectare is implausible, and that much lower figures might be more realistic to account for the large areas of some towns (especially in the north) that seem never to have been inhabited.[103] The population estimate that this

100 Desbordes (1974), (1985), Mangin *et al.* (1986), Mangin and Tassaux (1992) together with the surveys in the Colloque de Bleisbruck-Reinheim-Bitche *Les Agglomérations sécondaires de Gaule Belgique et des Germanies*, (October 1992).

101 Lyon: Audin (1986, 11); Vienne: Pelletier (1982, 226–7); Bordeaux: Etienne (1962, 145); Toulouse: Labrousse (1968, 375–8); Paris: Duval (1961, 249). Goudineau (1980b, 309–10) regards 5,000–6,000 as the norm, with a few cities such as Reims, Trier, Autun and Lyon being as high as 20,000–30,000.

102 Duncan-Jones (1982, 262–2) on various techniques.

103 Duncan-Jones (1982, 276–7) for a figure of 50–100 inhabitants/ha at Saturnia in Etruria; Jongman (1988, 111) estimated that Pompeii, covering 65 ha, sheltered a population of 8,000–12,000 inhabitants, giving a figure of between 123–187 inhabitants/ha. For Gallo-Roman cities, Goudineau (1980b, 309–10) argues for 150/ha as the upper limit. Others have used densities as high as 350/ha for urban centres, but the density calculated at St Romain-en-Gal was 100–120/ha (Pelletier 1982, 226) and since many areas within the street grids of some northern towns were probably not fully occupied, a figure around 100/ha seems to be preferred for many towns.

produces for most capitals is 5,000–6,000, but some cities were certainly larger, so the average should perhaps be reckoned closer to 8,000,
giving a total population for the *civitas* capitals of 800,000.

The secondary urban centres varied enormously in size, but on the
whole sites like Malain and Mandeure, with occupied areas of over 100
ha, bigger in other words than many *civitas* capitals, were extremely rare
and an average of 20 ha is a more realistic estimate, giving a maximum
population of 3,000 inhabitants, hence 1,200,000 for all the secondary
towns together. The resulting total population is of 2 million living in
towns in Gaul at the urban apogee. This figure has been produced by
multiplying the maxima for each variable. If, on the other hand, the average urban density were 100/ha and the number of secondary centres were
only 300 then the total would be under 1,200,000.[104] The number of
Gauls who inhabited towns can thus be very broadly determined as
between 1 and 2 million. My own preference is for a low value within
this range.

The population of the Gallic provinces themselves is equally uncertain. Recent estimates suggest a peak figure of around 12 million for
the four Gallic provinces.[105] On the basis of these estimates the proportion of the Gallic population that inhabited towns would be around
10 per cent. The approximate nature of these results is patent, yet they
nevertheless provide a basis for a comparison between Gaul and other
regions. Current estimates for Italy fluctuate around 30 per cent of the
population living in towns, and for Egypt a figure of 20–25 per cent has
been suggested. The latest estimate for Roman Britain, on the other
hand, is 6.5 per cent of the population living in towns.[106] These figures
make the total for the Gallic provinces seem plausible, and suggest the
range of variations that must have existed within them, between the more
urbanized south and east and the less developed northern and western
regions.

What do statistics of this kind mean, translated into everyday experience? One indication of what low levels of urbanism might be like is

104 Cf. King's (1990a, 108) 'very rough and possibly rather conservative' suggestion of a
    population of 1,180,000 (on the basis of about 7 towns of c. 20,000, 4 of c. 10,000,
    100 of c. 5,000 and 500 of c. 1,000).
105 Drinkwater (1983, 168–70) estimates 8 million rising to 12 for the Three Gauls, with
    useful discussion of the earlier estimates of Beloch, Jullian and Grenier. Extended to
    include Narbonensis, the figures rise to 9–14 million. King (1990a, 105–8) likewise
    extends Ferdière's (1988, I, 71–86) estimates for rural population density in the Gallic
    and German provinces to arrive at a figure of 11–12 million, or more cautiously 8–15
    million (excluding urban dwellers, rising to 9–16 million if they were included).
106 For Italy, see Jongman (1988, 65–7, 108–12); for Egypt, see Rathbone (1990,123),
    excluding from his calculation some villages that would qualify as towns under the
    criteria used here for Gaul; for Britain, see Millett (1990a, 185).

suggested by a consideration of Russia in the late eighteenth century. At the time, already half the population of Holland lived in towns, while in much of Europe the proportion of the population living in towns was around 20 per cent, and towns were key locations in the transformation of society, providers of education and professional services, the locations and sources of social conflict and economic growth for the whole of society. But in Russia, where only some 4 per cent of the population lived in towns, 'the greater part of the industrial tasks fell upon the villages, which were self supporting. Urban agglomerations did not dominate them or disturb them as they did in the West. There was as yet no competition between townsmen and peasants . . . in a poorly urbanized country, villages were necessarily forced to do everything by themselves'.[107] The figures are different and the social trajectory of eighteenth-century Europe was quite different to that of early imperial Gaul, yet the contrast between a world in which towns and country were highly integrated and a world in which towns and villages co-existed in relative isolation or as alternative providers of services in different areas is suggestive. That impression is strengthened when we consider the dispersal of towns in Gaul and the implications for the services they could offer as central places.

Central place theory predicts that centres offering equivalent services will be distributed evenly across a landscape, once allowance is made for variations in the terrain that lengthen or shorten journey times. But there are also absolute limits on the area for which a centre may supply services, based on the maximum journey times countrymen are prepared to travel in order to obtain those services. If the average distance between towns is greater that this then country dwellers will either do without those services or devise other ways in which they might be supplied.[108] The catchment area of a site varies according to the service in question and the frequency with which it is needed: country dwellers may well be prepared to make annual journeys to pay taxes or rarer long trips in search of justice or as pilgrimages. But services such as marketing or facilities for the repair and replacement of iron tools are needed so frequently that the centres that provide them must be relatively

107 Braudel (1981, 376–9). For other descriptions of the rural aspects of small towns in conditions of low urbanization, cf. Laslett (1971, 55–83), Weber (1979, 232–6).
108 The use of periodic markets is one obvious alternative, and one which de Ligt (1993) has shown was widely employed elsewhere in the empire. Although there is little certain evidence for such activities anywhere in the north-west provinces (cf. his appendix 2), it seems likely on *a priori* grounds that markets of this kind were important in many parts of Gaul. De Ligt also makes the point that these markets might be expected in urbanized areas as well as between them, and were one means by which rural populations had access to wider markets.

close to one another. A number of different figures for the maximum feasible distance between a rural site and a lowest order centre have been proposed on the basis of historical and comparative evidence. The most commonly needed services should be available, at least on regular basis, at no more than half a day's walk away and estimates of this distance vary, but on the whole they suggest a figure of about 5–10 km as a preferred journey time and hence a dispersal of 10–20 km between the lowest order central places.[109] Measures of the actual dispersal of towns in the Gallic provinces depend on the definitions of towns adopted, nevertheless some general idea can be gained. One recent study examined cities, in the sense of *civitas* capitals, together with a small number of the largest secondary centres, mostly towns that would later become independent or which were prominent in literary sources, and compared their dispersal in different regions of Gaul and Italy.[110] The dispersal of cities in central Italy averaged 11–16 km, while elsewhere in the peninsula and in Narbonensis they appeared at intervals of between 20 and 40 km. Only in central Italy, in other words, could cities themselves provide the lowest level of services to rural populations. But there is also a startling contrast between those dispersal rates and those of Comatan Gaul, where cities are between 50 and 100 km apart. In fact, the result is skewed by variations in the size of civic territories, and the addition of secondary towns reduces the dispersal to about 20–40 km for areas like Burgundy, the Berry and the Franche-Comté and 40–60 km for other northern areas, while Narbonensis approximates Italy even more closely.

The main contrast to emerge from these approaches is between urbanism in the Mediterranean world and the situation in the continental interior. The proportion of town dwellers in Narbonensis was probably broadly similar to that in most parts of Italy, but in any case most peasants lived close enough to a town to walk there and back in a day. The result was that urbanism had a profound influence over virtually all the population of those areas. In most of the Gallic interior, on the other hand, even the smaller towns were too widely dispersed to provide

109 Hodder (1972, 905) suggests lowest order markets might have been distributed at 10 km intervals; Hingley (1989, 112–14) gathers a range of comparative material to argue for an interval of 10–15 km; Bekker-Nielsen (1989, 32) argues for a journey distance of 20 km (i.e.: a dispersal of 40 km between lowest order centres), but this figure is derived from late antique and mediaeval itineraries which are arguably poorer guides than the figures he cites for Italian cultivators who would travel up to 10 km to their fields, and Chinese peasants who would travel 11 km to market with a wagon and 18 km with a mule.
110 Bekker-Nielsen (1989), using a list composed largely from Ptolemy's *Geography*, itself probably based on administrative sources.

much in the way of services to the population while those endowed with monumental architecture – the *civitas* capitals and the major secondary centres like Argenton, Alesia and Mandeure – were so far apart that a significant number of Gallic peasants must have visited them only a few times every year. Villages provided for most of the everyday needs of most Gauls. Yet it does not follow that towns were 'artificial' or alien to Gallo-Roman society in the north. They discharged important political, religious and cultural functions for the Gallic *civitates* as a whole, and for their elites in particular, many of whom seem to have divided their time between urban residences and their rural estates. Not least of their roles was to provide an environment within which some Gauls could behave as Romans and enjoy the civilized lifestyles they had learnt. But in another sense the towns of Gaul played little part in the lives of most of its inhabitants, who continued to inhabit a world of villages, in which activities like marketing, craft production and iron working were dispersed fairly evenly across the landscape.

Long-term geographical factors provide a partial explanation for this contrast. At a very general level, temperate Europe may be distinguished from the Mediterranean by relatively high levels of agricultural prosperity but poor internal communications. Those conditions exercised a constant influence between the Neolithic and the Industrial revolutions, inhibiting the growth of either large political units or large cities. Early modern urbanization came late and slowly to inland Europe and was characterized by the unusual prominence of middle-ranking cities and the small size of the largest cities,[111] except in areas with access to maritime and/or riverine communications systems. France in particular was characterized by regionalism and communal particularism much later than many European states.[112] Roman urbanism faced the same constraints. The small size of Comatan cities, their timber and earth architecture, their wide dispersal throughout a landscape composed mainly of villages and scattered farms, all these features may appear to us rather half-hearted, a poor man's urbanism or an imperfect attempt at becoming Roman. But perhaps it would be fairer to see them as an attempt to create civilization in a cold climate.

111 De Vries (1984). Compare the urban networks documented by Rozman (1973) and (1976), where imperial states created very steep hierarchies characterized by very large capitals and few medium sized cities.
112 Cf. generally Weber (1979), Braudel (1988). Fox (1971) contrasts this inertia in the continental centre of the country with the dynamism of the better located cities around its periphery.

6 The culture of the countryside

I   Beyond the city

What significance should the countryside have in an investigation of how Gauls became Romans? One common strategy employed by historians is to use the culture of the countryside to puncture the pretensions of the town. There is something to be gained rhetorically from setting Gallo-Roman cities against the vast backdrop of their rural hinterlands, if only to illustrate how few, small and far apart urban centres were in some parts of the Gallic provinces. It does not follow, however, either that Roman culture was restricted to the new cities of Gaul, or that the countryside was excluded from processes of cultural change.

In fact, every aspect of Gallic life was to some extent transformed by integration into the empire, including most spheres of rural life.[1] New crops were introduced, particularly for arboriculture, and the geographical range of some Mediterranean species, including the vine and the olive, was extended inland. New technologies were adopted, for example new methods of storing grain, of processing agricultural produce and of draining marshes. These changes were perhaps not as significant as the agricultural revolution that had begun and gathered pace in the centuries immediately preceding the Roman conquest. The first large scale production of metal agricultural tools was associated in the late iron age with demographic growth, attested by settlement evidence as well as by classical accounts of migrations and huge armies, and with agricultural expansion involving both some deforestation and the cultivation of heavier soils. But alongside its more modest impact on crops and agricultural technology, Roman rule introduced major changes in the way the countryside was managed and controlled. The entrenchment of the power of local elites, the emergence of a provincial aristocracy with interests spanning many *civitates*, the development of local and regional

---

1 For general accounts, see Ferdière (1988) with Leveau (1991). On Narbonensis, see Leveau, Sillières and Vallat (1993, 250–86). Briefer accounts are provided by Le Glay (1975) and Goudineau and Ferdière (1986).

markets in landed property and in agricultural produce, the imposition of the Roman law of property and of new tenurial, fiscal and monetary systems, all contributed to a series of social and economic transformations of rural life.

But a more important objection to viewing Roman culture in Gaul as a purely urban phenomenon is that the countryside did not constitute a separate world or a 'part society',[2] distinct from that of the Gallo-Roman town. To begin with, there are the implications of the low levels of urbanism discussed in the last chapter. If urbanization is considered as a special form of settlement differentiation, then low levels of urbanism imply a certain social proximity between town and country. Most Gallic cities provided little in the ways of services or goods that could not be obtained in the bigger secondary centres, and both large and small Gallo-Roman cities displayed a markedly rural character. Northern tribal capitals like Amiens possessed very extensive street grids, but they connected a loosely structured mosaic of open spaces, some probably cultivated, others simply gardens inserted into low density residential areas made up largely of one storey houses. Smaller urban centres, with populations of only a few thousand souls, were in many respects simply large peasant villages. Intra-mural cultivation, farms on the outskirts of towns, as at Vaison, and finds of agricultural equipment in urban contexts all suggest that the ten per cent or less of the Gallic population that did inhabit towns included many who were primarily or partly employed in agriculture.

Equally importantly, the wealthy, as will emerge, inhabited both the countryside and the towns. Their urban activities supported some artisans, but whenever large scale non-agricultural production is known of – for example, the manufacture of ceramic tableware and building materials, metallurgy and timber, the production of salt, preserved meats and fish, and of textiles, especially wool and linen – it mostly seems to have taken place in rural settings.[3] Equally the small scale of the establishments occupied by artisans in the towns suggests they produced for local, rather than regional or international markets.[4] Outside a few centres like Lyon, then, no large urban manufacturing class existed, and artisans are probably over-represented in funerary reliefs and

---

2 See Redfield (1956) for the term, referring to peasant cultures, conceived of as subordinated to and incomplete in respect of the Great Traditions of the states and societies within which they are embedded.
3 Whittaker (1990).
4 For artisan quarters, see Mangin (1985), who regards them as serving a wider market. The scale of the workshops concerned, however, is always very small. No large-scale industrial establishments are known from Gallo-Roman towns.

inscriptions. Nor were towns the only centres of consumption. The rich spent their money on residences and monuments, in the countryside as well as in the towns, and the surpluses produced in the countryside, agricultural and other, were directed to local and distant consumers as well as to urban populations. The implication of these observations is that Gallic economies and societies revolved much more around differences of wealth and power, than around any distinction between urban and rural, and many Gallo-Romans belonged, in some sense or other, to both worlds. To write of the culture of the countryside is not, then, to define a separate sphere of enquiry, so much as to adopt a different and complementary perspective from which to consider the societies and cultures of Roman Gaul.

One of the ways in which this perspective is complementary is that it is more sensitive than is an urban view to the diversity of Gallo-Roman cultures. Urban locales offer variety too – between north and south, between large cities and small towns, between colonies, *civitas* capitals and *vici* – yet in so far as Gallic towns were built to approximate to a common model or ideal of the Roman city, they were conscious attempts to minimize differences and the influence of local context. Gallic landscapes as a whole were not (usually) constructed in such a co-ordinated way, and so reflect more clearly the diversity of Gallo-Roman cultures. That diversity comprised much more than simply the degree to which a region was urbanized, and cannot be resolved into a scale of more or less Romanized landscapes. To illustrate the point, two landscapes may be considered that have been the object of recent and sophisticated studies, the lower valley of the Rhône and eastern Brittany.

The fragments of a series of inscribed maps, discovered in Orange but depicting a region that extended well beyond the *territorium* of that colony, provide a rare Roman view of a Gallic landscape, a view that has been refined and dated through aerial photography and excavation.[5] These 'cadasters', maps indicating the division of territory by units of ownership, were set up in Vespasian's reign and provide a snapshot of a landscape, of the lower Rhône valley, that had been centuriated about a century beforehand. Each unit demarcated is annotated with some indication of the fiscal and juridical status of the land within it in the Flavian period. Some areas were assigned to the colony and let out,

5 Piganiol (1962), with Salviat (1977), whose conclusion that the three 'cadasters' are contemporaneous is now widely accepted. Debate continues on the precise location of the centuriated areas mapped on each table, for which see Salviat (1986), with Chouquer and Favory (1991, 153–6) for rival views. For the archaeological dating of the centuriation to the last quarter of the last century BC or the beginning of the first century AD, see Bel and Benoit (1986). Favory and Fiches (1994) collect a number of recent papers based on archaeological research on the region.

sometimes to rich members of neighbouring communities; some remained
in the allotments which were assigned to veterans when the colony was
established; others (generally the least fertile) were designated as returned
to a pre-conquest people, the Tricastini. The emergence of some larger
properties both by the accumulation of small plots and by land reclama-
tion also seems likely.[6] The interpretation of these maps is not clear in
every respect, but the overall pattern is. At the end of the first century
AD, the plains of the Rhône were already a varied landscape, small
farms interspersed with larger ones, intensive production of grain on
the best soil and of wine along the valley, everywhere some olive production, smaller scale peasant agriculture on the poor soils and pastor-
alism in a few marginal areas.[7] Distinguishing a Roman from a 'native'
landscape, however, is not so easy. Among the great landowners some
seem descended from Italian immigrants, others from the indigenous
Vocontian population, to judge by their names. Many descendants of
veterans must have been less well off than the descendants of conquered Gauls. A society in which social status was based on wealth and
culture was much less disrupted by social and economic mobility than
one based on wealth and race. The real significance of cultural change
in the Rhône valley was that it neither created a unified society of equals,
nor allowed a fixed barrier to be set up between Roman and indigenous
landscapes, but rather allowed a single society to emerge based on uneven
distributions of wealth and marked by differences in culture.

No such documents reveal the Roman landscapes of eastern Brittany,
but a series of co-ordinated regional research programmes and surveys
has produced a detailed picture from archaeological evidence alone.[8]
Whereas the Rhône valley had in the Augustan period received a set of
highly monumentalized urban centres – both the veteran colonies built
from scratch, and indigenous centres like Nîmes and Vaison – in Brittany, even the *civitas* capitals of the Coriosolites and the Osismii were
barely monumentalized. Most Breton cities were either vast empty grid-
planned northern cities, like Corseul and Carhaix, or else small coastal
villages, like Alet and Quimper.[9] During the iron age, material culture
in Brittany conforms in general to standard La Tène styles, while settlement, with the exception of the *souterrain*, is conventional for northern
Gaul, except that stone walls complement ditches more frequently than
in other areas.[10] Eastern Britanny, in particular, has much the same

6 Pelletier (1976), Salviat (1986).
7 Leveau, Sillières and Vallat (1993), Laubenheimer (1985), Goudineau (1989).
8 Langouët (1991).   9 Galliou (1984, 59–86).
10 See Duval, Le Bihan and Menez (1990) on Brittany in the late La Tène. On settlement, see Le Bihan *et al.* (1990).

range of settlement types – typically large ditch complexes surrounding dispersed 'native farms' – as other north Gallic landscapes, and in some microregions, such as the Bassin de Rennes or in the northern part of the territory of the Coriosolites, iron age settlement was very dense indeed. At the end of the first century AD, much of this pattern may have seemed unchanged. *Civitas* capitals had been set up in the midst of this landscape. Corseul is the best known, a grid covering between 100 and 130 ha, organizing *insulae* of large private houses and probably some rudimentary monuments, although there seems to have been no theatre, and only a bath complex has certainly been identified. In the immediate environs of the town a cluster of Roman style suburban houses had been constructed in the first century. In so far as other Breton towns are known in detail, that pattern seems general. But most rural sites continued to be built and rebuilt in the same materials as had been used in the late iron age, even if the shape of the enclosures changed gradually from curvilinear plans to orthogonal ones.[11] Not until the middle of the second century AD did tiled roofs became common, and farms began in general to be constructed in Roman style. Richer soils again determined the density of settlement, and the areas that had been most populous in the iron age were transformed into '*villa* landscapes'.[12]

One way to interpret this landscape, and the contrast with the Rhône valley, would be in terms of mapping cultural change. That approach would draw attention to the relatively low level of Roman intervention experienced by Brittany by comparison with other regions of Gaul: there were no major troop concentrations, no veteran settlement, and no major routes crossed the Breton *civitates*. Those areas better integrated into a wider world – the east and the coastal fringe, in general, and the region around Rennes, in particular – showed more change than the west, or than the interior of the Armorican peninsula. Brittany was marginalized, both within the empire and within Gaul, never experienced as dramatic a penetration of Roman power as did the Tricastini, and consequently was slower to acquire and make use of Roman material culture. But it would be otiose to reiterate here in detail the discussion of cultural geography in chapter four. Two further points can, however, be made. First, the Roman culture of Brittany was not simply unusually under-urbanized. Romano-Breton towns were not islands of Roman culture in a native sea, and the peculiarity of Roman Brittany was not due to a failure of those towns to disseminate Roman culture more widely. In fact, both urbanism and rural settlement illustrate the same

11 Daire *et al.* (1991).   12 Gautier *et al.* (1991).

general response to Roman cultural norms, not quite resistance but an absence of enthusiasm or fervour in adopting them. Romano-Bretons were aware that they were on the margins of the empire and responded accordingly. Second, that marginalization itself was new. In the late La Tène, Britanny had been a fully participant region within the fragmented yet culturally unified world of the temperate European iron age. Cultural marginality was a consequence of the new place assigned Brittany in an imperial order. In that sense the culture of Roman Brittany is shown not to be a matter of the survival of primitive forms so much as a new creation of Roman power. It is important not to exaggerate. The settlement patterns of both iron age and Roman Brittany reflect perennial geographical factors that can be documented in other periods too.[13] But if the culture of Roman Brittany was Breton, it was also Roman, simply peripheral Roman.[14] East Brittany and the Rhône valley do not exhaust the types of landscape created in Roman Gaul, but the contrasts between them illustrate the sensitivity of landscape to social trends that are less easy to detect simply by comparing the kinds of towns created by each region in imitation of Roman norms.

Landscapes also differ from towns in that they are rarely created in a single co-ordinated effort, but instead reflect the cumulative impact of numerous individual choices. The centuriated landscapes of the south might seem an exception to this rule, yet even in the plains of the Rhône, individuals had remodelled the landscape to a sufficient extent, within less than a century of the centuriation, to prompt Vespasian to attempt a reassessment and new census. The development of an urban network and the roads that articulated it constrained the choices individuals made, yet the adoption of Roman items such as *tegulae* (Roman roof tiles) expresses personal taste rather than communal decision making. While the urbanizing of towns had to be the work of collectivities (directed of course by their elites), because it involved the planning of initial constructions, the allocation of plots and the approval or modification of euergetistic munificence, the culture of the countryside represents a more private aspect of cultural change. It also represents more spontaneous and creative innovation. Most Gallic landowners had little exposure to Roman models of rural life, in the way that Gallic town builders might look to the *coloniae* of the south or reflect on literary models.

13 Davies (1988), for example.
14 Galliou (1984), for Roman Brittany as a whole, stresses the extent of its integration into the Roman world, but perhaps at the expense of what distinguished Roman Brittany from other regions of Gaul. The case made for a complete change from the iron age situation, however, is unassailable. For a similar survey on the Coriosolites, see Langouët (1987).

II   The Gallo-Roman villa

Perhaps the best way of demonstrating the originality of the way Gallo-Roman landscapes were created is to examine the element which has traditionally been regarded as the most 'Roman' component of rural life in the provinces, that is the *villa*.[15] The definition of that term – a modern archaeological usage – has been a matter of much debate, but in general it is taken to refer to a settlement site, with a construction and design of broadly Roman style, located in the countryside. It is usually the centre of a working farm, often also providing a degree of comfort for the occupants, usually in the form of amenities such as baths and hypocausts, comparable to those available in town houses. Within this broad definition some scholars focus on the productive aspects of *villae*, others on their role as centres of conspicuous consumption.[16] Depending on which of these aspects is stressed, the definition may be loosened to include Roman-style residences in the country without working farms attached, or provincial farms with few Roman amenities other than tile roofs and stone sockles for their walls.

Not all these definitions are equally good. Except in the case of well excavated sites, it is unsafe to argue from design alone to any particular productive function. Even when agricultural structures have been excavated and floral and faunal remains studied, it may remain impossible to infer the tenurial systems and the character of agricultural labour employed, especially since there was no uniform *villa*-system or *villa*-economy common to Italy and the provinces.[17] The possibility that one individual may have owned more than one estate, or spent on one *villa* revenues obtained from other sources, also makes it dangerous to base sophisticated economic analyses on even the best excavated sites. In short, *villa* building represents expenditure of wealth acquired in ways that are no longer recoverable. It is thus safer to classify rural sites in terms of the amount and type of consumption they represent:[18] whether they are large or small, how they are situated, whether or not they have *tegulae*, mosaics and/or wall paintings, and whether bathhouses are

---

15 Percival (1976) remains the fundamental survey. For the Gallic provinces, Chevallier ed. (1982) collects a series of studies.

16 Cf. Percival (1976, 13–16) and Leveau, Sillières and Vallat (1993, 46–50) for discussion of various definitions.

17 See Whittaker (1980) for variations in labour systems.

18 Millett (1990a, 91–2). The papers collected in Branigan and Miles (1988) illustrate part of the range of economic activities practiced in connection with *villae* in just one province, Britain. For Gaul, other activities, including fish-sauce production, would need to be added. It is far from clear, however, that any of these activities were limited to farms run from *villae* as opposed to from 'native farms' or *vici*.

provided. Eastern Brittany is a case in point. There the process whereby the richest indigenous farms were gradually rebuilt in new architectures is better considered in terms of the spread of new styles of consumption than of the imposition of novel agricultural systems or a revolution in rural economies. For a sudden imposition of new patterns, it is necessary instead to look to the centuriated landscapes, which were always very restricted in scale within the Gallic provinces, and which seem not to have been immediately accompanied by *villa* building.[19]

It is possible to pursue this critique of modern usage of the category *villa* even further. Unlike the town, a cultural import the nature and organization of which were central to Roman discourse about the differences between civilization and barbarism, the *villa* was not regarded by Romans as a distinct cultural entity, and the term is used by Latin writers loosely for a range of rural buildings. While an ethic of civilized life in the country was developed, for example by the younger Pliny, the majority of sites termed *villae* by archaeologists do not conform to these ideals. Archaeologically, the morphological line between *villa* and 'native farm' is not always easy to draw.[20] Excavations in the Aisne valley at a site named Beaurieux, Les Grèves, show the gradual replacement of a late iron age 'native farm' by buildings which approximate closer and closer in each phase to a simple *villa*.[21] That pattern is evidently a common one. The range of material recovered by surface survey also illustrates the arbitrariness of any sharp line drawn between 'native farms' and *villae*. It is thus more precise to characterize the spread of the *villa* as an increasing taste for and use of Roman building materials, techniques and styles, rather than as the diffusion of a new social or economic form. That is not to say that new relations of production, new tenurial and agricultural systems, new technologies and so forth were not being introduced into the Gaulish countryside during the same general period in which *villae* were constructed, if not a little earlier. Simply the physical structures recovered rarely tell us a great deal about such changes, and were not necessarily essential for their success.

Iron age settlement in Gaul was enormously varied in nature. The La Tène period was characterized in many areas by a trend towards settlement nucleation in villages and *oppida*. But dispersed settlement certainly existed in the same period. Caesar's narrative makes frequent

19 Clavel's (1970) study of Béziers and its *territorium* suggests that the centuriated landscape set up when the colony was founded was overlain within a century by a settlement pattern in which the most visible elements were *villae* clustering around the city.
20 See Hingley (1989, 20–5) for a good discussion, including the recognition that abandonment of the term *villa*, although in some respects analytically desirable, 'is not a practical proposition'.
21 Haselgrove (1990b, 255), (1995).

incidental references to *aedificia*,[22] and recent research has uncovered traces of such isolated farms in a number of regions. In general they conform to the type already noted in eastern Brittany, massive post-built constructions surrounded by enclosures, and often at the centre of complex and extensive field systems demarcated by curvilinear ditches. Farms of this type have been found across northern France from Brittany, Champagne, Picardy and the Oise. Excavations such as that already mentioned at Beaurieux, Les Grèves and of an earlier structure at Verberie (Oise), show them to have been large structures which attest the presence in the countryside of the pre-conquest aristocracy.[23] Sites of this kind are, however, difficult to date. Around the valley of the Somme in Picardy, where conditions for aerial photography are especially good, hundred of structures of this kind, dubbed *fermes indigènes*, (native farms), have been discovered.[24] But excavation and survey of a small number of those sites indicate that many are post-conquest in date, and some were used until the third or fourth centuries. Surface survey has recovered *terra sigillata*, local wares of the Roman period and *tegulae* from many of these sites. Late prehistoric pottery, however, survives less well on the surface of ploughed fields, and it may be that surface survey systematically misses traces of earlier occupation on both *villa* sites and 'Roman period native farms'. It is likely, therefore, that isolated farms were common in both the iron age and Roman landscapes of some regions. It does not follow, however, that dispersed settlement was characteristic of all the landscapes of pre-Roman Gaul. In the Low Countries, small hamlets and villages were the norm.[25] Equally, the complete absence of any comparable structures in Narbonensis can no longer be regarded as the result of incomplete information. Detailed micro-regional studies around the iron age villages of Lunel-Viel and in the Vaunage, near Nages, have failed to find any trace of 'native farms' and it is safe to conclude that the pre-Roman settlement pattern consisted almost entirely of nucleated villages.[26] Less clear is the situation in the centre of France. Aerial photography has recorded

22 E.g. *de Bello Gallico* I.5, IV.19, discussed by Agache (1981, 49).
23 Haselgrove (1990b, 255) and Blanchet, Buchsenschutz and Méniel (1983). Buchsenschutz and Méniel (1984) illustrate the variety of agricultural structures during late prehistory. Further documentation is provided in the Acts of the second Colloque of AGER, published as Bayard and Collart (1996). I regret this volume appeared too late for me to make use of it here, but my discussion owes much to ideas and material presented at the conference, and I am sorry to be unable to acknowledge debts to individual contributors.
24 Agache (1978).   25 Roymans (1990, 185–6).
26 Raynaud (1990), Py (1990a), Favory and Fiches (1994) discussed by Leveau, Sillières and Vallat (1993, 260–4).

structures similar to the 'native farms' of northern France in some regions, such as the Berry. Their dates are uncertain, but it might be argued that their forms suggest a continuity with La Tène traditions. In Narbonensis, by contrast, small farms of the Roman period, like l'Ormeau à Taradeau, most closely resemble the houses on iron age *oppida*. In other regions, such as the Limousin and the Auvergne, incidentally areas where late La Tène nucleated settlements are much better attested than in the north, the absence of known isolated farms of iron age date may well reflect a real gap.[27] At this stage of research, it is perhaps safest to regard the iron age landscapes of Gaul as very varied in terms of settlement nucleation.

The emergence of new settlement patterns took different forms in different regions. In the north of Gaul, landscapes already characterized by dispersed settlement, like those of Brittany and the Somme, were transformed through the gradual replacement of indigenous farms by Roman style *villae*. Sometimes rebuilding involved small local shifts of site, but the overall pattern of settlement remained broadly similar. In present-day northern Belgium and Holland, villages and hamlets remained the norm, perhaps reflecting the constraints of local ecology and farming systems in which stock raising continued to play an important role. In the south, the iron age pattern of numerous small villages on eminences surrounding fertile plains was replaced by a dispersal of settlement. The first generation of isolated farms in Narbonensis appears in the second half of the last century BC, at about the same time, then, that the first Roman-style architecture appears on the southern *oppida* and that some of those sites, such as Vaison and Ambrusson, begin to shift down onto the surrounding plains.[28] But these first-dispersed farms seem not to have been *villae* in the conventional, that is the architectural, sense of the term, and Roman styles and materials replaced the architecture of the *oppida* only in the Augustan period.

'*Villa* landscapes' were not imposed in a single moment, in the same way as were, for example, centuriations or street grids. A small number of very large very early 'palatial' *villae* are known, such as Montmaurin, just south of Toulouse. But most *villae* probably emerged through the gradual adoption of new materials and of new plans in the course of successive modifications and rebuildings of existing farms. The point at

27 See Leday (1980, 155) and Provost (1993, 219–21) on the Berry; Ralston (1992, 123) on the Limousin; Mills (1985), (1986) on the Auvergne.
28 Leveau, Sillières and Vallat (1993, 263–4). Meffre (1994) provides a particularly graphic example from the plains around of Vaison. Intensive survey discovered only 2 possible sites from the late iron age in an area where 68 were established in the Augustan period and a further 90 during the early empire.

which a 'native farm' was transformed into a *villa* is to some extent a subjective judgement, depending on the relative weight given to plan, number of rooms, the presence of *tegulae* or of stone wall sockles, among other criteria. With these caveats, however, it is possible to give some indication of inter-regional differences in the spread of Roman architectural developments in the Gallic countryside.[29] Nothing like a *villa* is known from the Republican province. From the Augustan period, however, *villae* begin to be constructed on a large scale in the south and expansion continued until the end of the first century AD. Rare large rural residences were probably built in Roman style in most parts of Gaul from this period, either by Italian immigrants or by local magnates with special connections with Rome. But in general Roman architectural styles made little impact on the countryside of non-Mediterranean Gaul until the second half of the first century AD. By the end of that century, farms recognizable to us as *villae* were being built in Aquitaine, central France, the north east in the territory of the Treveri and the Mediomatrici, and in Picardy. Developments in the northwest, in Normandy and Brittany may have begun about the same time, but *villae* did not become common there until the second century. By the end of the second century, *villae* existed in most parts of Gaul, although the extent to which earlier architectural forms persisted varied considerably from one region to another. Moreover, all over Gaul many third century AD farms closely resembled those built at the turn of the millennium. One farm, excavated at Estrées-Deniécourt, remained in the fourth century AD in much the same style as that in which it had been built in the second century BC, and was never replaced with a *'villa'*.[30] It is necessary to insist once again that these changes were purely architectural in nature, and cannot be assumed to have entailed the imposition of any new social form or means of economic organization.

The creation of the Gallo-Roman *villa* thus comprised two distinct processes. The first, more noticeable in some regions than in others, was a general dispersal of settlement. Villages did not disappear, but in the spaces between them more and more scattered farms developed. That sequence might be put into relation with two processes discussed in the preceding chapter, the shift of some nucleated settlements down from the hills, and the development of greater hierarchy among centres. The settlements of Gaul became more differentiated, more specialized and more interconnected into an open network uniting scattered farms,

29 The best overall surveys are Percival (1976, 67–82), Wightman (1975) and Le Glay (1975), with the regional studies gathered in Chevallier (1982). A new systematic synthesis is badly needed.
30 Preliminary notice in de Saint-Blanquat (1992, 13–15).

hamlets, villages, small towns and cities. Just as in the case of cities and small towns, the physical relief and relative ease of communications both played a part in determining the precise forms taken by these very local networks. The second process that gave birth to the *villa* was a series of linked architectural changes that gradually transformed the physical structures at the centre of 'native farms'. Both processes were the product of individual choices made by landowners.

Because dispersal took place in the south before the architectural transformation, it seems safest to regard it as a response to new conditions of security, rather than the adoption of a new cultural preference for residing in the countryside. In much of the north, on the other hand, dispersed settlement was already the preferred pattern of residence, at least for some. Micro-regional surveys indicate that the dispersed settlement pattern that emerged in the south always included other sites besides *villae*, just as 'native farms' persisted in the north throughout the early empire. The significance of the second process of transformation, the architectural one, is rather different, then. The co-existence of *villae* with other kinds of farms, and the absence of any obvious technological or agricultural advantages of the former, makes it clear that new tastes are at issue, facilitated by the availability of new building technologies and by the acquisition by some landowners of the wealth necessary to make use of them. It does not follow that the conversion of 'native farms' into *villae* was seen as having the same cultural or political significance as city building, nor that it served the same functions in establishing new cultural identities for the Gauls as Romans.

One way of assessing the cultural significance of *villa* building in Gaul is to consider their (very diverse) designs in more detail. To begin with the range of sizes represented is very wide. The main buildings of Chiragan and Montmaurin in the Haute Garonne covered over a dozen hectares, comprised over a hundred rooms, and were equipped with bathhouses, hypocausts, wall paintings and mosaics. Areas of a couple of hectares are much more common and the smallest *villae* were simple structures of less than a dozen rooms. Those contrasts are revealing about the inadequacies of the modern category *villa*, and the consequent dangers of generalization about the social or economic status of '*villa* owners'. More significant culturally are the marked differences from one region to another between *villae* of roughly the same size.[31] *Villae* are known primarily from excavation or aerial photography, with the result that the most certain element is the ground plan, to which elements such as hypocausts or mosaics can occasionally be added. The

31 See Ferdière (1988, 156–99) for an illustrated survey.

elevations of *villae* are therefore largely conjectural, although it is certain that many were built on timber frames set into stone sockles, and that the larger ones would have had second storeys and occasionally towers of the kind illustrated on a wall painting from Trier. Equally, the central residences of *villae*, built more solidly and the focus of most excavations, are in general much better known than their outbuildings. Nevertheless, on the basis of surviving elements a number of broad types can be identified. One of the most distinctive is the hall *villa*, common in the north east of Gaul and in Britain, in which a central hall is surrounded with smaller rooms.[32] Over much of the north of Gaul the main buildings of *villae* are based along a corridor. Developments of this design included the construction of wings at either end of the corridor which extended forward to frame a yard, and in the Somme this design was extended into a huge trapezoidal complex with an outer and inner court flanked by smaller buildings extending for as much as five hundred metres ahead of the main residence. The general plan has been compared to those of sanctuaries in the same region.[33] Throughout central Gaul, a common plan is for *villae* to take the form of complexes built around courtyards, while in Narbonensis and southern Aquitaine, peristyles are common. It is important not to exaggerate the uniformity of design within each region, and well-surveyed areas like the Berry have produced examples of a variety of types.[34] But if the distributions of types are not always discrete and sometimes overlap, these regional preferences are common.

What sense should be made of this variation? Differences in climate may explain the failure of the peristyle to catch on in the north, but in general it is difficult to explain the emergence of regional styles in non-Mediterranean Gaul except in terms of varying cultural preferences, traditions and perhaps social structures. Only the very early *villae* and those of Narbonensis bear much resemblance *in detail* to designs current in Italy. The contrast with the close links between north Italian and Gaulish civic monuments is striking. Some southern *villae* bore the same close resemblance to town houses as did contemporary Italian ones, and in the case of the Maison au Dauphin at Vaison, a *villa* seems actually to have been transformed into a *domus* as the city expanded.[35] The south should perhaps be considered separately. There, contacts with Italy were much closer, and the presence in areas like the Rhône valley of Italian colonists and other immigrants provides one possible source of influence and cultural exchange. The origins and cultural

32 Smith (1978).
33 Agache (1982); see now Haselgrove (1995), building on work on site orientations.
34 Leday (1980).   35 Goudineau (1979).

connections of the earliest colonists are difficult to establish for certain, but Italian craftsmen are likely to have played a similar part in the construction of the earliest *villae* as they did in the building of the first civic monuments.

Northern *villae* represented a different tradition, or traditions,[36] despite attempts to elucidate northern *villa* plans with the aid of the Latin agronomists, or by the use of the terms *pars urbana* and *pars rustica* to differentiate the working parts of the farm from the residential areas. In Brittany and Picardy, for example, the resemblance with Italian structures can be effectively reduced to materials and construction techniques. The possibility that some regional designs reflected pre-Roman patterns of spatial organization has already been mentioned. It has also been suggested that the layout of Gallo-Roman farms may reflect differences of family structure in the north.[37] The evidence for Gallic kinship systems is so scanty[38] that such suggestions must remain speculative. It is in any case arguable that differences from Roman custom of this sort would have been swiftly broken down by the spread of Latin status and Roman citizenship, bringing with them Roman law which would have been unable to recognize institutions such as collective ownership of property by clans or usufruct rights shared within extended families, if such institutions indeed existed. Roman law would have provided individuals with the capacity to challenge such customary practices and the result would have been titles to property recognizable under the *ius civile*. Fiscal pressures may also have acted to assign each property a single owner liable for *tributum soli* on it.[39] Nevertheless, the architectural contrasts with Italian farms are sufficiently marked to make local tradition, innovation and perhaps social structure the likeliest sources of divergent designs. Northern *villae* would thus represent a local use of Gallo-Roman technology in ways that were determined by local tastes, rather than by a desire to emulate Roman models. A comparison might be made with a less widespread but interesting set of architectural changes that took place in the few landscapes where nucleated settlement

36 Lasfargues (1985), Blagg (1990).
37 Smith (1982), developing his 1978 paper in relation to Gaulish material, accepted by Hingley (1989), but see the important critique by Rippengal (1993).
38 Arguments by analogy from insular mediaeval law codes presuppose a degree of uniformity among Celtic speakers over time and space that remains to be demonstrated, and may seem unlikely on *a priori* grounds.
39 The impact of Roman law on the societies of the western provinces requires separate and fuller treatment. It is unclear, for example, whether it will have acted generally to strengthen the power of traditional leaders (as happened in favour of the Lairds during the Highland Enclosures) or whether it was more important as a force emancipating the poorer members of those societies from dependancy relations. For discussions, cf. Stevens (1970), Wightman (1978b), Whittaker (1980).

remained the norm. One such landscape was the sandy soiled area of northern Belgium and the Netherlands. There the predominant settlement forms were farmsteads and hamlets. Roman material is known from these sites, yet very few *villae* are known. In a small number of cases, for example Rijkswijk, the largest house within a hamlet was rebuilt using Roman materials and techniques during the second century. The absence of *villae* probably reflects both economic conditions and a cultural disposition to live in hamlets dominated by a single family. The rebuilding of their residences in Roman materials may reflect a different use of the same technology that was used elsewhere in the north to create grand houses in the countryside.[40] A second and better known example are the Vosges villages. Roman ceramics, inscriptions and sculpture are also known from these sites and they, too, made selective use of Roman building techniques, for example *tegulae*, to construct a local alternative to *villae*.[41]

The common chronology of these changes itself supplies powerful supporting arguments for this hypothesis. While the towns of Gaul were laid out in the formative period of provincial cultures, most rural residences (outside Narbonensis) were not transformed until a rather later period. It has already been suggested that material culture was deployed most urgently to assert new cultural identities during the period of most severe disruption to Gallic societies, and that displays of Roman goods were most effective in locations where Romans and Gauls encountered one another in public contexts, locations such as the provincial capitals and the new cities. It is less easy to see the transformation of rural architecture in the late first and second centuries AD as a part of that process. *Villae* and their analogues were scattered through landscapes rarely penetrated by Roman visitors; most can only have evoked Italian lifestyles very approximately and most were built in a period when differences between Gauls and Romans were less marked and less crucial. All these considerations combine to suggest that *villa* building in the north should not be interpreted in terms of assertions of Roman identity.

If most *villae* were not built in emulation of Roman rural residences, how may these architectural transformations be explained? One possibility is to see the *villae* of Narbonensis and the precocious, 'palatial' residences constructed in the early first century AD as setting a trend which gradually spread throughout Gaul. Gallo-Roman landlords improved their rural residences in order to compete with residences they knew of elsewhere in Gaul. That explanation is attractive in some

40 Roymans (1990, 190–1).   41 Petry (1982), Wightman (1985, 115–16).

respects. Secondly, an element of competitive building would help explain the development of regional traditions, as local aristocracies copied and tried to surpass each others' residences. The prominent locations of many Somme *villae* and their impressive façades and approaches suggest an element of ostentation, and the Roman culture of Gaul can only have encouraged emulative competition among the rich. Thirdly, we might see the architectural elaboration of these structures in new materials as in part an attempt to impress those poorer Gauls who were in various ways subordinated to the owners of the richest *villae*. The differences between regional styles, as well as the time intervals involved, suggest that neither early models nor Narbonensian precedents were followed slavishly. Another factor may have been the close relation between town and country in Gaul. Many or most of the elements in which *villae* differed from 'native farms' – mosaics, *opus caementicum*, wall paintings, bathhouses and tiled roofs – were already in use in town houses. The resemblance did not extend to the plans of rural residences. The general layout of *villae* in Gaul bore much less resemblence to that of the Gallo-Roman *domus* than did, for example, the *pars urbana* of *villae* like Settefinestre to the grand town-houses of Italian cities. The intention seems not so much to have been to transplant urban lifestyles into the country, *urbs in rure*, as to furnish rural residences with amenities and comforts also available in the town. The rebuilding of 'native farms' as *villae* thus reflects a deep internalization of Roman tastes, rather than a desire to imitate Roman style *in toto*.

III   Roman town and Gallic country?

For those who regard Romanization as a measurable quality, the countryside has often seemed under-Romanized, a reservoir of 'native survivals' or even of 'resistance' to Roman culture. This characterization is unacceptable for a number of reasons. Both modern and Roman preconceptions have probably played a part in fostering that impression. Modern images of 'the unchanging world of the peasant' have been powerful components of western ideologies, legitimating both paternalistic and exploitative attitudes to rural populations in Europe and especially beyond it, while many Romans saw a close connection between cities, civilization and the civilizing process.[42] For ancients and moderns alike, the countryside has often seemed to belong to the wild, the primitive antithesis of culture and civility. To be sure there are also concrete aspects of the archaeology of Roman Gaul which have

42 On *urbanitas*, see Ramage (1973).

seemed to support such an idea. In the formative period of Gallo-Roman culture, cities did offer Gauls privileged locations for the display of material culture as a means of asserting new identities. It has also been observed that areas remote from cities were slower to make use of cultural imports and innovation than suburban zones, and that *villae* in particular seem to have clustered around urban centres.

The phenomenon of *villae* clustering around towns is well attested in Gaul, as in other provinces of the Roman west.[43] In the territory of Béziers, for example, *villae* are commonest close to the colony.[44] That landscape had been centuriated at the foundation of the colony. But clustering also appears in eastern Brittany around Rennes, Corseul and Vannes.[45] It is important to note that *villae* cluster around small towns as well as around *civitas* capitals. Aerial survey in the Berry has revealed clusters around not only Bourges, but also Ernodurum, Allichamps and Levet,[46] and in the Franche-Comté around Mandeure, Port-sur-Saône, Seveux, Dammartin, Saint-Aubin, Grozon and Equevillon-Mont-Rivel.[47] 'Cluster' is in some sense an imprecise term, implying a discrete group of *villae*; it is more often the case that *villae* are simply more densely concentrated around towns than elsewhere in the landscape, with the innermost group – those within ten kilometres or so of the urban centre – often described as peri-urban or suburban *villae*.

Various explanations of this patterning have been offered. A number stress economic factors, suggesting that towns provided markets for rural produce and so enriched neighbouring farms more than distant ones, and encouraged them to reorganize their production on more 'rational' lines by importing 'the *villa* system' from Italy.[48] Despite the sophistication of some of these explanations, however, they face serious

43 Hodder and Millett (1980) conducted a systematic test of the proposition in southern Britain. No such survey has been carried out in Gaul: a sense of the incompleteness of our record of *villae*, together with a recognition of the arbitrariness of the distinction between *villae* and 'native farms', makes such a project difficult to achieve. For general discussion of this patterning in Gaul and other western provinces, however, see Leveau (1983b).
44 Clavel (1970).   45 Langouët and Jumel (1991), Naas (1991).
46 Holmgren and Leday (1982).   47 Mangin, Jacquet and Jacob (1986, 215, 228–9).
48 E.g. Gregson (1988), linking *villa* agriculture in Britain with the thesis that the Romano-British town promoted the spread of a disembedded economy at the expense of more traditional embedded systems, for which see Hodder (1979) and, for Gaul, Buchsenschutz and Ralston (1987). The antithesis between embedded and disembedded economies is, however, no longer seen as quite so clear cut by economic anthropologists, e.g. Appadurai (1986). Corbier (1986) adopts a different approach based on Kula's (1976) notion of a bisectorial economy, seeing the *villae* as capitalist enterprises producing for the market, and 'native farms' as the residence of subsistence peasants. Quite apart from the large size of some 'native farms', Kula's model, developed for feudal Poland, in fact depended on the geographical proximity and interdependence of the two analytically distinct kinds of economic activity.

difficulties. To begin with, the *villae* in question are not always very large sites, and the very fact they are densely packed suggests that they were not all the centres of large estates. Moreover, it is difficult to imagine that the populations of secondary towns at least, small in number and predominantly peasants, could have provided much of a market for agricultural produce. It might be possible to modify the thesis by stressing the importance of towns as centres from which surplus produce might be distributed to more distant markets, but in that case we might expect the road system to have exerted more of an influence on *villa* distribution, and less of a role to have been played by smaller towns, some of which were quite remote from the main arterial roads. A more fundamental objection is that *villae* represent a specific form of consumption, not of production. Farmhouses built in the Roman style do not provide evidence either for the profitability of the estates on which they stood, or for the manner in which those estates were farmed, and many *villae* may have been financed wholly or in part from other sources of wealth, while the presence of Roman building materials and techniques does not imply the importing of any system of agricultural production onto the territory around them.

If *villae* are instead treated as traces of a particular style of consumption, other explanations may be suggested. One possibility would be that landowners living near to towns acquired a taste for Roman style earlier or more completely than those who lived further away. For those who see Romanization as emanating from towns into the countryside, this is an attractive idea, and it has been suggested that provincial landscapes were frequently composed of Romanized areas, comprising towns surrounded by *villae*, scattered among hinterlands characterized by 'native' settlement types.[49] Hinterlands certainly did exist, interrupting and framing the plains, plateaux and large river valleys on which flourished both towns and dispersed and differentiated rural settlement. Upland areas like the Morvan, the Massif Central and the spine of the Breton peninsula had fewer *villae* than the surrounding areas, but the explanation is probably as much to be sought in terms of low levels of population and productivity, and in isolation from communication networks, as in cultural resistance or 'backwardness'. Areas of surviving forest, like the Ardennes, may also explain some areas of low *villa* density. It is less clear that there existed, within areas of broad ecological uniformity, juxtaposed and contrasting landscapes, differentiated primarily in cultural terms. Picardy has been thought to have been such an area, with 'native farms' located in some areas and *villae* in others,

49 See Leveau (1983a) for the best worked out version of this idea, debated with Goudineau in *Études Rurales* 89–91 (1983, 275–89).

but both surface survey and rescue archaeology have confirmed that these supposed contrasts in fact result from differences of soil type and depth, which have created variations in the visibility from the air of different settlement types. Clear boundaries between 'Roman' and 'native' landscapes are thus elusive in Gaul. The exception that proves the rule are the centuriated landscapes of the south, and even there both the Orange cadasters and the *villae* clustering around Béziers show how quickly those divisions broke down.

Clusters of *villae* around towns cannot to be explained, then, as islands of Roman culture in a sea of 'native' or 'Celtic' continuity. Instead, we might envisage a number of factors contributing to the phenomenon. It is possible, for example, that it was to begin with easier and cheaper to build in the Roman style in the vicinity of towns where supplies of building stone, timber and tiles, together with craftsmen with the requisite skills in using them, were easily at hand. Peri-urban *villa* building may have ridden piggyback, in other words, on urban construction. It may also be the case that landlords with more than one estate preferred to develop grandiose residences on those of their properties that were closer to towns, so as to enable them to enjoy urban amenities, and that those whose estates were remote from towns preferred to invest in urban *domus*, while others who lived nearby were content to reside in the vicinity and to rebuild their residences on a grander scale. The extent of the phenomenon can in any case be exaggerated. Despite the higher density of *villae* around some towns, *villae* were also common well away from urban centres and were in general very numerous in Gaul. Recent rescue excavation in Picardy has shown that even the hundreds discovered by aerial photography in the 1960s and 70s represent only a fraction of the real total.[50] The implication that there were well over a thousand *villae* in the medium-sized *civitas* of the Ambiani alone indicates just how widely distributed Roman-style architecture might be in Gallic countrysides.

It is in any case a mistake to focus attention too narrowly on towns and *villae* as the basic components of Gallic landscapes. Other organizations of rural space through centuriation, the road networks and physical geography require no further discussion. Rural sanctuaries and tiny shrines also played a part in organizing the countryside, mapping an old landscape of the sacred onto a new conception of the divine.

Underpinning all these human landscapes, too, were the physical structures that have been expressed in all historical periods in strong

---

50 De Saint-Blanquat (1992, 154–81) for one illustration (among many) of the density of the Gallo-Roman occupation as revealed by rescue excavation ahead of the construction of high speed rail links.

regional traditions. The more elements are considered, the more evident is the diversity of Gallo-Roman landscapes. Villages, for instance, remained common in some but not all areas, including Burgundy, Switzerland, north east Gaul, central Gaul and eastern Languedoc. Nor were all villages alike. In the Vosges, they formed the predominant settlement type and were relatively unspecialized. In Picardy, on the other hand, centres like the potters' settlement at Beauvraignes appear only as highly specialized components of landscapes that also include *villae*, 'native farms' and large and small towns. Where villages were rare, it is likely that a greater role in organizing rural population was played by a small handful of *villae* which were so large that each housed and employed well over a hundred individuals. Indeed large *villae* may have replaced villages in parts of Belgica, only to be replaced again by villages at the end of antiquity.[51] Yet another index of regional diversity is provided by the systems of land division used. The centuriated colonial landscapes of southern Gaul have already been discussed. Similar ones may have existed in some parts of the north, for example around the military base at Mirebeau, but the evidence for them is often poor. Much more common were landscapes where iron age field systems had been modified to slightly more regular forms, to create what have been termed 'Romano-indigenous' land divisions,[52] boundary systems, roughly rectilinear in form, that divided up farms of up to a couple of hundred hectares in size, often anchored to Roman roads. Such systems might be quite small scale, and located in close proximity to landscapes organized in other ways.

Towns, villages, roads, sanctuaries and land divisions were thus combined in numerous ways within the Gallic provinces. In so far as they reflected contrasts between regional societies that can only be guessed at today, it is probably pointless to try to build models either of a 'typical' Gallic landscape or of a 'typical' local society.[53] Some sense of the potential complexity of actual landscapes, however, may be gathered from the consideration of one well-studied micro-region, the Jurassian Finage, located at the south-western end of the Franche-Comté.[54] Here, the fertile plains of the Doubs and the Sablonne were

51 Wightman (1985, 107–19). For late antique developments, cf. now Percival (1992) with Van Ossel (1992).
52 Chouquer and Favory (1991, 171–82), with bibliography.
53 Cf., however, Crumley and Marquardt (1987) for the most ambitious attempt to date to capture the complexity of the workings of local societies in Gaul largely on the basis of landscape studies.
54 On the Finage, see Chouquer and Favory (1980), Chouquer and de Klijn (1989), Chouquer and Favory (1991, 205–7). Mangin, Jacquet and Jacob (1986, 120–7) discuss St Aubin and its context.

crossed by the main road from Châlon to Besançon. St Aubin, a small peasant village with a few public buildings, is located near the junction of this route with roads to Dijon and to Autun. To the south of it, the alluvial plains were centuriated and covered with small farms built in the Roman manner. To the north, on the other hand, the only visible land divisions are less regular, and the only farms visible are built in the iron age tradition. As the territory is less fertile, this may represent a marginalization of indigenous groups analogous to that experienced by the Tricastini near Orange. But the Finage is even more complex. To the east, beyond the centuriated area, are two much larger *villae*, perhaps the centres of relatively large estates, exercising considerable economic influence over neighbouring settlements. Finally, one *fanum* (a small shrine)is located at St Aubin, but there is another on the main road, about ten kilometres to the south west of the village. Some aspects of this reconstruction are provisional and much certainly remains unknown, but the complexity of the way space, and by implication society, was ordered is evident. The entirety of this landscape is no more than twenty kilometres long and ten wide.

IV   The Gallo-Roman aristocracy, between town and country

Perhaps the best argument against the notion that Gallo-Roman societies and cultures were divided between town and country is provided by consideration of the lifestyles of the new aristocracy of Roman Gaul. As elsewhere in the empire, the social distinctions that really mattered were those based on wealth, divisions manifested both in the towns of Gaul and in rural settings. The extent to which Roman culture and identity were appropriated by subordinate groups in Gaul will be the subject of the next chapter. But there are other reasons to privilege the culture of Gallic elites in this context. First, the capacity of the wealthy to represent their lifestyle and outlook was much greater than that of any other group. As a result, the mosaics, monuments, burials and wall paintings that provide the best evidence for the interpenetration of urban and rural culture relate most of all to the wealthy. Second, Gallo-Roman cities had relatively little in the way of an urban bourgeoisie whose values might contrast with those of a landed gentry.[55] Most Gallic cities were too small and their populations too involved in rural life. Some craftsmen and artisans, doctors and schoolteachers, and the skilled slaves of the larger urban *domus* inhabited a more urban world

---

55 See Drinkwater (1978) for a forceful argument to this effect.

than most Gauls, and in Lyon and the larger southern centres like Narbonne, Marseille and Vienne urban life must have resembled that of Italian *municipia*. But it will be the argument of this section that, in general, the tone of rural and urban culture alike was set by the same elite who self-consciously and ostentatiously kept a foot in both camps.

It is first necessary, however, to ask who the Gallo-Roman elites were. One powerful image in modern accounts of Roman Gaul is that of the Gallic landowner of extraordinary wealth, and it has been suggested that some form of continuity can be traced between the rich dynasts encountered by Caesar and the great aristocrats of late antiquity.[56] Very rich individuals doubtless existed in all periods, and it is likely that in Gaul, as in other provinces, Roman rule enabled a few individuals to become richer than had ever before been possible. On the other hand, the ways that wealth was acquired and spent varied considerably over time, no families can be shown to have remained wealthy and powerful over the centuries, and several periods of crisis can be identified which must have resulted in rapid redistributions of fortune among the aristocracy.[57]

There is in any case a danger of being dazzled by these super-rich whose very success has led to them receiving disproportionate attention. Other indications suggest that in many Gallic societies broad elite strata may have existed alongside, or even instead of a few families of enormous wealth.[58] The *villae* of Picardy, for example, provide evidence of well over one thousand substantial Roman-style country residences in the territory of the Ambiani. The density of sites suggests an average landholding of between 50 and 100 hectares, a modest but comfortable farm, and although it is likely that many local aristocrats may have owned more than one of these properties, it is difficult to see why a landowner should wish to develop residences on more than a couple of them, or why tenant farmers should invest in *villa* building. The

---

56 See Drinkwater (1978, 817–18) for a clear discussion of the thesis. Syme (1958, 454–63), Matthews (1975, 348–51), and Wightman (1978b) argue for continuity in various forms. Usually cited in this context are Dumnorix, Orgetorix and Vercingetorix's father (Caesar *de Bello Gallico* 1.17–19; 1. 2–4; 7.4); Gaius Iulius Rufus, the Santon magnate whose euergetisms to Saintes and Lyon are recorded on *CIL* XIII. 1036, *ILTG* 217; the Julio-Claudian magnates Valerius Asiaticus and Vindex; Solemnis, discussed in chapter two, and the priests of the altar in Lyon in general; Victoria, the mother of the Gallic emperor Victorinus, whose wealth secured the succession of Tetricus (on Victorinus see Drinkwater (1987, 39–41, 66–7); and in the fifth century Sidonius Apollinaris and his circle. For wealthy Gauls, see in general Drinkwater (1978) and (1979b).

57 Drinkwater (1987, 254–6).

58 See Millett (1990a, 49) for the importance of this variable in determining responses to Roman culture.

implication is that a broad class of *villa* owners existed, extending well beyond the hundred or so decurial families, let alone a handful of magnates. Some notion of stratification within the *villa*-owning classes is given by the estimate that about one in twenty of the Somme *villae* is very large, and less than half of those are luxurious in the sense of making use of marble and mosaics.[59] These results are difficult to generalize. Among the Treveri, *villae* seem more often to have been built on a luxurious scale. Local tastes influenced the forms ostentation took in each region, mosaics being unpopular in Britanny, many northern *villae* seemingly being designed to cover great areas and create grand façades, while great Burgundian and Aquitanian *villae* were distinguished by elaborations of design, especially in the form of peristyle courtyards.[60] The ratio of great magnates to the moderately well off probably varied considerably between *civitates*.

What identity did these groups own for themselves, urban or rural? The absence of literary accounts makes it difficult to say for certain until the fourth and fifth centuries AD, when the literary images of town and country conjured up by Ausonius and Sidonius Apollinaris evoke Plinian and Horatian ideals of rural residences built to permit the discerning to live in a civilized and urbane manner in the tranquillity and simplicity of a tamed countryside.[61] That evocation should perhaps not be taken at face value: a classicizing preoccupation with 'golden age' literary models was a feature of much late antique secular Latin literature, and might reasonably be interpreted as a response to threatened change, rather than as a reflection of continuity. But there are good *a priori* reasons for regarding Gallo-Roman elites as being active in both town and country. To begin with, in many areas of Gaul aristocrats were already present in the countryside before the conquest, building and inhabiting large 'native farms' which were monumental in the scale of their construction and enclosures, even if they did not resemble Roman *villae* in architectural terms. Contact with Roman ideals of civilized and humane behaviour would not have discouraged rural residence: the idealized aristocratic lifestyles presented by Cicero and the younger Pliny, among others, do not advocate the abandonment of the

---

59 See Wightman (1985, 111–14) for what follows. Compare the results of survey around Vaison which has revealed 67 sites with *tegulae* and fine wares, of which 19 were classified *villae* on architectural grounds, two of which covered over a hectare each, see Meffre (1994, 124–5).
60 Goguey and Goguey (1982).
61 See Février (1981) for the analysis of the late antique writers. For first century AD notions of '*urbs in rure*', see Purcell (1987) and Wallace-Hadrill (1991, 244–9).

countryside to the peasants, but rather represent aristocrats as moving backwards and forwards between town and country, their *urbanitas* manifested in a particular attitude to life in the country, not in a rejection of it. Naturally, the lives of the Gallo-Roman aristocrats of huge, barely urbanized northern *civitates* cannot have resembled in detail those idealized by those Roman senators, but the fact remains that there was nothing inherently un-Roman in rural residence, so long as it was conducted in a suitably grand and urbane manner.

In some cases, it is even possible to show the wealthy advertising their urban activities in a rural setting, or their rural interests in an urban one. A villa recently excavated at Liégeaud in the Limousin, 35 kilometres south east of Limoges, was decorated in the mid-second century with elaborate wall paintings that depicted a set of games, including gladiatorial combats, chariot racing and wild beast hunts.[62] A painted label suggests strongly that the paintings recorded actual games given as a *munus* by the *villa* owner. The wall paintings, the games and the Latin label make clear the extent to which the *villa* owner had appropriated Roman values. The record in a rural setting of urban munificence makes clear how important both worlds were to him. An answering image is perhaps to be found in the rural calendar depicted on a mosaic found in one of the luxurious *domus* of Saint-Romain-en-Gal, the 'new town' across the river from Vienne, the Allobrogian capital. The mosaic in question dates from the early third century AD, and consisted of twenty-four illustrations recording religious and agricultural activities in the countryside.[63] Another mosaic, from the town of Lillebonne in Normandy, presents a different aspect of man's relations with nature. It depicts scenes from a stag hunt, conducted with dogs, on horseback, using a tamed animal as a lure and accompanied by sacrifices. The social importance of hunting (and its marginal importance in diet) during the late la Tène period has been demonstrated from faunal remains, and the hunt remained an important part of aristocratic lifestyles in Gaul throughout the early empire.[64] Hunting was not a prominent part of traditional Roman ideals of rural life, as formulated in the late Republic, although as an important part of Greek

62 Dumasy-Mathieu (1991).
63 See *Recueil général...* (1957–), III 2, no. 368 for full publication. Ferdière (1988, vol. II, 4–14) discusses the mosaic in relation to comparable documents.
64 On the La Tène, see Méniel (1987, 89–100); on the Gallo-Roman period, see Ferdière (1988, vol. II, 163–81). Arrian devotes a good part of his *Kynegetikos* to the hunting practices of the Keltoi which he regards as one of the more important of his *addenda* to Xenophon's treatise.

aristocratic lifestyles it was to be adopted by some Roman aristocrats and emperors.[65] It might well be that the evident importance of the hunt in Gaul does reflect some local emphases in the ways nature was perceived and enjoyed. But the prominence of hunting in the art forms patronized by the Gallo-Roman aristocracy does not signify a rejection of urban life. As the Lillebonne mosaic shows, images of the hunt were as acceptable in urban residences as images of gladiators were in rural *villae*.

The same sense of an elite equally at home in the city and on its rural estates emerges from consideration of elite burial practice.[66] Italian norms tolerated both burial in *mausolea* on the outskirts of cities and burial on a landowner's own estates. Both practices can be exemplified from Gaul. While the majority of Gallo-Roman burials of those of humbler status were in cemeteries around settlements or in close proximity to them, a number of isolated rural monuments are known recording the rural burial of very prominent individuals who had held civic offices and priesthoods in neighbouring cities.[67] There is even one case of an equestrian family, the Domitii Aquenses, probably belonging to the colony of Aix, but buried in a magnificent monument on their estates near Rognes.[68] Isolated rural burials for the very prominent were also a feature of some iron age traditions in Europe.[69] A series of rich burials in and around the Berry and dating to the last three quarters of the last century BC and the first half of the first century AD, provides a good example of a phenomenon which, with variations, can be attested very widely in northern Europe.[70] The Berry tombs take the form of square chambers, perhaps covered with mounds, and contain the remains of the deceased together with weapons, ceramic table services, metal drinking services, *amphorae* and food. The latest in the group was decorated with wall paintings and located only a few hundred metres from a 'native farm' and a *villa* building. During the second century, rural monuments became very common in two areas of Gaul in the north east, especially around Trier and extending down to Burgundy, and in the south-west, particularly south of the Garonne. There are hints of different but analogous isolated tombs elsewhere in Gaul.[71]

The nearest thing that survives to a Gallo-Roman aristocrat's account of himself is a document relating to just such a monument. The

65 On the history of hunting in antiquity, see Lane Fox (1996). A full account of hunting in the Roman period would have to take into account mosaic evidence from North Africa and the contrast between hunting and the trapping of animals for *venationes* in (mostly) urban amphitheatres. Only hunting proper was an aristocratic pursuit.
66 Février (1981), Hatt (1951, 164–212) with Ferdière (1993).
67 Février (1981), Ferdière (1993).   68 Burnand (1975).
69 Collis (1977), Metzler *et al.* (1991), Cliquet *et al.* (1993).
70 Ferdière and Villard (1993).   71 Galliou (1989, 31–3) on Breton *mausolea*.

text, known as the 'Testament of the Lingon', is preserved only in a tenth century manuscript found in the library of Basel in the late nineteenth century. The original may have been inscribed on a funerary monument but may equally be a fragment of a will.[72] On onomastic and linguistic grounds the document is dated to the second century AD, and the text makes clear that the author is a citizen of the Lingones, a community with a large territory whose capital was modern Langres. The stated concern of the author is to specify precisely how he shall be buried, how his tomb shall be constructed and what cult shall be paid at it after his death. That concern is echoed by literary and epigraphic texts from throughout the Roman world, and in other regions, this led individuals to construct tombs for themselves in their own lifetime or to establish foundations to fund civic celebrations on their birthdays. But the Lingon, whose name does not survive in the text, chose instead to specify in great detail what he required. The projected monument is described in detail, and he specifies the materials to be used for each section of it, 'imported marble of the best quality' or 'best quality bronze' for the statue, marble from Luni in Italy for the altar. The text goes on to describe the provisions to be made for the days when the monument is open for cult observance and the duties and remunerations of his freedmen who will tend it and maintain it. The monument is to be inscribed with the names of the magistrates of the year it was begun and with the Lingon's age at his death. If these provisions are not respected and the tomb is allowed to fall into decay or is encroached on by other tombs, his heirs are to pay a fine to the *civitas* of the Lingones. The nature and timing of the commemorative cult is described, and required of his descendants and freedmen, and finally he requests to be burnt along with his hunting equipment, which is listed in great detail.

If we ask what image the Lingon leaves of himself, both deliberately and implicitly, it is difficult to classify him as Gaul or Roman, rural magnate or civic notable. The design and materials of his monument attest his thoroughly Roman taste, as do the devices by which he attempts to ensure posthumous cult. The centrality of hunting perhaps looks back to the late iron age burials of the Berry, and evokes the rural lifestyles of the pre-conquest elite, while the fine paid to the Lingon *civitas* and the dating by their magistrates tacitly accepts the civic order of society. The point is not that he was 'wholly Roman' (although he was arguably as Roman as anyone was), and some local traditions do

---

72 *CIL* XIII 5708 = *ILS* 8379. Le Bohec (1991) for a new text with translation, commentary and collected interpretative essays, cf. also Hatt (1951, 66–71).

seem to be represented in his self-portrayal. The lifestyle of Roman aristocrats from Gaul was, doubtless, different in important ways from that of their Italian counterparts, or that of elites of more urbanized regions, some of whom who drew on Greek, Syrian or other local traditions. The point is rather than the Lingon's 'Romanity' is not compromised by his local identity, and there is no concern to conceal 'un-Roman' elements of his lifestyle, nor does any fault line appear between his rural lifestyle and his urban connections. Viewed in these terms, the image that emerges from his testament accords perfectly with the argument of this chapter that there was no great gulf between Romanized cities and Gallic hinterlands, and that a culturally and socially unified Gallo-Roman elite dominated both spheres, perhaps with little consciousness of the divergent cultural traditions that had contributed to their lifestyle and outlook.

7   Consuming Rome

I   A new world of goods

The testament of the Lingon, discussed in the previous chapter, demanded that the altar beside his tomb be built of marble from Luni in Italy. The stipulation reveals not only a desire for the best quality stone but, more significantly, a knowledge of where the best marble was to be found. That discrimination is part of the Lingon's self-representation, as an aristocrat of taste who recognizes and demands quality. But it also serves as a reminder of the complexity of the cultural competence that Gallo-Roman aristocrats had had to acquire in order to consume in accordance with their new identities in the imperial order. Like all upwardly mobile groups they must have found their new positions bewildering at first, as they were presented with unfamiliar choices from all the good things of the empire. Consumption was problematic enough for Italian elites in this period, but the new aristocracies of the western provinces faced additional difficulties as they struggled to avoid provincialism. The reputation of Valerius Asiaticus, a Julio-Claudian senator from Vienne, renowned not only for his wealth but also for his ostentatious display of it, suggests that at least some of them did get it wrong.[1]

Consumption was problematic principally because it was one way in which Romans expressed their public identities. The late Republic and early empire were characterized by fierce debates about what kinds of consumption were appropriate for members of the Roman elite. Deviation exposed individuals to charges of *luxuria* or *parsimonia*, and the creation of a consensus about consumption was made more difficult by the growth of personal fortunes and by increasing rates of social mobility. Moreover the period was characterised by debate over the extent to which various levels of familiarity with different components of Greek culture were either necessary for the educated man or else compromised

---

1 Tacitus *Annales* 11.1–3, Cassius Dio 60.27 and alluded to in *ILS* 212. Dio and Tacitus agree on his exceptional wealth and the jealousy it aroused. It is less clear how far his provincial origin contributed to his disgrace.

his Roman identity.[2] Diet, sexuality, dress, domestic and public architecture, entertainment and literary taste were just some of the areas in
which these contests were played out. Changes in consumption were
not confined to the elite. Many of their social subordinates were also
drawn into the transformation of the material culture of the empire.[3]
At first sight much of this activity may be classified as emulation, an
appropriation of elite culture by those who aspired to share their social
eminence and power. But it would be a mistake to regard these appro-
priations simply as 'Veblen effects', a gradual trickle down of material
culture from one social level to another.[4] Aspirations to elite status were
not realistic for many of those who changed their patterns of consumption, and the cultures they created were not faithful replicas of those of
their social superiors. The culture of freedmen, for instance, was not
simply an imperfect imitation of that of their former masters, even if
satirists like Petronius might represent it as such. Certainly they drew
on the varieties of consumption they had encountered while slaves, but
the new *personae* they created were not designed only for the eyes of
their patrons, with whom most of them could never compete, but also
for those of their former fellow slaves; their new peers, both freeborn and
freed; their own slaves; and their spouses and children. Perhaps most
importantly their consumption was driven by their own self-esteem,
each representing to himself what he had become.[5] The culture of noble
Romans provided an inspiration and a resource from which others might
select items with which to fashion their own distinctive social *personae*.

Roman society was not unique in the role played by consumption
in creating social identities. Arguably, Romans were more free to create
new *personae* in this way than the members of many other historical
societies, in which cultural style was often used to signal ethnic differences or social rank.[6] Some items of Roman material culture did operate

2 Wallace-Hadrill (1988), Edwards (1993), Toner (1995, 117–23).
3 Wallace-Hadrill (1990a).
4 Veblen (1926) outlined the thesis that the elite set trends in consumption that progressively spread 'down' through society as a result of successive emulations, and thereby
   prompted changes in elite consumption. A 'Veblen effect' is a manifestation of this
   dynamic. Cf. Miller (1982) for a similar thesis argued in relation to archaeological
   examples. For a full critique of Veblen's thesis, see Campbell (1987) and (1993).
5 Corroborative evidence might be the notorious over-representation and extravagant
   nature of libertine funerary monuments. The alternative view, that that cultural incom-
   petence and unrealistic social aspirations inspired 'vulgar ostentation', is elitist. See
   Campbell (1987) on consumption aimed to realize cultural ideals for the consumer's
   own satisfaction rather than to earn others' approval.
6 Hodder (1982), drawing on Barth (1969), shows how such symbols are used more prominently at times of social stress, when claims to a given identity bring tangible advantages
   and are often contested. Douglas and Isherwood (1978, 47) make the point that 'emulation is not a human universal' and that some kinds of social organization, in particular
   those with strong socially or institutionally sanctioned prescriptive rules, limit it severely.

as signals of this kind. Depending on context, the *toga* was a sign of adulthood, of masculinity, of female deviance, of citizenship, of traditional virtue, of civil as opposed to military *personae*, of constitutional rather than monarchic style, or of the civilized condition of some provincial peoples. But few items were as semantically laden as the *toga*, and even the laws and debates on *luxuria* never succeeded in defining Roman consumption to a significant degree. Roman society was in this respect much more like modern societies in which consumption is an important strategy for self-actualization, a means to create a distinctive individual identity.[7] Naturally choices are never exercised in a semantic vacuum. For consumption to convey meaning, even to oneself, it must operate within a set of conventions, which can usefully be regarded as constituting a system of communications.[8] Some caveats are appropriate.[9] Individuals are not always discriminating enough to choose well or to appreciate the choices of others. Nor is personal preference irrelevant, even if in practice personal preferences are rarely formed without any reference to wider frameworks of meaning.[10] Finally, some goods are desirable in themselves, either because they provide sensual physical comforts, or because they offer more efficient means to old ends: wine might come into the former category, weatherproof roofing tiles into the latter.[11] It is easy to over-simplify the means by which new styles of consumption come about. Nevertheless, consumption offered an important means by which all Gauls, apart from the very poorest, might participate in the new order of things and fashion new identities for themselves.

Pragmatically, viewing Romanization as a change in patterns of consumption provides us with a way to approach the vast quantity of bric-à-brac that comprises the most tangible and common traces of the everyday experiences of the mass of the Gallo-Roman population.[12]

7 Miller (1987), Campbell (1987).
8 Douglas and Isherwood (1978) for consumption as communication. Consumption as communication and consumption as self-actualization are not mutually exclusive aims. The personal ideals a consumer pursues are generally socially constructed, while individuals usually make use of goods which have already been invested with significances.
9 For archaeological debates on the selection and use of goods in this way, cf. Hodder (1989) and Conkey and Hastorf (1990), especially the papers by Sackett and Wiessner, with references to their earlier work. Cf. also the seminal paper by Wobst (1977). For an example of analysis in these terms, see Miller (1985). Perhaps the main conclusion to be drawn from these debates is that accounts of style that reduce it entirely to its communicative aspect are as flawed as accounts of consumption solely in terms of conspicuous display. The communicative potential of both, however, is uncontestable.
10 Bourdieu (1977) shows how consumption is patterned even when there are apparently few constraints on choice.
11 See Mintz (1993) on food. See Meadows (1994) for suggestive remarks on how this might be applied to Romanization.
12 Deetz (1977) and Braudel (1981) demonstrate respectively the archaeological and historical potential of the mundane and the banal.

The point is conveniently illustrated by consideration of the enormous range of small objects of metal, glass and pottery that comprise the greater part of the Gallo-Roman collections of any provincial museum in France. To get a more precise idea, it is worth considering a few recent archaeological projects in detail. One of the most carefully recorded is an excavation in the car park of the town hall of Besançon, the site of Vesontio, the iron age and Gallo-Roman capital of the Sequani.[13] The structures on the site were not unusual for a northern *civitas* capital. Two groups of late La Tène structures were found, dated to between 120 and 40 BC, succeeded, after a brief abandonment, by Roman buildings which at the start of the first century were organized into a street grid. Subsequently the area was a mixture of residential housing just outside the precinct of a large urban temple. This part of the city underwent several rebuildings in the late first and early second centuries but was abandoned sometime around AD 160. But the interest of the site is in the quantity and nature of the small finds recovered from 20,000 cubic metres of earth. A total of 837 objects were recovered, *excluding* pottery, glass, coins and iron nails. Of these, 93 originated in the 70 odd years of pre-Roman occupation and the remaining 744 from the two centuries of Roman Vesontio. That comparison is a crude one, and the La Tène levels were not poor. *Fibulae* (brooches used to fasten clothing), rings, bracelets, needles, a piece of a helmet, a fragment of mirror and metal horse fittings were recovered, as well some imported Italian metalwork. But with the Roman period both the volume and the variety of finds increases enormously. Items of personal adornment again are common: *fibulae*, bracelets (including examples in glass and ivory), beads, pins, a mirror and ear-rings. Also common are domestic items such as knives, spoons, bone knife handles, a pestle and large numbers of iron rings, handles, supports and attachments for wooden boxes and other items, part of a balance (with weights) and part of a lock. A few fragments of wooden furniture survive, as do a fair number of bone gaming counters and dice. Finally there is a large quantity of tools. Most of the iron implements were too corroded to be identified, but scissors, needles of various sorts, pins, moulds for bronze work and an oculist's box of salves were found. If the number of items per year are compared, the average for the iron age is just over one object per year, and for the Roman period almost four times as much.

Bric-à-brac of this kind might seem mundane and insignificant compared with the monumental buildings of Gallic cities and sanctuaries or the *villae* and tombs of the aristocracy, but they offer a glimpse of

13 Guilhot and Goy (1992).

the extent to which the creation of a new provincial culture affected the daily lives of the great majority of the population. Vesontio was the capital of one of the largest communities, but indications of the extraordinary range of objects and artefacts made and used by humbler Gallo-Romans can be found on any site of the period. The village of Lunel-Viel near Nîmes has also produced *fibulae*, metal bracelets, rings, mortars, knives, sickles, spoons, hooks, bronze nails, horse-fittings, a scalpel, glass rings and ornaments, bone hairpins, a spatula, gaming counters and of course a mass of pottery, including finewares, coarse wares and *amphorae*.[14] A similar range of goods has been recovered at the small town of Entrains (Nièvre): tools, blades, weights and keys of iron; statuettes, jewellery and fittings of bronze; pins, gaming tokens and an oculist's box of bone as well as pipe-clay figurines, loom weights, coins and ceramics.[15] Some of these objects were probably votives and grave goods. Grave goods from the cemetery of Argentomagus, a small town in central Gaul, include rings, beads, gaming tokens, a mirror, buttons, lamps, antler medallions, a bone knife handle, a mortar and of course ceramics.[16] Perhaps most surprising is the range of goods recovered from the wreck of a 25 metre long boat that sank at the mouth of the harbour of St Peter Port on Guernsey some time in the late third century AD.[17] Little trace remains of the cargo, but the possessions of the crew and the equipment of the boat included 80 coins, fish hooks, buckles, pins, studs, the bronze hinge of a box, pieces of textile and rope, and a number of wooden implements including tool handles, a spatula, pieces of joinery and a lathe-turned maple wood bowl. The ceramic (mostly local wares) included cooking pots, flagons, bowls, beakers and some *amphorae*. The examples could be multiplied indefinitely.

What can be made of this wealth of mundane and inexpensive consumer goods? To begin with the contrast with the late iron age needs to be put into perspective. Ceramics, *fibulae*, ornaments and iron tools are all found on late La Tène sites. The material culture of the iron age was not only sophisticated, but it was developing in the direction of diversity and quantity well before the Roman conquest. There was a steady increase in the quantity of iron work produced and the uses to which iron was put, while the potter's wheel and enamel and glass working were already common in Europe. The material culture of Roman Gaul owed much to that of the La Tène period, and in particular instances, like that of the *fibula*, was closely modelled on it. Nevertheless, Rome introduced many innovations in technology and many new kinds of

14 Raynaud (1990, 261–76).   15 Devauges (1988), cataloguing museum collections.
16 Allain *et al.* (1992).   17 Rule and Monaghan (1993).

objects, from games to medical instruments, and from tiles to new textiles. Ceramics, as will emerge later in this chapter, are a particularly sensitive indicator of both these changes. Besides, the sheer quantity of small objects increased enormously, to the extent that archaeologists are forced to approach Roman sites in ways very different from those applied to prehistoric settlements.[18]

These changes cannot be ascribed to deliberate policy on the part of the conquerors, and they are too widespread and rapid to be the work of the new Gallo-Roman elites, who would in any case have disdained many of these new goods. Equally, although some innovations may have immediately been seized on as means of realizing existing goals, the advantages of all of them were not self-evident but had to be learnt. Understanding this 'consumer revolution'[19] raises questions about the means by which more humble members of Gallo-Roman societies made use of the new material culture available, and their motivations for doing so. Consumption will have served many goals, but I shall argue that an important motivation for the Gallic masses was to transform themselves into new kinds of people suitable to inhabit a new world. That new goods and technologies were employed in this way in early imperial Gaul is strongly suggested by comparison with the rather different patterns of consumption of Mediterranean products characteristic of the pre-conquest period.

II   Roman goods beyond the empire

The presence and significance of Mediterranean imports on late La Tène sites in temperate Europe has been much discussed.[20] Wine *amphorae*, of the types known as Greco-Italic and especially Dressel 1A and 1B, and the fine pottery termed Campanian ware are found in many regions of late iron age Gaul, and Italian bronze drinking vessels have been found in smaller quantities. Virtually all these goods were produced in central Italy, mostly in Etruria and Campania, and some at

---

18 See Harris (1993) for an economic approach to this wealth of objects.
19 The phrase is that of McKendrick *et al.* (1982), referring to the new demand for manufactures among the humbler classes of eighteenth-century England that preceded and to some extent enabled the mass production of the Industrial Revolution. More recently, changes in non-elite consumption have been traced back to the seventeenth (Schama 1987) and sixteenth (Mukerji 1983) centuries, and a distinction drawn between the emergence of materialist styles of consumption, and its (much more recent) generalization. For a collection of recent perspectives, see Brewer and Porter (1993).
20 For what follows, see Woolf (1993c). For general accounts of Mediterranean wine in late iron age Europe, cf. Clemente (1974), Roman (1983), Tchernia (1983), Fitzpatrick (1985), (1989), Cunliffe (1988), Laubenheimer (1990).

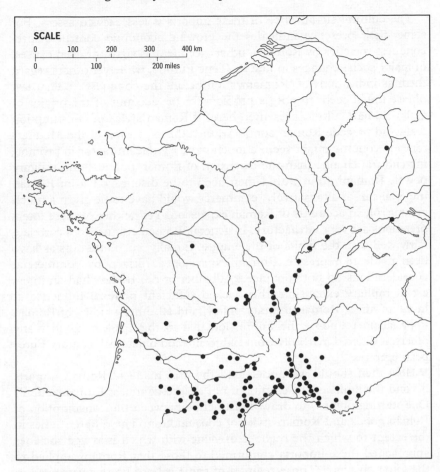

Fig. 7.1   Campanian ware in Gaul

least were imported into parts of temperate Europe in considerable numbers well before the Roman conquest. Wine *amphorae* appear on iron age sites in France and southern Germany from the early second century BC, and in some regions became common on virtually every site during the last century BC, when it is estimated that between 50,000 and 100,000 hectolitres of wine were imported into Gaul each year.[21] Some sites have produced tens of thousands of *amphorae*. Numerous wrecks of vessels transporting wine have been discovered off the Mediterranean coast of France. The scale of the exchanges represented by these discoveries is undeniable.

21 Will (1987), Fitzpatrick (1989), Hesnard (1990), Laubenheimer (1993).

The cultural significance of these imports is less easy to assess. For some, their presence indicates the growing economic control of pre-conquest societies by Romans, others see them as signs, or even causes, of major social changes in late La Tène Europe, while yet others regard them as indications of 'Romanization before the conquest'.[22] That last phrase might seem to pose a problem for the account of the origins of Gallo-Roman culture presented here. If Roman styles of consumption really did precede Roman conquest, then the expansion of the Mediterranean economy might seem a much more significant factor in promoting cultural change than the extension of Roman political and military power. Romanization would then need to be disengaged from Roman imperialism, or alternatively, commerce would have to be given a much greater role in accounts of Roman expansion. Yet neither of these interpretations are very satisfactory. In general, Roman culture does correlate fairly well with the limits of the empire. Equally, such attempts as have been made to represent Roman expansion as driven by commercial considerations do not convince.[23] Whether or not traders had an interest in military expansion, they lacked sufficient political influence at home to affect Roman military policy, and all other studies of Roman imperialism reinforce the impression that in this respect, as in many others, it differed markedly from eighteenth and nineteenth century European empires.[24]

How then should we understand the uses made of Roman imports beyond the limits of the empire, if not as 'pre-conquest Romanization'? One starting point is to draw a distinction between the consumption of Roman goods and Roman styles of consumption. The difference lies in the extent to which the regimes of value with which iron age societies approached these imports conformed to those that Romans applied to the same objects.[25] Those regimes of value cannot be reconstructed in detail, but both classical accounts and a contextual approach to Mediterranean artefacts found at iron age sites suggest strongly that iron age populations used these imports in ways that were quite distinctive, and that the values they gave these exotics were rather different to those accorded them in the Roman world.

---

22 For the latter formulation, see Haselgrove (1984b). For critical assessments of the case for the wine trade prompting major social changes in Europe, cf. Fitzpatrick (1989), Woolf (1993c).
23 Clemente (1974), Nash (1987), Cunliffe (1988).
24 Woolf (1993d). For the relationship between Roman trade and Roman imperialism in Gaul, see the fuller discussion in chapter 2 above. For the contrast with more recent empires, cf. Brunt (1965) and Woolf (1990a).
25 Compare Renfrew's (1975, 87–94) distinction between transfers of goods with information and transfers of goods without information, further developed by van der Leeuw (1983).

The Gauls' taste for Mediterranean wine is a prominent feature of classical accounts of pre-conquest societies. A trope of Greek and Roman ethnography was that Gauls over-valued wine to an absurd degree. Italian traders were said to have profited from this to purchase slaves at ridiculously low prices.[26] The social context of drinking most often described contrasted markedly from the Greek *symposium* or Roman *cena*, in which wine drinking took place among individuals of notionally equal status. Gallic feasts were described as occasions in which the powerful disbursed food and wine to their dependants as one among many displays of wealth. Phylarchus wrote that no-one at a Gallic feast touched his food until the king had touched his portion, and in another fragment he told the story of how one chief, Ariamnes, set up huge enclosures throughout his kingdom at which anyone who wished was fed meat, barley meal and wine. The disbursement was said to have lasted for an entire year.[27] Poseidonius, writing in the last century BC, wrote of feasts at which the Gauls sat on the ground in a circle around whomever was most distinguished in war, birth or wealth. The host sat alongside him with armed retainers in attendance sharing the food. The rich drank Italian and Massiliot wine, without mixing it with water, in contrast to Greek and Roman practice. Poseidonius also tells how another Gallic chief, Louernios the Arvernian, set up an enormous enclosure at which wine and food was distributed to all comers over a period of several days.[28] Gallic feasts were said to be characterized by ritualized combats for prestige, some of them to the death. Some individuals even volunteered to be killed on the spot in return for contributions of silver, gold and wine which were then distributed to their descendants.[29] Classical writers assimilated the personal dependants, variously called *soldurii* or *ambacti*, who formed the retinue of the chief, to *parasitoi*, literally those who ate with their leader.[30]

These stories need to be handled with care. Little distinction was made by classical ethnographers between all the different groups they termed Celts or Gauls, and accounts may often have been transferred from one group to another. It was also usual for ethnographers to concentrate on the bizarre and distinctive elements of alien societies.

26 Diodorus 5.26.   27 Both quoted in Athenaeus IV.150d–f.
28 Athenaeus IV.151e–152f.   29 Athenaeus IV.154b–c.
30 Caesar *de Bello Gallico* 6.15, 3.22 (cf. Athenaeus VI.249b, quoting a similar version from Nicolaus of Damascus). Also Athenaeus VI.246c, again quoting Poseidonius. On these forms of dependancy, see Daubigney (1979), (1983) and the essays gathered in Daubigney (1984) and (1993), especially Lewuillon in the latter. The range of rival anthropological readings of these passages perhaps reflects the limitations of this evidence as much as the contrasting theories of gift exchange, kinship and dependancy used to interpret it.

The prominence of feasts may also be exaggerated by the fact that few ethnographies have survived complete, and an important source for their fragments is Athenaeus' *Deipnosophists*, a work with a particular interest in stories of food and dining. Despite these caveats, feasts, in which imported wine played a prominent part, do seem to have been important in some pre-conquest societies, and wine *amphorae* were even depicted on some Celtic coins.[31] Significantly, Greek and Roman observers did not see these feasts and wine drinking as a sign that Gauls shared classical values and customs: instead they presented the bizarre and excessive uses that the Gauls made of wine as confirmation of their barbarism.

A sense of the distinctive uses made of Mediterranean imports in iron age Europe also emerges from archaeological considerations. First of all, the range of imports is extremely limited. Wine, Campanian ware and bronze tableware constitute virtually the only categories of goods imported into Europe from the Mediterranean world.[32] Secondly, regions differed considerably in the range of these goods that are found, in the scale of imports and in the uses made of them. The simplest illustration that classical goods were not imported as a package is provided by the different distributions of each category of imports. Bronze vessels and drinking equipment are the least well documented, but enough survive to indicate that they were imported into areas of central Europe where few or no *amphorae* have been found, and do not seem to have reached all the areas in the west and north to which wine was traded.[33]

The situation is clearer with Campanian ware, a hard, shiny, black tableware which dominated western Mediterranean markets for fineware between the late third century and the end of the last century BC. The stylistic criteria and dietary practices to which this pottery catered were the product of long interactions within the Mediterranean world.[34] Most Campanian ware was produced in central Italy, perhaps exploiting the concentration of wealth and communications on the city of Rome, but similar wares were produced all around the western Mediterranean, some conventionally described as imitations, others as the products of secondary centres. Campanian ware had been found at some fifty Gallic sites by 1985,[35] most of them in Mediterranean France with extensions

31 Laubenheimer (1990, 71–5).   32 See Fitzpatrick (1989, 35–8) for fuller discussion.
33 See Kunow (1983) for Italian metalwork in iron age Europe, and Collis (1984, 137–46) for maps and discussion.
34 For Campanian ware, see Morel (1981b), summarized in Morel (1981a). On the economic factors behind central Italian dominance of the western Mediterranean, see Morel (1981c).
35 See Morel (1985, 181) for a map, superceding those in Nash (1978a, 113) and Collis (1984, 144).

up the Rhône valley and across the Gallic Isthmus. The number continues to rise. Little has been recovered north of the Massif central. Campanian ware appears both earlier (from the second century) and in much greater quantity on the southern *oppida*. At Nages, some 30–40 sherds were found for each cubic metre excavated, and imported Campanian ware was the most commonly inscribed ceramic in the south, perhaps suggesting it was used by local elites. On inland sites, by contrast, Campanian ware appears only in the first century BC and in very small quantities, comprising, for example, 0.5 per cent of the total ceramic from Feurs in the Forez. Equally, while Campanian was imitated in southern Gaul, it made little impact on local production in non-Mediterranean France.

Wine *amphorae* have the largest distribution of all Mediterranean imports, produced in the same regions as Campanian ware, but distributed as far north as the Netherlands and central Britain.[36] But their ubiquity in Gaul conceals major regional variations. In south-west France around the Aude, and in Burgundy, *amphorae* appear at virtually all sites and on the largest they number in tens and hundreds of thousands. Some of these sites, such as Châlon-sur-Saône, may have been transhipment points where wine was decanted into lighter, more perishable containers, but others, including the *oppida* at Essalois in Forez, Mont Beuvray in Burgundy and Vieille-Toulouse in the south west, can only have been sites at which very large quantities of wine were consumed. The chronology of the imports – beginning in the second century BC (before Campanian ware) and peaking in the last century BC – makes it clear the consumers were Gauls, rather than Roman soldiers, and the scale of consumption shows it cannot have been limited to the elite.[37] Elsewhere in Gaul, *amphorae* are much rarer and were correspondingly more exclusive in use. In Brittany, as in southern Britain, very few sites have produced more than two or three *amphorae*. *Amphorae* appear as grave goods in the richest tombs of northern Gaul. However wine was used in these societies, it cannot have been consumed in quite the same social contexts as it was in the south. Cost and availability presumably influenced the ways wine was used in the north (although some areas seem to have refused to import it[38]), but the result was a mosaic of different use patterns and regimes of value throughout iron age Europe.

36 See Fitzpatrick (1985), with (1987) for a critical study of the distribution map.
37 Tchernia (1983), *pace* Middleton (1983). Tchernia (1986, 85–7) estimates that an average figure of between 60,000 and 150,000 hectolitres of Italian wine was imported into Gaul each year in the century or so in which Dressel 1 *amphorae* were produced (mid-late second century to mid-late first century BC). The figure is necessarily very approximate but gives some idea of the scale of trade and of consumption.
38 Fitzpatrick (1985), Caesar *de Bello Gallico* 4.2.

Mediterranean imports in pre-conquest Gaul represented a selection from the goods potentially available, and the choice of imports and the ways they were used exhibit major inter-regional variations. The importance of highlighting the freedom of the Gauls to choose is in the contrast this makes with the pattern of imports into Roman Gaul. Before the conquest, iron age populations did purchase Mediterranean goods, but for their own ends, not in order to reproduce classical cultural practices nor to appropriate new identities modelled on those of the society from which the imports originated. We cannot hope to understand why each group came to desire particular varieties of Mediterranean goods. Metalwork was perhaps already a means of acquiring and displaying status within some La Tène societies, and wine has, maybe, its own attractions. Significantly, none of these goods – not even Campanian ware – could be produced by the Gauls themselves with La Tène technology. What is clear is that Mediterranean imports were not acquired as devices to turn Gauls into Romans.

Similar patterns of selective and limited imports of Mediterranean goods are exhibited by many other societies beyond the borders of the empire.[39] With the development of frontier systems that were effectively static, a broad band of territories developed – up to two hundred kilometres in width – stretching from Ireland and northern Scotland, through southern Scandinavia and central Europe to the Black Sea, within which Roman pottery, coins, wine *amphorae*, metalwork, brooches and occasionally even buildings are found. This 'buffer zone' has been interpreted both as a periphery of the Roman economy, and as one half of a zone of dynamic economic activity created by the frontier, the other half of which was within the empire.[40] Yet the products imported into different sectors of this zone vary in type and quantity and in some sectors they are virtually non-existent. Up to a point these variations may be explained by variations in depositional factors within this zone. But the contrasts between the variety and quantity of imports in different sectors of the 'buffer zone' strongly suggest that local choice played a large part in determining what uses each group made of the opportunities offered by the availability of Roman goods.

39 Fulford (1985), Pitts (1989), Fitzpatrick (1989), Parker-Pearson (1989).
40 See Hedeager (1987) for the world-systems interpretation, see also Cunliffe (1988). Whittaker (1989) and (1994, 98–131) for the frontier studies perspective. Fulford (1989) points out the empirical difficulties in establishing the existence of the interior half of the postulated frontier zone, while he then argues (1992) for a system of frontier supply that drew on a much wider hinterland. More empirical studies of the distribution of Roman goods within the empire are needed before it is possible to decide for certain just how localized the impact of frontier supply was on provincial economies.

That variable use of Roman imports fits into much wider cultural patterns characteristic of all late iron age Europe. Iron age societies shared a common repertoire of cultural forms, but each group selected and combined forms in a unique way.[41] That pattern is evident in the discontinuous distributions of writing, of coinage, and of painted pottery, while the same sense of a shared cultural vocabulary manifested in countless local variations, is conveyed by La Tène ritual, art and fortification. Local communities distinguished themselves not with distinctive elements, but with distinctive combinations produced by bricolage from a common cultural stock. Roman imports were simply added to that repertoire in the last two centuries BC, broadening the range of material culture from which each community might fashion local identities and cultural styles.[42]

III   The consumer revolution

The material culture of Roman Gaul was very different to its iron age precursors. Not only was it richer and more various but it was also ordered by a new regime of values and tastes. If material culture is viewed as a sign system, an ordered complex of symbols that conveys meaning to the knowledgeable, the contrast with the material culture of the iron age is twofold. First, the complexity and differentiation of the new sign system was much greater, with all that that implies for the acquisition of cultural competence, of discrimination and of good taste. Second, at least the central components of the regimes of value manifested in this sign system were no longer local, nor even regional, but were those of the entire Latin West. The fact that the anonymous Lingon felt the need to parade his discrimination might imply it had been learnt at a price, but his worth could have been measured by the culturally competent members of provincial societies of over half the empire.

The Roman symbol system encountered by the Gauls was itself undergoing major transformation around the turn of the millennia. Imperial expansion, economic growth, the broadening of the imperial elite, the intensification of the Roman fascination with Greek culture, and the transition to autocracy all contributed to what has been dubbed 'the Roman cultural revolution'.[43] These developments were not confined to

41 Woolf (1997).
42 See Willis (1994) for an illuminating study of imports into iron age Britain along these
    lines.
43 Wallace-Hadrill (1989b), reviewing Zanker (1988); cf. Nicolet (1988). Note that both
    the latter works concentrate their attention on Augustus, whose role as product of
    these changes receives less attention than his role as producer of them.

the city of Rome or to the principate of Augustus, nor were they co-ordinated from the centre of power. If the redefinition of Roman culture, Roman history and Roman identity was centred on the capital, it also embraced the formative period of provincial cultures, both in the East and in the West.[44] Put otherwise, as Rome became an imperial society – as opposed to a conquest state ruling over subject peoples – it acquired an imperial culture accessible to at least some members of all provincial and Italian societies. Latin literature preserves fragments of a discourse that sought to regulate and assess these experiments. Pliny's *Natural History* provides a good example. His work is preoccupied with distinguishing 'natural' uses of the earth's bounty – those in accordance with *humanitas* and *natura* – from transgressive abuses.[45] But it also included long lists of products from particular regions and systematic comparisons of particular goods, such as wine or oil, which ranked, classified and evaluated the products of each region. The material available to Pliny, and his desire to inventory it, illustrates how complex and problematic consumption had become by the middle of the first century AD.

The stages by which Gallic consumption was drawn into this revolution emerges graphically from recent studies of imports of container *amphorae* after the end of independence. The same urban excavation in Besançon again provides a convenient starting point. Around 97 per cent of the *amphorae* from the iron age phases, dated to 120–40 BC, were Dressel 1 wine *amphorae* from central Italy, the remainder being wine *amphorae* from Spain. The proportions remain much the same in the succeeding phase (40–30 BC), although now 1 per cent carried Gallic wine and 1 per cent wine from Rhodes. Change shows much more clearly in the material from 30–1 BC, in which Italian wine *amphorae* have dropped to 82 per cent, Spanish ones remained around 3 per cent, Gallic and Rhodian wine vessels remained at the same low levels, but for the first time *amphorae* containing other products make an appearance, namely olive oil (6 per cent) and fish sauces (4 per cent), both from Spain. Over the first and second centuries AD, Dressel 1 remain numerous, but the fact that this type of *amphora* was no longer being produced shows that they are residual, *amphora* fragments that attest to the scale of earlier imports and have become mixed up in later assemblages. Once these are excluded, the trends that stand out are the virtual disappearance of Italian wine from the start of the first century,

---

44 See Woolf (1994b) on developments in the East and Ward-Perkins (1970) on the importance of this period in the West.
45 Cf. Beagon (1992) and Wallace-Hadrill (1990b) with slightly different emphases to that stressed here.

the growth of first Spanish and then Gallic wines, and the continued consumption of eastern wines and fish sauces and oil from Spain. Throughout the first and second centuries eastern wine *amphorae* consistently make up around 3 per cent of the non-residual *amphorae*, and Spanish oil *amphorae* account for between 20 and 30 per cent. Where there is change is in the growing importance of Gallic wine at the expense of Spanish. Spanish wines probably never disappeared completely (unless the later examples are residual), but the vast majority of Spanish imports after the Augustan period consist of fish sauces and oil.[46]

Interpreting these statistics is not easy. To begin with, relative proportions of different kinds of *amphorae* are not easily translatable into absolute numbers or quantities of goods consumed. In addition, not all *amphorae* from the site at Besançon have been identified and provenanced, some *amphorae* carried more than one kind of produce, and barrels may have come to play an important role that their non-survival has obscured.[47] Nevertheless, the broad trends outlined above have been established with some certainty. Where iron age societies had imported wine alone, in the Roman period *amphorae* came to bring a wider range of goods, more conventionally Roman in their range, and even in wine consumption a variety of vintages were consumed in Gaul, just as they were in Italy. Besançon gives a fair idea of consumption on civilian sites in non-Mediterranean Gaul, and of the timing of the change. Recent re-examination of almost 200 *amphorae* recovered on Mont Beuvray in the nineteenth century excavations found only one Spanish wine *amphora*, only one carrying fish sauce and only four carrying Spanish wine: all the remainder were Dressel 1 *amphorae*, the stamps on which dated them to the first century BC.[48] Even such a precocious consumer of Roman goods as the Aeduan capital had little taste, then, for anything other than central Italian produce before the site was abandoned around the turn of the millennium. Much the same picture emerges for the south from the study of the *amphorae* recovered in recent excavations at St Romain-en-Gal, across the Rhône from Vienne, and from Lyon, to which material from the Rhineland has been compared.[49] The

46 From 11 per cent in the period AD 1–15, Gallic wine *amphorae* rise to nearly 43 per cent throughout the periods AD 15–65 and AD 65–120, and in the last phase, AD 120–65, they make up half the non residual *amphorae*. See Guilhot and Goy (1992, 188–212).
47 On all these difficulties, see Tchernia (1986), and on Gaul in particular, see Laubenheimer (1990).
48 Laubenheimer (1991). It is possible, of course, that these proportions reflect the relative availability of goods rather than tastes, but that seems unlikely in view of Bibracte's seemingly good access to Roman goods of other kinds and in view of the presence of Spanish produce on early military sites.
49 Dangréaux and Desbat (1987), Desbat and Martin-Kilcher (1989), Desbat and Dangréaux (1993). For other studies, see Laubenheimer (1992).

Rhône valley sites offer a series of assemblages from the period 30–20
BC to the period AD 180–220. All show the same roughly constant level
of consumption of oil and fish sauces as Besançon. Equally clear is the
dramatic rise in the proportion of Gallic wine *amphorae*, from virtually
none in 30–20 BC to dominating the market by the end of the first
century AD, preceded by a brief period in the early first century when
Spanish wine *amphorae* increase as a proportion of the total while Italian ones decline in relative terms. Italian wines perhaps survived longer
in the south, while consumption of oil and fish sauces was a little
greater and began earlier in the military camps of the Rhineland, but
the same broad trends are visible. Across Gaul the transition from a
single imported *amphora* type to the wider range that expresses a greater
variety of products and provenances, is consistently dated to the period
between 30 and 1 BC. Good contexts from the preceding twenty years
are scarce, and it may be that fish sauces appear a little later than oil,
and eastern wines a little earlier, but the relative rapidity of the change
in taste is evident.[50]

The picture given by *amphorae* is partial, but even so implies wide
changes in lifestyle. Olive oil was used not only for cooking – supple-
menting animal fat and as a basic ingredient in many Roman recipes –
but also for lighting as the basic fuel for the cheap terracotta lamps that
were ubiquitous in the Roman world, and it was an essential accom-
paniment of Roman bathing.[51] Fish sauces provided a condiment and a
savoury ingredient of various dishes. The changes in wine consumption
are even more revealing. One component of these changes is the rise of
provincial productions, first in Spain and then in Gaul itself. But, just
as in the case of the early modern and modern 'consumer revolution',
changes in production were interdependent with changes in demand.

Iron age consumption of wine was (at least in Roman terms) indis-
criminate. Virtually all wine originated in central Italy and was of much
the same quality. Diodorus and Athenaeus, both of whose accounts
probably derive in these passages from Poseidonius' account written in
the early last century BC, describe wine consumption as restricted to
Gallic elites, whose social subordinates drank locally produced beer.[52]
That picture is certainly an oversimplification for some areas, where a
genuine mass consumption of wine, perhaps disbursed by elite members,
existed.[53] But the social distinction between wine and beer drinking is
probably broadly correct. The appearance of eastern wines, however,
indicates the adoption of a new regime in which all wines were not

50 Hesnard (1990).   51 See Le Gall (1983) for a short discussion.
52 Diodorus 5.26, Athenaeus 4.152c.   53 Tchernia (1983).

equal and in which wine itself offered a medium of social differentiation. The fourteenth book of Pliny's *Natural History* is largely concerned
with classifying wines by age, flavour and provenance. That system
corresponds in many respects to our own, with local *vins ordinaires*, a
series of *grands crus* and speciality wines. Gaul produced some of the
latter two categories as well as quantities of the former. Pliny describes
the distinctive taste and qualities of several wines grown around Vienne;
he writes that they were highly rated locally and within Gaul, like those
of Béziers, but not abroad.[54] Marseille had produced wine for centuries, and in the early empire it became famous for a sweet, strong wine
which was produced in only small quantities and priced as highly as
Falernian, one of the great Italian vintages.[55] Gallic imports of eastern
wines, some of the most highly praised vintages of the Roman world,
illustrate that some Gauls too had become discriminating in their choice
of wines. Most wine drunk was produced locally, of course, and distributions of different categories of Gallic *amphorae* make it possible to
distinguish an intermediate group of productions with regional markets
– the Languedoc, say, but not Provence. But the overall pattern of
consumption is thoroughly Roman. It is probable that similar patterns
will emerge for other products. Narbonensis, for example, imported
Baetican oil – reckoned among the best varieties by Pliny – even after
local olive oil production is well attested.[56] Container *amphorae* reveal
two major features of the transformation of consumption patterns in
Gaul. The first is the replacement of a series of local regimes of value
with those of the new imperial culture of consumption. The second
is the rhythm of change. A rapid formative period is evident in which
tastes, values and consumption changed utterly, but it took some time
for local production to supply these new tastes, allowing Italian and Spanish wines brief export booms.[57] The initial change of taste was sudden
enough, however, to justify the term 'consumer revolution'.

IV   The consumer revolution in ceramics

Wine and oil were not confined to the elites of the Roman world, but
their relative expense makes them poor guides to how far down the
social or economic scale new styles of consumption spread. A more
sensitive indicator for those purposes is pottery, used by virtually every
sector of Roman societies for the preparation, storage and serving of

54 Pliny *NH* 14.18, 26, 57, 67.
55 Bertucchi (1992). See Laubenheimer (1990, 77–110) for Gallic production in more
    detail, building on Laubenheimer (1985).
56 Brun (1986).   57 Woolf (1992b) for the general pattern.

food. The same general features of the Roman consumer revolution can be noted through this medium: first the ceramics of Roman Gaul were much more differentiated than those of the iron age, and second new tastes in ceramics appeared equally suddenly, with a similar time lag before they could be wholly satisfied from local production.

Ceramics are capable of enormous differentiation. Some of these differences derived from function – some vessels were designed for various kinds of cooking, like the red Pompeian ware used to bake bread; others, like *amphorae* and *dolia*, were produced for the transport and storage of goods; tablewares were suited to particular styles of serving food and drink; and Gallo-Roman kilns also produced tile and brick for various kinds of construction, roofs, hypocausts, bathhouses, hearths and so forth. Other differences derived from the technologies of production – most obviously potters' wheels of different speeds and kilns firing at higher or lower temperatures, but also the use of slips and glazes, and the selection and preparation of clays. Finally, variation was generated by a wide range of different decorative techniques. All but the very poorest had access to some kind of pottery, and those who could expressed their social position and tastes through selection within the variety of ceramics available. Pottery thus makes manifest a series of social categories and claims about status that are inaccessible through most other sources.[58]

Iron age ceramics conformed to the general pattern of late La Tène culture, with local variations on a common technological and cultural repertoire. Perhaps the best indication of what might be achieved were tall slender pedestal jars, produced on a wheel in a thin, hard ceramic. In some areas, these vessels were decorated with bold multi-colour designs, commonly geometric or zoomorphic patterns. Alongside the pedestal jars, the most popular forms were tall ovoid storage jars and broad open conical bowls. A fair proportion of pottery, however, was not produced on the wheel, characteristically being thick and unfinished with rough inclusions. Some wares were probably used for cooking and storage, while the pedestal jars and bowls seem designed for serving food and are often included in funerary deposits.[59] This ceramic tradition was common to much of late iron age Europe, although regional variants existed such as the *jatte d'Aulnat* produced in the

58 See Miller (1985) for a sophisticated ethno-archaeological study of ceramics used in this way; cf. Hodder (1982). The best study of this kind conducted on Gallic material is Bats (1988b) (on Olbia). Some of these ideas are used by Okun (1989a) and (1989b).
59 No good synoptic work on late La Tène pottery exists, and the best studies are generally in the reports of well excavated sites. Vaginay and Guichard (1988) provide some of the best recent analysis in the report of excavation at Feurs in the Forez.

Auvergne or the *vase de Besançon*. A greater range of forms and decorations was employed in the south, where Iberian traditions were influential in the Languedoc and south of the Garonne, and Massaliot models were imitated east of the Rhône. An additional influence has already been noted: Campanian ware was exported into the region, as it was in smaller quantities up the Rhône-Saône corridor, and in the south attempts were made to produce it locally.

Mediterranean wares differed from those of temperate Europe in form, decoration and in the technology which produced them.[60] Many of the differences in form reflected differences in the ways food was prepared and consumed. Baking dishes and mortars, for example, were used in styles of cooking which were unknown north of the Alps, and tableware included individual place settings and plates, reflecting the manners of the *cena* and the *symposium*. Decoratively, wares like Campanian ware and its eastern analogues were the latest representatives of a tradition of glossy wares that had been developing for centuries from Greek origins. By the second and first centuries BC, the finest Mediterranean tableware was no longer ceramic but gold and silver plate. As a result the influence of metalwork is evident in all Hellenistic finewares: the colours, black followed by red; the glossy finishes; the moulding of wares such as Megarian bowls, which imitated embossed and engraved designs; and probably many of the forms.[61] In terms of technology, Mediterranean wares were virtually all produced on the fast wheel and fired at high temperatures in large kilns that allowed a variety of kinds of ventilation to produce various colours of finished product. Mediterranean wares were generally harder, finer and had none of the rough inclusions of iron age products. The desire to imitate plate had also produced a number of minor technological refinements including the use of slips, moulds and later appliqué.

Roman styles of tableware were not left untouched by the transformation of imperial culture at the end of the last century BC. For the last two centuries of the Republic, Campanian ware had been ubiquitous in the western Mediterranean. That ware is better characterized as a certain style than as a particular production, since it was produced in a large number of centres, even if trends were set by the mass productions of first Campania, then of Etruria and Cales just north of Naples. This style consisted of black gloss plates and bowls, usually used alongside thin-walled goblets. At some point soon after 50 BC, however, this

60 For introductions to Hellenistic wares, see Lévêque and Morel (1981), (1987) and, briefly, Hayes (1991).
61 Vickers (1986) for studies of the history of this relationship, better studied in relation to Greek than Roman ceramics.

style was very rapidly replaced by a taste for Arretine ware, the first in a series of red-gloss tablewares collectively termed *terra sigillata*. Many of the forms were similar to those of Campanian ware, and in most respects Arretine was simply the latest product of the same tradition. The details of the change are obscure. The technical advances that enabled the production of a red gloss and also of moulded bowls derived from eastern Mediterranean precedents, but whether the change should be seen as the result of migrations of potters, of a new style of pottery production, as an aspect of general imitation of eastern styles, or as an echo of a contemporaneous shift in taste from silver to gold plate remains controversial.[62] At all events, the change was rapid and widespread, and the area that adopted the new style was greater than that for any other production in the ancient world. *Sigillata* outcompeted its predecessors not only throughout the Mediterranean world (setting the style for new eastern *sigillata* wares as well as ousting Campanian wares), but also throughout Rome's new European empire.

Within Gaul, Arretine ware was distributed much more widely than Campanian ware. Finds of Campanian ware are concentrated in Mediterranean Gaul, and in lesser quantities through the Carcassone Gap into southern Aquitaine and up the Rhône valley to Burgundy.[63] Arretine occurs in all these areas, but also north of the Massif Central in western France, on the Loire, in the Paris Basin and especially in the north east.[64] The sites where it occurs are not confined to those where Roman troops were based,[65] although once garrisons became based on the Rhine they provided important markets for *terra sigillata*. In Italy, Arretine ware is present in the countryside as well as in the cities, and at lower status sites as well as at *villae*, a point that confirms its relatively low value and wide social dissemination as a poor man's luxury. It does not follow that its value was immediately the same for Gauls as it was for Italians. In some parts of Gaul, notably the west and north, Arretine ware is rare, relative to later *sigillata* productions.[66] Nevertheless, the rapidity of the spread of a taste for ceramic made in that style is striking.

A precise chronology for this change is again offered by Besançon.[67] Campanian wares are the only non-local ceramics until the period 60–40 BC when a few other Italian products appear, but the major change

---

62 See Pucci (1973), (1981a) for a new organization of production; Goudineau (1981) for technical aspects; Vickers (1994) for imitation of gold; Wells (1992) for a critical overview.
63 See Nash (1978a, 113), Collis (1984, 144) and Morel (1985, 181) for maps.
64 See Hofman (1976, 43–5) for maps, revised in Hofman (1992).
65 Wightman (1977), *pace* Ritterling (1906).   66 See Marsh (1981) for figures.
67 Guilhot and Goy (1992).

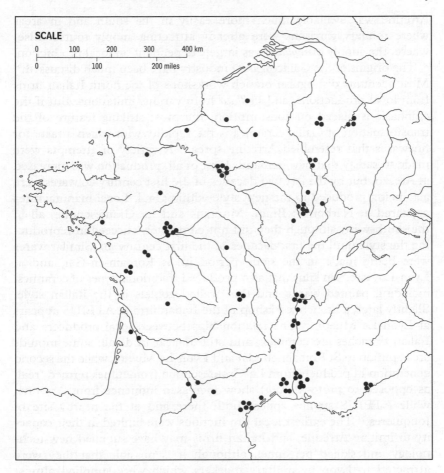

Fig. 7.2   Arretine ware in Gaul

occurs in the period 30–1 BC when *sigillata* appears, along with imitations of *sigillata*, thin-walled cups and mortars. In the material from AD 1–15, *sigillata* makes up 13 per cent of the total ceramic, excluding *amphorae*, and a locally produced imitation, *terra nigra*, appears alongside Italian imports. The ceramics from this site add to a general impression that, even if much early Arretine ware in Gaul was brought by or for Roman garrisons, it rapidly spread to civilian sites. But in this case the Besançon pottery represents a more markedly regional pattern. A taste for the kind of pottery represented by Arretine ware spread throughout Gaul from about 30 BC onwards, but the actual ceramics used to satisfy that taste varied enormously from one region to another.

Arretine was available much more easily in the south and in areas where military garrisons were already attracting supply routes. Elsewhere, the supply of *sigillata* was largely dependent on local production.

The origins of the Gallic *sigillata* industry have been much discussed.[68] Most accounts distinguish branch workshops of the north Italian firms from local productions, and *sigillata* from various imitations. But if the emphasis is placed on consumption, the most striking feature of the transformation of Gallic ceramics is the rapidity with which a taste for finewares that resembled Arretine spread. A variety of attempts were made to satisfy that new demand. First of all, production was increased at Arezzo, but by the last two decades of the first century BC wares were also being produced in the new style within Gaul. Local manufactures appeared at Narbonne, Bram, Montans and La Graufesenque, all in the south-west, although they did not completely succeed in reproducing the style until the first decades of the first century AD. Similar wares were being made in the same period in St Romain-en-Gal, and at Lyon-Loyasse,[69] in kilns that also produced traditional types of ceramics, including painted wares, and thin walled goblets in the Italian style. Slightly later, a branch workshop of the Italian firm of ATEIUS appears at Lyon-La Muette.[70] The relationships between local producers and Italian branches are complex, and still unclear in detail: some moulds are common to St Romain-en-Gal and Lyon-La Muette, while the second generation of products from La Graufesenque (sometimes termed 'real' as opposed to proto-*sigillata*) show increased influence from Arretine, while ATEIUS stamps appear both there and at the nearby site of Jonquières.[71] The earliest local productions were limited in their capacity to imitate Arretine, and Italian firms may have supplied new technology and skilled personnel, although it is possible that they were attracted to Lyon by military markets which were supplied almost entirely from there, and which may not have been satisfied with Gallic 'proto-*sigillata*'.

Whatever the complexities of the organization of the industry, as far as consumption is concerned it is the new taste that is significant. Other wares were also produced around the turn of the millenia with this taste in mind. Imitations of *sigillata* appear in Switzerland as soon as imported Arretine arrived, in the last two decades of the first

---

68 See Bémont and Jacob (1986) for the most recent work, with Guéry (1990) and Wells (1992).
69 See Vernhet (1986), Passelac (1986) on the earliest southern Gallic productions; Desbat and Savay-Guerraz (1986) for St Romain-en-Gal, Goudineau (1981, 126–7) for Lyon-Loyasse.
70 Vertet (1986).   71 Hoffman and Vernhert (1992).

century BC.[72] In Belgica and the Rhineland, a series of wares termed Gallo-Belgic (*terra rubra* and *terra nigra*) were produced from about 30 BC. These developed from late La Tène traditions, adding some forms from *sigillata* and a few techniques such as potters' stamps and, in the case of *terra rubra*, oxidizing firing that produced a red colour.[73] Similar wares were produced in central France and elsewhere, typically appearing at the same moment as the first imports of Arretine, and lasting only until local *sigillata* industries were set up in each area. Just as in the case of wine, then, the new taste spread much more rapidly than the capacity of Italian or even south Gaulish producers to satisfy it.

The uses for which these new wares were designed is partly implicit in their forms. Plates, goblets and *mortaria* illustrate the spread of Roman styles of preparing and serving food throughout the Gallic provinces. Equally the spread of Pompeian red ware signals a shift from the consumption of grain through porridge to its consumption as bread. Of course, these wares might also be used for functions for which they were not designed, culinary or other. One such secondary use was as grave goods in the richly furnished burials of the Augustan and Tiberian elite. At Fléré-la-Rivière, for example, the body was accompanied by weapons and by an elaborate bronze drinking service, but the burial chamber also contained a selection of ceramic table ware, plausibly interpreted as the equipment for a banquet in the after world for which food and *amphorae* of wine were also supplied. The vessels included only a few pieces of *sigillata*, but a quantity of *terra nigra*. The assemblage seems typical of aristocratic burials of the Berry.[74] In many respects – the underground chamber, the *amphorae*, the feasting equipment and food, for example – rich burials of this kind were simply a continuation of a tradition now well attested for the late La Tène over much of France and neighbouring regions. Examples include the Welwyn group from south-east England and Clémency in modern Luxembourg.[75] But while the ceramics from the burial at Clémency consisted of wheel spun tall ovoid jars and bowls, along with coarser cooking wares, at Fléré-la-Rivière the finewares were either imports or imitations which in decoration and form (plates, for example) resembled *sigillata*.

This usage is revealing for a number of reasons. First, the presence of Roman-style ceramic tableware in burials like the very early imperial aristocratic tombs of the Berry represents the incorporation of Roman-style goods into a very un-Roman context. Richly furnished burials in

72 Paunier (1986).
73 On these wares, see Greene (1979, 106–27) and Rigby (1973). Tuffreau-Libre (1992, 39–42, 55–74) provides a clear introduction to these developments.
74 Ferdière and Villard (1993).   75 Stead (1967), Metzler *et al.* (1991).

underground chambers covered by *tumuli* did not exhibit the same consciousness of Roman propriety as the monument of the Lingon would have done. Second, the presence of these wares in aristocratic graves shows in Gaul that they were not (yet) simply poor man's luxuries. *Sigillata* was worthy of a Gallic noble in precisely the same period as plate tableware was the preferred usage of Roman aristocrats and as *sigillata* was used in great quantities by those of much lower status in Italy and in Rhineland garrisons like Haltern. Finally, the prominence of Roman style wares in funerals and in feasting illustrates the kind of contexts in which it was important to possess Roman tableware. Both contexts were public ones, occasions for display equivalent to the preconquest feasts and funerals described by classical observers.

The availability of *sigillata,* and of other imported wares like thin walled goblets, varied considerably from one region to another, mainly as a function of distance from areas into which it was imported in bulk, such as zones where Roman troops were stationed in numbers or from areas like the Rhône valley or southern Gaul where it was produced. The high value accorded *sigillata* in the rich burials of Berry at the turn of the millennium is one such indicator. It took even longer to penetrate parts of Belgica. A burial outside a rich farmhouse at Trinquies around AD 70 contained a thirteen-piece service of *sigillata,* presumably still a status indicator.[76] The desire in much of the centre and the north to possess this ware in preference to Gallo-Belgic ceramic and similar imitative wares may be part of the reason for the extraordinary success of the productions at La Graufesenque that begin exporting in bulk throughout Gaul in the middle of the first century AD, but the costs of transport must account for its continued rarity in the north. As mass productions and smaller local productions developed, the gap between the significance of *sigillata* for Italians and soldiers and its value for Gauls must have narrowed. The reduction of this gradient was complete in Narbonensis by the middle of the century, but the time lag for the north may have been as much as two generations.

During the formative period of Gallo-Roman culture, the significance of imported *sigillata* and *sigillata*-style ceramics is patent. The rich could signify their eminence through use of these ceramics in more or less public contexts, both Roman-style *cenae,* to which their near peers were invited, and funerals, at which a greater proportion of the population was plausibly present. But such occasions might signify not only wealth but an adherence to a new, Roman, set of manners. The attractions of

76 Bayard (1993).

Roman culture, whether used to impress the conquerors or to identify oneself with them in the eyes of one's rivals, provides an explanation for the rapidity of this change of taste. What Roman observers would have made of these displays is, of course, unknowable. It would have been possible to regard this absurd over-valuation of ordinary tableware as a barbarous use of civilized things, analogous to the pre-conquest Gauls' consumption of Italian wine, but it may also have seemed a laudable if perhaps unintentionally comic aspiration to *humanitas*.

Sigillata and its imitations were not the only ceramics in use in Gaul, and their significance was formed in contra-distinction to that of other tablewares. At Besançon, alongside the imported tablewares, and the locally produced wares that imitated them, the majority of the ceramic resembled late La Tène wares until the middle of the first century AD. Throughout Gaul, the transformation of ceramic assemblages at the very end of the last century BC is marked not by a new uniform style, but by increased diversity of forms, fabrics, decorations and methods of construction. Late La Tène tradition wares, including a few non-wheel turned productions, continued to be made and used in the north at least until the late first century AD. Traditional styles continued longer in forms used to prepare food, even when they were supplemented by specialized vessels such as mortars.[77] The vessels that changed the most, and most rapidly, were those used in formal public contexts. Painted wares, for example, were among the earliest late La Tène ceramics to disappear. Ceramic was already a differentiated medium in the late iron age, and its transformation resulted in a more differentiated medium as well as in the replacement of some varieties by Roman-style alternatives. That process stands as a paradigm for what happened to entire Gallic cultural systems during the formative period of Gallo-Roman civilization.

V   Mass consumption and regional traditions

The notion of a formative period is a difficult one, easily confused with a period deemed 'classic' by successive generations, ancient or modern. What is meant here by the term is simply a period of rapid change in which a new cultural matrix was laid down, a general structure within which change continued to occur, if at a more gradual pace. Iron age

77 Okun (1989b), although the suggestion that this distinction relates to gender roles is speculative.

cultures of Gaul were rapidly remodelled and drawn into an empire-wide system of structured differences, but that system itself changed gradually over the early imperial period. Ceramics once again are a sensitive indicator to the evolution of this system after the formative period, as the new styles came to lose their significance as a cultural marker and become identified more with social status and eminence. Unlike the changes of the formative period, however, these later developments took place at a regional scale and gave rise to a new geographical diversification of culture.

Two trends stand out in ceramics, first the replacement in the course of the first century AD of the remaining late La Tène tradition wares by new varieties of ceramics, and second, the increasingly wider dispersal of the production and consumption of *terra sigillata*, that is to say locally produced wares which were accepted by Gallo-Romans as authentic enough to exclude effective competition by *sigillata* from other regions. The replacement of late La Tène tradition ceramics was complete in most areas by the last quarter of the first century AD.[78] This is a considerable simplification, as different traditional wares disappeared in each area at slightly different times, and some wares, such as those not manufactured on a wheel or those for which Gallo-Belgic wares and *sigillata* were substituted, disappeared very rapidly. In general terms, however, by the end of the first century AD, about 60 per cent of most ceramic site assemblages comprise new 'common wares' produced locally. Most were hard, thin-walled wares with a smooth fabric often beige or grey in colour, and were produced with a technology that included the fast wheel and large kilns that fired evenly and at high temperatures. Technically, then, they show the influence of Roman ceramics. Many were made in potters' villages where a dozen or so kilns were used at the same time, but others were produced in towns or on large farms. Some 500 workshops are presently known within Gaul, operating on a variety of scales. Stylistically, in terms of both forms and decoration, they drew freely on both Mediterranean and La Tène traditions. There are also marked inter-regional variations. In central and eastern Gaul, for example, micaceous wares are very common, while in parts of the north a smooth grey fabric is more characteristic. The range of forms also varies between regions, often preserving the odd late La Tène style form, but also characterized by local inventions. As far as can be seen, the regions served by each workshop seem to have become smaller in the course of the second century. Part of the explanation must be in the high costs of overland transport, but those were a

---

78 See Tuffreau-Libre (1992, 75–94) for what follows.

constant in all periods. More significant was the increasingly wide-spread availability of the expertise and equipment needed to produce high quality ceramics.

It is against the background of these developments that the continued spread of *sigillata* production needs to be set. The dissemination of technical expertise was instrumental in this case too, since after Lyon-La Muette there are no further 'branch workshops', and all subsequent production of *sigillata* in Gaul was the work of local potters, not so much out-competing Gallo-Belgic wares, other imitations and imports as learning to satisfy the same taste better themselves. Recent work has made clear that the mass productions of La Graufesenque, Lezoux and north eastern centres like Rheinzabern were simply the most successful of more than fifty local *sigillata* productions.[79] The beginning of these productions can be traced from southern Gaul to central Gaul – Poitou as well as the Auvergne – by the middle of the first century AD, northwards and eastwards by the end of the century, and into the Rhineland before AD 150. No production centres are yet known south of the Garonne, east of the Rhône or in Brittany or the Paris basin, but most other areas had some local productions.

Most Gallic *sigillata* producers supplied only local consumption, but a small number managed for a short time to sustain extraordinary mass-productions which were very widely distributed. La Graufesenque in the second half of the first century AD, Les Martres-de-Veyre at the beginning of the second, Lezoux in the mid-second century and some north-eastern centres a little later are the best known examples. All of these centres had produced a little *sigillata* for some time before their periods of mass production, and they usually continued to produce a little for some time afterwards. Their successive distributions reach smaller and smaller areas and all are skewed northwards, the production centres being far to the south of the centres of the distribution.[80] There has been fierce debate about the significance of these patterns. The suggestion that these centres were in some sense competing in a highly integrated 'world market' in *sigillata* now seems less likely to be correct.[81] An integrated market in commodities with such a low value per unit of weight seems unlikely in view of the costs of ancient

---

79 Bémont and Jacob (1986).   80 King (1981).
81 See Pucci (1981a) for a recent restatement of this as a component of the thesis that provincial competition contributed to a crisis in Italian agriculture in the first century AD, for critiques of which see Purcell (1985), Tchernia (1986), Patterson (1987). This thesis can be traced back to Rostovtzeff (1926) and, in respect of *terra sigillata*, has been criticized by Finley (1985, 34 and 137), Goudineau (1974) and Marsh (1981, 206–12). The view taken here owes much to all these works.

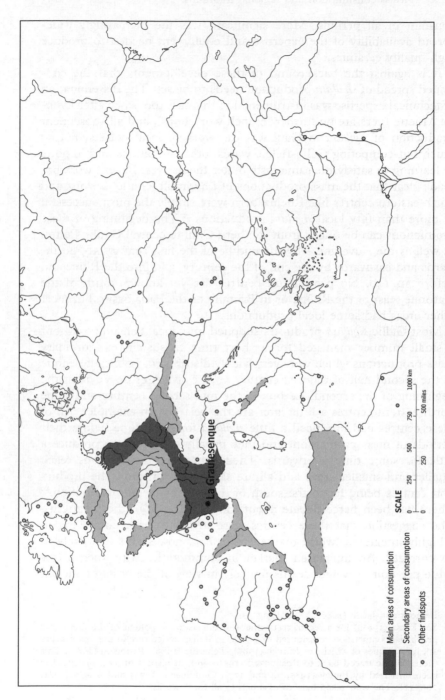

SCALE

0	250	500	750	1000 km
0	250	500	750 miles

● La Graufesenque

■ Main areas of consumption

▨ Secondary areas of consumption

○ Other findspots

Fig. 7.3 Distribution of *terra sigillata* produced at La Graufesenque

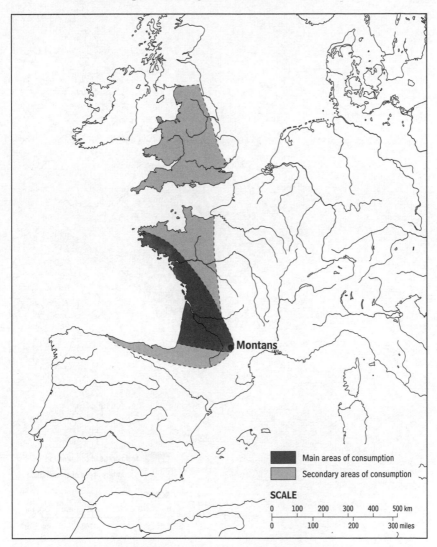

Fig. 7.4 Distribution of *terra sigillata* produced at Montans

overland transport. It has in any case been shown that new centres did
not emerge by capturing market share from their predecessors. A study
of the supply of *sigillata* to London and other centres suggests that peaks
of production did not respond to demand among *distant* consumers.[82]

82 Marsh (1981).

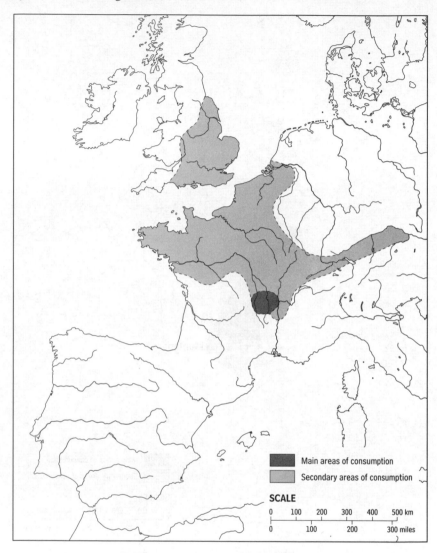

Fig. 7.5   Distribution of *terra sigillata* produced in central Gaul

Arretine production was already in decline before the rise of south Gallic *sigillata* and the latter before the rise of central Gallic productions.[83] Quite simply, the total amount of *sigillata* produced in Gaul varied dramatically from one decade to another.

83 Goudineau (1981), Marsh (1981).

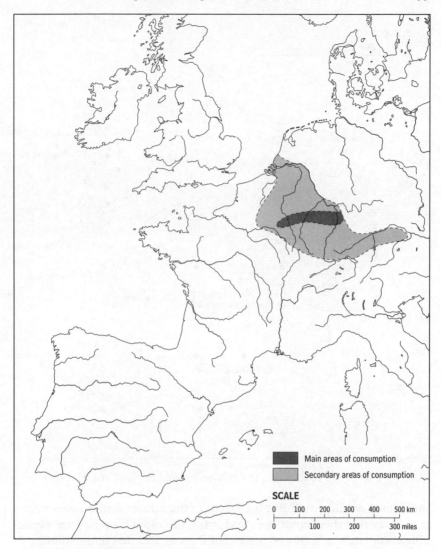

Fig. 7.6 Distribution of *terra sigillata* produced in eastern Gaul

The failure of production and demand to co-vary might be explained in two ways. One possibility is that an additional enabling factor was needed in order for the mass producers to exploit a distant market. Suitable candidates would be a temporary subsidy on either transport costs or production costs. Both have been suggested, and either or both may have played some part in giving one centre an advantage over its

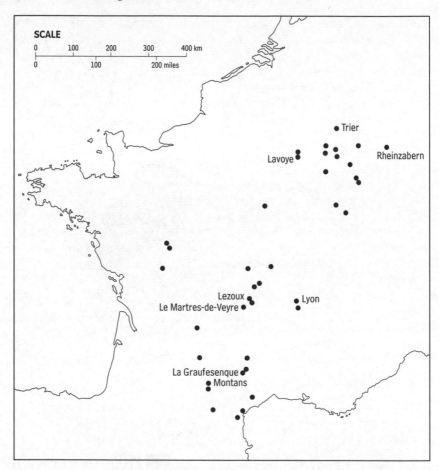

Fig. 7.7   Production sites of *terra sigillata* in Gaul and Germany

immediate neighbours.[84] But the extent of the earliest distributions makes it unlikely that their rapid rises and still more rapid collapses are explicable completely in terms of the establishment and de-commissioning of military supply routes, and it is difficult to imagine what could cause the costs of either labour or materials to vary so widely in pre-industrial conditions. Transport costs would always favour production for local markets, and the long term trend to smaller and smaller distributions of

84 Middleton (1983) argues that military supply routes gave some production centres a significant advantage over others. Reduced costs of production would have involved either cheaper labour (unlikely in an economy where most potters were also involved in agriculture), wood, water or clay. Picon and Vertet (1970) and Bet and Vertet (1986) suggest superior clay sources as a reason for Lezoux's success.

sigillata and other ceramics alike, probably reflects an increased localization of production, much as it does for wine. The Gallic sequence is in this respect wholly typical of developments in the production of *sigillata* elsewhere in the empire.[85]

The second possibility is that the wide distributions of the mass productions in fact reflect secondary markets, and that the main demand was always local. In that case, changes in local patterns of consumption would have an indirect effect on supply to distant secondary markets. This seems a much more satisfactory solution. It remains to establish what changes in local demand might account for sudden expansions in the scale of production. The most likely hypothesis is that the taste for *sigillata* had, in these regions, become generalized within local societies, through emulation of the local elites. This was certainly the case in the south, where *sigillata* is abundant, and may have been true elsewhere. With a large local demand, production might increase and be able to supply in addition the secondary markets represented by the northerly skewed distributions, in other words, markets in areas of Gaul where *sigillata* remained a rare and valued indicator of social eminence and cultural accomplishment. Once local markets were saturated with *sigillata*, however, production would have collapsed, whether or not local production of similar wares had been established in the former secondary markets. That cycle may have been repeated several times in the Gallic provinces.

The fragmentary and incomplete aspect of these processes reveals a good deal about the nature of these cultural changes. In several regions of Gaul it seems that *terra sigillata* was never produced locally despite the high costs of land transport. It seems unlikely, given the widespread availability of the requisite technology by the middle of the second century, that local production would have been impossible. The most likely explanation may be that in these areas the taste for *sigillata* was never generalized. It does not follow that regions like Aquitaine were not susceptible to Roman culture: in other respects, architecture or plastic art, for example, it might be considered precocious. Elsewhere, for example the north east, *sigillata* seems not only a generalized taste but even a popular (as opposed to an elite) one.[86] The designs become

---

85 On Spain: Mayet (1984); on Africa: Tortorella (1987) with Hayes (1972), (1980); on Italian production after Arezzo: Pucci (1981b) and the general discussion in Woolf (1992b).

86 The value of *sigillata* in the provinces is currently a matter of debate. Mayet (1984, 238–42) regards Spanish *sigillata* as 'la vaisselle de table courante des classes aisées et une vaisselle exceptionelle pour les moins favorisés' (presumably throughout the period of its use). Curk (1990) argues that it was available to all social strata in the former Yugoslavia, and Millett (1990a, 123–6) shows it was ubiquitous in southern

simpler and the decoration less elaborate, and hence less costly to produce and purchase. Perhaps where mass consumption of *sigillata* had occurred as successive groups imitated the behaviour of local elites, those elites may themselves have abandoned a material culture that had become symbolically debased through its appropriation by their social inferiors. Many members of the Gallo-Roman elite will in any case already have abandoned *sigillata* by the late second century in favour of the gold and silver plate tableware used by their peers in Italy.[87] Such cyclical trends in taste are well attested elsewhere.[88] What they illustrate in Roman Gaul, however, is the breakdown of a consensus of taste. *Sigillata* had simply become a part of the local repertoires of the numerous Gallo-Roman potteries, responding like other wares to local dynamics of tastes and styles.

The significance of these developments for changing patterns of consumption in Gaul is enormous. The consensus of taste created within the formative period stands out in contrast to the diversity that both preceded and followed it. Had *sigillata* simply become cheaply available everywhere, and had retained more of a unity of style, this might have suggested a slow spread of Roman tastes and values throughout Gallo-Roman society. Certainly, like inscribed tombstones or roof tiles, ceramic in this tradition became more and more widely available through the second century, perhaps bringing with it changes in diet and manners, and iron age patterns had certainly been replaced more thoroughly by the mid-second century than they had by the mid-first in this sphere. Yet the incompleteness of the process suggests that these later changes were driven by something other than the desire for a quintessentially *Roman* good that had motivated the first elite consumers of *sigillata*. Because this later imitation was accompanied by regionalization, it makes better sense to see the process in terms of local cultural

Britain. In Italy, it seems agreed that Arretine was not a prerogative of the wealthy and that the Italian *sigillata* that succeeded it was designed for an even more lowly clientèle; see Goudineau (1974). Part of the difficulty in deciding who used *sigillata* may derive from attempts to divide consumers into rich (with luxuries) and poor (with coarseware). In fact, there was probably a spectrum of statuses, economic as well as social, in most parts of the empire. Nothing excludes the possibility that the same ware might serve as an everyday table service for one group and as a poor man's luxury for another. Those *sigillatae* which include both decorated and plain vessels may represent some differentiation between intended consumers.

87 See Martin-Kilcher (1989) on the spread of plate in Gaul. The high value of plate and the ease with which it may be recycled naturally leads to its under-representation in archaeological contexts, except in periods in which either hoarding or votive deposits are common.

88 Cf. Miller (1982) for the cycle. But for a less deterministic approach to these processes, see also Kopytoff's (1986) notion of a cultural biography, which charts the changing significances and values of an object in the course of its lifetime.

dynamics. The ceramics of the Gallic masses took the form they did because various forms, decors, eating habits and so forth evoked the lifestyle of the local elites, rather than of Romans. Gallo-Romans may not have seen the difference, of course. By the second century AD, Gallic elite members *were* Romans, and any imitation of their manners by their subordinates was perfectly understandable in Roman terms.

The consumption of the Gallo-Roman elites was not immune to growing regionalism. The diversity of local traditions of tomb building and of the design of the elaborate rural residences termed *villae* has already been discussed. Wall paintings provide yet another example, one recently documented in considerable detail.[89] The first Pompeian style is hardly present in Gaul, examples being known only at Glanum, Marseille and perhaps Lattes. Between 50 and 30 BC wall painting (now of the second style) becomes much more common in the south, and from the early first century AD the third style appears, beginning in the Rhône valley within a decade of its invention in central Italy. By the middle of the century, the third style had spread throughout southern Gaul, Burgundy, Aquitaine and into the north. Only the north-west has so far produced no examples. Dating by Pompeian styles is a little imprecise. It is unclear, for example, how rapidly tastes did change and how far some patrons and artists were ahead of or behind the times. But the rough chronology and the sequence of regions affected conforms to the general patterns of cultural change noted in other media. Most interesting is the sequel to the spread of Italian styles throughout Gaul.[90] At Pompeii, the final, fourth, style appears in the third quarter of the first century AD, but with the exception of Narbonne, no Gallic site has produced examples of these developments. Instead, the wall paintings created in Gaul from the second half of the first century are developments of some elements of the third style, and within this neo-third style regional schools rapidly developed.

The re-emergence of regional traditions within Gallo-Roman civilization is paradoxical. On the one hand, it makes clear the very great extent to which Roman tastes and values had been assimilated. Creative variation within a tradition requires a much greater cultural competence than slavish imitation. On the other hand, it makes plain that the primary use of Roman-style material culture was no longer to demonstrate cultural competence to the representatives of a still alien ruling power. Roman goods had probably served from an early date as a means by

89 See Barbet (1987) for this outline. The pace of research is rapid, however, and may be followed in the Actes of the seminars regularly held by the Association française pour la peinture murale antique.
90 Eristov (1987).

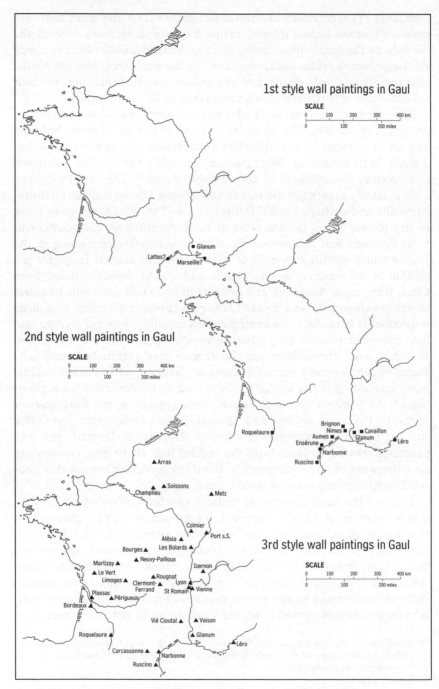

Fig. 7.8   1st, 2nd and 3rd style wall paintings in Gaul

which members of the new Gallo-Roman aristocracies might establish
their power and status before their local subordinates. Before the end of
the first century AD that seems to have become their prime significance.
Gauls were now Romans, and had less to prove, fear or gain once the
crises of the formative period were over. Material culture became once
again, as it had been in the iron age, a means of realizing local goals,
whether that meant competition with one's peers, imitation of one's
betters, or cowing one's inferiors. The nature of these local traditions
had been irrevocably transformed, of course. If the cultures of Roman
Gaul were once again regional, they were also provincial, a part of a
greater imperially structured civilization.

8   Keeping faith?

I   Gallic gods, Roman rites

Did any place remain where Gallo-Romans remained Gauls above all?
Put otherwise, did some form of Celtic or Gallic identity persist beneath a public veneer of Romanized manners and culture, perhaps in
the remoter parts of the country, or in the depths of forests or in mountain valleys? The argument of this book has so far made the opposite
case. Roman and Gallic identities *were* opposed during an early – but
brief – formative period; thereafter that opposition was supplanted by
more familiar Roman contrasts, between rich and poor, educated and
uneducated, military and civilian and so forth. Cultural distinctions
echoed these social changes, so that the construction of theatres and
temples or the possession of mosaics and consumption of fish-sauce
rapidly came to signify good taste and social eminence, rather than
adherence to a set of cultural norms associated first and foremost with
alien conquerors. The villas of Brittany and the material culture of the
Vosges villages seem to offer little support for the idea of islands of
residual 'Celticism' in a Gallo-Roman sea. The spread of Roman style,
right down to the most basic tableware, shows that even the poorest
had learned to be impoverished in a Roman manner.

Historians who have taken a different line have most often based
their case on Gallo-Roman religion. It is easy to see why this has been
the case. To begin with, the gods of the Gallo-Romans included deities
with names – Sucellus and Epona, Nehalennia and Rosmerta – largely
unknown elsewhere in the empire. Their iconography is also often
unfamiliar. One deity for instance, perhaps Sucellus,[1] is usually represented holding a mallet in one hand, a small jar in the other and wearing
the *sagum* (a Gallic cloak). Some symbols – such as the wheel, the
ram-headed serpent or the god with a torc (a gold neck ring) who sits
cross-legged, crowned with the antlers of a stag – appear on both

---

1 Boucher (1988). The deity is often syncretized in the south with Silvanus.

proto-historic and early Gallo-Roman art.[2] Even classical deities appear
with unfamiliar epithets, for example Mercurius Dumias, the chief god
of the Arverni, who was worshipped in a temple on the Puy-de-Dôme,
or Hercules Magusanus, popular on the lower Rhine among the Batavi,
the Tongri and also soldiers serving locally.[3] The survival of many of
these symbols and names into the third century AD or even later seems
to contrast markedly with, for example, the disappearance of La Tène
styles of ceramic or architecture. Secondly, it is clear that in many cases
Gallo-Roman temples were constructed on sites that had been religious
centres from long before the conquest. The sanctuaries of Ribemont-
sur-Ancre and Gournay-sur-Aronde in northern France are good examples
of this phenomenon. In both cases cult activity and some structures are
attested as early as the middle La Tène, and despite an interruption of
use at Gournay, both were succeeded by Gallo-Roman temples, in the
case of Ribemont a huge sanctuary complex. Numerous other examples
could be cited, despite the fact that more substantial Gallo-Roman
temples have often made the archaeology of iron age cult centres
beneath them difficult to interpret.[4] Thirdly, there is the role played by
religion in the political conflicts of the first generations of Roman rule.
Under this heading might be put the installation of the imperial cult at
Lyon by Drusus after a period of unrest (along with the hostile reaction
to similar cult centres in Britain and Germany in times of revolt); the
involvement of the religious leaders Mariccus and Veleda in rebellions
during the first century AD;[5] and above all the suppression of the Druids
by Roman authorities. Analogies have been suggested with millenarian
movements opposed to European colonial rule in Africa, and the notion
of 'religious resistance to Romanization' has been formulated, encompassing not only overt political opposition based on or supported by
religious authority, but also the appropriation of Roman deities through
assimilation to pre-Roman cults.[6]

2 Deyts (1992) for a good introduction to the material and its difficulties. See Megaw
  (1970) on iron age art, in particular religious representations.
3 For Mercury Dumias, see Trixier (1985) and now the *Carte Archéologique* 63/2, 212–45;
  for Hercules Magusanus, see Genevrier (1986), Roymans and Derks (1994).
4 A number of recent conference proceedings bring together new work on both iron age
  and Roman sanctuaries. For the former, see Buchsenschutz *et al.* (1989) and Brunaux
  (1991), for the latter, see Goudineau *et al.* (1994), with Faudet (1993) and Faudet and
  Bertin (1993).
5 Tacitus *Hist.* 2.61, 4.61.
6 For millenarian revolts, see Dyson (1971) and Webster (1995). For religious resistance
  and the notion of the Africanization of Roman cults, see Bénabou (1976a), who is discussed critically by Garnsey (1978) and, with more sympathy, Rives (1995a, 132–53).
  Clavel-Lévêque (1972) and Carré (1981) discuss examples of the resistance approach
  applied to Gallo-Roman religion, although this has been criticized by Lavagne (1979)
  and Le Glay (1984).

It is important to be clear what is at issue here. The proposition that the Gallic provinces of the empire had distinctive cults is uncontroversial.[7] Local and regional cults were a characteristic feature of Roman imperial culture everywhere, comparable to local languages, local architectural styles and so on.[8] Nor is it surprising that these distinguishing features owed something, at least to begin with, to the diversity of the cultures and societies incorporated in the empire. Nor is the crucial question whether or not these local or regional cults contributed to local and regional identities – they did in Gaul, as they did everywhere, including the cities of Italy and Rome itself. The central issue is this: did local identities, formed or maintained at least in part by cult, in any sense undermine or offer an alternative to Roman identity? The experience of other regions suggests that the possibility should not be excluded *a priori*; if the civic cults of the Roman colony of Pompeii cannot plausibly be construed as incompatible with Roman identity, some Greeks and some Jews did on occasion find in their peculiar religious traditions a basis around which alternative identities might be constructed.[9] It remains legitimate, then, to ask whether or not worship of Hercules Magusanus necessarily implied a certain reservation in respect of Rome and the Romans that the worship of Hercules pure and simple did not. That question is often addressed rather subjectively. Proponents of total assimilation point to the name Hercules and the Latin inscriptions through which his cult is known, while others stress the epithet as a sign of the limits of Romanization. Different elements of iconography, letter forms or temple architecture can be recruited by either side in the same way. But to attempt to measure the '*romanitas*' of each Gallo-Roman cult would be to debate in such cases whether the glass is half full or half empty. A more pragmatic approach is to ask what impact Roman imperial institutions and ideas had on the religious dimensions of iron age culture, and how this encounter influenced the

---

7 Toutain (1906–20, vol. 3, 193–470) and Clavel-Lévêque (1972) provide surveys of the whole range of cults attested in Roman Gaul; see also Duval (1976).

8 For the general pattern of religious life in the empire, see Beard, North and Price (forthcoming) chapter 9. I am grateful to the authors for allowing me to consult it prior to its publication.

9 On religious components of revolts, see Bowersock (1986) and especially Momigliano (1986). But even in these cases, although religious symbols and authority might be used against Rome, the cults were not intrinsically anti-Roman, at least not according to the apologetical writings of Philo and Josephus and the Greek imperial panegyricists, or (more tellingly) in the eyes of Roman patrons of Jewish and Greek cults. For the role of Judaism in Jewish revolts, see Goodman (1987). Cult might equally be used, as in the Greek imperial cult, to construct loyalty instead of resistance, and to negotiate new identities in relation to Rome, a central theme of Price (1984) and also treated by Rogers (1991b) and Elsner (1992).

ways in which Gallo-Romans came to approach the divine and to make sense of their world in relation to it.

Evidence for the rituals conducted by the La Tène populations of Gaul is available in abundance, to the extent that it is often difficult to identify excavated structures and deposits that do not have some religious significance. That difficulty may reflect a genuine ubiquity of ritual in iron age everyday life.[10] It is also possible to identify a group of common cult practices, variants of which occur across a very large area of temperate Europe and seem to be related to a ritual tradition that can be traced at least as far back as the bronze age. Among the characteristic features of this ritual tradition are deposits of weapons and other metal valuables, often in rivers or lakes, but also on occasion in sanctuaries.[11] Human and animal remains are often associated with such deposits and accompany pottery or domestic tools in pits and in the enclosure ditches of shrines, hillforts and other settlements.

What is really distinctive about these deposits is less their contents than the elaborate ways in which they were structured. For example, the sorts of objects deposited in rivers and those included as grave goods sometimes formed opposed categories. In some deposits, the species of animals deposited were carefully selected from the range of those consumed on settlement sites. Very often bodies, human as well as animal, were subjected to manipulation after death but before decomposition: the choice of parts selected for deposition is not always explicable simply in terms of the separation of edible and inedible portions. Parts of bodies – again both human and animal – were sometimes displayed. At Gournay-sur-Aronde, the interior enclosure ditch was lined with wood and filled by an accumulation of semi-articulated remains, separated by species, with cattle skulls by the entrance, human remains in the corners and a mixture of sheep and pig bodies separating them. Incomplete horse skeletons also punctuated the assemblages. Wild animals were excluded and domestic animals were distinguished into species that were eaten and those that were not.[12] Human bodies might be treated in equally complex fashions. At nearby Ribemont-sur-Ancre, human long bones were piled up into an enormous ossuary, and in the hypostyle porticoes of the southern *oppida* human skulls were displayed.[13]

10 Duval (1989) and Hill (1993) offer suggestive general discussions of this phenomenon.
11 See Bradley (1990) for a lucid and insightful analysis of this tradition, especially focusing on watery deposits, and Furger-Gunti (1982) for an analysis of metal 'hoards'.
12 On Gournay, see Brunaux et al. (1985). For the complexity of the selection of species, individuals and body parts on northern French sites, see Méniel (1991).
13 On Ribemont, see Cadoux (1984b); on *salles hypostyles*, see Arcelin (1992b) with Dedet (1992, 273–5) for a link to mortuary rites.

Other structured depositions left no immediately visible trace: the disposal of selected assemblages (or bodies) in watery sites, for example, or the placing of human or animal remains in pits that were subsequently sealed.[14] These assemblages reflect only a small part of iron age ritual, that which has left traces in the material record, and their interpretation is not straightforward.[15] Analysis of the residues of structured deposits indicates they were at least partly organized in relation to oppositions between males and females, humans and animals, and the wild and the domesticated, but it is difficult to proceed far beyond this very general and perhaps unsurprising conclusion.

If this cultic technology was generalized in some form across much of Europe, the actual rules by which deposits were structured varied enormously from one region to another, and even in the same region did not remain static throughout late prehistory. Change might involve a shift in the deposition of weapons from graves to rivers or *vice versa*, or else participation in more general trends, such as a gradual distancing of mortuary from other cults, a rise in the prominence of sanctuaries, changes in religious imagery, and a standardization in the nature of deposits, marked by the use of coins and the ingots known as currency bars.[16] It is difficult to strike the right balance between acknowledging the prominence of a few recurrent motifs – such as structured depositions of the kind described above, or the various forms of special attention given to the human head[17] – and recognizing the essentially local context of iron age cults.[18] Perhaps the best formulation would be 'local variation within a shared tradition', a formulation that might well be applied to much of the culture of iron age Europe.

Sanctuaries, which by the late iron age are attested throughout Europe, provide a good example of this local combination of familiar elements. Perhaps the most uniform element was a clear delineation of space by ditches, banks, walls or a combination of these. These barriers

---

14 Fitzpatrick (1984), Wait (1985), Bowden and McOmish (1987), Hill (1989) and Cunliffe (1992) on the basis of British material. The significance of similar material is perhaps still less often recognized in France but see Coudart *et al.* (1981) and Py (1993, 135–6 and 193–6).

15 Brunaux (1986) has a good discussion of one example.

16 Bradley (1990, 171–81) and King (1990b) provide overviews, with different emphases. Bradley's (181–9) cautious discussion of the reasons for these trends might be preferred to King's explanation, which is mainly in terms of Mediterranean influences.

17 See Megaw (1970) and Green (1986) for a similar style of analysis.

18 Recent reviews, e.g. Fitzpatrick (1991), Webster (1995), have rightly emphasized the problems inherent in combining material from societies widely separated in space and time to create some composite iron age or 'Celtic' religion. For the similar problems facing attempts to use the (relatively recently constructed) notion of 'Celtic society', cf. Champion (1987), Merriman (1987), Hill (1989), Taylor (1991) and Chapman (1992).

feature in isolated sanctuaries and in many of those on settlement sites, but not noticeably on terrace sites like Roqueperteuse or other cult places connected with natural features such as river sources or mountains.[19] Possibly they operated to construct sacred space where no obvious sacred place already existed, although a connection with the cultic deposits at the boundaries of settlements is also possible.[20] Many sanctuaries seem to have consisted of little more than this delimited space, making them difficult to distinguish from other enclosures.[21] Other sanctuaries, like the Picard examples already mentioned, are much richer. At Gournay, and perhaps on Mont Beuvray, sanctuaries appear within larger settlements, as they regularly do on the southern *oppida*,[22] but the majority were in isolated, if often visually prominent, locations. In a few cases structures appear in the late iron age which can reasonably be termed temples: the porticoes at Entremont, St Blaise, Ensérune and Nîmes were stone built monumental structures, and a wooden structure had replaced a group of pits at Gournay by the late second century BC. The square enclosures and the architecture of some temples, such as the possible shrines at Nages and Roque-de-Viou, recall the *fana* that often succeeded them in the Gallo-Roman period.[23] But the rituals conducted within them were very different.

If we can see more and more clearly how iron age peoples worshipped their gods, the identity of those gods and the kind of meaning that Gallic rituals gave to the world remain obscure. A few religious representations have survived from late iron age Gaul, and some of them, like the god of Bouray, were perhaps cult images. Other religious art was on portable objects, weapons above all but also coins and other

---

19 For Roqueperteuse, see now Dijoud *et al.* (1991).
20 For the latter (in Britain), see Bowden and McOmish (1987), Hingley (1990).
21 See Brunaux (1989) on *Viereckschanzen*. This category of site is currently highly problematic. The traditional view asserts the existence of a category of square sacred enclosures, similar to that excavated at Holzhausen in Bavaria, characterized by their form and by the absence or virtual absence of internal structures or deposits in them. Critics argue that the category is now defined in such vague terms that a variety of very different structures have been included, and that evidence for cultic activity in many is very scarce. For a variety of views, see Buchsenschutz *et al.* (1989).
22 For Gournay, see Brunaux *et al.* (1985). A Gallo-Roman temple is attested at Mont Beuvray: some iron age material was recovered from beneath it, and the structure known as the Camp de Marc Antoine has been interpreted as a *Viereckschanze*, but the recent excavations on both sites have failed to find certain evidence of La Tène sanctuaries on Bibracte. The evidence is much better for other parts of late iron age Europe, in particular for southern Britain and Bohemia. For the south, with much better evidence, see Arcelin *et al.* (1992) and the case studies gathered in the same volume.
23 On Nages and Roque de Viou, see Py (1992). For Gallo-Roman *fana*, see Faudet (1993), Faudet and Bertin (1993) and Goudineau *et al.* (1994).

metalwork,[24] which may have been used in a variety of ways; as objects of worship, as sacrifices or as ex-votos.[25] Many sacred images were not anthropomorphic but took the form of animals, animal-human hybrids, trees or symbols such as the sun wheel.[26] Motifs like the human head or triple images of various kinds also had some religious significances. But no myths have survived from the iron age, and none of the methods used to reconstruct Gallic cosmologies are wholly convincing.[27] Caesar stated that the Gauls worshipped Mercury above all, and after him Apollo, Mars, Jupiter and Minerva, and that they regarded themselves as descended from Dispater,[28] and Lucan supplies some indigenous names; Teutates, Esus and Taranis.[29] But classical testimony of this sort is difficult to use, partly since it is rarely clear which Gauls are meant by each reference and partly since observations were naturally filtered through a whole series of Roman preconceptions. On the whole classical observers either focused on the bizarre; on human but not animal sacrifice, on sacred lakes and groves[30] but not temples, and on

24 Megaw (1970) argues for a primarily religious role for all iron age art but cf. Green (1986) and Taylor (1991). Some pieces, such as the Gunderstrup Cauldron from Denmark, published most recently and with full bibliography by Bergquist and Taylor (1987), certainly draw on a rich vocabulary of religious symbols and myths.

25 Cult images might include the god of Bouray and the stone head found in a sanctuary at Mseké Zehrovice in Bohemia. See Megaw and Megaw (1988) for a cautious discussion of this and comparable examples from Závist and elsewhere. Possible votives might include the Gundestrup cauldron, and a variety of objects inscribed in Gallo-Greek letters with ethnonyms, interpreted as votives at foreign shrines by Goudineau (1991b). But the portability of these images means that few if any have been found *in situ*. Caesar *de Bello Gallico* 6.17 and Lucan *Pharsalia* 3.412 mention *simulacra*, which in a Roman context would mean cult images.

26 Green (1986).

27 The problems may be summarized briefly. Attempts to discern general features of 'Celtic' or Indo-European religion risk missing potentially significant geographical and chronological variations, especially given the considerable evidence for variation and change in both iron age ritual and Gallo-Roman religion, as discussed in Fitzpatrick (1991), and the best studies of this kind limit their range as closely as possible (and certainly exclude early mediaeval Irish texts). Megaw (1970), Duval (1976) and Green (1986) are among cautious practioners of this approach. Other studies attempt to sort iron age cult into 'strata' of varying antiquity, e.g. Celtic or Indo-European sky gods, Neolithic mother goddesses and so forth; see Hatt (1986) and (1989) and Brunaux (1988, 71–3) for versions of varying plausibility. But schematic models of this sort are unverifiable and fail to explain how different elements were associated in cult practice or belief. Post-conquest material is often used to reconstruct iron age religion, but this procedure risks begging the most important questions about the iron age/Roman transition.

28 *de Bello Gallico* 6.17–18, but it is unclear to which native gods these names corresponded, or how widely Caesar's comments are applicable.

29 *Pharsalia* I.444–446. The Berne scholiast supplies (inconsistent) classical equivalences for these deities, and specifies the forms of human sacrifice appropriate to each. The source of his information and its reliability are unknown.

30 See Dyson (1970) for discussion of one example (discussing Strabo 4.1.13), Webster (1994) for another.

Druids rather than the more recognizable priests of the kind who had a role in the election of Aeduan magistrates,[31] or else they familiarized alien cults to the point where they become unrecognizable. Iron age religion was probably polytheistic, deities were differentiated by attribute and perhaps by function,[32] and each local Gallic cosmology may have been articulated by myth. A pantheon could well have had a place in organizing the iron age cosmos,[33] and it seems likely that the cosmos was organized partly in relation to a sacred geography to judge from the existence of early Gallo-Roman topical cults like that of Dea Bibracte at Autun, of Matrebo Glaneikabo at Glanum[34] and of Mercury Dumias in the Auvergne. Political entities too may have been reflected in the heavens, in the form of tribal cults and perhaps deities.[35] Finally, many

31 The bibliography on the Druids is immense, and much of it speculative. Druids were already mythologized in the ancient world – as natural philosophers at the edge of the world, like the Brahmins or the Ethiopian Gymnosophists, and as savage practisers of human sacrifice or magicians – and have been again on several occasions since. No archaeological evidence exists for Druidism, and there is little reliable classical testimony of which the most important is Caesar *de Bello Gallico* 6.13–14, Mela 3.2.18–19, Strabo 4.4.4–5 and Diodorus 5.31. Chadwick (1966) and Piggott (1968) provide good critical introductions to the historiographical tradition. Among recent (and very different) attempts to reconstruct the reality, cf. Letta (1984), Zecchini (1984), Clavel-Lévêque (1985) and Brunaux (1988, 57–65). Caesar *de Bello Gallico* 7.33 probably refers to other priests, as does the title *gutuater* attested in early Gallo-Roman epigraphy.

32 Much confusion has been caused by the assumption, e.g. by Benoit (1959) and Thevenot (1968), that all Gallo-Roman Martes, for instance, refer to a single (concealed) Celtic deity, who then necessarily acquires a very wide range of attributes and functions. In fact, a narrow range of Roman gods were syncretized with a very large number of deities of indigenous origin, whose cults were mostly very localized. Attempts to discern the essence or function of 'the Celtic Mercury' and others are misconceived; see Webster (1995) for a useful critique of 'polyvalence'.

33 Arguments based on the divine family portrayed in the Irish legends, e.g. those of Guyonvarc'h and Le Roux (1986), ignore the possibility that these texts were influenced by classical literature; see Champion (1985).

34 Dea Bibracte: *CIL* XIII.2651–3, Matrebo Glaneikabo: *RIG* G.64.

35 Uncertainty over the social and political organization of late La Tène societies naturally makes this hypothesis difficult to investigate, although a number of studies, e.g. Brunaux (1988) and (1995), have attempted to explicate late iron age religion by reference to social evolutionary trajectories assumed to be common to iron age Europe and various other societies, in particular archaic Greece. The cost of this method is a loss of a sense of the historical specificity of late prehistoric Europe. Correlations between the location of iron age sanctuaries and political boundaries have yet to be demonstrated convincingly since studies such as Marchand (1991) rely heavily on Roman period sanctuaries and Gallo-Roman communal boundaries. Many iron age sanctuaries originated in any case in the mid La Tène, long before most archaeologists would claim that states were emerging in northern France, a point that casts into some doubt the various attempts in Brunaux (1991) cf. Brunaux (1995), to find in third or second century BC Gaul similar relations between sanctuaries and political growth to those claimed for eighth century BC Greece by de Polignac (1984), (1991) and (1994). The combination of Roman period data with social evolutionary schemata to show the social embeddedness of iron age religion is also a feature of Roymans' otherwise excellent (1988) survey of northern Gallic cults.

cults were very localized, to judge from the topical cults of the Roman period and the very large number of deities with Celtic names who are attested in only one Gallo-Roman inscription or a single valley.[36] It might follow that no single cosmology was shared by the Gauls and that, as in the case of ritual, different patterns were created in each region from roughly the same building blocks.[37]

What of the attitudes of the Roman conquerors?[38] Roman polytheism did not constitute an exclusive system: other gods were deemed to exist, to be powerful and potentially as interested in human affairs as were the gods of the Romans. One way of dealing with them was through *interpretatio*, the assertion of some form of equivalence between a foreign deity and a Roman one.[39] Alternatively, Romans might recognize the distinctiveness of an alien god and accord her or him cult. This might follow *evocatio*, the ritual by which enemy gods were persuaded to defect to Rome; the institution of public cult to an imported deity such as Mater Magna or Aesculapius; or it might simply be a private initiative, like the dedications made by soldiers to local gods all over the empire.[40] But in all these cases the cult paid was thoroughly Roman. Private individuals were theoretically free to pay proper cult to any deity,[41] but the rites through which any gods were worshipped, publicly or privately, were a matter of public concern, and deviance, alien or domestic, was ridiculed, censured and on occasion punished.[42]

These concerns naturally intersected with Roman debates about world conquest and the civilizing process.[43] As Roman power grew it became common to interpret world empire as the result of a divine mandate,[44] and Pliny the Elder's notion of Italy as *divinely* ordained to propagate

36 See Toutain (1906–20, vol. 3, 292–331) for these local cults.
37 Brunaux (1988, 66–7) asserts the independence of tribal *panthea*, but his use of Dumézilian Indo-European categories to generate a new unitary order does not convince.
38 For the religious dimension of Roman imperialism, see above all Rüpke (1990) and also Brunt (1978, 163–7) and Beard (1994, 763–8). For the imperial period, see Gordon (1990), to which I am indebted for much of what follows.
39 On *interpretatio*, see Wissowa (1916–19) and the last section of this chapter below. On the variety of forms interpretatio might take, see Le Glay (1984, 162).
40 There seems to have been no concern on the Romans' part to appropriate systematically the gods of the conquered. Many enemy gods never received cult in Rome, while some of those imported came from beyond the empire. The phenomenon is better seen as a consequence of the expansion of Rome's cultural horizon than of her empire, as expansion stimulated theological speculation. See, for instance, Cicero *de Divinatione* 1.41.90 for an example involving Druidism, and in general Beard (1986).
41 A freedom insisted on by Henig (1986) in relation both to choice of deities and the particular equivalences asserted in private *interpretationes*.
42 North (1979), Garnsey (1984).   43 Gordon (1990, 235–8).
44 Brunt (1978). North (1993) suggests similar views may have been important even in the middle Republic.

humanitas is an unsurprising formulation.[45] The civilizing process, thus conceived, did not entail the propagation of a particular cosmology or theology, but rather of a particular ritual tradition and its associated sensibilities such as *pietas* and *religio*. Conversely, the cults of the barbarians, like those of peasants and other social inferiors, were stigmatized as *superstitio*.[46] This marginalization of religion that differed from that of the elite of Rome was based not on a failure to worship the right gods, but on a failure to worship any gods in the right way. Just as Romans conceived of a continuum between *humanitas* and barbarism, so too different forms of deviance were regarded differently. Zoomorphic and aniconic representations of deities were generally regarded as odd, but their use persisted, in Egypt and in the Near East as well as in Gaul, whereas human sacrifice was suppressed everywhere. Different degrees of civilized behaviour were seen as appropriate to different groups in society. *Coloniae* and *municipia* were expected to organize their public cults and priesthoods on Roman lines, but *peregrine* communities seem to have been allowed more latitude, at least to judge from the diversity of religious titulature.[47] These relationships were perhaps rarely conceptualized as clearly as they were by Pliny, but they nevertheless informed the attitudes and behaviour of Romans when they confronted Gallic religion. The worship of Taranis, Epona and Sucellus was as acceptable as that of Mars, Apollo and Minerva, but not if they were portrayed as animals or horned gods, not if the ritual involved structured deposits like those displayed at Gournay and on Entremont, and not if the cult demanded human sacrifice. The broad lines of the eventual compromise between Roman sensibilities and La Tène religion are already clear. It remains to be asked how it was achieved.

II   The creation of Gallo-Roman religion

Pliny the Elder tells the story of how the Greek sculptor Zenodorus was paid the fantastic sum of 40 million HS by the Arverni to create a colossal bronze statue of Mercury.[48] Since Zenodorus went on to perform an imperial commission for Nero in Rome, his activities in the Auvergne can be dated to the first half of the first century AD, and the

---

45 Pliny *NH* 3.39, cf. Virgil *Aeneid* 6.851–3, both discussed in ch. 3 above.
46 On the development of this term and its significance, see Calderone (1972), Grodzynski (1974) and Scheid (1985). Under the early empire it was used to denote excessive cult, often vain attempts to sway the gods based not on a proper understanding of the relationship between gods and men, but on irrational fear. Frequently opposed to *religio* it was naturally used as a label for various religious deviancy, usually located in the more private areas of Roman religion or among barbarians.
47 Beard, North and Price (forthcoming) ch. 9.   48 Pliny *Natural History* 34.45.

statue was quite possibly intended to stand in the huge temple of
Mercurius Dumias being constructed on the summit of the Puy-de-
Dôme at the time. The decision to commission a new cult statue would
have been taken by the decurions of the Arverni, meeting in their new
capital of Augustonemeton, modern Clermont Ferrand, at the foot of
the Puy. The sum paid and the Arvernian choice of Zenodorus, one of
the most famous artists of the day, illustrate both their commitment to
provide the best possible Hellenistic-style image for their tribal god, and
also their cultural *savoir-faire*. They may, of course, have been acting on
advice. If so the most likely candidate for advisor would be the governor, Dubius Avitus, for whom Zenodorus made two cups during his
stay in Gaul. Agricola's encouragement of British communities to construct temples is not the only parallel for a governor's participation in
such matters.[49] Either way the re-imaging of Arvernian Mercury provides
a rare snapshot of one of the ways in which Gallo-Roman religion was
created, a process in which Gallic elites, Mediterranean craftsmen and
Roman governors each played a part.

A second snapshot is provided by the foundation of the cult centre of
the Tres Galliae at Lyon in 12 BC.[50] The literary accounts of the event
are brief, and in some respects contradictory, but it seems that the
initiative came from the imperial prince Drusus (presumably in con-
sultation with the emperor) and that it responded to unrest following
census-taking in Gaul;[51] in just the period, then, when Roman power
was being extended deeper and deeper into the Gallic communities.
The sanctuary was one of the first of its kind in the West, a cult centre
dedicated to the imperial cult and organized on wholly Roman lines,
with an altar and aristocratic priests who performed sacrifices and gave
gladiatorial games as a public service. Established on neutral ground at
the confluence of the Rhône and Saône, under the hill on which a
Roman colony had been established a generation before and easily
accessible from most parts of Gaul through the new Agrippan road
network, the sanctuary was to be the venue for an annual assembly, to
which representatives would be sent from every state in the three northern Gallic provinces, an assembly at which cult would be paid to Rome
and Augustus, elections would be held for officers of the cult and the

---

49 Tacitus *Agricola* 21. For the religious functions of governors, see Eck (1992), and for
   other examples of governors offering provincials advice on cult, see Dorner (1935),
   Price (1984, 69–71), and Rives (1995a, 76–84).
50 On the foundation of the sanctuary of the Three Gauls, see Larsen (1955, 126–44),
   Deininger (1965, 21–24) and Christopherson (1968), the latter perhaps underestimat-
   ing the religious component of the cult. Turcan (1982) and Fishwick (1987–1992, 97–
   102) provide good recent accounts.
51 Livy *Periochae* 139, Dio 54. 32, Suetonius *Claudius* 2.

annual priest, and a council would provide the Gallic communities with a collective voice. Despite modern attempts to find predecents for the assembly and its activities in pre-conquest traditions, its organization strongly suggests that the immediate models were Greek provincial assemblies, such as the *koinon* of Asia, modified, principally in matters of ritual, by Rome.[52] If the initiative and organization came from Rome, the cult was enthusiastically embraced by the new elites of Gaul. The career of Solemnis shows how delegates were drawn from the most prominent of civic decurions, and the priesthood at the altar came to be seen as the highest distinction possible within Gaul.[53] The standard was set by the first priest, Gaius Julius Vercondaridubnus, a representative of the Aedui, Rome's oldest allies in the Three Gauls. At the altar, and in the associated cult organization and provincial council, the noblest Gauls had the opportunity to compete for prestige on a wider stage than any *civitas* could offer. While in Britain and Germany similar institutions were to be seen as symbols of Roman oppression, in Gaul euergetistic competition rapidly provided the sanctuary at Lyon with monuments like the amphitheatre constructed by the Santon noble Gaius Julius Rufus in Tiberius' reign.[54] Eventually, gladiatorial games escalated in cost to the point where the emperor and the senate had to intervene to ensure the priesthood did not become prohibitively expensive,[55] but that crisis testifies to the success, not the failure, of the cult. The rise of Lyon to effective capital of the Three Gauls was due largely to the success of the neighbouring sanctuary.[56]

It will never be possible to reconstruct all the preliminary exchanges, conversations, requests, hints and negotiations that preceded the establishment of these cults in the form in which we first see them.[57] For that

52 For pre-Roman traditions, see Christopherson (1968) and, more cautiously, Deininger (1965, 23) and Fishwick (1987–92, 99–102). The *koinon Asiae* had annually elected high priests who gave gladiatorial games, presided over imperial cult and also an assembly: Deininger (1965, 16–19).

53 On the priests of the altar, see Maurin (1978, 181–204), Deininger (1965, 99–107).

54 For resentment focused on provincial cult centres at Cologne and Colchester, see Tac. *Ann.* 1.57 and 14.31. For the amphitheatre at Lyon, see Maurin (1978, 181–2) on the basis of *CIL* XIII.1036 and *ILTG* 217.

55 Oliver and Palmer (1955), with Millar (1977, 195). Although the inscription recording this ruling of AD 177/8 was found at Italica in Spain, the references to the priests of the Gauls in lines 14 and 56 strongly suggests that the generalized measure was a response to a representation from the *concilium Galliarum*.

56 Drinkwater (1976) notes that the colony was not originally intended to serve this role. After the construction of the Agrippan road network and the Rhine frontier, its success also probably owed something to its location on important communications routes. Formally, Lyon remained capital of Lugdunensis alone.

57 Rogers (1991a) for such an attempt in another part of the empire, but cf. Mitchell (1993, 210 n. 73).

reason alone, it is pointless to attempt to weigh up local against central initiatives, at least as far as public cult is concerned. But the active participation of both sides in remodelling Gallic religion is evident. That process began at the end of the last century BC.[58] Earlier Mediterranean influences have been detected at the sanctuary at Glanum,[59] but the links are with Greek Marseille rather than Rome, and the sanctuary of the fountain at Nîmes was not remodelled until the turn of the millenium.[60] Further north developments lagged a little behind. At Ribemont, a middle and late La Tène sanctuary continued to be the site of rituals like those attested at Gournay until the first decades of the first century AD, before being replaced by a large temple in the middle of the first century:[61] this sequence seems typical for both small and large sanctuaries in the region. The same chronology is even evident in the private dedication of thousands of ex-votos at Chamalières in the Auvergne and at the source of the Seine.[62] The fact that the ex-votos were of wood and their watery contexts have certainly encouraged the search for iron age origins, but at neither site has any indication been found that cult preceded the reign of Augustus, and the rites involved are perfectly comprehensible in terms of Roman ritual traditions.[63]

It is perhaps not surprising that the formative period of Gallo-Roman culture is evident in matters of religion. The same new elites who were at that very period laying out the huge street grids of the tribal capitals, having their sons taught Latin and importing all the accessories of civilized life from the Mediterranean, also presided over the reworking of the public cults of the gods. For Tacitus, civilizing the Britains had involved encouraging the building of temples, *fora* and noble houses (*domos*).[64] The inclusion of religion in this process is another argument against viewing the transformation of Gallic culture simply in terms of emulation, unless we are prepared to regard the Gallic elites as uncommitted to their gods, cynical manipulators of cult for their own political or economic advantage. That view is untenable. An analogous interpretation

---

58 On lack of earlier change in the Republican province, see Carré (1981).
59 Roth Congès (1992b).
60 Guillet et al. (1992) with Célié et al. (1994) for the general background.
61 Cadoux (1991), Wightman (1986, 567–9).
62 See Vatin (1972) and Romeuf (1986) on Chamalières, still not fully published. See Deyts (1983) on the material from the source of the Seine.
63 Scheid (1992, 31–5). Bourgeois (1991, 211–15) argues that the only pre-Roman components of these cults are the names of the deities involved. The argument that prehistoric deposits in water are mostly accidental, however, cannot be accepted. It seems preferable to follow Bradley (1990), in seeing the prehistoric deposits as sacrificed objects, but to regard the very different statuettes and images of body parts of the Roman period as monuments of the fulfilment of a vow made to a deity.
64 Tacitus *Agricola* 21, discussed in chapter 3 above.

of the Roman aristocracy's attitude to religion has now been largely rejected, and there seems no reason to regard Gallic elites differently. Religion in all societies operates to make sense of the world and of human experience:[65] it is precisely because of its capacity to do so that it may also be made to serve social or political ends. The transformation of Gallo-Roman religion thus exposes the inadequacies of any account of the origins of provincial cultures based solely on the material or political interests of provincials or Romans. The rituals that resulted in the bizarre deposits at Gournay and the display of human skulls at Entremont had made some kind of sense of the world. We can hardly imagine what that sense was, yet it is evident that the partial abandonment of those rites entailed a cost and that Gallo-Roman religion must have offered more in return than the perfunctory approval of a distant governor, perhaps spiritual as well as material goods.

Discerning the precise mechanisms through which Gallic religion was re-invented is not easy. The problem is the familiar one of accounting for the common cultural outcome of multiple independent initiatives without invoking any central policy designed to achieve that end,[66] but the case of religion offers new ways of approaching it. A good starting point is an examination of the kind of power exercised by the religious authorities of the empire over provincial religion, always remembering that that religion comprised not only the public cults offered Mercurius Dumias on the Puy-de-Dôme but also the votives left by private individuals at the shrine of Chamalières at its foot. Religious authority at Rome, like other kinds of public power, was fought over between senate, people and individual aristocrats under the republic and acquired under the principate by emperors who sometimes chose to associate other bodies, especially the senate, in their decisions.[67] It is less clear what the scope of this authority was felt to be. The cults of the city of Rome were certainly included and, at least since the Bacchanalian controversy of the early second century BC, some religious jurisdiction over all Italy had been assumed. How this overview was conceived is unclear, as is the relationship between authority in Rome and authority

65 Cf. Geertz's famous (1966) definition of religion as 'a system of symbols which acts to establish powerful, pervasive, and long-lasting moods and motivations in men by formulating conceptions of a general order of existence and clothing these conceptions with such an aura of factuality that the moods and motivations seem uniquely real.' See Price (1984) for a study of Roman cult in these terms.
66 Woolf (1992a).
67 See North (1976), with discussion of the role of priests and the Sybilline books. On the transition to the principate, see Beard (1990, 47–8). Other parties were involved: Beard (1994, 745–9) discusses *popularis* attitudes to religion, and naturally the senate continued to be formally associated with the emperor's authority in this sphere as in others; see also Talbert (1984, 386–91).

over the cults of *coloniae*, partly defined at their foundation, but also in part managed by their own decurions. Uncertainties of this sort are even more a feature of the imperial period, when the erosion of civic authority over cult seems not to have been answered by the provision of any supra-civic religious authority. Early in the principate, provinces and cities wishing to initiate cults to members of the imperial house tended to seek permission from the current emperor, but whether these consultations were required or merely prudential is unclear.[68] Municipal and colonial charters show that the organization and finances of the public cults of provincial communities were first of all the responsibility of civic authorities, but they conferred no explicit rights of religious (any more than of political) autonomy; governors could and did intervene.[69] The inconclusive debates over the legal basis of the persecution of Christians illustrate the difficulties in deciding who had responsibility for religious activity (private as well as public) in provincial communities. Emperors seem in practice to have been prepared to intervene in the cults of the provinces on the same basis that they intervened in other matters; rarely, then, and often in reaction to some stimulus, notionally in accordance with local tradition and the status of the provincials concerned, but usually also in line with Roman precedent, religious principles, and, of course, interests.

Gaul provides one of the best examples of such intervention in the case of the Druids. Caesar's account of them shows no particular hostility, presenting them as exegetes of an arcane wisdom whose vocation set them apart from worldly affairs except in so far as they intervened to settle disputes. Although he notes their role in human sacrifice, he devotes more space to discussing their doctrine and the schools through which it was transmitted, and Druids are conspicuous by their absence from his narrative of war and politics in Gaul. Likewise, Cicero, in his treatise *On Divination*, has Quintus cite Druidical beliefs as an illustration that divination is not neglected 'even by barbarians'.[70] Much classical testimony is along similar lines, but a group of early imperial writers describes a more hostile attitude and policy. The Elder Pliny, in

---

68 Price (1984, 66–8).

69 For *coloniae* in Gaul, cf. Scheid (1991) and Van Andringa (1994) largely on the basis of the *Lex Ursonensis*. Religious affairs were probably, but not certainly, dealt with on one of the missing portions of the *Lex Irnitana*, for which see Galsterer (1988, 79–80). On the role of decurions, see also Rives (1995a, 28–35). Eck (1992) discusses gubernatorial jurisdiction over religion.

70 Caesar *de Bello Gallico* 6.13–16, Cicero *de Divinatione* 1.90. This image of the Druids as natural philosophers does, however, continue to appear in later writers, as discussed by Piggott (1968, 76–87), although for Tacitus *Hist.* 4.54 Druids connoted *superstitio* and magic above all.

a discussion of the history of magic, relates how traces of it survived in early Italy and how even in Rome it was not until 97 BC that human sacrifice was banned.

But in both Gallic provinces it survived, right up until our own day. For it was the principate of Tiberius Caesar that got rid of their druids and all kind of bards and healers. But why should I record all this about an art that has crossed the ocean and fled to the emptiness of nature? Today Britain is obsessed by magic and practises it with such pomp that it might seem to have given it to the Persians. So widespread is magic throughout the whole world, even if its exponents disagree or are ignorant of each other. It is impossible to calculate how much is owed to the Romans for suppressing these atrocities, according to which the most religious rite was to kill a man, and the healthiest practice was to devour him (*Natural History* 30.4).

The context, then, is Pliny's conception of Rome extending *humanitas* through the world, the abolition of human sacrifice first in Rome, then in Gaul and not yet in Britain, marking the advance of the civilizing process at the expense of *superstitio*. Mela's account of how human sacrifice had been replaced in his own day by a token shedding of blood fits within the same framework.[71] Finally, Suetonius describes how Claudius abolished the cruel religion of the Druids that Augustus had forbidden citizens to take part in. Significantly, the comment is made in a chapter largely concerned with Claudius' assertion of traditional, Roman moral values.[72] Druidism in these passages is never associated with arcane wisdom or juridical functions but always with human sacrifice, which some classical writers stated could only take place in the presence of Druids.[73] Even if these passages do present problems for knowing exactly how and when Druidism was abolished, they strongly

71 Mela 3.18. See Rives (1995b) for discussion of the location of human sacrifice within the Roman moral universe.
72 Suetonius *Claudius* 25. The chapter also describes Claudius' actions to enforce traditional respect of status in Roman society by punishing ungrateful freedmen and negligent masters; his defence of traditional privilege through the imposition of penalties on freedmen claiming to be knights and on peregrines pretending to be citizens; his differentiation between the treatment of provincials on the basis of their moral conduct, by punishing the Lycians for their *discordiae*, rewarding the Rhodians for their *paenitentia*, exempting Trojans from tribute for the sake of their ancestral ties and ancient privileges, and expelling the Jews from Rome for the disturbances they had been encouraged to cause by Christ; and his respect for the ancient cults of Eleusis, Eryx and Rome herself. Suetonius' comment that all this was done not on Claudius' own initiative but on the advice of his wives and freedmen illustrates that the conduct described in this chapter was regarded as generally credit-worthy, the proper exercise of imperial authority in support of civilization and traditional values and against barbarous novelty.
73 Caesar *de Bello* Gallico 6.13, Strabo 4.4.5, Diodorus 5.31.4. The extent to which these testimonies draw on the same sources is contentious, for which see Nash (1976a).

suggest that Roman hostility was based on the incompatibility of Druidical ritual with civilized and Roman standards.[74] Certainly druidical opposition to Roman rule is not recorded until after the Julio-Claudian persecution.

The persecution of the Druids and Drusus' establishment of the federal cult centre at Lyon show that the Roman contribution to the formation of Gallo-Roman religion should not be discounted. But most cult was neither imposed nor banned by Rome and so reform from above is implausible as a general explanation. Much of the imperial contribution must rather have been through informal encouragement of the kind that may be suspected to lie behind the invitation extended to Zenodorus by the Arvernian senate, and through the provision of models for cult that might be imitated by Gallo-Roman elites.

By accident or design, Rome provided the Gauls with several models of proper cult. The cult performed at the Altar of Lyon is an obvious case, an act of worship in which the most influential members of Gallic communities participated, before returning to their cities where many held local priesthoods of Rome and Augustus.[75] Lyon was also the focus for a parallel set of cults, those conducted by the *conventus civium Romanorum consistentum*.[76] These associations of Roman citizens are attested in a number of Gallic communities in the first century AD, when they seem to have been catered not so much for newly enfranchised local aristocrats as for Roman citizens from elsewhere in the empire who were resident in Gaul. Both at Lyon and in their host communities, these Roman residents exemplified the proper organization and conduct of Roman religion. A third set of models was provided by the public cults of the *coloniae* of the south, themselves modelled on the cults of Rome. Perhaps the best example is provided by a marble altar originally set up in the forum of Narbonne in AD 12.[77] Inscribed on

74 See Last (1949) for a succinct and convincing statement, cf. Garnsey (1984, 13) and Gordon (1990, 243) with slightly different emphases. Other motives for the suppression have been suggested, both political and social, and not all of them wholly incompatible with the view suggested here. Goodman's (1987, 239–44) argument (following Nash 1976a, 125) that Romans objected to a separate priestly class is plausible (although there is little agreement about the birth and wealth of Druids). But his proposition that Romans deduced religious fanaticism from this feature of Gallic society seems unnecessary in view of the explicit testimony linking the persecution of Druids to human sacrifice. Letta (1984), on the other hand, accepts that Romans objected to human sacrifice above all, but goes on to argue that no full scale persecution ever took place.

75 Cf. Maurin (1978, 193–7), Drinkwater (1979a, 94–5) and Chastagnol (1980, 189–91) for slightly different views on these priesthoods and their titulature.

76 Audin *et al.* (1954, especially at 303–35), with Maurin (1978, 150–1).

77 *CIL* XII 4333 = *ILS* 112, on which see Kneißl (1980), Gayraud (1981, 358–65), Cels-Saint-Hilaire (1986) and Fishwick (1987–92, 379–80).

the front of the altar is a colonial statute of AD 11 that details the public cult to be paid there to the Numen of Augustus, consisting of a series of annual sacrifices to be conducted by priests selected according to their social status, who would provide incense and wine for the colonists on Augustus' birthday and other holidays, including the anniversary of Augustus' reconciliation of the *iudicia* of the decurions and the *coloni* of Narbo. The reasons for this intervention in the politics of the colony are unclear, but all the other details are as conventional as might be expected for a Roman colony. On one side of the altar is added the text of the dedicatory statement, made for Augustus, his family, the senate and people of Rome and the colonists and resident foreigners (*incolae*) of Narbo, and laying down the laws that regulate cult at the altar (including private cult) by determining which rituals are acceptable. That text is brief but includes the statement that the laws shall otherwise be the same as those of the altar of Diana on the Aventine. That clause is analogous to passages in the Flavian municipal law that provide for some legal issues to be decided as if the *municipes* were subject to the Roman *ius civile*. At Narbonne it is a reminder that the cults of *coloniae* were the cults of Roman citizens, but it also serves to insert this new cult into a genealogy of ritual.[78] The new cults descend from those of Diana on the Aventine, just as hers descended from a Massiliot model, itself based on the cults of Artemis of Ephesos. The law does not simply establish new cults, but also specifies that they are not entirely new, but also part of an ancient cultic tradition.

It is possible that new cults were established in Gallo-Roman *civitates* in just so formal a manner right from the start. But perhaps it is more likely that to begin with the creation of new cults in the communities of Roman Gaul was more haphazard, by simple imitation of the cults practised by Romans in their midst or in neighbouring *coloniae* and at the altar, and in the light of the advice and reactions of Roman officials and residents. Priestly functions seem to have been exercised by the chief magistrates of the Bituriges even in the period when they were still termed *vergobrets*,[79] and priests entitled *gutuaters* set up marble votive altars in the new Aeduan capital of Autun.[80] A more systematic reorganization of public cults probably awaited the municipalization of

78 See Cels-Saint-Hilaire (1986, 486–7) for a similar point. Gayraud (1981, 360) discusses another instance from Salona. Compare, too, line 21 of *CIL* XII 6038, a Flavian law probably designed to set up provincial cult in Narbonensis (for which see now Williamson 1987b), which refers back to the regulations governing the *flamen Augusti* for details of how to treat the *flamen provincialis*.
79 Allain *et al.* (1981).
80 *CIL* XIII 11225 & 11226, dedicated in the first century to Augustus and Deo Anvallo. At least one of the priests has the *tria nomina*.

the Gallic communities. The granting of a charter, whether municipal or colonial, required the civic authorities to determine the public cults of the community and then to take responsibility for their management. No civic charters have survived from the Gallic provinces, but analysis of the cults of several communities in terms of examples from Spain is suggestive.[81] The *duoviri* and the *decuriones* had responsibility for fixing the religious calendar of the community, determining which public cults would be celebrated and organizing the election of priests, and each year the *duoviri* appointed *magistri* to supervise the sanctuaries. The decisions made were naturally very Roman in form. A communal sanctuary seems to have been established at which cult was paid to the tribal diety, syncretized in a form presumably decided by the decurions although often apparently on the basis of quite detailed knowledge of the Roman pantheon. Associated with this cult was the cult of the gods of each of the *pagi*, the subdivisions of the Gallo-Roman state, along with the imperial cult in one form or another. At Rennes, for example, the second century basilica of the temple of Mars Mullo also housed statues dedicated to the *numina pagorum*: their bases specify the deities in question, so Mars Vicinnus was the patron of the *pagus Carnutenus*, Mercury Atepomarus of the *pagus Matans* and so forth, but they were also dedicated in honour of the imperial house.[82] At Trier, the suburban sanctuary at Irminenwingert seems to have functioned as the centre of the colony's cult to Lenus Mars, but beside the main temple were a series of *exedra*, each comprising stone seats on three sides of a square behind an altar for each Treveran *pagus*.[83] Cults of either the *genius pagi* or of named tutelary deities, usually associated with imperial cult, are also attested in the territory of the Helvetii and other states.[84] This pattern of public cults conducted at the city, with the participation of sub-divisions of the state and incorporating elements of imperial cult, can be attested throughout the empire.[85]

The new religious order was expressed physically in a new monumentality of the sacred. New sanctuaries and temples were constructed, as at Lyon and in Autun, while old ones, like Ribemont and the fountain

81 Scheid (1991) and Van Andringa (1994). The method is easier to apply to *coloniae* since religious matters are hardly dealt with by the surviving portions of the Flavian law dealing with Latin *municipia*. The chronology of the extension of the Latin right and municipalization throughout Gaul is problematic, but it was probably widespread by the end of Claudius' reign, if not earlier; see Maurin (1978, 154–60).
82 Chastagnol (1980).
83 Scheid (1991). Similar structures have been found beside the temple of Mercury on the Puy-de-Dôme.
84 Étienne (1992), Van Andringa (1994).
85 See, for example, the Demostheneia of Oenoanda described in Rogers (1991a).

at Nîmes, were transformed by the construction of new buildings, new images and a new organization of space. The fact that many of these developments have already been discussed in previous chapters shows the centrality of temple building to both urbanization and the transformation of Gallo-Roman landscapes. The scale of religious architecture is, however, striking. The great circular temple of Besançon, built between AD 65 and 120, had an enclosure over ninety metres in diameter and was one of several in the city. At the centre of Roman Vienne was a monumental complex over three hectares in area comprising a *forum* enclosed by two *areae sacrae* (sacred precincts), while the sanctuary of the fountain at Nîmes may have been more impressive than the *forum* and civic centre proper. Most striking of all today is the tower of Vesunna in Périgueux, a circular structure just over thirty metres in diameter, originally surrounded by a sacred precinct 140 by 120 metres in area.[86] Gregory of Tours described the third century destruction by barbarians of a similarly massive temple at Clermont Ferrand, a temple with walls thirty feet thick, floors decorated with marble and mosaics, and roofed in lead.[87] If many temples did not acquire their greatest development until the late second century or later, they were nonetheless prominent in the earliest cities. Dedications of temples, altars and other sacred structures account for about half the building inscriptions found in the Gallic and German provinces, and the dedicators were for the most part local benefactors.[88] The financing as well as the management of the new cults were the responsibility of the new Gallo-Roman elites, then. Nor were their activities restricted to the capitals of the Gallo-Roman communities: in small towns, in villages and even on their own estates the wealthy constructed sanctuaries and temples, often associated with theatres.[89]

The responsibilities of the decurions did not end with the cults performed on behalf of the state and its component parts and the sanctuaries constructed for them. Other public cults existed, for example the ceremonies performed by *seviri Augustales*, and cult was also conducted publicly by groups whose relationship to the state was slightly more remote, such as *collegia* like the *dendrophoroi* of Lyon, the inhabitants of *vici* that were not formally subdivisions of the state, and the enigmatic cult associations termed *curiae* that existed throughout much of northern

86 For Besançon: Guilhot and Goy (1992, 18–19 and 78–9); on Vienne: André *et al.* (1991); on Nîmes: Gros (1984), (1991); on the tower of Vesunna: Lauffrey (1990). For a recent survey, see Bedon *et al.* (1988, 119–71).
87 Gregory of Tours *Historia Francorum* I. 32.
88 Frézouls (1984, 41–3) provides the figures. The sums involved are discussed by De Kisch (1979, 271–2).
89 Bouley (1988), Fauduet (1993), Goudineau *et al.* (1994).

Gaul.[90] Finally, as the law of the altar of Narbonne shows, even cult performed by individuals was theoretically subject to regulation by the civic authorities, perhaps especially when it was performed publicly as in the forum of Narbonne.

The cults created and sanctioned by the decurions were paid to a mixture of traditional and Roman gods. The sanctuary of the Altbachtal at Trier provides an excellent example.[91] At the edge of the city a complex of dozens of temples, mostly *fana* of the Gallo-Roman type equipped with altars and often *exedrae* (monumental benches), and a theatre, grew up in an organic fashion over the two hundred years following the foundation of the city. The cult complex was naturally under the control of the decurions, but unlike the Lenus Mars sanctuary there is no sign it functioned as a cult centre for the colony. Most of the gods whose cults are attested by epigraphy have indigenous names, among them Intarabus, Aveta, Ritona, Vorio and Epona. Alongside them were classical deities including Diana and Mercury and a few double-named; some of the latter, like 'Vertumnus or Pisintus' indicated considerable knowledge of Roman cults on the part of the syncretizers. Images range from a classical bronze Mercury to a Jupiter column and terracottas of female deities holding baskets of fruit and accompanied by a small dog. Even Mithras makes a late appearance. The Altbachtal sanctuary provides a graphic image of the complexity of Gallo-Roman religion and of the impossibility of separating out the Gallic from the Roman within it.

The grand monuments and great sanctuaries should not overshadow humbler but parallel transformations of the ritual system. Animal sacrifice continued, even if human sacrifice was forbidden and semi-articulate skeletons were no longer displayed in and around sanctuaries. Romans themselves practised forms of animal sacrifice, after all, but the deposition of portions of animals in pits probably represents a partial continuation of local rites.[92] Deposits also typically contain a number (sometimes very large) of whole pots, often specially selected from those in use on settlement sites and occasionally inscribed; coinage, sometimes mutilated; rare miniature weapons; and more frequently statuettes, which often represent wild animals.[93] As in the iron age, the precise rites varied considerably from one locality to another.

90 For the *collegia* of Lyon, see Waltzing (1895–1900, 558–64). Burnand (1994) discusses *vici* with no juridical status. Others did have magistrates and some may have operated as the capitals of *pagi*, for which see Drinkwater (1979a). For the *curiae* of the north, who may be connected to the organization of *civitates* by *pagus*, see Rüger (1972) and (1983).
91 See Wightman (1970, 215–8) and Scheid (1995) for recent appraisals.
92 Brunaux (1995, 159).
93 A number of these rituals are described in contributions to Goudineau *et al.* (1994). No synthetic survey of the cult practices of Roman Gaul yet exists.

Yet other rituals seem to be new, or at least made archaeologically visible by the new forms they took. The wooden votive statuettes deposited at the springs of Chamalières and at the source of the Seine from very early in the first century AD have already been mentioned. Elsewhere in Gaul, Roman figurative imagery was put to other uses and manifested in other media. From the middle of the first century AD, terracotta statuettes began to be produced in a number of areas, but especially in the valley of the Allier.[94] Standing only ten or twenty centimetres high they portrayed a range of deities, wild and domestic animals and birds and also human types and busts. The iconography is a mixture of Greco-Roman and indigenous images. Venus is by far the most common type, and Minerva, Mercury and Hercules also appear as well as Victory and Abundance, and images of gladiators and of soldiers. Epona and increasingly various mother-goddesses also appear, and among the animals there are lions and three-horned bulls alongside more mundane stags, ducks, hares and fighting cocks. Indigenous iconographic elements are identifiable by their departure from Roman norms, not by their resemblance to any pre-Roman versions. Representations of gods in this way were as new as the uses to which the statuettes were put.[95] Many were grave goods or markers for relatively humble graves, like those in one of the cemeteries of Argentomagus;[96] others have been recovered from sanctuaries where they may have been votives or substitutes for or commemoration of sacrifices; on domestic sites they perhaps stood in *lararia*, household shrines.[97] Statuettes of the same kind were produced in other regions in stone, rather than clay,[98] and small bronzes may have performed similar roles.[99] But it is the relative cheapness of wood and terracotta that is striking in emphasising the rapidity with which new rites and new images were adopted for use in private cult by individuals of modest means. The same point can be made in relation to the adoption of new burial rites already discussed, or to the appearance of curse tablets and (rather later) votive altars.

At first sight, it might be tempting to order all these changes in terms of the different degrees of penetration of Roman rites and beliefs in different sections of the population, the decurions of the *coloniae* and

94 Bémont et al. (1993).   95 Brunaux in Bémont et al. (1993, 135–8).
96 Allain et al. (1992).
97 Lintz in Bémont et al. (1993, 139–42) discusses differences in the types associated with each kind of context.
98 Deyts (1994). The choice of media probably reflected in part the distribution of workable stone and clay deposits.
99 Boucher (1976), in discussing these, stresses the predominance of classical iconography and subjects by comparison with figurines in other media, and the greater influence of Italian techniques and styles on local productions.

municipia creating a new Roman religion for Gaul, while peasants and those who lived in remote areas clung to traditional practices as far as it was possible and safe to do so. Without doubt, Gallo-Roman elites, and others in close contact with Romans for example auxilary veterans, did play leading roles in remodelling the religious life of the Gauls. Equally, rough carvings in local stone and wood were cheaper and probably less prestigious than marble altars or bronze figurines and so attest to the cults of poorer Gallo-Romans. But that picture needs to be nuanced.

To begin with, the Gallo-Roman elite, when they established cults like that of Vesonna at Périgueux or those of the Altbachtal at Trier, were among the most active syncretizers. Even Roman administrators on occasion might pay cult to indigenous Martes, and Roman soldiers often worshipped locally syncretized gods and the Matres.[100] The implications of the Gallo-Roman elites' concern to keep faith with the old gods at the same time as embracing the new will be considered in the next section. It is worth remarking here, however, that since Roman religion was collective, the notion of one religion for the educated and another for the masses is inappropriate: Mars Camulus was the god of *all* the Remi, decurions and peasants alike. Similarly, cult was paid to such gods in association with the *numina* of the emperors and other imperial cults, vows were made to deities such as Apollo Augustus, Nemausus Augustus, the Matres Augustae, and dedications to Augusto Marti Britonio or Deo Augusto and emperors were portrayed in the likeness of these gods.[101] Imperial cults worked by associating, in one way or another, the emperors and existing cults, so in this sphere, too, religious stratification on class lines was not possible. Finally, although the public cults presided over by Gallo-Roman priests and magistrates doubtless often took the form of sacifices that would have been familiar to all Romans, the participation of a Vergobret of the Bituriges at a dedication in a ritual pit at Argentomagus during Tiberius' reign is a warning against assuming that the elite shunned older ritual traditions.[102] Turning now to the participation of the masses in Gallo-Roman religion, while it is true that indigenous gods were most likely to be worshipped by dedicators without the three names of real or pretended Roman

100 Wightman (1986, 577–84). Millett (1995) points out that double-named deities are rare in Britain and most are mentioned in dedications by Roman administrators and soldiers. Webster (1995) makes a similar point. Double-named gods are in any case relatively rare compared to gods with indigenous names or gods with Roman ones; see Zoll (1994), (1995).
101 Le Glay (1991), Turcan (1996). The ubiquity of the emperor's name and face was not peculiar to Gaul, nor is it a sign that all monumental complexes, rural and urban, were designed primarily to serve the imperial cult, *pace* Gros (1991), Finker and Tassaux (1992). Rather the emperor was inserted here, as elsewhere, into countless cultic contexts.
102 Allain *et al.* (1981). For the site, see Coulon (1996).

citizenship,[103] it was not the case that those worshippers confined their attention to indigenous deities. Popular cults were very diverse, directed to local and indigenous deities of course, but also to syncretized deities like Silvanus-Sucellus in Narbonensis, to the Matres, to Hercules, to Cybele in southern cities and everywhere to the imperial house and the emperor's *numina*.[104] Indeed if Latin dedications in the Gallic and German provinces are taken as a whole, the gods most commonly named are Jupiter, Mercury, Mars, Apollo, Hercules, Fortuna, Mithras, Cybele and Silvanus.[105]

Despite the leading role in all these transformations played by the new Gallo-Roman elites, it is difficult to believe that such wide-ranging changes could have taken place had the majority of Gauls held stubbornly to their ancestral rites or even had they remained passive and uninvolved. Although magistrates had jurisdiction over private as well as public cult neither they nor the Roman administration could in practice have compelled conformity. Yet recognizably Roman forms of religious activity were widely adopted in precisely the same period as an older ritual tradition was being in part abandoned, as sanctuaries were taking on a markedly new physical form, and as the gods were being given new names and, for the first time, faces. The inevitable conclusion is that Roman religion had an attraction for Gauls that was also based on the primary function of religion, to make sense of the world and of human experience of it. Whether or not the term conversion is used to describe it,[106] a revolution in practice and belief had occurred in Gaul.

103 Toutain (1906–20, vol. 3, 437–54). Correlations between worshippers without the *tria nomina* and indigenous or syncretized deities are better attested in the south, for which see Lavagne (1979) on cults of various Martes, and (on the basis of a smaller sample) Carré (1981), than in the north, for which see Wightman (1986, 583). On the need to revise Toutain's conclusions, see Le Glay (1984). It is rarely possible to analyze these samples in terms of the chronological development of the phenomenon, but a gradual shift towards the cult of Roman deities seems likely, for which see below section III.

104 Le Glay (1984) offers a masterly demonstration that, throughout the West, popular and indigenous cults were not identical. For doubts about the distinctiveness of rural religion in the Roman period, see North (1995).

105 MacMullen (1981, 5–7). The measure is certainly crude and obscures major interregional contrasts, for example between the cult payed by soldiers in the north-east and those of civilian Gaul, or that between Narbonensis and the interior. Contrasts existed within those regions too, but the broad conclusion, that Roman gods were very widely worshipped, is inescapable.

106 Nock (1933) and Goodman (1994) conventionally reject the use of the term in connection with classical religion. To be sure, Gauls were not invited to exchange *in toto* one belief system for another, there was no clear boundary across which they might pass to acquire a new identity, and no specifically religious institution concerned itself with the recruitment of converts. The resemblances remain, however, and Goodman's (1994, 14) definition of a proselytizing mission as 'a universal mission to bring people perceived as outsiders into a particular community and to convert them to views held by that community' would be applicable to Roman conceptions of their celestial vocation if 'rites practised' were substituted for 'views held'.

III   A new heaven and a new earth

Let us begin from this assumption, that the Romans of Gaul believed in their gods and that their religion gave meaning to their world. It is difficult to believe that the Gauls exchanged a religious system that made good sense of the world for one that made less sense of it. It follows that Roman cults must either have made equally good sense of the world or that they offered a superior understanding. The rapidity with which private cults in particular changed strongly suggests that, during the formative period of Gallo-Roman civilization, Roman religion came to be understood to be better as well as different. Yet Gallo-Roman religion did not entail the utter rejection of existing paths to the sacred. That pattern of encounter is in any case only really plausible if one religion made exclusivist claims of the kind familiar from the history of Judaism, Christianity and Islam, but even the Isiac religion and other revelatory 'mystery' cults seem to have claimed that the understandings they offered supplemented rather than replaced prior religious knowledge. If the structures – cognitive and institutional – of Roman polytheism help explain why Romans did not require the Gauls to abandon their gods, it remains to be asked why the Gauls wished to retain them. Any account of why Gauls chose to worship in a Roman way must therefore take into account the persistence of divine names that were not Roman in origin; the construction of new temples on sites that had long been sacred; and the use of new representational arts and of writing to portray deities who had never had images before.

The crisis of iron age religion derived from many sources. Some were wholly secular in origin, for example the census to which Drusus' creation of the federal cult at Lyon responded. Others, like the suppression of human sacrifice and the Druidical priesthood that Romans associated with it, may have been seen as more direct attacks on Gaulish religion. The destruction of a native religious elite, particularly if the Druids really had monopolized religious knowledge[107] and had been essential for the performance of some central rituals, would have been enormously damaging. Other new impositions mingled secular and religious demands, such as the requirement imposed on communities

---

107 The second-century AD calendar found at Coligny, published in *RIG* III and on which (cautiously), see Olmsted (1992), is sometimes cited as a sign of surviving traditional religious lore and practice. The lettering and design of the calendar is apparently modelled on Roman calendars, even if the division of time embodied in it may reproduce pre-conquest traditions. The possibility that some religious lore survived the suppression of Druidism cannot be excluded, then, but it is also possible that the calendar is a late and erudite antiquarian reconstruction, to be compared with the renewed interest in Druidism attested in the fourth century AD; see Bachelier (1960).

who wished to receive municipal or colonial status to organize public cults and priesthoods on Roman lines. For the new Gallo-Roman elites, there was also the disturbing confrontation with Roman attitudes to much of the iron age ritual tradition, to sacrifices of the kind performed at Gournay for example. Privately, as the attitudes expressed in numerous passages of Juvenal and Tacitus show, Romans were intolerant of much ritual practice that was not explicitly forbidden by the religious authorities of the state. Those attitudes must have posed difficulties for Gallic elite members concerned to transform themselves and their children into Romans and to win esteem and approval from their new masters.

Roman religion also posed an explicit intellectual challenge to the leaders of the Gauls. At the federal sanctuary, in schoolrooms like those in Autun and from the speeches of Roman governors and commanders, Gallic leaders will have acquired an understanding of the Roman conception of a divine mandate for the empire, of Roman success on earth depending on the maintenance of proper relations with the gods, and of the intimate links between the civilizing process and the right rites. It is impossible to say for certain whether similar claims of divine sanction for the pre-conquest order had been made by the Druids or others, although it is likely,[108] but in any case Roman success seemed to confirm Roman claims about the worship of the gods. That sense that the destruction of the Druids and the victory of Rome demonstrated the inadequacy of ancestral cults and accepted wisdom may well have been more widely felt in Gallic society. Perhaps, the efficacy of Roman rites having been demonstrated in the most dramatic fashion possible, they were rapidly applied by private individuals to more immediate problems: the recovery of lost goods, the cure of illness, the cursing of enemies and the securing of divine protection on the eve of a journey.[109] But the elite, as in so much else, had a special stake in the new order. Euergetistical priesthood offered them a new monopoly of authority within Gallo-Roman societies. Interest and religious obligation coincided for them as happily, then, as they did for the imperial elite. For them, the internalization of Roman religion and Roman ideas about

108 Gordon (1990, 235–40) discusses the 'theodicy of good fortune', the notion that the existing order is not contingent but rather favoured by heaven. The corollary might seem to be a 'theodicy of bad fortune', that the failure of a society and a priesthood be taken as an indication of heaven's displeasure. A suggestive parallel is offered by the rapidity of the collapse of New World empires, themselves highly dependent on religious legitimation, after the initial successes of the conquistadores.

109 De Sury (1994), demonstrating the use of Roman rituals in Gallic sanctuaries. For curative springs, cf. Pliny *NH* 31.2 & 12 and Landes (1992) with Scheid (1992); for curses, see Lejeune (1985); for vows for a safe return, see Hondius-Crone (1955) and Stuart (1971) on the Nehallenia temples which provide documentation for votives dedicated on the eve of a journey.

civilization offered a new history in which the conquest of the Gauls by Romans made sense and was justified, and a new future in which Gallic Romans might, with the favour of the gods, have an honourable place.

Yet the ancestral religion was not abandoned altogether. The inter-mingling of Roman and indigenous traditions is often discussed in terms of *interpretatio*, conceived of as a translation of the gods of one people into the religious idiom of another. The original phrase is Tacitean,[110] but current usage is confused and perhaps blurs distinctions between a whole series of different expedients used by various groups for various purposes and in different circumstances. Translation is, after all, a procedure that maintains the distinctiveness of two languages. As such it is appropriate as a metaphor for a Roman making Roman sense of an alien cosmology (as Caesar was doing when he stated that the Gauls worshipped Mercury above other gods) and for any parallel activity on the part of Gauls to make sense of Roman gods in indigenous terms. The latter activity is, however, difficult to establish since it is rarely possible to distinguish which deities were being worshipped through any given iron age rites, and those rites were in any case disappearing in this period. The so called *interpretatio Gallica* or *Celtica*[111] is rather different, since this (modern) term is usually applied when Gauls are believed to have been using Roman names or images as a sort of disguise for con-tinued worship of an indigenous god. If such a disguise was successful, of course, it is now impenetrable, since the name and image of Jupiter standing for Taranis is indistinguishable from that used for the worship of Jupiter. An image of Jupiter accompanied by that of a wheel, however, poses rather different problems, for the wheel signifies a non-standard association for Jupiter, yet fails to disguise Taranis. It is far from obvious, however, that it should be interpreted as an 'incomplete' or 'unsuccess-ful' disguise.[112] It is perfectly likely, if unverifiable, that Gauls did on occasion translate Roman gods just as Romans translated some Gallic ones. But in most cases, translation is not an appropriate metaphor, since what was being created was in fact a new language in which elements of the old had a place alongside innovations.

---

110 Tacitus *Germania* 43, explaining the basis of the equation in terms of similar charac-teristics of the indigenous and Roman gods being equated. For a fundamental dis-cussion of the term, see Wissowa (1916–19).

111 E.g. Grenier (1956).

112 In some cases the disguise thesis is clearly untenable. Scheid (1995) shows how some syncretisms in the sanctuary of the Altbachtal at Trier show an impressive awareness of the attributes and functions of the Roman gods chosen as 'equivalents' for local deities. That sanctuary was, however, apparently founded well after the conquest and was under the control of the decurions of a Roman colony, and the results cannot be generalized to all *interpretationes*.

The decision by the Treveran *decuriones* to initiate public cult to Mars Lenus, the creation of images of Jupiter with the wheel in Narbonensis, and the setting up by individual merchants of votive altars to Dea Nehalennia on which she was portrayed anthropomorphically but accompanied by a small dog pose the problem precisely, and it is not one of translation but of syncretism.[113] A deliberate decision was made in each case to combine elements drawn from two symbolic systems in order to represent the gods. Syncretism took many forms. It was not the case, for example, that a written description always expressed a Roman identity and the iconography a Gallic one. Either a name or an image might combine old and new elements. Nor can these combinations be regarded as in some sense 'bilingual', announcing two identities to two potential audiences, since some of the media used, such as Latin epigraphy, were accessible to only a few. Nor was combination obligatory, as classical statuettes of Venus illustrate, as well as those dedications on which the deity's name is wholly indigenous, although it may be inscribed and in Latin and perhaps prefixed with the title Dea or Deus. It was possible to dedicate to Mercury, to Mercury Dumias or to Rosmerta. Nor was the distinction determined by dedicant or context, since dedications to pairs such as Mercury and Rosmerta are common. One of the most famous of early Gallo-Roman religious monuments is a pillar set up in Tiberius' reign by the shippers of the Parisii and dedicated to Jupiter the Greatest and Best.[114] The techniques of construction are Roman, as is the Latin epigraphy and the notion of the dedication, but the gods on the column, and the images and names by which they are represented, are a mixture of classical and indigenous, Venus, Fortuna, Vulcan, Castor and Pollux, but also Mars together with the local goddess Boudana, Cernunnos complete with horns and a torc, Smertrios attacking a serpent, Tarvos Trigaranus (the bull with three cranes), Esus cutting down a tree and a series of figures that are difficult to identify. On this monument, classical and indigenous gods are distinguished but placed in relation to each other, by juxtaposition (and in the one case by divine marriage). Establishing public cult to Mars Lenus, or portraying Nehalennia in human form, also asserted relationships of this kind.

There were rules, or at least conventions, governing these combinations. For example, in the north east, male gods were usually given Roman or dual names while most goddesses remained un-syncretized.[115]

113 For discussion of modern syncretism, see Stewart and Shaw (1994), emphasising the creative nature and ubiquity of religious borrowings, mostly in the context of nineteenth- and twentieth-century colonialism.
114 Deyts (1992, 146–9), Duval (1956).
115 Derks (1991), with comments by Zoll (1994).

It is also common in inscriptions for the classical name to precede the indigenous, which might then function much as an epithet did in classical religion, so Mars Mullo, Apollo Grannius and Mercurius Dumias. There was, however, no objection to syncretizing the same classical god with a number of indigenous deities in the same region – or even, as at Rennes, in the same sanctuary – to the extent that in some areas virtually all the male gods were Martes or Mercurii.[116] Similarly the new iconography followed certain rules. Deities were portrayed anthropomorphically, but animals like Epona's horse and Nehalennia's dog might feature alongside them in depictions, together with conventional classical motifs such as *cornucopiae*. Tripling of images was acceptable, indeed relatively common in the case of 'mother goddesses'. Inscriptions might be added, in which case they were virtually always in Latin. One way to understand these conventions or rules is as manifestations of the same prescriptive attitude that governed sacrifice and other rituals. Representing the gods, in other words, was itself an act of ritual,[117] perhaps especially since the majority of these images were used in cult, whether in sanctuaries or *lararia*, as grave goods or in commemorating the discharging of a vow.

References made to the ancestral traditions of *both* Gauls and Romans were thus deliberate. A number of Roman religious customs permitted and perhaps encouraged these strategies: the notion that each place had its own gods, for example, as expressed in the cult of the *genius loci*; the acceptance of alien gods as real; the practice of translation (*interpretatio*), which was in some respects analogous to, although not identical with, syncretism; the Romans' use of epithets to give more precise meanings to cults; even the notion of the juxtaposition of images and names, a device used widely to insert the emperor into ancient cults and temples.[118]

The theme might be explored further in relation to sacred space.[119] From the Augustan period on, a new landscape of the sacred was created in which new and old elements alike had their places. All settlements, from Lyon to the lowliest of the Vosges villages, had communal

---

116 On the popularity of these two gods for syncretism in different regions, cf. Benoit (1959), Thevenot (1968, 52–3), and for a case study, see Merten (1985).
117 Sperber (1975).
118 In this sense, Gordon (1990, 243) and Webster (1995) are right to note that *interpretatio* operated ideologically to sustain the power relations out of which the empire was constituted, although it is perhaps too simple to see it primarily as an imperialist strategy. The debate over whether it impoverished (Clavel-Lévêque 1972) or enriched (Letta 1984) Gallic polytheism depends on the use of criteria that are essentially subjective.
119 For such an approach see Alcock (1993, 172–99).

shrines, and all political entities, such as *coloniae, civitates* and *pagi,* had official cults on the standard Roman model.[120] Not all public cults were based, like those of the Treveri, in urban or suburban temple complexes: the main Arvernian sanctuary was on the Puy-de-Dôme, an extinct volcano above Clermont-Ferrand. Some rural sanctuaries, for example Ribemont-sur-Ancre and Gournay-sur-Aronde, were at sites which had been religiously important before the conquest, and a number were founded in physical locales which were believed to be especially numinous, most famously at the sources of rivers. There is no reason to believe that rural sanctuaries were vested with particular political functions,[121] even if they benefited from the euergetism of rich devotees and were centres at which worshippers gathered at regular intervals. A minority of Gallo-Roman rural sanctuaries were very large complexes, such as Ribemont in Picardy, Grand in the Vosges or Sanxay in Vienne,[122] which probably attracted worshippers from well outside the *civitates* in which they were situated. But the majority were very small structures – often called *fana* or 'Romano-Celtic' temples – and usually consisted of a single room, the *cella,* round, square or octagonal in plan, often surrounded by a gallery and a sacred enclosure.[123] Some contained stone, and perhaps wooden, cult statues and votive offerings, like those of Roman shrines, but the overall design usually showed little classical influence, and parallels for most elements of the plan can be found among the very diverse small temples known from iron age Europe.[124] Architecturally the phenomenon is best understood as the replacing of previous structures in new materials and using new techniques, rather as was argued for *villae.* Some were constructed on ancient sites like Ribemont and Bibracte, others on new sites like Autun and in the

---

120 Scheid (1991) provides a demonstration of this in relation to the Treveri. Drinkwater (1979a) stresses the prominence of priesthoods in inscriptions that record local careers. For the 'standard Roman model', see Gordon (1990).

121 Picard's (1973), (1975) and (1976) suggestion, accepted by Nicolini (1976) that the largest sanctuaries were founded by Gallic aristocrats to provide civic amenities for dispersed rural populations, is no longer widely accepted. It has become clear that many of these 'isolated' *conciliabula* were in fact the monumental centres of small towns, for which see Aeberhardt (1985), Desbordes (1985), and that there was no evidence at Gallic rural sanctuaries for any non-religious functions of the kind attributed to *conciliabula* in Italy, for which see Jacques (1991).

122 On Ribemont: Cadoux (1984a), (1991); for Grand: most recently Bertaux (1993) and the account in *Dossiers d'Archéologie* 162 (1991) entitled *Grand. Prestigieux sanctuaire de la Gaule*; for Sanxay: Aupert (1992) with further bibliography.

123 Fauduet (1993) has the most up to date survey, together with the papers gathered in Goudineau, Fauduet and Coulon (1994) and the atlas of sites collected by Fauduet and Bertin (1993).

124 But see Horne (1986) for some exceptions. Brunaux (1991) offers some sense of the variety of iron age sanctuaries.

Altbachtal sanctuary, and many were scattered throughout the country-side, in isolated spots, as roadside shrines or associated with *villae*. Over six hundred are now known in Gaul, and in some *civitates* more than twenty have been located, most constructed at much the same time as the cities and small towns of Gaul. Romano-Celtic temples did not represent an 'indigenous' cult structure, then, nor a rural one. Instead they illustrate the very wide extension of the system of fusions, com-binations and replacements that constituted Gallo-Roman religion. No religion of the town, no Roman cults against a backdrop of a barbaric rites; rather a new ritual system developed from numerous currents but representing a unified if complex whole. The new cults retained the capacity to imbue with meaning features of the world that had been changed little or not at all by Roman conquest, such as old gods, old places, the cults of the tribe and perhaps of the ancestors. But they also offered a religious understanding of the conquest of Gaul, of the new order and of the place within it of the Gauls and their elites and of Romans and their emperor.

Gallo-Roman cults were not frozen in this role of mediators between indigenous and Roman religious sensibilities. All religions survive only by repeated re-creation and re-representation in the course of which elements that have become objectionable may be shed and new ones added. Such re-evaluations may have been a particular feature of the first century AD, when religion provided support for both assimilation and also occasional armed rebellion against Rome. Other changes can be traced over the subsequent period, most of them representing a wider adoption of Roman rituals by private individuals. In the north-east the dedication of votive altars, which in the first century had been a practice restricted to soldiers and those Gauls who had served as auxiliaries, became more widespread in Gallo-Roman society.[125] An-other example is provided by the Jupiter columns of which over 150 survive in the Rhineland and the Mosel valley. These monuments – set up in cities, in sanctuaries and on rural estates – carried either an image of Jupiter enthroned or else a god struggling with serpent-footed giants. The other deities portrayed on the columns were a mixture of familiar Roman types and local divinities, combined in a form that was thor-oughly local but shows the influence of various Roman types, such as a first century column in honour of Nero set up at Mainz.[126] Further south, the diffusion of the cult of Mater Magna within Narbonensis is

125 Derks (1991).
126 Bauchhenß and Noelke (1981). On the Nero monument, see Bauchhenß (1984).

another example of the spread of a cult from Rome into Gaul.[127] Occasionally these new cults established relationships with older ones, as the presence of Egyptian astrological tablets at the sanctuary of Apollo Grannius at Grand and the incorporation of Cybele into civic cults at Die illustrate.[128] More often, as in the case of the worship of Mithras or Isis, the new cults seem to have been practised in Gaul in much the same forms as they were elsewhere. But if Gallo-Roman religion in the second and third centuries included many new elements, most of Roman origin, there is no sign of any attempts to modify cults like those of Mars Lenus that had been created in the formative period of Gallo-Roman culture. Rather, Gallo-Romans were participating in the evolving history of the religious life of the Roman West as a whole, even occasionally contributing a cult, like that of the horse-goddess Epona,[129] to that wider complex of rituals and beliefs. Innovations did more often come from beyond the Gallic provinces than from within them, but that is perhaps better seen as an expression of the Gauls' location within the empire, and of the relatively passive role played by the Western provinces of the empire (Italy and Rome included) in the religious history of this period, rather than as a sign of the continued civilizing of Gallo-Roman cults. Gallo-Romans had practised Roman religion since the formative period, but that religion was itself changing, and the Gauls, like other Romans, changed with it.

127 Turcan (1972), (1986). Walter (1974) surveys the spread of Mithraism in Gaul. For the wider context of these developments, see North (1992).
128 See Abry et al. (1993) on Grand; Turcan (1972) on Cybele at Die.
129 Oaks (1987).

9   Being Roman in Gaul

I   Becoming Roman

The culture of Roman Gaul had its origin in a single historical moment, a formative period shared with other provincial cultures in the
East and the West, itself one aspect of a much broader reconfiguration
of Roman power and culture.[1] That formative period lasted a short
century that spanned the turn of the millenia and centred around the
principate of Augustus, although the shift to autocracy was only one
component of these transformations. The life and manners of the south
of Gaul, conquered at the end of the second century BC, were thus
transformed at much the same time as those of the interior which
Caesar added to the Roman empire almost seventy years later. Naturally it took the Gauls some time to satisfy the new cultural aspirations
learnt in that period. The technology gap was formidable, and the cost
of building a new civilization ruinous. But little by little imported wine
and marble were replaced by local products, and stop-gap solutions like
wooden *fora* and imitation *sigillata* were replaced with the real thing.
Eventually, distinctively Gallo-Roman cultural forms appeared, some,
like *villae* and *fana*, the results of Mediterranean technology applied to
traditional structures, others simply local creations, like Gallo-Roman
theatre-amphitheatres and the Jupiter columns of the north-east, that
developed within the increasingly loose complex that formed Roman
imperial culture. That increasing looseness is also evident in the appearance of regional traditions in everything from burial rites to ceramic
tablewares. The regional diversity of Gallo-Roman culture in the second and third centuries AD recalls that of the very different cultures of
the late La Tène period. Cultural diversity is unsurprising, the default
condition of the perpetual creativity of human societies, especially when

1 See Ward-Perkins (1970), Woolf (1995) for this perspective and (1994b) for a study
   of its distinctive manifestation in the Greek East. On this transformation of imperial
   culture, see most recently Zanker (1988) with Wallace-Hadrill (1989b) and Nicolet
   (1988).

unrestrained by modern communications and industrial production, and uncoerced by the cultures of the nation-state. Regional diversity has in any case long been characteristic of France, a product in part of an environment that, without insulating populations, has permitted their circumscription into local communities and traditions.[2] It is the brief convergence of Roman provincial cultures during the formative period that demands explanation.

Various factors have been invoked to account for that moment of convergence. The initial stimulus was the extraordinary disruption of Gallic societies by the extension of Roman power into Gaul. Trade, and even military conquest, were relatively minor and early components of this process. The formative period coincides more closely with a structural transformation manifested in the imposition of much more intense structures of exploitation and control, institutions that bound Gallic communities and individuals more and more tightly within the empire of cities and the empire of friends. The census, the levy, new taxes, new constitutions, the spread of a cash economy, of Roman education, of citizenship and of law, and the *pax Romana* itself were just the most prominent features of this penetration of Gallic societies by Roman power. But imperialism, even understood in these terms, provides only a partial explanation for cultural change. Also important were the attitudes that accompanied it, the notion of a civilizing process, that divinely sanctioned ideology of the Roman empire, or the idea that Roman identity was intimately connected with *mores*, and the significance that those attitudes gave to culture as a basis for patronage and privilege. Roman imperialism and the attitudes that accompanied it provided the opportunity for some groups in Gallic society – notably the emergent aristocracies of the new Gallo-Roman communities, but also auxiliary soldiers, the neighbours of veteran colonists and others in close contact with Romans – to make strategic use of Roman culture to acquire privileged places for themselves in the new order of things. Those uses were more complex than simple emulation, even if they were seen as such by Romans confident of their own civilization. Roman civilization also offered more sensual attractions, and a consolation for conquest. Nevertheless, the public contexts of the earliest manifestations of this process – civic centres and monuments, equipment for dining and burial and so forth – suggest that, to begin with, Roman culture satisfied public needs more than private desires. Other enabling factors can be inferred by comparing the Gallic experience to that of

2 See Fox (1971) on this enduring feature of inland France. For a historical perspective, see Weber (1979) and Braudel (1988).

other provincial populations. There is no sign, for example, that Rome had to make concessions to the defining symbols of Gallic identities as they did to the customs of the Jews or the language of the Greeks. Even the gods of the Gauls might be accommodated within Roman religion, if they were prepared to give up their traditional priests and a part of their ancestral rites.

Romans, too, played a part in the creation of Gallo-Roman culture that was not limited to tolerant approbation of those who civilized themselves. Emperors, governors, landowners, teachers, architects, sculptors, craftsmen, traders, colonists, soldiers, and many others, played active roles in the creation of Gallo-Roman civilization. That process confirmed the imperial conceits of some Romans, and made some rich, especially during that initial period when the demand for Roman goods seems to have been insatiable. The pace and profits of the civilizing process inevitably slowed, as the capacity of Gaul to produce Roman goods of its own increased, and as the need to prove oneself Roman declined with the Gauls' progressive integration into the empire. By stages now difficult to measure, the styles and goods that had once symbolized Roman and not Gaulish, civilized and not barbarian came to mean rich not poor, and educated not boorish. But by the late first century, an elite who regarded themselves as both Gallic and Roman were advertising their social status with a culture of exclusion that was thoroughly Roman in form. Naturally, areas existed which were in some senses 'backward' and 'peripheral', but that status reflected their location in an imperial geography of civilization, and they were far from cultural Galapagos Islands, inhabited by remnant La Tène societies. Nothing could have been more Roman (in the sense of characteristic of living in the Roman empire) than to be culturally peripheralized.

It is meaningless to ask, then, how Roman (let alone how Romanized) were the Gauls. Those Roman aristocrats who had taken on themselves the burden of regulating civilization had defined Roman culture in such a way that it might function as a marker of status, not of political or ethnic identity. That situation has not been uncommon in the past,[3] but its rarity in more recent times may have led us to misunderstand Roman culture in the provinces. Modern national cultures are organized around a distinction between metropolitan sophistication and

3 Gellner (1983), although his schematic representations of the cultural anatomy of modern and pre-industrial states are best treated as ideal types. Cultures of exclusion (promoted by dominant social groups) and cultures of inclusion (unifying political communities) have co-existed in most societies, although Gellner is right to note the dramatic shift in their relative importance. The Roman solution was not the only one possible, however, as the experience of Hellenistic kingdoms demonstrates.

uncultivated provincialism.[4] That situation existed to a much more limited extent in the Roman empire, and by the middle of the first century claims based on relative civilization were over-riding those based on Roman or Italian identity, not just in Claudius' speech on behalf of the leading citizens of Gaul, but much more widely, as leading provincials from all over the empire were recruited successively into each level of the imperial ruling hierarchy.[5] By the middle of the second century AD, cultural distinctions between powerful men from different parts of the empire were much less marked than those maintained between them and their social subordinates everywhere.[6] A symbolic centre did exist in the Roman cultural system, but it was located not in any one place or region but rather in the set of manners, tastes, sensibilities and ideals that were the common property of an aristocracy that was increasingly dispersed across the empire. Naturally there were geographical expressions of this system. The city of Rome occupied one central position in the empire of the imagination, the emperor's court (wherever it happened to be at the time) another, and conversely, distant provinces like Germania and northern Britain might stand (in literary contexts) for the limits of civilization. But from the Roman aristocrat's perspective, civilization was to be found anywhere that he was, and he was surrounded everywhere by the primitive or degenerate beliefs and manners of peasants, artisans, slaves and the like. Modern analysts might prefer a more inclusive notion of imperial culture, one perhaps that embraced the experience of the excluded majority. Yet even from that viewpoint the uncivilized Gauls have their counterparts in the uncivilized masses of every province, and also of Italy. The Gallic provinces, in this respect, were as Roman – but also as un-Roman – as any part of the empire.

II   Becoming Roman, becoming different

An immense cultural gap separated the Gallo-Romans from their ancestors. The building and adornment of cities; the red tile roofs that

4 A claim implicitly accepted by those in some modern regions who reject the nation-state on the basis of the antiquity (real or imagined) of their own culture, for which see Trevor-Roper (1983). For the spread of the notion that national communities were or should be co-terminus with cultural ones, see Anderson (1983).
5 A full discussion of the issue would require consideration of the shifting valency of Roman and Italian identities in this period. The *locus classicus* is Statius *Silvae* 4.5.45–8. For some preliminary discussion, see Woolf (1990b, 223–7).
6 The existence of two high cultures, Greek and Latin, slightly complicates the picture, as do the close cultural links between former slaves and their ex-masters. The prominence of cultures of exclusion also reflects to some extent the threat posed to elite exclusiveness by upwardly mobile individuals, especially in the cities of the empire where large numbers of individuals are difficult to classify as either rich or poor.

replaced thatch on farms, temples and town houses; statues of men and gods; and meals cooked in olive oil, flavoured with fish sauces, and accompanied by wine (now mixed with water) sipped from shiny red pottery goblets were among the external manifestations of this distance. Where older ways persisted they were marginalized, revalued as signs of a lack of sophistication, of *urbanitas*, rather than as signs of un-Roman behaviour or cultural resistance. Nor were these changes simply a convenient façade, concealing a core of Gallic sensibility. Material culture is not, in any case, so easily separable from mentality, habit and moral culture. The novelty of Gallo-Roman society was also expressed in new tastes, new senses of style, of cleanliness and of propriety. The Gauls had also gained a new conception of the divine and lost any sense of a past distinct from that of the Romans, and in the process they had become a different people. It is possible in any case that the category of 'Gauls' had no agreed meaning before the conquest,[7] and that it was classical ethnographers and Roman administrators who had invented the identity on which the *imperium Galliarum* of AD 69–70 was based and floundered.[8]

But the creation of Gallo-Roman culture made the Gauls different in other ways. The new order was itself much more highly differentiated than iron age societies had ever been. Becoming Roman did not involve becoming more alike the other inhabitants of the empire, so much as participating in a cultural system structured by systematic differences, differences that both sustained and were a product of Roman power. This aspect of cultural change can be explored in several ways. At one level it comprised the differentiation of roles and spaces within Gallo-Roman society. Gauls thus became more different from each other, as they became more Roman. The emergence in the first century AD of divides between rich and poor, artisans and peasants and slaves and freedmen marks the appearance of a more complex society, within which some individuals had new opportunities to change their roles, homes and identities. Economic growth and participation in much larger systems created a differentiation of its own.[9] Naturally it is the most

---

7 Goudineau (1983b). For modern analogies, see Ardener (1972).
8 As in the case of the Italian identity at the time of the Social War. If provincial boundaries and cults promoted the Roman view of the Gauls as a single people, with a collective identity which provided the basis for the anti-Roman coalition, they also asserted differences between Gauls and Germans which operated as a powerful argument for Gallic loyalty to Rome; see Tacitus *Histories* 4.54–79. Julius Sabinus' claim to be descended from Julius Caesar and his adoption of the title 'Caesar' illustrates the Roman form in which the *imperium Galliarum* was conceived.
9 For a similar approach to the complexification of Anglo-Saxon society and ensuing social mobility, cf. Runciman (1984), and, applied to Rome, Woolf (1996a).

dramatic examples – the rise of senators like Valerius Asiaticus, for example – that attract the most attention, but most mobility was far more localized within the Gallic provinces.[10] Countrymen moved into the new towns, and craftsmen and traders and some landowners moved between them, settling as *incolae* in neighbouring or distant communities. The capacity to escape the local community in this way was a direct result of the Roman peace in Gaul, and it was the common cultural framework of Gallo-Roman culture that made it possible. Finally, greater differentiation was reflected in the specialized place occupied by the Gallic provinces within the empire as a whole.

These themes are neatly brought together and illustrated by consideration of the development, over the first century AD, of an increasingly distinct militarized zone in the north-east.[11] Even if the traditional picture of unbroken tranquillity needs to be nuanced a little, the Gallic provinces were nevertheless probably as typical as any area was of the peaceful, productive core of the empire, protected by and sustaining the military, and supplying the emperors and imperial aristocracies with the wealth on which *pax*, *luxuria* and *indulgentia* depended. Yet for many Gauls, becoming Roman took place in a rather different environment, in the course of military service of one kind or another. That experience evolved over time. During the Caesarian and triumviral wars, Gallic aristocrats had led irregular levies in support of Roman armies, and although the organization of both the *auxilia* and the imperial command structure underwent gradual transformations, there were always Gauls serving in the Roman military as commanders, volunteers and conscripts. The epigraphic evidence is not as abundant for Gaul as it is for other regions, but it seems clear that the Rhine legions were increasingly recruited from Narbonensis, their accompanying auxiliaries were largely drawn from northern and eastern Gaul, and conversely, most Gauls who joined the army were stationed on the northern frontier, in Germany or Britain.[12] The Roman culture of the German frontier zone bore a superficial resemblance to that of the cities and landscapes of the Gallic provinces, but on closer inspection there are marked differences.

10 Krier (1981), Wierschowski (1995).
11 On the significance of these developments, see Drinkwater (1983, 64–9), stressing the establishment of separate German provinces. Those arrangements were simply one stage in a longer process whereby frontier arrangements became institutionalized and the Gauls and Germanies more differentiated.
12 On the development of the *auxilia*, see Holder (1980) and Saddington (1982). Mann (1983, 25–8) shows that the German legions were largely recruited from Italy and Narbonensis, with the balance shifting in favour of the latter in the course of the first century. Holder (1980, 110–19) discusses the prominence of Belgic Gauls in the *auxilia*, throughout the first century, and argues that the majority were stationed on the Rhine.

Patterns of epigraphic commemoration illustrate graphically the bonds that held together one of the few ancient societies not based on kinship. Rank, unit affiliation and comradeship supplanted social status, community of origin and familial relationships on the mortuary epigraphy of the north-east, just as they did in the social life of the camps.[13] Analysis of faunal remains and transport *amphorae* reveals distinctions between the diet of military populations and that of surrounding populations;[14] graffiti reveal the local forms of Latin that provided recruits with a *lingua franca*;[15] and military calendars and private dedications alike list distinctive festivals and cults.[16] The culture of the frontier zones may usefully be considered as civilization without cities. While in the eastern provinces soldiers were often billetted in cities,[17] in the north-west permanent stone-built legionary bases began to be constructed from the late first century AD, equipped with main roads and side streets, 'public' juridical and religious areas around the *praetorium*, and, scattered around the edge of the camp, bathhouses and amphitheatres, cemeteries and shrines. The army provided education, too, and offered mobility – social, economic and geographical – but the Romans it produced were rather different to those that emerged from the civil societies of the Gallic provinces.

Likewise those populations among whom Roman soldiers lived had their own peculiar experiences of becoming Roman. For those who inhabited the *canabae*, the informal settlements that grew up around the forts, there was a variety of close relationships with soldiers, which may have been commercial, filial, sexual, or amicable. Their experience was the underside of the civilization of the troops, a chaotic mixture of those aspects of civic and familial life that had been carefully edited out of the design of the 'military cities'. Others in the vicinity lived lives closer to those of the farmers and artisans of the Gallic provinces, but were exposed to a rather different series of models of Roman life than those presented by the Narbonensian *coloniae*, or in the Gallic interior, where few Romans from other provinces or from Italy ever penetrated. The nature of each different 'contact culture' inevitably left its trace on the new provincial cultures that emerged in each region.[18] Other communities in the frontier zones were transformed into almost wholly

---

13 Saller and Shaw (1984) on commemoration patterns. MacMullen (1984b) on the social organization of military life; see also MacMullen (1963).
14 King (1984), Desbat and Martin-Kilcher (1989).   15 Adams (1994).
16 See Rüpke (1990, 165–98) on the official cult of the army, Derks (1991), (1995) and Zoll (1994), (1995) on private cults patronized by soldiers.
17 Isaac (1990, 269–82).
18 See Foster (1960) for the notion of contact culture. The distinctive development of frontier societies is the main theme of Whittaker (1994).

militarized societies. The Batavians of the Low Countries provide a good example. Encouraged to maintain their military customs, they were recruited in great numbers into the Roman *auxilia* and were used both on the Rhine and in Britain. Their cults, and especially their burials, show how their position in the new order had entailed a distinctive selection from both iron age and Roman culture.[19] Often these different worlds were physically juxtaposed, as in the complex of forts, *canabae* and civilian native settlements around Nijmegen.[20] The culture of the militarized zones of the empire is an enormous subject. The object of introducing it here is simply to indicate some of the variety in the Gallic experience of becoming Roman. There were so many kinds of Romans to become that becoming Roman did not mean assimilating to an ideal type, but rather acquiring a position in the complex of structured differences in which Roman power resided.

Cultural distinctions in the West traced, for the most part, the contours of Roman power.[21] While the complexity, wealth and antiquity of pre-Roman cultures might be expected to have made major differences to the speed or completeness with which indigenous forms were replaced by Roman ones, it is striking how similar the sequence seems to have been in the huge tribal communities of inland Gaul to that in the tiny hilltop villages of southern Iberia or the ancient Punic cities of Tripolitania. The same seems true for Rome's temperate empire as far east as the Black Sea. To be sure, local traditions left a trace in the forms of houses, in regional distributions of cults and rural settlement patterns, in the languages spoken by most of the inhabitants of the empire. But in most respects western cultures were artefacts of Roman imperialism. It is difficult to see any explanation other than the equal contempt in which all these cultures were held by Rome. Elsewhere, the picture is more complex. The place occupied by the Greeks in Roman conceptions of civilization seems to have resulted in a distinctly different handling of provincial communities. Nevertheless, the formative period is evident here, too, although it took different forms, limited in those areas of Greek culture which were central to Greek self-definition in this period, such as language and cult, although more noticeable in fields like civic constitutions, architecture and technology.[22] Roman attitudes to Jews, Syrians and Egyptians were less clear cut, a result of a mixture of respect for antiquity and contempt for the present day, but

19 Roymans (1993).
20 See Bloemers (1990) for a clear discussion, suggesting in addition that Xanten and Tongres might be comparable.
21 Woolf (1997).
22 Woolf (1994b), perhaps understressing the religious dimension of interaction.

without the history of interchange that mediated a similar relationship with Greeks.[23] The compromises differed according to Roman assessments of each group's claims to antiquity and civilization, and according to the different ways in which each group constructed its identity. Discussion of these regions is beyond the scope of this study, but some of the factors adduced in it – the idea of a formative period, the importance of Roman notions of civilization and of the specific ways in which culture participated in the construction of identity – may be applicable in the East as well as in the West.

III   Roman culture and the Roman empire

Rome was not the most seductive of ancient civilizations. Hellenism, in different ways, fascinated Lydians and Carians, Macedonians and Italians, Parthians, Jews and Romans among many others, even when there were few obvious material or political benefits, while Judaism and Christianity exercised even more powerful attractions, enticing some individuals to jeopardize relatively privileged positions in their own communities and in the empire in exchange for membership of minorities who were at best tolerated and occasionally persecuted. Yet if the Greek world seems at times to have been surrounded by a penumbra of would-be Greeks, with others keen to imitate specific aspects of Greek culture from architecture to athletics, the limits of early imperial Roman culture were much more precise. A few items were imported into late La Tène Gaul as they were later into Free Germany or Ireland, but the phenomenon of becoming Roman, in the sense in which it has been discussed here, was firmly limited by the boundaries of the empire.

One possible explanation for the limits of Roman culture would be that noone had ever really wished, in their heart of hearts, to become Roman as an end in itself. Togas and baths, inscriptions and mosaics would then be no more than the props for an elaborate ruse played on the Roman elite, and Tacitus' comment in the *Agricola* would need to be turned on its head, since it was the Romans who mistook servility for civilization.[24] That view is superficially attractive for a number of reasons: it stresses the active role played by the subjects of the empire in the creation of an imperial culture, it offers to expose the conquerors'

23 The nature of pre-Roman identities is not always clear in these regions, and in many areas the issue was further complicated by the prior encounter with Hellenism, which often provided a bridge to Roman culture, for which see Millar (1993) and, for a later period, Bowersock (1990).

24 See Reece (n.d.) for a similar perspective on Roman Britain.

perceptions of the civilizing process as an ideology that deceived themselves more than anyone else, and it entails a view of culture as a means of adaptation employed strategically by individuals and communities to achieve material goals. This explanation will naturally appeal to those committed to any of those positions on general grounds – among them most New Archaeologists, many Marxists, a few post-colonial historians, and those prehistorians and Romanists most concerned to emancipate themselves from historical and classical paradigms at any price. The argument of this book, however, does not support such an explanation. The contrast between the uses made of Roman-style culture in the formative period, and those characteristic of the succeeding two centuries strongly suggests that Roman values *were* internalized by the Gallo-Roman elite. Otherwise it is difficult to understand the continuing use of Roman culture after the crisis in which its use had been adopted. A deception that lasted generations is unimaginable. No means existed for reproducing such a tradition in secret alongside publicly owned values rehearsed in education, in political rhetoric and action, in acts of euergetism and so forth.

The implausibility of the 'thin veneer' view of Gallo-Roman culture has been a leitmotif of this study. Certainly Roman culture did not remain frozen in the shape it had taken in the formative period, and its evolution encompassed both a growth of regional diversity and a shift in the terms in which Roman identity was defined. The re-appearance from the third century of some stylistic forms of pre-Roman origin has been taken as evidence for a 'Celtic renaissance',[25] but there is nothing to suggest that La Tène motifs on common ceramics – if indeed that description of Argonne ware is accepted – had any political connotations, and the phenomenon is best seen as a feature of that loosening of Roman culture that has already been remarked on. Cultural conformity was less of an issue precisely because anxieties about Gallic membership of the empire were less acute. The same attitude is expressed in the opinion of a jurist writing just after Caracalla's extension of citizenship to most of the inhabitants of the empire, that the trusts known as *fideicommissa* were valid even if made in the Celtic language.[26] This relaxation of the definition of Roman culture can be exemplified from all over the empire in this period, along with other changes such as the de-centring of urbanism within notions of civilization, and the increasing importance attached to education. Yet when the military crisis of the third century finally spread to the Gallic provinces, the local elites and the military commanders of the region set up their own emperors

25 MacMullen (1965), but cf. King (1990a, 172–9). 26 Digest 32.1.11.

not as a rejection of Rome but in order to protect Roman life in Gaul from the barbarians.[27] Roman culture can hardly have been adopted simply as a gesture of loyalty to the empire if Gauls would resort to rebellion in order to remain Roman.

The problem, then, is to understand why Roman identity remained so attractive to those within the empire, yet failed to enchant those beyond it. One starting point is provided by the comparison already drawn with Hellenism, Judaism and Christianity. The seductiveness of those cultural movements did not derive from any material rewards open to those who adopted Greek, Jewish or Christian identities, but rather from the content and organization of those cultural systems. Roman culture equally demands to be treated in terms of its content and structure as well as of any pragmatic advantages Roman identity offered to adherents. This is an area where cultural analysis is under-developed, but it is helpful to return to the notion of culture as organized around symbolic centres, points in an interconnected symbol system which are less open to negotiation and change than others, values which operate as points of reference in relation to which other values may be calculated, concepts which articulate the symbol system, spaghetti junctions in a semantic field through which all travellers pass frequently and where chains of significance meet, intersect and depart again. Symbolic centres do not all occur in the same area of culture. For Greeks of the Roman period, for instance, language, cults and a mythology through which religion was linked to descent, often via the Homeric poems, were central to cultural definition, while for Jews, religion was central but language less so.[28] The stress Romans placed on customs (*mores*) and the central articulating function acquired by the notion of civilization (*humanitas*) have already been discussed. One explanation for the limits of Roman culture would be to posit a similar centrality for the relationship conceived between Roman civilization and the Roman empire, between being Roman in a cultural sense and being a member of the Roman political community. Such a notion might be contrasted with the weaker association of cultural and political identity in the case of the Greeks, for whom panhellenism rarely provided the basis for common political action. Roman identity, on the other hand, had not been formulated in conditions of political pluralism, and at least since the late Republic, political dissidents had been represented as culturally deviant, whether barbarizing like Sertorius or hellenizing like Anthony,

27 Drinkwater (1987), with a good discussion of the implication of the iconography of the coins of Postumus and his successors.
28 Schwartz (1995).

or flirting with both as in the case of Catiline. *Humanitas* may have been formulated as a universalizing concept, but Roman identity was perhaps more jealously guarded and closely defined, to the extent that it was simply not available beyond the limits of the empire. That intimate relationship between Roman civilization and Roman empire is also a reminder of the centrality of imperialism in the Roman culture of the principate.

Any temptation to elevate these defining features of early imperial culture into enduring constants should, however, be resisted. Just as Hellenism came in the East to mean paganism, and Greek-speaking Christians in Byzantium came to define themselves as Romans, so, too, in the West the content and structure of Roman culture underwent changes. At some point in the fifth century AD Roman cultural identity became finally dissociated from any particular political membership,[29] and the ethnic 'Roman' came to refer to a people scattered throughout a series of barbarian kingdoms, rarely in positions of power but maintaining, for a time, separate legal and educational systems, and distinguished by their own language, religion (now Catholic Christanity) and literature. Perhaps the political division of the empire had made it thinkable that the Romans might live in several different polities even before the fragmentation of the West, and perhaps the introduction of barbarians into the empire had already raised Roman awareness of themselves as a group distinguished by culture above all, an impression that Christianity will have reinforced in areas that came under the control of pagans or heretics. At some moments in this process of redefinition, a Sidonius might identify himself with the attitudes and lifestyle of a Pliny, but the conceit was purely literary. Being Roman no longer meant the same thing in a changing Gaul.

29 For the most recent attempts to trace this process, see Drinkwater and Elton (1992) and Harries (1994).

Index of works cited

Abrams, P. (1978) 'Towns and economic growth: some theories and problems', in Abrams and Wrigley, eds. (1978), 9–33

Abrams, P. and Wrigley, E. A. eds. (1978) *Towns in Societies. Essays in economic history and historical sociology*, Cambridge

Abry, J. H., Buisson, A. and Turcan, R. eds. (1993) *Les tablettes astrologiques de Grand (Vosges): et l'astrologie en Gaule romaine*, Paris

Abu Lughod, J. L. (1989) *Before European Hegemony. The world system AD 1250–1350*, Oxford

Adams, J. N. (1994) 'Latin and Punic in contact? The case of the Bu Njem ostraka', *JRS* 84: 87–112

Aeberhardt, A. (1985) 'Sanctuaires ruraux et pré-urbanisation en Charente', in Chevallier ed. (1985), 47–59

Agache, R. (1978) *La Somme pré-romaine et romaine*, Amiens

(1981) 'Le problème de fermes indigènes pré-romaines et romaines en Picardie', in Buchsenschutz ed. (1981), 45–50

(1982) 'Les grandes villas stereotypées de la Gallia Belgica: reflet des systèmes politiques, économiques et sociaux?' in Chevallier ed. (1982), 3–10

Alcock, S. E. (1993) *Graecia Capta. The landscapes of Roman Greece*, Cambridge

Alföldi, A. (1952) 'The moral barrier on the Rhine and the Danube', in *The Congress of Roman Frontier Studies 1949*, E. Birley ed., Durham, 1–16

Alföldy, G. (1986) 'Latinische Bürger in Brigantium und im Imperium Romanum', *Bayerische Vorgeschichtsblätter* 51: 187–220

Allain, J., Fauduet, I. and Tuffreau-Libre, M. (1992) *La nécropole du champ de l'image à Argentomagus*, (*RAC* supplément 3 = Mémoires du Musée d'Argentomagus 1), Saint Marcel

Allain, J., Fleuriot, L. and Chaix, L. (1981) 'Le vergobret des Bituriges à Argentomagus; essai d'interprétation d'une fosse cultuelle', *RAE* 32: 11–32

Allen, D. F. (1980) *The Coins of the Ancient Celts*, D. Nash ed., Edinburgh

Anderson, B. (1983) *Imagined Communities. Reflections on the origin and spread of nationalism*, London, (revised edition 1991)

André, P., Desbat, A., Lauxerois, R. and Le Bot-Helly, A. (1991) 'Données nouvelles sur la Vienne Augustéene', in Goudineau and Rebourg eds. (1991), 61–77

Appadurai, A. ed. (1986) *The Social Life of Things. Commodities in cultural perspective*, Cambridge

Arcelin, P. (1992a) 'Société indigène et propositions culturelles massaliotes en basse Provence occidentale', in Bats *et al.* eds. (1992), 305–36

(1992b) 'Salles hypostyles, portiques et espaces cultuels d'Entremont et de Saint-Blaise (B.-du-Rh.)', *Documents d'Archéologie Méridionale* 15: 13–27

Arcelin, P., Dedet, B. and Schwaller, M. (1992) 'Espaces publics, espaces religieux protohistoriques en Gaule méridionale', *Documents d'Archéologie Méridionale* 15: 181–242

Ardener, E. W. ed. (1971) *Social Anthropology and Language*, (ASA monograph 11), London

(1972) 'Language, ethnicity and population', *Journal of the Anthropological Society of Oxford* 3 (3): 125–32; reprinted in E. W. Ardener (1989) *The Voice of Prophesy and Other Essays*, M. Chapman ed., Oxford, 65–71

Audin, A. (1965) *Lyon, miroir de Rome dans les Gaules*, Paris

(1986) *Gens de Lugdunum*, (Collection *Latomus* 190), Brussels

Audin, A., and Burnand Y. (1959) 'Chronologie des épitaphes romaines de Lyon', *REA* 61: 320–52

Audin, A., Guey, J. and Wuillemeier, P. (1954) 'Inscriptions latines découvertes à Lyon', *REA* 56: 297–346

Audouze F. and Buchsenschutz, O. eds. (1988) *Architectures des âges des metaux: fouilles récentes*, (Dossiers de Protohistoire 2), Paris

Audouze F. and Buchsenschutz, O. (1989) *Villes, villages et campagnes de l'Europe celtique. Du début du IIe millénaire à la fin du Ie siècle av. J.-C.*, Paris; English translation (1991) *Towns, Villages and Countryside of Celtic Europe, From the Beginning of the Second Millennium to the End of the First Century BC*, London

Aupert, P. (1992) *Sanxay. Un grand sanctuaire rural gallo-romain*, (Guides Archéologiques de la France 25), Paris

Aupert, P. and Sablayrolles, R. (1992) 'Villes d'Aquitaine, centres civiques et religieux', in *Villes et Agglomérations . . .* , 283–92

Bachelier, E. (1960) 'Les Druides en gaule romaine IV', *Ogam* 12: 91–100

Badian, E. (1958) *Foreign Clientelae 264–70 BC*, Oxford

(1966) 'Notes on Provincia Gallia in the Late Republic', *Mélanges d'archéologie et d'histoire offerts à André Piganiol*, Paris, 901–18

(1968) *Roman Imperialism in the Late Republic²*, Oxford

Balmelle, C. (1992) 'L'habitat urbain dans le Sud-Ouest de la Gaule romaine', in *Villes et agglomérations . . .* , 335–64

Balsdon, J. P. V. D. (1939) 'Consular provinces under the late Republic', *JRS* 29: 57–73, 167–83

(1979) *Romans and Aliens*, London

Barbet, A. (1987) 'La diffusion des Ier, IIième et IIIième styles pompéians en Gaule', in *Pictores per provincias*, (Cahiers d'archéologie romande 43 = *Aventicum* 5), Avenches, 7–27

Barratt, J. C. (1997) 'Romanization: a critical comment' in Mattingly ed. (1997) 51–64

Barrett, J. C., Fitzpatrick, A. P. and Macinnes, L. eds. (1989) *Barbarians and Romans in North-West Europe from the Later Republic to Late Antiquity*, (BAR IS 471), Oxford

Barruol, G. (1969) *Les peuples préromains du sud-est de la Gaule*, (*RAN* supplément 1), Paris

(1976) 'La resistance des substrats pré-romaines en Gaule méridionale', in Pippidi ed. (1976), 389–405

Bartel, B. (1980) 'Colonialism and cultural responses: problems related to Roman provincial analysis' *World Archaeology* 12: 11–26

(1985) 'Comparative historical archaeology and archaeological theory', in *Comparative Studies in the Archaeology of Colonialism*, S. L. Dyson ed., (BAR IS 233), Oxford, 8–37

Barth, F. ed. (1969) *Ethnic Groups and Boundaries. The social organisation of culture difference*, London

Basso, K. H. and Selby, H. A. eds. (1976) *Meaning in Anthropology*, Albuquerque

Bats, M. (1986) 'Le vin italien en Gaule au IIe – Ier s. av. J.-C.: problèmes de chronologie et de distribution', *DHA* 12: 391–430

(1988a) 'La logique de l'écriture de l'une société à l'autre en Gaule méridionale protohistorique', *RAN* 21: 121–48

(1988b) *Vaisselle et alimentation à Olbia de Provence (v. 350–50 av. J.C.). Modèles culturels et catégories céramiques*, (*RAN* supplément 18), Paris

(1992) 'Marseilles, les colonies massaliètes et les relais indigènes dans le trafic le long du littoral méditerranéen gaulois VI-Ier siècle av. J.-C.', in Bats *et al.* eds. (1992), 263–78

Bats, M., Bertucchi, G., Congès, A. and Treziny, H. eds. (1992) *Marseilles grecque et la Gaule*, (Études Massaliètes 3), Aix

Bauchhenß, G. (1984) *Die grosse Iuppitersäule aus Mainz*, (Corpus Signorum Imperii Romani Deutschland II.2), Mainz

Bauchhenß, G. and Noelke, P. (1981) *Die Jupitersäulen in der germanischen Provinzen*, (*BJ* Beiheft 41), Bonn

Bayard, D. (1993) 'Sépultures et villae en Picardie au Haut-Empire: quelques données récentes', in Ferdière ed. (1993), 69–80

Bayard, D. and Collart, J.-L. eds. (1996) *De la ferme indigène à la villa romaine. La romanisation des campagnes de la Gaule* (*Revue Archéologique de Picardie* numéro spécial 11): Actes du deuxième colloque de l'Association AGER tenu à Amiens (Somme) du 23 au 25 Septembre 1993, Amiens

Bayard, D. and Massy J. L. (1983) *Amiens Romain. Samarobriva Ambianorum*, (*Revue Archéologique de Picardie* Numéro Special), Amiens

Beagon, M. (1992) *Roman Nature. The thought of Pliny the Elder*, Oxford

Beard, M. (1986) 'Cicero and divination: the formation of a Latin discourse', *JRS* 76: 33–46

(1990) 'Priesthood in the Roman Republic', in *Pagan Priests. Religion and power in the ancient world*, M. Beard and J. North eds., London, 19–48

(1994) 'Religion', in *CAH*² VIII: 729–68

Beard, M., North, J. and Price, S. R. F. (forthcoming) *Religions of Rome*, 2 vols. Cambridge

Bedon, R. (1984) *Les Carrières et les Carrièrs de la Gaule Romaine*, Paris

Bedon, R., Chevallier, R. and Pinon, P. (1988) *Architecture et urbanisme en Gaule romaine*, 2 vols., Paris

Bee, R. L. (1974) *Patterns and Processes. An introduction to anthropological strategies for the study of sociocultural change*, New York

Bekker-Nielsen, T. (1989) *The Geography of Power. Studies in the urbanisation of Roman north-west Europe*, (BAR IS 477), Oxford

Bel, V. and Benoit, J. (1986) 'Les limites du cadastre B d'Orange. Etude sur les régions de Montélimar et Saint-Paul-Trois-Châteaux', *RAN* 19: 79–100

Bémont, C. and Jacob, J. P. eds. (1986) *La terre sigillée gallo-romaine. Lieux de production du Haut Empire: implantations, produits, relations*, (DAF 6), Paris

Bémont, C., Jeanlin, M. and Lahanier, Chr. eds. (1993) *Les figurines en terre cuite gallo-romaines*, (DAF 38), Paris

Bénabou, M. (1967) 'Une éscroquerie de Licinius au dépense des Gaulois', *REA* 69: 221–27

(1976a) *La résistance africaine à la romanisation*, Paris

(1976b) 'Résistance et romanisation en Afrique du Nord sous le Haut-Empire', in Pippidi ed. (1976), 367–75

Bénard, J. and Mangin, M. (1985) 'Les étapes de la romanisation d'une agglomération indigène du centre-est des Gaules: l'exemple d'Alésia', in Chevallier ed. (1985), 103–16

Bénard, J., Mangin, M., Goguey, R. and Roussel, L. eds. (1994) *Les agglomérations antiques de Côte d'Or*, (ALB 522), Paris

Benoit, F. (1959) *Mars et Mercure*, Aix

Bérard, F. and Le Bohec, Y. (1992) *Inscriptions Latines de Gaule Lyonnaise*, (Collection Centre d' Etudes romaines et gallo-romaines n.s. 10), Paris

van Berchem, D. (1978) 'Un banquier chez les Helvètes', *Ktema* 3: 267–74

Bergquist, A. and Taylor, T. (1987) 'The origin of the Gundestrup cauldron', *Antiquity* 61: 10–24

Bertaux, C. (1993) 'Pèlerinage au sanctuaire antique du Grand', in Abry *et al.* eds. (1993), 25–38

Bertin, D. and Guillaumet, J.-P. (1987) *Bibracte. Ville gauloise sur le mont Beuvray*, (Guides archéologiques de la France 13), Paris

Bertucchi, G. (1992) *Les amphores et le vin de Marseille*, (*RAN* supplément 25), Paris

Bet, P. and Vertet, H. (1986) 'Centre de production de Lezoux', in Bémont and Jacob eds. (1986), 138–44

Bickerman, E. J. (1952) 'Origines Gentium', *CPh* 47: 65–81; reprinted in E. J. Bickerman (1985) *Religion and Politics in the Hellenistic and Roman World*, Como, 399–417

Biró, M. (1975) 'The inscriptions of Roman Britain', *Acta Archaeologica Academiae Scientarum Hungaricae* 27: 13–57

Blagg, T. F. C. (1990) 'First-century Roman houses in Britain and Gaul', in Blagg and Millett eds. (1990), 194–209

Blagg, T. F. C. and King, A. C. eds. (1984) *Military and Civilian in Roman Britain. Cultural relationships in a frontier province*, (BAR IS 130), Oxford

Blagg, T. F. C. and Millett, M. eds. (1990) *The Early Roman Empire in the West*, Oxford

Blanchet, J.-C., Buchsenschutz, O. and Méniel, P. (1983) 'La maison de La Tène moyenne à Verberie (Oise)', *Revue Archéologique de Picardie* 1: 96–126

Blázquez, J. M. (1989) '¿Romanizacion o asimilacion?', in *Nuevos Estudios sobre la Romanizacion*, J. M. Blázquez ed., Madrid, 99–145

Bloemers, J. H. F. (1990) 'Lower Germany: plura consilio quam vi: proto-urban settlement developments and the integration of native society', in Blagg and Millett eds. (1990), 72–86

Bohannon, P. and Plog, F. eds. (1967) *Beyond the Frontier. Social process and cultural change*, New York

Bost, J.-P. and Fabre, G. (1988) 'Aux origines de la province de Novempopulanie: nouvel examen de l'inscription d'Hasparren', *Aquitania* 6: 167–78

Boucher, S. (1976) *Recherches sur les bronzes figurés de Gaule pré-romaine et romaine*, (BEFAR 208), Rome

  (1988) 'L'image et fonctions du dieu Sucellus', *Le Monde des images en Gaule et dans les provinces voisines*, (*Caesarodunum* 23), Paris, 77–85

Boudet, R. (1987) *L'âge du fer récent dans la partie méridionale de l'estuaire Girondin (du Ve au Ier s. av. n. ère)*, Périgueux

Bouley, E. (1983) 'Les théâtres cultuels de Belgique et des Germanies. Réflexions sur les ensembles architectoniques théâtre-temples', *Latomus* 42: 546–71

Bourdieu, P. (1977) *Outline of a theory of practice*, Cambridge (French original 1972)

  (1984) *Distinction. A social critique of the judgement of taste*, London (French original 1979, Paris)

Bourgeois, C. (1991) *Divona I. Divinités et ex-voto du culte gallo-romain de l'eau*, Paris

Bowden, M. and McOmish, D. (1987) 'The required barrier', *SAR* 4: 76–84

Bowersock, G. W. (1986) 'The mechanics of subversion in the Roman provinces', in *Opposition et résistance à l'empire d'Auguste à Trajan*, A. Giovannini ed. (Entretiens Hardt 33), 291–320

  (1990) *Hellenism in Late Antiquity*, Cambridge

Bowman, A. K. (1992) 'Public buildings in Roman Egypt', *JRA* 5: 495–503

Bowman, A. K. and Thomas, J. D. (1991) 'A military strength report from Vindolanda', *JRS* 81: 62–73

Bradley, R. (1990) *The Passage of Arms. An archaeological analysis of prehistoric hoards and votive deposits*, Cambridge

Braemer, F. (1959) *Les stèles funéraires à personnages de Bordeaux Ier aux 3ième s.*, Paris

Brandt, R. and Slofstra, J. eds. (1983) *Roman and Native in the Low Countries. Spheres of interaction*, (BAR IS 184), Oxford

Branigan, K. and Miles, D. M. eds. (1988) *The Economies of Romano-British Villas*, Sheffield

Braudel, F. (1981) *Civilisation and Capitalism I. The structures of everyday life*, London (French original 1979, Paris)

  (1988) *The Identity of France I. History and environment*, London (French original 1986)

Braund, D. C. (1980) 'The Aedui, Troy and the Apocolocyntosis', *CQ* n.s. 30: 402–423

Brewer, J. and Porter, R. eds. (1993) *Consumption and the World of Goods*, London

Briquel, D. (1981) 'Deux propositions nouvelles sur le rituel d'ensevelissement de Grecs et de Gaulois au Forum Boarium', *REL* 59: 30–7

Broise, P. (1976) 'L'urbanisme vicinal aux confins de la Viennoise et de la Séquanaise', *ANRW* II 5: 602–29

Broom, L. *et al.* eds. (1954) 'Acculturation: an exploratory formulation', *American Anthropologist* 56: 973–1000; reprinted in Bohannon and Plog eds. (1967), 255–86

Brun, J.-P. (1986) *L'oléiculture antique en Provence. Les huileries du département du Var*, (*RAN* supplément 15), Paris

Brunaux, J.-L. (1986) 'Le sacrifié, le défunt et l'ancêtre', in *Actes du 8ième colloque AFEAF, Angoulême mai 1984*, (*Aquitania* supplément 1), Bordeaux, 317–26

(1988) *The Celtic Gauls. Gods, rites and sanctuaries*, London (French original 1987)

(1989) 'Les enceintes carrés sont elles des lieux de culte?' in Buchsenschutz *et al.* eds. (1989), 11–14

ed. (1991) *Les sanctuaires celtiques et le monde méditerranéen*, (Dossiers de Protohistoire 3), Paris

(1995) 'Religion gauloise et religion romaine. La leçon des sanctuaires de Picardie', *Cahiers du Centre Glotz* 6: 139–61

Brunaux, J.-L., Méniel, P. and Poplin, F. (1985) *Gournay 1. Les fouilles sur le sanctuaire et l'oppidum (1975–1984)*, (*Revue Archéologique de Picardie* Numéro Special), Amiens

Brunt, P. A. (1959) 'The revolt of Vindex and the fall of Nero', *Latomus* 18: 531–59; reprinted with revisions in Brunt (1990) 9–32, 481–7

(1960) 'Tacitus on the Batavian revolt', *Latomus* 19: 494–517; reprinted with revisions in Brunt (1990) 33–52, 481–7

(1961) 'Charges of provincial maladministration under the early empire', *Historia* 10: 189–223; reprinted with revisions in Brunt (1990) 53–95, 487–506

(1965) 'Reflections on British and Roman imperialism', *CSSH* 7/3: 267–88; reprinted with revisions in Brunt (1990) 110–33, 506–11

(1971) *Italian Manpower, 225 BC–AD 14*, Oxford

(1974) 'Conscription and volunteering in the Roman imperial army', *Scripta Classica Israelica*, 1: 90–115; reprinted with revisions in Brunt (1990) 188–214, 512–13

(1975) 'Did Imperial Rome disarm her subjects?', *Phoenix* 29: 260–70; reprinted in Brunt (1990) 255–66

(1976) 'The Romanization of the local ruling classes in the Roman empire', in Pippidi ed., 161–73; reprinted with revisions in Brunt (1990) 267–81, 515–7

(1978) 'Laus imperii', in Garnsey and Whittaker eds. (1978), 159–91; reprinted with revisions in Brunt (1990) 288–323

(1981) 'The revenues of Rome', *JRS* 71: 161–72; reprinted with revisions in Brunt (1990) 324–46, 531–40

(1990) *Roman Imperial Themes*, Oxford

Buchsenschutz, O. ed. (1981) *Les structures d'habitat à l'Age du Fer en Europe tempérée. L'évolution de l'habitat en Berry*, (Actes du colloque de Châteauroux, Bouges-le-Château, Levroux, 27–29 octobre 1978), Paris

(1984) *Les Structures d'habitats et fortifications de l'Age du Fer en France septentrionale*, (Memoires de la Société Prehistorique Française 18), Paris

ed. (1988) *L'évolution du canton de Levroux d'après les prospections et les sondages archéologiques*, Levroux

Buchsenschutz, O. and Colin, A. (1990) 'Contribution des habitats de la Gaule chevelue à la chronologie de la Tène finale', in Duval, Morel and Roman eds. (1990), 217–25

Buchsenschutz, O. and Méniel, P. eds. (1994) *Les installations agricoles de l'âge du fer en Ile-de-France*, (Etudes d'Histoire et d'Archéologie 4), Paris

Buchsenschütz, O., Olivier, L. and D'Aillières, A.-M. eds. (1989) *Les Viereck-schanzen et les enceintes quadrilaterales en Europe celtique*, (Actes du IXe colloque de l'AFEAF, Chateaudun, 16–19 mai 1985), Paris

Buchsenschutz, O. and Ralston, I. B. M. (1981) 'Les fortifications de l'age du fer dans le centre de la France', *Revue Archéologique* n.s. 1: 45–66

(1986) 'En relisant la Guerre des Gaules', in *Actes du 8ième colloque AFEAF, Angoulême mai 1984*, (*Aquitania* supplément 1), Bordeaux, 383–7

(1987) 'Réflexions sur l'économie de Gaule d'après César et les données archéologiques', in *Mélanges offerts au Docteur J.-B. Colbert de Beaulieu*, Paris, 163–72

Buckley, B. (1981) 'The Aeduan area in the third century', in King and Henig eds. (1981), 287–315

Burghardt, A. F. (1979) 'The origin of the road and city network of Roman Pannonia', *Journal of Historical Geography* 5: 1–20

Burnand, Y. (1961) 'Chronologie des épitaphes romaines de Vienne (Isère)', *REA* 63: 291–313

(1975) *Domitii Aquenses. Une famille de chevaliers romains de la région d'Aix-en-Provence* (*RAN* supplément 5), Paris

(1982) 'Senatores Romani ex Provinciis Galliarum orti', in *Epigrafia e Ordine Senatorio* II, Rome, 387–437

(1990a) 'Personnel municipal dirigeant et clivages sociaux en Gaule romaine sous le Haut-Empire', *MEFRA* 102 (2): 542–71

(1990b) 'Les alliances matrimoniales des sénateurs et chevaliers gallo-romains', in *Parenté et strategies familiales dans l'antiquité romaine*, J. Andreau and H. Bruhns eds., (CEFR 129), Rome, 295–309

(1992) 'La datation des épitaphes romaines de Lyon: remarques complémentaires', in Bérard and Le Bohec eds. (1992), 21–7

(1994) 'Remarques sur quelques problèmes institutionnels du pagus et du vicus en Narbonnaise et dans les Trois Gaules', *Latomus* 53: 733–47

Burnham, B. C. (1986) 'The origins of Romano-British small towns', *OJA* 5: 185–203

(1987) 'The morphology of Romano-British "small towns"', *Archaeological Journal* 144: 156–90

(1994) 'Les "petites villes" de la Bretagne romaine: présentation de l'état des connaissances actuelles', in Petit *et al.* (1994a), 227–38

Burnham, B. C. and Wacher, J. S. (1990) *The Small Towns of Roman Britain*, London

Cadoux, J.-L. (1984a) 'Le sanctuaire gallo-romain de Ribemont-sur-Ancre (Somme): état de recherches en 1983'. *Revue du Nord* 66: 125–45

(1984b) 'L'ossuaire gaulois de Ribemont-sur-Ancre. Premières observations, premières questions', *Gallia* 42.1: 53–78

(1991) 'Organisation spatiale et chronologie du sanctuaire de Ribemont-sur-Ancre (Somme)', in Brunaux ed. (1991), 156–63

Calderone, S. (1972) 'Superstitio', *ANRW* II 2: 377–96

Campbell, C. (1987) *The Romantic Ethic and the Spirit of Modern Consumerism*, Oxford

(1993) 'Understanding traditional and modern patterns of consumption in eighteenth century England: a character action approach', in Brewer and Porter eds. (1993), 40–57

Campbell, J. B. (1984) *The Emperor and the Roman Army 31 BC–AD 235*, Oxford

Carré, R. (1981) 'Cultes et idéologie religieuse en Gaule méridionale', *MHA* 5: 131–42

Célié, M., Garmy, P. and Monteil, M. (1994) 'Enceintes et développement urbain: Nîmes antique des origines au 1er s. ap. J.-C.', *JRA* 7: 383–96

Cels-Saint-Hilaire, J. (1986) 'Numen Augusti et Diana de l'Avetin. Le témoinage de l'ara Narbonensis', in Lévêque and Mactoux eds. (1986), 455–502

Cepas, A. (1989) *The North of Britannia and the North-West of Hispania. An epigraphic comparison*, (BAR IS 470), Oxford

Chadwick, N. K. (1966) *The Druids*, Cardiff

Champion, T. C. (1985) 'Written sources and the study of the European iron age', in T. C. Champion and J. V. S. Megaw eds. *Settlement and Society. Aspects of West European prehistory in the first century BC*, Leicester, 9–22

(1987) 'The European iron age: assessing the state of the art', *SAR* 4: 98–107

Champion, T. C., Gamble, C., Shennan, S. and Whittle, A. (1984) *Prehistoric Europe*, London

Chapman, M. (1982) '"Semantics" and "the Celt"', in *Semantic Anthropology*, D. Parkin ed. (ASA monograph 22), London, 123–43

(1992) *The Celts. The making of a myth*, Basingstoke

Chastagnol, A. (1980) 'L'organisation du culte impérial dans la cité des Riedones à la lumière des inscriptions de Rennes', in *La civilisation des Riedones* A.-M. Rouanet-Liesenfelt ed., (*Archéologie en Bretagne* supplément 2), Brest, 187–99; reprinted in Chastagnol (1995), 29–35

(1981) 'Une firme de commerce maritime entre l'Isle de Bretagne et le continent gaulois à l'époque des Sévères', *ZPE* 43: 63–6; reprinted in Chastagnol (1995), 221–4

(1995) *La Gaule romaine et le droit Latin. Recherches sur l'histoire administrative et sur la romanisation des habitants*, (*Scripta Varia* 3 = Collection du Centre d'Etudes Romaines et Gallo-Romaines 14), Lyon

Chevallier, R. ed. (1976) *Le vicus Gallo-romain*, (*Caesarodunum* 6), Paris

ed. (1982) *La villa romaine dans les provinces du nord-ouest*, (*Caesarodunum* 17), Paris

ed. (1985) *Les debuts de l'urbanisation en Gaule et dans les provinces voisines*, (*Caesarodunum* 20), Paris

Chilver, G. E. F. (1957) 'The army in politics', *JRS* 47: 29–35

Chouquer, G., Clavel-Lévêque, M., Dodinet, M., Favory, F. and Fiches, J. L. (1983) 'Cadastres et voie domitienne. Structures et articulations morpho-historiques', *DHA* 9: 83–112

Chouquer, G. and Favory F. (1980) *Contribution à la recherche des cadastres antiques*, (ALB 236), Paris

(1991) *Les paysages de l'antiquité. Terres et cadastres de l'Occident romain*, Paris

Chouquer, G. and de Klijn, H. (1989) 'Le Finage antique et mediéval', *Gallia* 46: 261–98

Christ, K. (1959) 'Römer und Barbaren in den hohen Kaiserzeit', *Saeculum* 10, 261–98

Christol, M. (1995) 'De l'Italie à la Gaule méridionale, un transfert: l'épigraphie latine', *Cahiers du Centre Glotz* 6: 163–81

Christol, M. and Goudineau, C. (1987) 'Nîmes et les Volques Arécomiques au 1er siècle av. J.C.', *Gallia* 45: 89–103

Christopherson, A. J. (1968) 'The provincial assembly of the Three Gauls in the Julio-Claudian period', *Historia* 17: 351–66

Clarke, D. L. (1979) *Analytical Archaeologist*, London

Clarke, G. (1965) 'The Treveri and the tribute in Tacitus', *Historia* 14: 335–41

Clavel, M. (1970) *Béziers et son territoire dans l'antiquité*, Paris

Clavel-Lévêque, M. (1972) 'Le syncrétisme gallo-romain: structures et finalités', in F. Sartori ed., *Praelectiones Patavinae*, Rome, 91–134; reprinted with revisions in Clavel-Lévêque (1989) 337–87

    (1974) 'Les Gaules et les Gauloises: pour une analyse du fonctionnement de la Géographie de Strabon', *DHA* 1: 75–93; reprinted with revisions in Clavel-Lévêque (1989) 285–306

    (1975) 'Pour une problématique des conditions économiques de l'implantation romaine dans le midi gaulois', *CLPA* 24: 35–75; reprinted with revisions in Clavel-Lévêque (1989) 27–82

    (1976) 'Urbanisation et cités dans l'Occident antique: voies privilegées, impérialisme et transitions', *Cahiers de l'Institut Maurice Thorez* 19: 239–46

    ed. (1983a) *Cadastres et espace rurale*, Paris

    (1983b) 'Pratiques impérialistes et implantations cadastrales', *Ktema* 8: 185–251

    (1985) 'Religion, culture, identité. Mais où sont les druides d'antan . . . ?' *DHA* 11: 557–604; reprinted with revisions in Clavel-Lévêque (1989) 389–456

    (1989) *Puzzle gaulois: les Gaules en mémoire, images, textes, histoire*, (ALB 396) Paris

Clemente, G. (1974) *I Romani nella Gallia meridionale (II-I sec. a.C.). Politica ed economia n'età dell'imperialismo*, Bologna

Clifford, J. and Marcus, G. E. eds. (1986) *Writing culture. The poetics and politics of ethnography*, Berkeley

Cliquet, D., Remy-Watte, M., Guichard, V. and Vaginay, M. eds. (1993) *Les Celtes en Normandie. Les rites funéraires en Gaule (IIIème – Ier s. av. J.-C.)*, (Actes du 14ième colloque de l'AFEAF Evreux 1990 = *RAO* supplément 6), Rennes

Colbert de Beaulieu, J.-B. (1962) 'Les monnaies gauloises au nom de Togirix', *RAE* 13: 98–118

Colin, A., Fichtl, S. and Buchsenschutz, O. (1995) 'Die ideologische Bedeutung der Architektur der Oppida nach der Eroberung Galliens', in Metzler *et al.* eds. (1995), 159–67

Colin, M.-G. ed. (1987) *Les enceintes Augustéennes dans l'Occident romain*, (Actes du colloque international de Nîmes 9–12 Octobre 1985 = *Bulletin Annuel de l'École Antique de Nîmes* 18), Nîmes

Collins, J. H. (1972) 'Caesar as political propagandist' *ANRW* I 1: 922–66

Collis, J. R. (1977) 'Pre-Roman burial rites in north-western Europe', in *Burial in the Roman World*, R. Reece ed. (CBA research report 22), London, 1–13

Collis, J. R. (1984) *Oppida. Earliest towns north of the Alps*, Sheffield
Collis, J. R. and Ralston, I. B. M. (1976) 'Late La Tène defences', *Germania* 54: 135–46
Colloque de Dijon (1974) *L'idéologie de l'impérialisme romain*, Paris
Conkey, M. and Hastorf, C. eds. (1990) *The Uses of Style in Archaeology*, Cambridge
Connerton, P. (1989) *How Societies Remember*, Cambridge
Corbier, M. (1986) 'Grande proprietà fondiaria e piccole aziende: la Gallia settentrionale in epoca romana', in *Società romana e impero tardo-antico. III Le Merci*, A. Giardina ed., Rome, 687–702
   (1987) 'L'écriture dans l'espace public romain', in *L'Urbs. Espace urbain et histoire 1er siècle av. J.C. – III siècle ap. J.C.*, (Actes du colloque international organisé par le CNRS et l'Ecole française à Rome 8–12 mai 1985 = CEFR 98), Rome, 27–60
   (1988) 'L'impôt dans l'empire romain', in *Forms of Control and Subordination in Antiquity*, T. Yuge and M. Doi eds., Tokyo, 259–74
Cormack, R. (1990) 'Byzantine Aphrodisias: changing the symbolic map of a city', *PCPhS* n.s. 36: 26–41
Cottam, S., Dungworth, D., Scott, S. and Taylor, J. eds. (1994) *TRAC 94. Proceedings of the fourth annual theoretical Roman archaeology conference Durham 1994*, Oxford
Coudart, A., Dubouloz, J. and Le Bolloch, M. (1981) 'Un habitat de La Tène ancienne dans la vallée de l'Aisne à Menneville (Aisne)', in *L'âge du fer en France septentrionale*, V. Kruta ed. (Memoires de la Société Archéologique Champenoise 2), Reims, 121–30
de Coulanges, N. D. F. (1891) *Histoire des institutions politiques de l'ancienne France*, Paris
Coulon, G. (1996) *Argentomagus. Du site gauloise à la ville gallo-romaine*, Paris
Crawford, D. J. (1976) 'Imperial Estates', in *Studies in Roman Property*, M. I. Finley ed., Cambridge, 35–70
Crawford, M. H. (1981) 'Italy and Rome', *JRS* 71: 153–6
   (1985) *Coinage and Money under the Roman Republic. Italy and the Mediterranean economy*, London
Crumley, C. A. (1974) *Celtic Social Structure: the generation of archaeologically testable hypotheses from literary data*, (Anthropological Papers of the Museum of Anthropology, University of Michigan 54), Ann Arbor
Crumley, C. L. and Marquardt, W. H. eds. (1987) *Regional Dynamics: Burgundian landscapes in historical perspective*, San Diego
Cunliffe, B. W. (1988) *Greeks, Romans and Barbarians. Spheres of interaction*, London
   (1992) 'Pits, preconceptions and propitiation in the British iron age', *OJA* 11.1: 69–83
Curchin, L. A. (1991) *Roman Spain. Conquest and assimilation*, London
Curk, I. M. (1990) 'Welche Bevölkerungsschichten haben vorwiegend Sigillaten (aus Rheinzabern) gebraucht – Beobachtungen aus Nord-West-Jugoslawien?' *RCRFActa* 27–8, 29–31
Curtin, P. D. (1984) *Cross Cultural Trade in World History*, Cambridge
Daire, M.-Y., Gautier, M. and Langouët, L. (1991) 'Le substrat rural protohistorique en Haute-Bretagne', in Langouët ed. (1991), 165–82

Dangréaux, B. and Desbat, A. (1987) 'Les amphores du dépotoir flavien du Bas de Loyasse à Lyon', *Gallia* 45: 115–53

D'Arms, J. H. (1981) *Commerce and Social Standing in Ancient Rome*, Cambridge, Mass.

Daubigney, A. (1979) 'Reconnaissance des formes de la dépendance gauloise', *DHA* 5: 145–89

   (1983) 'Relations, marchandes méditerranéenes et procès des rapports de dépendance (magu- et ambactes) en Gaule protohistorique', in *Modes de Contacts et Processus de transformation dans les sociétés anciennes*, (Actes du colloque de Cortone 1981, CEFR 67), 659–83

   ed. (1984) *Archéologie et rapports sociaux en Gaule*, (ALB 290), Paris

   ed. (1993) *Fonctionnement social de l'âge du fer. Opérateurs et hypothèses pour la France.* (Table-ronde internationale de Lons-le-Saunier (Jura) 24–26 octobre 1990), Lons-le-Saunier

Dauge, Y. (1981) *Le Barbare. Recherches sur la conception romaine de la Barbarie et de la civilisation*, (Collection *Latomus* 176), Brussels

Davies, W. (1988) *Small worlds. The village community in early mediaeval Brittany*, London

Dayet, M. (1962) 'Qui était Togirix?' *RAE* 13: 82–98

Dedet, B. (1992) *Rites funéraires protohistoriques dans les Garrigues languedociennes*, (*RAN* supplément 24), Paris

Dedet, B. and Fiches, J. L. eds. (1985) *Les enceintes protohistoriques de Gaule méridionale*, (A.R.A.L.O. cahier 14), Caveirac

Deetz, J. (1977) *In Small Things Forgotten. The archaeology of early American life*, New York

Deininger, J. (1965) *Die Provinziallandtage der römischen Kaiserzeit von Augustus bis zum Ende des dritte Jahrhunderts n. Chr.*, (Vestigia: Beiträge zur alten Geschichte 6), Munich

Derks, T. (1991) 'The perception of the Roman pantheon by a native elite: the example of votive inscriptions from Lower Germany', in *Images of the Past. Studies on ancient societies in northwestern Europe*, N. Roymans and F. Theuws eds., Amsterdam, 235–65; reprinted in abbreviated form in *MEFRA* 104.1: 7–23 as 'La perception du panthéon romain par une elite indigène: le cas des inscriptions votives de la Germanie Inférieure'

   (1995) 'The ritual of the vow in Gallo-Roman religion', in Metzler *et al.* (1995), 111–27

Desbat, A. (1990) 'Etablissements romains ou précosement romanisés de Gaule tempérée', in Duval, Morel and Roman eds. (1990), 243–54

Desbat, A. and Dangréaux, B. (1992) 'La distribution des amphores dans la région lyonnaise. Étude des deux sites de consommation', in Laubenheimer ed. (1992), 151–6

Desbat, A. and Martin-Kilcher, S. (1989) 'Les amphores sur l'axe Rhône-Rhine à l'époque d'Auguste', in Lenoir *et al.* eds. (1989), 339–65

Desbat, A. and Savay-Guerraz, H. (1986) 'Saint Roman-en-Gal', in Bémont and Jacob eds. (1986), 127–8

Desbordes, J. M. (1974) 'Jalons pour l'étude des noyaux urbains dans l'antiquité gallo-romaine: exemples régionaux', *Cahiers archéologiques de Picardie* 97–102

Desbordes, J. M. (1985) 'La typologie des sites urbaines dans la cité des Lemovices', in Chevallier ed. (1985), 145–56

De Kisch, Y. (1979) 'Tarifs de donation en Gaule romaine d'après des inscriptions', *Ktema* 4: 259–80

Devauges, J. B. (1988) *Entrains gallo-romain*, Entrains

DeWitt, N. J. (1940) *Urbanisation and the Franchise in Roman Gaul*, Lancaster, Pennsylvania

Deyts, S. (1983) *Les bois sculptées des sources de la Seine*, (*Gallia* supplément 42), Paris

(1992) *Images des dieux de la Gaule*, Paris

(1994) 'Différents types de statuaire en pierre, offrandes et ex-voto, principalment dans le nord-est de la France', in Goudineau *et al.* eds. (1994), 153–60

Dijoud, F. *et al.* (1991) 'Le sanctuaire protohistorique de Roqueperteuse', *Documents d'Archéologie Méridionale* 14: 17–88

Doreau, J., Golvin, J.-C. and Maurin, L. (1982) *L'amphithéâtre gallo-romain de Saintes*, Bordeaux

Dörner, F. K. (1935) *Der Erlass des Statthalters von Asia Paullus Fabius Persicus*, Greifswald

Douglas, M. and Isherwood, B. (1978) *The World of Goods. Towards an anthropology of consumption*, London

Drinkwater, J. F. (1976) 'Lugdunum – "natural capital" of Gaul?' *Britannia* 6: 133–40

(1978) 'The rise and fall of the Gallic Julii', *Latomus* 37: 817–50

(1979a) 'A note on local careers in the three Gauls under the early empire', *Britannia*, 10: 89–100

(1979b) 'Gallic personal wealth', *Chiron* 9: 237–42

(1983) *Roman Gaul. The Three Provinces, 58 BC–AD 260*, London

(1984) 'Peasants and bagaudae in Roman Gaul', *Classical Views* 28: 349–71

(1985) 'Urbanization in the Three Gauls: some observations', in *Roman Urban Topography in Britain and the western Empire*, F. Grew and B. Hobley eds. (CBA Research Report 59), London, 49–55

(1987) *The Gallic Empire. Separatism and continuity in the north-western provinces of the Roman empire*, (*Historia* Einzelschriften 52), Stuttgart

Drinkwater, J. F. and Elton, H. eds. (1992) *Fifth Century Gaul: A crisis of identity?*, Cambridge

Dumasy, F. and Fincker, M. (1992) 'Les édifices de spectacle', in *Villes et agglomérations . . .* , 293–321

Dumasy-Mathieu, F. (1991) *La villa du Liégeaud et ses peintures. La Croisille-sur-Brance (Haute Vienne)*, (DAF 31), Paris

(1994) 'Les agglomérations sécondaires de la cité des Bituriges Cubi', in Petit *et al.* (1994a), 215–22

Duncan-Jones, R. P. (1981) 'The wealth of Gaul', *Chiron* 11: 217–20

(1982) *The Economy of the Roman Empire: Quantitative Studies*², Cambridge

(1990) *Structure and Scale in the Roman Economy*, Cambridge

Duthoy, R. (1976) 'Recherches sur la répartition géographique et chronologique des termes sevir Augustalis, Augustalis et sevir dans l'Empire romain', *Epigraphische Studien* 11: 143–214

Duval, A. (1989) 'Monde des morts, monde des vivants. Qu'appele-t-on "sanctuaire" à l'époque de la Tène?' in Buchsenschutz *et al.* eds., (1989), 161–4

Duval, A., Le Bihan, J. P. and Menez, Y. eds. (1990) *Les Gaulois d'Armorique. La fin de l'age du fer en Europe tempérée*, (Actes du XII Colloque d'AFEAF, Quimper, mai 1988 = *RAO* supplément 3), Rennes

Duval, A., Morel, J.-P. and Roman, Y. eds. (1990) *Gaule Interne et Gaule Méditerranéene aux IIe et Ier siècles avant J.C. Confrontations Chronologiques*, (*RAN* supplément 21), Paris

Duval, P.-M. (1956) 'Le groupe de bas-reliefs des Nautae Parisiaci', in *Monuments Piot* 48, 64–90; reprinted in P. M. Duval (1989) *Travaux sur la Gaule (1946–1986)*, (CEFR 116) 2 vols, Rome, 433–62

   (1961) *Paris Antique*, Paris

   (1976) *Les dieux de la Gaule²*, Paris

   (1986) *Receuil des Inscriptions Gauloises III: Les Calendriers (Coligny, Villards d'Héria)*, (*Gallia* supplément 45), Paris

Dyson, S. L. (1970) 'Caepio, Tacitus and Lucan's sacred grove', *CPh* 65: 36–8

   (1971) 'Native revolts in the Roman empire', *Historia* 20: 239–74

   (1975) 'Native revolt patterns in the Roman empire', *ANRW* II 3: 138–175

   (1985) *The Creation of the Roman Frontier*, Princeton

Ebel, C. (1976) *Transalpine Gaul. The emergence of a Roman province*, Leiden

Eck, W. (1991) 'Die Struktur der Städte in den nordwestlichen Provinzen und ihr Beitrag zur Administration des Reiches, in *Die Stadt in Oberitalien und in dem nordwestlichen Provinzen der römischen Reiches*, W. Eck and H. Galsterer eds., Mainz, 73–84

   (1992) 'Die religiösen und kultischen Aufgaben der römischer Statthalter in der hoher Kaiserzeit', in Mayer and Gomez Pallarès eds. (1992), 151–60

Edwards, C. (1993) *The Politics of Immorality in Ancient Rome*, Cambridge

Egger, R. (1961) *Die Stadt auf dem Magdalensberg. Ein Grosshandelsplatz*, Vienna

Eisenstadt, S. N. and Roniger, L. (1984) *Patrons, Clients and Friends. Interpersonal relations and the structure of trust in society*, Cambridge

Elsner, J. (1992) 'Pausanias: a Greek pilgrim in the Roman world', *Past and Present* 135: 3–29

Engels, D. (1990) *Roman Corinth. An alternative model for the classical city*, Chicago

Eristov, H. (1987) 'Les peintures murales provinciales d'époque flavienne', in *Pictores per provincias*, (Cahiers d'archéologie romande 43 = *Aventicum* 5), Avenches, 45–55

Erskine, A. (1990) *The Hellenistic Stoa. Political thought and action*, London

Étienne, R. (1962) *Bordeaux Antique*, Bordeaux

   (1992) 'Culte de la civitas – culte des pagi dans les Trois Gaules', in Mayer and Gomez Pallarès eds. (1992), 171–6

Fallers, L. (1955) 'The predicament of the modern African chief: an instance from Uganda', *American Anthropologist* 57: 290–305

Fauduet, I. (1993) *Les temples de tradition celtique en Gaule romaine*, Paris

Fauduet, I. and Bertin, D. (1993) *Atlas des sanctuaires Romano-Celtiques de Gaule*, Paris

Favory, F. and Fiches, J.-L. eds. (1994) *Les campagnes de la France méditerranéenne dans l'Antiquité et le haut Moyen Age. Études microrégionales*, (DAF 42), Paris

Fear, A. T. (1996) *Rome and Baetica. Urbanization in southern Spain c.50 BC–AD 150*, Oxford

Ferdière, A. (1988) *Les campagnes en Gaule romaine*, 2 vols., Paris

ed. (1993) *Monde des Morts, Monde des Vivants en Gaule Rurale (1er s. av.-Ve s. ap. J.-C.)*, (Actes du Colloque ARCHEA/AGER, février 1992 = *RAC* supplément 6), Tours

Ferdière, A. and Villard, A. (1993) *La tombe augustéene de Fléré-la-rivière (Indre) et les sépultures aristocratiques de la cité des Bituriges*, (*RAC* supplément 7), Saint Marcel

Ferdière, A. and Zadora-Rio, E. eds. (1986) *La prospection archéologique. Paysage et peuplement*, (DAF 3), Paris

Ferrary, J.-L. (1988) *Philhellenisme et Impérialisme. Aspects idéologiques de la conquête romain du monde hellénistique*, (BEFAR 271), Rome

Février, P. A. (1973) 'The origins and growth of the cities of southern Gaul to the third century', *JRS* 63: 1–28

(1980) 'Vetera et nova: le poids du passé, les germes de l'avenir, IIIe–VIe siècle', in Février et al., 393–493

(1981) 'Villes et campagnes des Gaules sous l'empire', *Ktema* 6: 359–72

Février, P. A., Fixot, M., Goudineau, C. and Kruta, V. (1980) *L'Histoire de la France Urbaine. I La ville antique*, Paris

Fiches, J.-L. (1979) 'Processus d'urbanisation indigènes dans la région de Nîmes (VII–I s. av. n. è.)', *DHA* 5: 35–54

(1986) *Les maisons gallo-romaines d'Ambrusson (Villetelle-Hérault). La fouille du secteur IV*, (DAF 5), Paris

Fiches, J.-L. and Nin, N. (1985) 'Les fortifications indigènes de Gaule mediterranéenne après la conquête romaine', in Dedet and Fiches eds. (1985), 39–50

Finker, M. and Tassaux, F. (1992) 'Les grands sanctuaires "ruraux" d'Aquitaine et le culte impérial', *MEFRA* 104.1: 41–76

Finley, M. I. ed. (1976) *Studies in Roman Property*, Cambridge

(1985) *The Ancient Economy*², London

Firth, R. (1965) 'A note on mediators', *Ethnology* 4: 172–89

Fishwick, D. (1987–92) *The Imperial Cult in the Latin West. Studies in the ruler cult of the western provinces of the Roman empire*, 4 vols., Leiden

Fitzpatrick, A. P. (1984) 'The deposition of La Tène iron age metalwork in watery contexts in southern England', in *Aspects of the Iron Age in central and southern Britain*, B. W. Cunliffe and D. Miles eds. (Oxford University Committee for Archaeology monographs 2), Oxford, 178–90

(1985) 'The distribution of Dressel 1 amphorae in north-west Europe', *OJA* 4: 343–50

(1987) 'The structure of a distribution map: problems of sample bias and quantitative studies', *RCRFActa* 25/26: 79–112

(1989) 'The uses of Roman imperialism by the Celtic barbarians in the later Republic', in Barrett et al. eds. (1989), 27–54

(1991) '"Celtic (Iron Age) religion": traditional and timeless?' *SAR* 8: 123–29

Forni G. (1953) *Il reclutamento delle legioni da Augusto a Diocletiano*, Milan

Foster, G. M. (1960) *Culture and Conquest. America's Spanish heritage*, Chicago

Fox, G. W. (1971) *History in Geographic Perspective. The other France*, New York

France, J. (1993) 'Administration et fiscalité douanières sous le règne d'Auguste: la date de la création de la Quadragesima Galliarum', *MEFRA* 105.2: 895–922

Frederiksen, M. (1966) 'Caesar, Cicero and the problem of debt', *JRS* 56: 128–41

Freeman, P. W. M. (1993) ' "Romanisation" and Roman material culture', *JRA* 6: 438–45

    (1996) 'British imperialism and the Roman empire,' in Webster and Cooper eds. (1996), 19–34

    (1997) 'Mommsen through to Haverfield: the origins of studies of Romanization in late 19th -c. Britain,' in Mattingly ed. (1997), 27–50

Frere, S. S. (1977) 'Town planning in the western provinces', *Beiheft zum Bericht der römisch-germanisch Kommission* 58: 87–104

Freyburg, H.-U. (1988) *Kapitalverkehr und Handel im römischen Kaiserreich (27 v. Chr.- 235 n. Chr.)*, Freiburg im Breisgau

Frézouls, E. (1984) 'Evergétisme et construction urbaine dans les Trois Gaules et les Germanies', *Revue du Nord* 66: 27–54

    (1991) 'Villes Augustéennes de l'Est et du Nord-Est de la France', in Goudineau and Rebourg eds. (1991), 107–15

Fulford, M. G. (1985) 'Roman material in barbarian society c. 200 BC–AD 400', in *Settlement and Society. Aspects of West European prehistory in the first millenium BC*, T. C. Champion and J. V. S. Megaw eds., Leicester, 91–108

    (1989) 'Roman and barbarian: the economy of Roman frontier systems', in Barrett *et al.* eds. (1989), 81–95

    (1992) 'Territorial expansion and the Roman Empire', *World Archaeology* 23: 294–305

Furger-Gunti, A. (1982) 'Der "Goldfund von St-Louis" bei Basel und ähnliche keltische Schatzfunde', *Zeitschrift für Schweizerische Archäologie und Kunstgeschichte* 39: 1–47

Gagé, J. (1964) *Les classes sociales dans l'empire romaine*, Paris

Galliou, P. (1984) *L'Armorique romaine*, Braspars

    (1989) *Les tombes romaines d'Armorique. Essai de sociologie et d'économie de la mort*, (DAF 17), Paris

Galsterer, H. (1986) 'Roman law in the provinces: some problems of transmission', *L'impero Romano e le strutture economiche e sociali delle province*, M. H. Crawford ed. (Biblioteca di Athenaeum 4), Como, 13–27

    (1988) 'Muncipium Flavium Irnitanum: a Latin town in Spain', *JRS* 78: 78–90

Galsterer-Kröll, B. (1973) 'Zum ius Latii in den keltischer Provinzen des Imperium Romanum', *Chiron* 3: 277–306

Garcia, D. (1990) 'Urbanisme et architecture de la ville de Lattara aux IIe–Ier s. av. n. è. Premiers observations', *Lattara* 3: 303–16

Garmy, P. (1992) 'Tradition et noveautés dans les cadres de la vie urbaine au début de l'empire romain', in *Villes et agglomérations . . .* , 223–35

Garnsey, P. D. A. (1978) 'Rome's African empire under the principate', in Garnsey and Whittaker eds. (1978), Cambridge, 223–54

    (1984) 'Religious toleration in classical antiquity', in *Persecution and Toleration*, W. J. Scheils ed. (Studies in Church History 21), Oxford, 1–27

Garnsey, P. D. A., Hopkins, K. and Whittaker, C. R. eds. (1983) *Trade in the Ancient Economy*, Cambridge

Garnsey, P. D. A. and Whittaker, C. R. eds. (1978) *Imperialism in the Ancient World*, Cambridge.

Gautier, M., Jumel, G., Langouët, L., Leroux, G. and Provost, A. (1991) 'L'occupation rurale en Haute-Bretagne à l'époque gallo-romaine', in Langouët ed. (1991), 183–208

Gautier, P. (1981) 'Le citoyenneté en Grèce et à Rome: participation et integration', *Ktema* 6: 166–79

Gayraud, M. (1981) *Narbonne Antique, des origines à la fin du IIIième siècle*, Paris

Gechter, M. (1990) 'Early Roman military installations and Ubian settlements in the Lower Rhine', in *The Early Roman Empire in the West*, T. Blagg and M. Millett eds., Oxford, 97–102

Geertz, C. (1960) 'The Javanese Kijaji: the changing role of a cultural broker', *CSSH* 2: 228–49

   (1966) 'Religion as a cultural system', in *Anthropological approaches to the study of religion*, M. Banton ed. (ASA monograph 3), London, 1–46; reprinted in C. Geertz (1973) *The Interpretation of Cultures. Selected essays*, London, 87–125

Gellner, E. (1983) *Nations and Nationalism*, Oxford

Genevrier, M.-L. (1986) 'Le culte d'Hercule Magusanus en Germanie Inférieure', in *Les grandes figures religieuses, Fonctionnement pratique et symbolique dans l'antiquité*, (ALB 329), P. Lévêque and M.-M. Mactoux eds., Paris, 371–8

Giddens, A. (1979) *Central problems in social theory. Action, structure and contradiction in social analysis*, London

   (1984) *The Constitution of Society. Outline of the theory of structuration*, Cambridge

Gleason, M. W. (1995) *Making Men. Sophists and self-presentation in ancient Rome*, Princeton

Goguey, R. (1978) 'La forteresse de légionnaires de Mirebeau', in *Travaux militaires . . .* 329–33

Goguey, R. and Goguey, D. (1982) 'Villas gallo-romaines à cour peristyle en Bourgogne', in Chevallier ed., (1982) 125 (résumé only)

Goguey, R. and Reddé, M. (1995) *Le camp légionnaire de Mirebeau*, (Römisch-Germanisches Zentralmuseum, Forschungsinstitut für Vor- und Frühgeschichte, monograph 36), Mainz

Golvin, J.-C. (1988) *L'amphithéâtre romain. Essai sur la théorisation de sa forme et des fonctions* (2 vols.), Paris

Gonzalez, J. (1986) 'Lex Irnitana: a new copy of the Flavian municipal law', *JRS* 76: 147–243

Goodman, M. D. (1987) *The Ruling Class of Judaea. The origins of the Jewish revolt against Rome, AD 66–70*, Oxford

   (1994) *Mission and Conversion. Proselytizing in the religious history of the Roman empire*, Oxford

Gordon, R. (1990) 'Religion in the Roman empire: the civic compromise and its limits', in *Pagan Priests. Religion and power in the ancient world*, M. Beard and J. North eds., London, 235–55

Goudineau, C. (1974) 'La céramique dans l'économie romaine', *Dossiers d'Archéologie* 6: 103–9

Goudineau, C. (1975) 'La romanisation des institutions en Transalpine', *CLPA* 24: 26–34
(1976) 'Le statut de Nîmes et des Volques Arécomiques', *RAN* 9: 105–14
(1978) 'La Gaule transalpine', in *Rome et la conquête de la monde mediterranéen*, C. Nicolet ed., Paris, 679–99
(1979) *Les fouilles de la Maison au Dauphin. Recherches sur la romanisation de Vaison-la-Romaine*, (*Gallia* supplément 37), Paris
(1980a) 'Le reseau urbain', in Février *et al.* eds. (1980), 74–109
(1980b) 'Les villes de la paix romaine', in Février *et al.* (1980), 237–391
(1981) 'La céramique Aretine', in Lévêque and Morel eds. (1981), 123–30
(1983a) 'Marseilles, Rome and Gaul from the third to the first century BC', in Garnsey, Hopkins and Whittaker eds. (1983), Cambridge, 76–86
(1983b) 'La notion de patrie Gauloise durant le Haut-empire', in *La Patrie Gauloise (d'Agrippa au VIième s.)*, (Actes du Colloque de Lyon, 1981), Lyon, 149–60
(1988) 'Le pastoralisme en Gaule', in *Pastoral Economies in Classical Antiquity*, C. R. Whittaker ed., (*PCPhS* supplément 14), Cambridge, 160–70
ed. (1989) *Aux origines de Lyon*, Lyon
(1991a) 'Introduction', in Goudineau and Rebourg eds. (1991), 7–15
(1991b) 'Les sanctuaires gaulois: relecture d'inscriptions et de textes', in Brunaux ed., (1991), 250–6
(1996) 'Gaul', *CAH²* vol. X, Cambridge, 464–502
Goudineau, C., Fauduet, I. and Coulon, G. eds. (1994) *Les sanctuaires de tradition indigène en Gaule romaine*, (Actes du colloque d'Argentomagus), Paris
Goudineau, C. and Ferdière, A. (1986) 'La période gallo-romaine', in *Archéologie de la France rurale de la Préhistoire aux temps modernes*, A. Coudart and P. Pion eds., Paris, 74–89
Goudineau, C. and Peyre, C. (1993) *Bibracte et les Éduens. À la decouverte d'un peuple gaulois*, Paris
Goudineau, C. and Rebourg, A. eds. (1991) *Les villes Augustéennes de Gaule*, (Actes du Colloque international d'Autun 6–8 juin 1985), Autun
Grant, E. ed. (1986) *Central Places, Archaeology and History*, Sheffield
Green, M. (1986) *Gods of the Celts*, Gloucester
Greene, K. (1979) *Usk. The pre-Flavian finewares*, Cardiff
Gregson, M. (1988) 'The villa as private property', in Branigan and Miles eds. (1988), 21–33
Grenier, A. (1931–60) *Manuel d'Archéologie Gallo-Romaine*, 4 vols., Paris
(1936) 'Tibère et la Gaule', *REL* 14: 373–88
(1937) 'La Gaule Romaine', in *Economic Survey of Ancient Rome*, III, T. Frank ed., Baltimore, 379–644
(1956) 'La triade Capitoline en Provence', in *Studi in onore di A. Calderini e R. Paribeni*, Milan, 139–42
Griffin, M. T. (1982) 'The Lyons tablet and Tacitean hindsight', *CQ* 32: 404–18
Griffith, G. T. (1935) *The Mercenaries of the Hellenistic World*, Cambridge
Grodzynski, D. (1974) 'Superstitio', *REA* 76, 36–60
Gros, P. (1976) 'Hellénisme et romanization en Gaule Narbonnaise', in *Hellenismus in Mittelitalien*, P. Zanker ed., Göttingen, 300–14

Gros, P. (1984) 'L'Augusteum de Nîmes', *RAN* 17: 123–34
   (1991) 'Nouveau paysage urbain et cultes dynastiques: remarques sur
   l'idéologie de la ville Augustéene à partir des centres monumentaux
   d'Athènes, Thasos, Arles et Nîmes', in Goudineau and Rebourg eds. (1991),
   127–40
   (1992) 'Rome où Marseille? Le problème de l'hellénisation de la Gaule transalpine aux deux derniers siècles de la République', in Bats *et al.* eds.
   (1992), 369–79
Guéry, R. (1990) 'La terre sigillée en Gaule', *JRA* 3: 361–75
Guilhot, J. O. and Goy, C. eds. (1992) *20,000 metres³ de l'histoire. Les fouilles du
   parking de la mairie de Besançon*, Besançon
Guillet, E. *et al.* (1992). 'Une découverte récente: le portique de Nîmes', *Documents d'Archéologie Méridionale* 15: 57–116
Guyon, J. (1991) 'From Lugdunum to Convenae: recent work on Saint-Bertrand
   de Comminges', *JRA* 4: 89–122
Guyonvarc'h, Ch.-J. and Le Roux-Guyonvarc'h, F. (1986) 'Remarques sur la
   religion gallo-romaine: rupture et continuité', *ANRW* II 18.1: 423–55
Haarhoff, T. (1920) *Schools of Gaul. A study of pagan and christian education in
   the last century of the western empire*, Oxford
   (1938) *The Stranger at the Gate*, London
Hainsworth, J. B. (1962) 'Verginius and Vindex', *Historia* 11: 86–96
Hall, E. (1989) *Inventing the Barbarian. Greek self-definition through tragedy*,
   Oxford
Harries, J. (1994) *Sidonius Apollinaris and the fall of Rome AD 407–85*, Oxford
Harris, W. V. (1971) *Rome in Etruria and Umbria*, Oxford
   (1979) *War and Imperialism in Republican Rome 327–70 BC*, Oxford
   ed. (1984) *The Imperialism of mid-Republican Rome*, (MAAR 29), Rome
   (1989) *Ancient Literacy*, Harvard
   ed. (1993) *The Inscribed Economy. Production and distribution in the Roman
   Empire in the light of instrumentum domesticum*, (*JRA* supplement 6), Ann
   Arbor
Hartog, F. (1988) *The Mirror of Herodotus. The representation of the other in the
   writing of history*, Berkeley (French original 1980)
Haselgrove, C. C. (1984a) 'Warfare and its aftermath as reflected in the precious
   metal coinage of Belgic Gaul', *OJA* 3: 81–105
   (1984b) 'Romanization before the conquest: Gaulish precedents and British
   consequences', in Blagg and King eds. (1984), 1–64
   (1987a) 'Culture process on the periphery: Belgic Gaul and Rome during the
   late Republic', in *Centre and Periphery in the Ancient World*, M. Rowlands,
   M. Larsen and K. Kristiansen eds., Cambridge, 104–24
   (1988) 'Coinage and complexity: archaeological analysis of socio-political
   change in Britain and non-Mediterranean Gaul during the later iron
   age', in *Tribe and Polity in late Prehistoric Europe*, D. B. Gibson and M. N.
   Geselowitz eds., New York, 69–96
   (1990a) 'The Romanization of Belgic Gaul: some archaeological perspectives', in Blagg and Millett eds. (1990), 45–71
   (1990b) 'Late iron age settlement in the Aisne valley: some current problems
   and hypotheses', in Duval, Le Bihan and Menez eds. (1990), 249–59

Haselgrove, C. C. (1995) 'Social and symbolic order in the origins and layout of Roman villas in northern Gaul', in Metzler *et al.* (1995), 65–75

Hassall, M. (1978) 'Britain and the Rhine provinces: epigraphic evidence for Roman trade', in *Roman Shipping and Trade*, (CBA Research Report 24), J. du Plat Taylor and H. Cleere eds., London, 41–8

Hatt, J.-J. (1951) *La tombe gallo-romaine*, Paris

(1959) *Histoire de la Gaule romaine (120 av. J. C. – 451 ap. J. C.). Colonisation où colonialisme?*, Paris

(1986) 'Les deux sources de la religion gauloise et la politique religieuse des empéreurs romains en Gaule', *ANRW* II 18.1: 410–22

(1989) *Mythes et dieux de la Gaule. I. Les grandes divinités masculines*, Paris

Haverfield, F. (1912) *The Romanization of Roman Britain*[2], Oxford

Hayes, J. W. (1972) *Late Roman Pottery*, London

(1980) *A supplement to late Roman Pottery*, London

(1991) 'Finewares in the Hellenistic world', in *Looking at Greek Vases*, T. Rasmussen and N. Spivey eds., Cambridge, 183–202

Heather, P. (1994) 'Literacy and power in the migration period', in *Literacy and Power in the Ancient World*, A. K. Bowman and G. D. Woolf eds., Cambridge, 177–97

Hedeager, L. (1987) 'Empire, frontier and the barbarian hinterland: Rome and northern Europe from AD 1–400', in *Centre and Periphery in the Ancient World*, M. Rowlands, M. Larsen and K. Kristiansen eds., Cambridge, 125–40

Henig, M. (1986) 'Ita intellexit numine inductus tuo: some personal interpretations of deity in Roman religion', in Henig and King eds. (1986), 159–169

Henig, M. and King, A. eds. (1986) *Pagan Gods and Shrines of the Roman Empire*, (Oxford University Committee for Archaeology monograph 8), Oxford

Herescu, N. I. (1960) 'Les constantes de l'humanitas Romana', *Rivista di cultura classica e medioevale* 2: 258–77

(1961) 'Civis humanus. Ethnos et ius', *Atene e Roma* 6: 56–82

Herman, G. (1987) *Ritualised Friendship and the Greek City*, Cambridge

Hermon, E. (1993) *Rome et la Gaule transalpine avant César, 125–59 av. J.-C.*, (Diáphora 3), Naples

Herrin, J. (1987) *The Formation of Christendom*, Oxford

von Hesberg, H. (1991) 'Die Monumentalisierung der Städte in den nordwestlichen Provinzen zu Beginn der Kaiserzeit', in *Die Stadt in Oberitalien und in dem nordwestlichen Provinzen der römischen Reiches*, W. Eck and H. Galsterer eds., Mainz, 179–99

Hesnard, A. (1990) 'Les amphores', in Duval, Morel and Roman eds. (1990), 47–54

Hill, J. D. (1989) 'Rethinking the iron age', *SAR* 6: 16–24

(1993) 'Can we recognise a different European past? A contrastive archaeology of late prehistoric settlement in southern England, *Journal of European Archaeology* 1: 57–75

Hingley, R. (1982) 'Roman Britain: the structure of Roman imperialism and the consequences of imperialism on the development of a peripheral province', in *The Romano-British Countryside*, (BAR BS 103), D. Miles ed., Oxford, 17–52

Hingley, R. (1989) *Rural Settlement in Roman Britain*, London
   (1990) 'Boundaries surrounding iron age and Romano-British settlements',
      SAR 7: 96–103
   (1996) 'The "legacy" of Rome: the rise, decline and fall of the theory of
      Romanization,' in Webster and Cooper eds. (1996), 35–48
Hodder, I. R. (1972) 'Locational models and the study of Romano-British
      settlement', in *Models in Archaeoology*, D. L. Clarke ed., London, 887–909
   (1975) 'The spatial distribution of Romano-British towns', in *The Small Towns
      of Roman Britain*, (BAR BS 15), W. Rodwell and T. Rowley eds., Oxford,
      67–74
   ed. (1978) *The Spatial Distribution of Culture*, Cambridge
   (1979) 'Pre-Roman and Romano-British tribal economies' in *Invasion and
      Response: the case of Roman Britain*, (BAR BS 73), B. C. Burnham and
      H. Johnson eds., Oxford, 189–96
   (1982) *Symbols in Action*, Cambridge
   ed. (1989) *The Meanings of Things. Material culture and symbolic expression*,
      London
Hodder, I. R. and Hassall, M. (1971) 'The non-random spacing of Romano-
      British walled towns', *Man* 6.3: 391–407
Hodder, I. R. and Millett, M. (1980) 'Romano-British villas and towns: a
      systematic analysis', *World Archaeology* 12: 69–76
Hoffman, B. and Vernhet, A. (1992) 'Imitations de decors aretins à La
      Graufesenque', *RCRFActa* 31–2: 177–93
Hoffman, B. (1976) 'Diffusion en Gaule romaine des marques sur sigillée italique
      depuis l'époque de César jusqu'au règne de Tibère', in Chevallier ed.,
      (1976), 39–46
   (1992) 'Rappel de quelques marques italiques précoces trouvées en Gaule',
      RCRFActa 31–2: 255–99
Hohenberg, P. M. and Lees, L. H. (1985) *The Making of Urban Europe 1000–
      1950*, Harvard
Holder, P. A. (1980) *Studies in the Auxilia of the Roman Army from Augustus to
      Trajan*, (BAR IS 70), Oxford
Holmgren, J. and Leday, A. (1982) 'L'implantation des villas gallo-romaines
      dans la Champagne berrichonne', in Chevallier ed., (1982), 127–39
Holy, L. and Stuchlik, M. eds. (1980) *The Structure of Folk Models*, (ASA
      monograph 20), London
Hondius-Crone, A. (1955) *The Temple of Nehalennia at Domburg*, Amsterdam
Hopkins, K. (1961) 'Social mobility in the later Roman empire: the evidence of
      Ausonius', *CQ* 11: 239–49
   (1965) 'Elite mobility in the Roman empire', *Past and Present* 32: 12–26;
      reprinted in M. I. Finley ed. (1974) *Studies in Ancient Society*, London,
      103–120
   (1978) 'Economic growth and towns in classical antiquity', in Abrams and
      Wrigley eds. (1978), 35–77
   (1980) 'Taxes and trade in the Roman empire (200 BC–AD 200)', *JRS*
      70: 101–25
   (1983) *Death and Renewal*, (Sociological Studies in Ancient History 2),
      Cambridge

Horne, P. (1986) 'Roman or Celtic temples?' in Henig and King eds. (1986), 15–24

Hostetler, J. A. (1964) 'Persistance and change patterns in Amish society', *Ethnology* 3: 185–198; reprinted in Bohannon and Plog eds. (1964), 289–306

Howgego, C. (1992) 'The supply and use of money in the Roman world 200 BC to AD 300', *JRS* 82: 1–31
    (1994) 'Coin circulation and the integration of the Roman economy', *JRA* 7: 5–21

Humbert, M. (1981) 'Le droit Latin impérial: cités Latines où citoyenneté Latine?' *Ktema* 6: 207–26

Hurst, H. R. (1988) 'Gloucester', in *Fortress into City. The consolidation of Roman Britain in the first century AD*, G. Webster ed., London, 48–73

Isaac, B. (1990) *The Limits of Empire. The Roman army in the East*, Oxford

Jacobsen, G. (1995) *Primitiver Austausch oder freier Markt? Untersuchungen zum Handel in den gallisch-germanischen Provinzen während der römischen Kaiserzeit*, (Pharos 5), St Katherinen

Jacques, F. (1977) 'Les cens en Gaule au IIe siècle et dans la première moitié du IIIe siècle', *Ktema* 2: 285–328
    (1991) 'Statut et fonction des conciliabula d'après les sources latines', in Brunaux ed. (1991), 58–65

Jacques, F. and Scheid, J. (1990) *Rome et l'intégration de l'Empire 44 av. – 260 ap. J.-C.*, Paris

Johnston, D. (1985) 'Munificence and Muncipia: bequests to towns in classical Roman law', *JRS* 75: 105–125

Jones, R. F. J. (1987) 'A false start? The Roman urbanisation of western Europe', *World Archaeology* 19: 47–58

Jones, R. F. J., Bloemers, J. H. F., Dyson, S. L. and Biddle, M. eds. (1988) *First Millennium Papers. Western Europe in the first millennium AD*, (BAR IS 401), Oxford

Jongman, W. (1988) *The Economy and Society of Pompeii*, Amsterdam

Jullian, C. (1908–26) *Histoire de la Gaule* 8 vols., Paris

Kaster, R. A. (1988) *Guardians of Language: the grammarian and society in late antiquity*, Berkeley
    (1995) *C. Suetonius Tranquillus' De Grammaticis et Rhetoribus, edited with a translation and commentary*, Oxford

Keay, S. J. (1992) 'The "Romanisation" of Turdetania', *OJA* 11.3: 275–315

Kemp, W. (1994) 'Ritual, power and colonial domination. Male initiation among the Ngaing of Papua New Guinea', in Stewart and Shaw eds. (1994), 108–26

Kennedy, H. (1985) 'From "polis" to "madina": urban change in late antique and early islamic Syria', *Past and Present* 106: 3–27

Kidd, I. G. (1988) *Posidonius II. The commentary*, 2 vols., Cambridge

King, A. C. (1981) 'The decline of Samian ware manufacture in the north-west provinces: problems of chronology and interpretation', in King and Henig eds. (1981), 187–218
    (1984) 'Animal bones and the dietary identity of military and civilian groups in Roman Britain, Germany and Gaul', in Blagg and King eds. (1984), 187–218

King, A. C. (1990a) *Roman Gaul and Germany*, London

(1990b) 'The emergence of Romano-Celtic religion', in Blagg and Millett eds. (1990), 220–41

King, A. C. and Henig M. eds. (1981) *The Roman West in the third century. Contributions from Archaeology and History*, (BAR IS 109) Oxford

Knapp, R. C. (1977) *Aspects of the Roman Experience in Iberia 206–100 BC*, Valladolid

Kneißl, P. (1980) 'Entstehung und Bedeutung der Augustalität. Zur Inschrift der ara Narbonensis CIL XII 4333', *Chiron* 10: 291–326

(1988) 'Zur Wirtschaftsstruktur des römischen Reiches: Das Beispiel Gallien', in *Alte Geschichte und Wissenschaftsgeschichte. Festschrift für Karl Christ am 65. Geburtstag*, P. Kneißl and V. Losemann eds., Darmstadt, 234–55

Kopytoff, I. (1986) 'The cultural biography of things: commoditization as process', in A. Appadurai ed. (1986), 64–91

ed. (1987) *The African Frontier. The reproduction of traditional African societies*, Indianapolis

Kremer, B. (1994) *Das Bild der Kelten bis in augusteische Zeit: Studien zur Instrumentalisierung eines antiken Feindbildes bei griechischen und römischen Autoren*, (*Historia* Einzelschriften 88), Stuttgart

Krier, J. (1981) *Die Treverer ausserhalb ihrer Civitas*, Trier

Kula, W. (1976) *An Economic Theory of the Feudal System*, London (Polish original 1962)

Kunow, J. (1983) *Der römische Import in der Germania libera bis zu den Marcomannenkreigen*, Neumünster

(1990) 'Relations between Roman occupation and the Limesvorland in the province of Germania Inferior', in Blagg and Millett eds. (1990), 87–96

Labisch, A. (1975) *Frumentum Commeatusque. Die Nahrungsmittelversorgung der Heere Caesars*, Meisenheim am Glan

Labrousse, M. (1968) *Toulouse Antique*, Paris

de Laet, S. J. (1966) 'Claude et la romanisation de la Gaule', *Melanges . . . Piganiol* II, Paris, 951–61

Lambert, P.-Y. (1992) 'Diffusion de l'écriture gallo-grecque en milieu indigène', in Bats *et al.* eds. (1992), 289–94

Landes, C. ed. (1989) *Le Gout du théâtre à Rome et en Gaule romaine*, Lattes

ed. (1992) *Dieux guérisseurs en Gaule romaine. Catalogue de l'exposition de Lattes*, Lattes

Lane Fox, R. (1996) 'Ancient hunting: from Homer to Polybios,' in *Human Landscapes in Classical Antiquity. Environment and Culture*, G. Shipley and J. Salmon eds., London, 119–53.

Langouët, L. ed. (1987) *Les Coriosolites. Un peuple armoricain de la periode gauloise à l'époque gallo-romaine*, Saint-Malo

ed. (1991) *Terroirs, territoires et campagnes antiques. La prospection archéologique en Haute Bretagne. Traitement et synthèse des données*, (*RAO* supplément 4), Rennes

Langouët, L. and Jumel, G. (1991) 'Les campagnes gallo-romaines de la civitas des Coriosolites', in Langouët ed. (1991), 127–34

Langouët, L. and Provost, A. (1991) 'Les relations ville-campagne: le cas de Corseul et de Rennes', in Langouët ed. (1991), 209–13

Laroche, C. and Savay-Guerraz, H. (1984) *Saint-Romain-en-Gal. Un quartier de Vienne antique sur la rive droite du Rhône*, (Guides Archéologiques de la France 2) Paris

Larsen, J. A. O. (1955) *Representative Government in Greek and Roman History*, Berkeley

Lasfargues, J. ed. (1985) *Architectures de terre et de bois. L'habitat privé des provinces occidentales du monde romain. Antécedents et prolongements: Protohistoire, Moyen Age et quelques expériences contemporaines*, (DAF 2), Paris

Laslett, P. (1971) *The World we have Lost*[2], Cambridge

Last, H. (1949) 'Rome and the Druids: a note', *JRS* 39: 1–5

Lattimore, O. (1962) 'The Frontier in History', in *Studies in Frontier History*, O. Lattimore ed., London, 469–91

Laubenheimer, F. (1985) *La production des amphores en Gaule Narbonnaise*, (ALB 327) Paris

(1990) *Le temps des amphores en Gaule. Vins, huiles, sauces*, Paris

(1991) *Les amphores de Bibracte. Le materiel des fouilles anciennes*, (DAF 29), Paris

ed. (1992) *Les amphores en Gaule. Production et Circulation*, (ALB 474), Paris

(1993) 'Au dossier du vin italien en Gaule (IIe–Ier siècles av. J.-C.)', in Daubigney ed. (1993), 57–64

Lauffrey, J. (1990) *La Tour de Vésone à Perigueux*, (*Gallia* supplément 49), Paris

Lavagne, H. (1979) 'Les dieux de la Gaule Narbonnaise. "Romanité" et romanisation', *Journal des Savants* 155–97

Leach, E. R. (1954) *Political Systems of Highland Burma*, London

(1976) *Culture and Communication. The logic by which symbols are connected. An introducton to the use of structuralist analysis in social anthropology*, Cambridge

Le Bihan, J. P., Bardel, J.-P., Menez, Y. and Tanguy, D. (1990) 'Les établissements ruraux du second âge du fer en Armorique', in Duval, Le Bihan and Menez eds. (1990), 97–113

Le Bohec, Y. ed. (1991) *Le Testament du Lingon*, (Collection Centre des Etudes Romains et Gallo-Romains n.s. 9), Paris

ed. (1993) *Militaires romains en Gaule civile*, (Collection Centre des Etudes Romains et Gallo-Romains n.s. 11), Paris

Leday. A. (1980) *Rural settlement in central Gaul in the Roman period* , (BAR IS 71), Oxford

van der Leeuw, S. E. (1983) 'Acculturation as information processing', in Brandt and Slofstra eds. (1983), 11–38

Le Gall, J. (1980) *Alesia. Archéologie et histoire*[2], Paris

(1983) 'La diffusion de l'huile espagnole dans la Gaule du Nord', in *Producción y commercio del aceite II*, J. M. Blázquez-Martinez and J. Remesal-Rodriguez eds., Madrid, 213–23

Le Glay, M. (1975) 'La Gaule romanisée', in *Histoire de la France rurale I*, G. Duby and A. Wallon eds., Paris, 195–285

(1977) 'Remarques sur l'onomastique gallo-romaine', in *L'Onomastique Latine*, Paris, 269–77

(1984) 'Les religions populaires dans l'Occident romain', *Praktika of the 8th International Congress of Greek and Latin Epigraphy I*, Athens, 150–70

(1991) 'Le culte d'Auguste dans les villes Augustéenes . . . et les autres', in Goudineau and Rebourg eds. (1991), 117–26

Lejeune, M. (1983) 'Rencontres de l'alphabet grec avec les langues barbares au cours du 1er millénaire avant J. C.', in *Modes de Contacts* . . . , 731–53

(1985) 'Textes gauloises et gallo-romains en cursive latine: II. Le plomb de Larzac', *Etudes Celtiques* 22: 95–177

Lejeune, M. and Marichal, R. (1976–7) 'Textes gauloises et gallo-romaines en cursive Latine I', *Etudes Celtiques*, 15: 151–7

Lenoir, M., Manacorda, D. and Panella, C. eds. (1989) *Amphores romaines et histoire économique. Dix ans de recherche.* (Actes du colloque de Sienne, CEFR 114), Rome

Le Roux, P. (1982) *L'armée romaine et l'organisation des provinces ibériques*, Paris

Letta, C. (1984) 'Amministrazione romana e culti locali in età altoimperiale, il caso della Gallia', *RSI* 96: 1001–24

Leveau, P. (1983a) 'La ville antique "ville de consommation"? Parasitisme social et économie antique', *Etudes Rurales* 89–91, 275–83 with response by C. Goudineau, 283–9

(1983b) 'La ville antique et l'organisation de l'espace rural: villa, ville, village,' *Annales ESC* 38: 920–42

ed. (1985) *Les origines des richesses depensées dans la ville antique*, (Actes du Colloque d'Aix-en-Provence, mai 1984), Aix

(1991) 'Les campagnes en Gaule', *JRA* 4: 295–8

(1994) 'La recherche sur les agglomérations secondaires en Gaule narbonnaise', in Petit *et al.* eds. (1994a), 181–96

Leveau, P., Sillières, P. and Vallat, J.-P. (1993) *Campagnes de la Méditerranée romaine*, Paris

Lévêque, P. and Mactoux, M.-M. eds. (1986) *Les grandes figures religieuses, fonctionnement pratique et symbolique dans l'antiquité*, (ALB 329), Paris

Lévêque, P. and Morel, J.-P. (1981) *Céramiques hellenistiques et romaines I*, (ALB 242), Paris

(1987) *Céramiques hellenistiques et romaines II*, (ALB 331), Paris

Lévi-Strauss, C. (1963) *Structural Anthropology*, London (French original 1958)

Lewuillon, S. (1993) ' "Contre le don". Remarques sur le sens de la réciprocité et de la compensation sociale en Gaule', in Daubigney ed., (1993), 71–89

de Ligt, L. (1993) *Fairs and markets in the Roman empire. Economic and social aspects of periodic trade in a pre-industrial society*, Amsterdam

Lintott, A. W. (1980) 'What was the "imperium Romanum"?', *Greece and Rome* 28: 53–67

Löffler, R. (1971) 'The representative mediator and the new peasant', *American Anthropologist* 73: 1007–92

MacDonald, W. L. (1986) *The Architecture of the Roman Empire II. An Urban Appraisal*, New Haven

Mackie, N. (1990) 'Urban munificence and the growth of urban consciousness in Roman Spain', in Blagg and Millett eds. (1990), 179–92

MacMullen, R. (1959) 'Roman imperial building in the provinces', *HSCP* 64: 207–35

(1963) *Soldier and Civilian in the Later Roman Empire*, Cambridge, MA

(1965) 'The Celtic renaissance', *Historia* 14: 93–104; reprinted in MacMullen (1990) 41–8, 286–90

(1968) 'Rural romanization', *Phoenix* 22: 337–41

MacMullen, R. (1981) *Paganism in the Roman empire*, New Haven
    (1982) 'The epigraphic habit in the Roman empire', *AJPh* 103: 233–46
    (1984a) 'Notes on Romanization', *BASP* 21: 161–77; reprinted in MacMullen
        (1990) 56–66, 291–5
    (1984b) 'The legion as a society', *Historia* 33: 440–56; reprinted in MacMullen
        (1990) 225–35, 368–74
    (1990) *Changes in the Roman Empire. Essays in the ordinary*, Princeton
Macready, S. and Thompson, F. H. eds. (1985) *Archaeological Field Survey in
    Britain and Abroad*, London
    eds. (1987) *Roman Architecture in the Greek East*, London
Mangin, M. (1981) *Un quartier des commerçants et artisans d'Alesia. Contribution
    à l'histoire urbain en Gaule*, (Publications de l'Université de Dijon 60), 2
    vols., Paris
    (1983) 'Agglomérations secondaires du Centre-Est et acculturation sous le
        haut empire', in *La Patrie Gauloise (d'Agrippa au VIIème s.)*, (Actes du
        Colloque de Lyon, 1981), Lyon, 39–54
    (1985) 'Artisanat et commerce dans les agglomérations secondaires du Centre-
        Est de la Gaule sous l'empire', in Leveau ed. (1985), 113–31
    (1994) 'Les agglomérations secondaires dans les régions de Franche-Comté
        et de Bourgogne', in Petit *et al.* (1994a), 45–79
Mangin, M., Jacquet, B. and Jacob, J.-P. eds. (1986) *Les agglomérations secondaires
    en Franche Comté romain*, (ALB 337), Paris
Mangin, M. and Tassaux, F. (1992) 'Les agglomérations secondaires de
    l'Aquitaine romaine', *Villes et agglomérations . . .* , 461–96
Mann, J. C. (1983) *Legionary Recruitment and Veteran Settlement during the
    Principate*, London
    (1985) 'Epigraphic consciousness', *JRS* 75: 204–6
Marchand, C. (1991) 'Sanctuaires picards et territoire', in Brunaux ed. (1991),
    14–18
Marichal, R. (1988) *Les graffites de la Graufesenque*, (*Gallia* supplément 47),
    Paris
Marrou, H.-I. (1965) *Histoire de l'Education dans l'Antiquité*[6], Paris (1st Edition
    1948)
Marsh, G. (1981) 'London's Samian supply and its relationship to the develop-
    ment of the Gallic Samian industry', in *Roman Pottery Research in Britain
    and North-West Europe*, A. C. Anderson and A. S. Anderson eds. (BAR IS
    123), Oxford, 173–238
Martin-Kilcher, S. (1989) 'Services de table en metal précieux du 1er au 5e
    siècle après Jésus-Christ', in *Trésors d'orfèvrerie gallo-romains*, F. Baratte
    and K. S. Painter eds., Paris, 15–20
Matthews, J. F. (1975) *Western Aristocracies and Imperial Court. AD 364–425*,
    Oxford
Mattingly, D. ed. (1997) *Dialogues in Roman Imperialism. Power, discourse and
    discrepant experience in the Roman Empire*, (*JRA* supplement 23), Ports-
    mouth, RI.
Maurin, L. (1978) *Saintes Antique*, Saintes
    ed. (1988) *Les fouilles de 'Ma Maison'. Etudes sur Saintes Antique*, (*Aquitania*
    supplément 3), Paris

Maurin L. (1991) 'Les villes Augustéennes de l'Aquitaine occidentale: Bordeaux, Périgueux, Saintes', in Goudineau and Rebourg eds. (1991), 45–59

(1992) 'Remparts et cités dans les trois provinces du Sud-Ouest de la Gaule au Bas-Empire (dernier quart du IIIe siècle-début du ve siècle)', in *Villes et Agglomérations* . . . 365–89

May, R. (1986) *Saint-Bertrand -de-Comminges. (Antique Lugdunum Convenarum). Le point sur les connaissances*, Toulouse

Mayer, M. and Gomez Pallarès, J. eds. (1992) *Religio Deorum. Actas del colloquio internacional de epigrafia. Culto y sociedades en occidente*, Barcelona

Mayet F. (1984) *Les céramiques sigillées hispaniques. Contribution à l'histoire économique de la Péninsule Ibérique sous l'empire romain*, Paris

McKendrick, N., Brewer, J. and Plumb, J. H. (1982) *The Birth of a Consumer Society. The commercialization of eighteenth century England*, London

Meadows, K. (1994) 'You are what you eat. Diet, identity and Romanization', in Cottam *et al.* eds. (1994), 132–40

Meffre, J.-C. (1994) 'Espace rural autour de Vaison-la-Romaine (Vaucluse): habitats et morphologie agraire à l'époque gallo-romaine', in Favory and Fiches eds. (1994), 117–37

Megaw, J. V. S. (1970) *Art of the European Iron Age. A study of the elusive image*, New York

Megaw, R. and Megaw, J. V. S. (1988) 'The stone head from Msecke Zehrovice: a reappraisal', *Antiquity* 62: 630–41

Meid, W. (1983) 'Gallisch oder Lateinisch? Soziolinguistische und andere Bemerkungen zu populären gallo-lateinischen Inschriften,' *ANRW* II.29.2: 1019–44

Méniel, P. (1987) *Chasse et élevage chez les gaulois, 450–52 av. J.C.*, Paris

(1991) 'Les animaux dans les sanctuaires gaulois du Nord de la France', in Brunaux ed. (1991), 257–67

Merriman, N. (1987) 'Value and motivation in prehistory: the evidence for "Celtic Spirit"' in *The Archaeology of Contextual Meaning*, I. Hodder ed., Cambridge, 111–16

Merten, H. (1985) 'Der Kult des Mars im Trevereraum', *TZ* 48: 7–113

Mertens, J. (1985) 'Les debuts de l'urbanisation dans le Nord de la Gaule', in Chevallier ed. (1985), 261–80

Metzler, J., Millett, M., Roymans, N. and Slofstra J. eds. (1995) *Integration in the Early Roman West. The role of culture and ideology*, (Dossiers d'Archéologie du Musée National d'Histoire et d'Art 4), Luxembourg

Metzler, J., Waringo, R., Bis, R. and Metzler-Jens, N. (1991) *Clémency et les tombes de l'aristocratie en Gaule Belgique*, (Dossiers d'Archéologie du Musée National d'Histoire et d'Art 1), Luxembourg

Meyer, E. A. (1990) 'Explaining the epigraphic habit in the Roman empire', *JRS* 80: 74–96

Middleton, P. S. (1979) 'Army supply in Roman Gaul', in *Invasion and Response: the case of Roman Britain*, (BAR BS 73), B. C. Burnham and H. Johnson eds., Oxford, 81–97

(1983) 'The Roman army and long-distance trade', in *Trade and Famine in Classical Antiquity*, P. D. A. Garnsey and C. R. Whittaker eds. (*PCPhS* supplement 8), Cambridge, 75–83

Millar, F. G. B. (1977) *The Emperor in the Roman World*, London

(1983) 'Empire and city, Augustus to Julian: obligations, excuses and status', *JRS* 73: 76–96

(1987) 'Empire, Community and Culture in the Roman Near East: Greeks, Syrians, Jews and Arabs', *Journal of Jewish Studies* 38: 143–64

(1990) 'The Roman coloniae of the Near East: a study of cultural relations', in *Roman Eastern Policy and Other Studies in Roman History*, H. Solin and M. Kajava eds., Helsinki, 7–58

(1993) *The Roman Near East 31 BC–AD 337*, Cambridge, MA

Miller, D. (1982) 'Structures and stratagems: an aspect of the relationship between social hierarchy and cultural change', in *Symbolic and Structural Archaeology*, I. R. Hodder ed., Cambridge, 89–98

(1985) *Artefacts as Categories*, Cambridge

(1987) *Material Culture and Mass Consumption*, Oxford

Miller, D. H. and Savage, W. W. (1977) 'Ethnic stereotypes and the frontier: a comparative study of Roman and American experience', in Miller and Steffen eds. (1977), 109–37

Miller, D. H. and Steffen, J. O. eds. (1977) *The Frontier I. Comparative studies*, Oklahoma

Millett, M. (1986) 'Central places in a decentralised Roman Britain', in Grant ed. (1986), 45–7

(1990a) *The Romanization of Britain. An essay in archaeological interpretation*, Cambridge

(1990b) 'Romanization: historical issues and archaeological interpretation', in Blagg and Millett eds. (1990), 35–41

(1995) 'Re-thinking religion in Romanization,' in Metzler *et al.* eds. (1995), 93–100

Mills, N. (1985) 'Iron age settlement and society in Europe: contributions from field surveys in central France', in Macready and Thompson eds. (1985), 74–100

(1986) 'Recherches sur l'habitat et la société au cours de l'âge du fer en Auvergne (France)', in Ferdière and Zadora-Rio eds. (1986), 121–30

Mintz, S. W. (1993) 'The changing roles of food in the study of consumption', in Brewer and Porter eds. (1993), 261–73

Mitchell, S. (1993) *Anatolia. Land, men and gods on Asia Minor. Volume I. The Celts and the impact of Roman rule*, Oxford

Moberg, C.-A. (1987) 'Quand l'archéologie rencontre les rencontres d'alphabets (quelques réflexions sur des monnaies épigraphes celtiques)', in *Mélanges offerts au Docteur J-B. Colbert de Beaulieu*, Paris, 639–49

Mócsy, A. (1970) *Gesellschaft und Romanisation in der römischen Provinz Moesia Superior*, Amsterdam

Modes de Contacts . . . (1983) *Modes de contacts et processus de transformation dans les sociétés anciennes*, (Actes du colloque de Cortone 1981, CEFR 67), Pisa

Momigliano, A. (1975) *Alien Wisdom. The limits of hellenisation*, Cambridge

(1986) 'Some preliminary remarks on the "religious opposition" to the Roman empire', in *Opposition et résistance à l'empire d'Auguste à Trajan*, A. Giovannini ed. (Entretiens Hardt 33), 103–33

Mommsen, T. (1886) *History of Rome V. The provinces of the Roman Empire from Caesar to Diocletian*, London (German original 1885)

Morel, J.-P. (1981a) 'La céramique Campanienne: acquis et problèmes', in Lévêque and Morel eds. (1981), 85–112

(1981b) *Céramique Campanienne. Les Formes*, (CEFR 244), Rome

(1981c) 'La produzione della ceramica Campana: aspetti economici e sociali', in *Società romana e produzione schiavistica* II, A. Giardina and A. Schiavone eds., 81–97

(1985) 'Le céramique campanienne en Gaule interne', in *Les âges du fer dans la vallé de la Saône*, L. Bonnamour, A. Duval and J.-P. Guillaumet eds. (AFEAF Actes 7 = *RAE* supplément 6), Paris, 181–87

Morris, I. (1992) *Death-Ritual and Social Structure in Classical Antiquity*, Cambridge

Mrozek, S. (1973) 'A propos de la répartition chronologique des inscriptions latines dans le Haut-Empire', *Epigraphica* 35: 13–18

(1988) 'A propos de la répartition chronologique des inscriptions latines dans le Haut-Empire', *Epigraphica* 50: 61–4

Mukerji, C. (1983) *From Graven Images. Patterns of modern materialism*, New York

Murray. O. (1991) 'History and reason in the ancient city', *PBSR* 59: 1–13

Naas, P. (1991) 'Les campagnes gallo-romaines de la civitas de Venetes', in Langouët ed. (1991), 143–56

Nash, D. (1976a) 'Reconstructing Poseidonius' Celtic ethnography', *Britannia* 7: 111–26

(1976b) 'The growth of urban society in France', in *Oppida: the beginnings of urbanisation in Barbarian Europe*, (BAR IS 11), B. W. Cunliffe and T. Rowley eds., Oxford, 95–133

(1978a) *Settlement and Coinage in central Gaul c.200–1 BC*, (BAR IS 39), Oxford

(1978b) 'Territory and state formation in central Gaul', in *Social Organisation and Settlement*, (BAR IS 47), D. Green, C. C. Haselgrove and M. Spriggs eds., Oxford, 455–75

(1978c) 'Plus ça change . . . : currency in Central Gaul from Julius Caesar to Nero', in *Scripta Nummaria Romana. Essays presented to Humphrey Sutherland*, R. A. G. Carson and C. M. Kraay eds., London, 12–31

(1981) 'Coinage and state development in central Gaul', in *Coinage and Society in Britain and Gaul: some current problems*, (CBA Research Report 38), B. W. Cunliffe ed., London, 10–17

(1985) 'Celtic territorial expansion and the Mediterranean world', in *Settlement and Society. Aspects of west European prehistory in the first millenium BC*, T. C. Champion and J. V. S. Megaw eds., Leicester, 45–67

(1987) 'Imperial expansion under the late Republic', in *Centre and Periphery in the Ancient World*, M. Rowlands, M. Larsen and K. Kristiansen eds., Cambridge, 87–103

Neumann, G. and Untermann, J. (1980) *Die Sprachen im römischen Reich der Kaizerseit*, (*BJ* Beiheft 40), Bonn

Nicolet, C. (1988) *L'Inventaire du Monde. Géographie et Politique aux Origines de l'Empire Romain*, Paris; English translation (1991) *Geography, Space and Politics in the Early Roman Empire*, Ann Arbor

Nicolini, G. (1976) 'Les sanctuaires ruraux de Poitou-Charentes: quelques exemples d'implantation et de structure interne,' in Chevallier ed. (1976), 256–72

Nicols, J. (1987) 'Indigenous culture and the process of Romanisation in Iberian Galicia', *AJPh* 108: 129–51

Nixon, C. E. V. and Rodgers, B. S. (1994) *In Praise of Later Roman emperors. The panegyrici Latini*, Berkeley

Nock, A. D. (1933) *Conversion. The old and the new in religion from Alexander the Great to Augustine of Hippo*, Oxford

North, J. A. (1976) 'Conservatism and change in Roman Religion', *PBSR* 44: 1–12

(1979) 'Religious toleration in Republican Rome', *PCPhS* n.s. 25: 85–103

(1981) 'The development of Roman imperialism', *JRS* 71: 1–9

(1992) 'The development of religious pluralism', in *The Jews among Pagans and Christians*, J. Lieu, J. A. North and T. Rajak eds., London, 174–93

(1993) 'Roman reactions to empire', *Scripta Classica Israelica* 12: 127–38

(1995) 'Religion and rusticity', in *Urban society in Roman Italy*, T. J. Cornell and K. Lomas eds., London, 135–50

Oaks, L. S. (1987) 'Epona in the Aeduan landscape. Transfunctional deity under changing rule', in Crumley and Marquardt eds. (1987), 295–333

Obermayer, A. (1971) *Kelten und Römer am Magdalensberg*, Vienna

Okun, M. L. (1989a) *The Early Roman Frontier in the Upper Rhine Area. Assimilation and acculturation on a Roman frontier*, (BAR IS 547), Oxford

(1989b) 'An example of the process of acculturation in the early Roman frontier', *OJA* 8: 41–54

Oliver, J. H. and Palmer, R. E. A. (1955) 'Minutes of a meeting of the Roman Senate', *Hesperia* 24: 320–49

Olmsted, G. (1992) *The Gaulish Calendar: a reconstruction from the bronze fragments from Coligny, with an analysis of its function as a highly accurate lunar/solar predictor as well as an explanation of its terminology and development*, Bonn

Ortner, S. (1984) 'Theory in anthropology since the sixties', *CSSH* 26: 126–66

Osborne, R. G. (1991) 'Pride and prejudice, sense and subsistence: exchange and society in the Greek city', in Rich and Wallace-Hadrill eds. (1991), 119–45

Parker-Pearson, M. (1989) 'Beyond the pale: barbarian social dynamics in western Europe', in Barrett *et al.* eds. (1989), 198–226

Passelac, M. (1986) 'Les premiers ateliers', in Bémont and Jacob eds. (1986), 35–8

Patterson, J. R. (1987) 'Crisis: what crisis? Rural change and urban development in imperial Appennine Italy', *PBSR* 55: 115–46

Paunier, D. (1986) 'La production de terre sigillée en Suisse au 1er s. de notre ère', in Bémont and Jacob eds. (1986), 265–8

Pelletier, A. (1976) 'La superficie des exploitations agraires dans le cadastre d'Orange', *Latomus* 25: 582–5

(1982) *Vienne antique de la conquête romaine aux invasions alamanniques*, (Roanne)

Percival, J. (1976) *The Roman Villa. An historical introduction*, London

(1992) 'The fifth-century villa: new life or death postponed?' in Drinkwater and Elton eds. (1992), 156–64

Perring, D. (1991) 'Spatial organisation and social change in Roman towns', in Rich and Wallace-Hadrill eds. (1991), 273–93

Petit, J.-P., Mangin, M. and Brunella, P. eds. (1994a) *Les agglomérations secondaires. La Gaule Belgique, les Germanies et l'Occident romain*, Paris

eds. (1994b) *Atlas des agglomérations secondaires de la Gaule Belgique et des Germanies*, Paris

Petry, M. F. (1982) 'Vici, villae et villages: relations triangulaires à la limite des territoires mediomatrique et triboque', in Chevallier ed. (1982), 211–12

Pflaum, H.-G. (1948) *Le Marbre de Thorigny*, Paris

(1960–61) *Les carrières procuratoriennes équestres sous le haut empire romain*, Paris

(1978) *Les fastes de la province de Narbonnaise*, Paris

Picard, G.-Ch. (1973) 'La romanisation des campagnes gauloises', in *Atti de colloquio sul tema La Gallia Romana*, (Academie Nazionale de Lincei, Quaderno 158), Rome, 139–50

(1975) 'Observations sur la condition des populations rurales', *ANRW* II 3: 98–111

(1976) 'Vicus et conciliabulum,' in Chevallier ed. (1976), 47–9

Picon, M. and Vertet, H. (1970) 'Les compositions des premières sigillées de Lezoux et le problème des céramique calacaires', *RAE* 21: 207–18

Piganiol, A. (1962) *Les documents cadastraux de la colonie romaine d'Orange*, (*Gallia* supplément 16), Paris

Piggott, S. (1968) *The Druids*, London

Pinon, P. (1988) 'L'urbanisme gallo-romain', in Bedon, Chevallier, and Pinon eds. (1988), vol. 2, 4–42

Pippidi, D. M. ed. (1976) *Assimilation et résistance à la culture gréco-romaine dans le monde ancien*, Paris

Pitts, L. F. (1989) 'Relations between Rome and the German "Kings" on the middle Danube in the first to fourth centuries AD', *JRS* 79: 45–58

de Polignac, F. (1984) *La naissance de la cité grecque*, Paris

(1991) 'Convergence et compétition: aux origines des sanctuaires de souvraineté territoriale dans le monde grec', in Brunaux ed. (1991), 97–105

(1994) 'Mediation, competition and sovereignty: the evolution of rural sanctuaries in Geometric Greece', in *Placing the Gods: sanctuaries and sacred space in ancient Greece*, S. E. Alcock and R. G. Osborne, eds., Oxford, 3–18

Pounds, N. J. G. (1969) 'The urbanization of the classical world', *Annals of the Association of American Geographers* 59: 135–57

Press, I. (1969) 'Ambiguity and innovation: implications for the genesis of the cultural broker', *American Anthropologist* 71: 205–17

Price, S. R. F. (1984) *Rituals and Power. The Roman imperial cult in Asia Minor*, Cambridge

Provost, M. (1993) *Le val de Loire dans l'Antiquité*, (*Gallia* supplément 52), Paris

Pucci, G. (1973) 'La produzione della ceramica aretina, nota sull'industria nella prima età imperiale', *Dialoghi di Archeologia* 7: 255–93

(1981a) 'La ceramica Italica (Terra sigillata)', in *Società romana e produzione schiavistica* A. Giardina and A. Schiavone eds., Rome, vol. II, 99–121

(1981b) 'Le officine ceramiche tardo-italiche', in Lévêque and Morel eds. (1981), 135–157

Purcell, N. (1985) 'Wine and wealth in ancient Italy', *JRS* 75: 1–19

Purcell, N. (1987) 'Town in country and country in town', in *Ancient Roman Villa Gardens*, E. B. MacDougall ed., Dumbarton Oaks, 185–203
   (1990) 'The creation of provincial landscape: the Roman impact on Cisalpine Gaul', in *The Early Roman Empire in the West*, T. Blagg and M. Millett eds., Oxford, 7–29
Py, M. (1990a) *Culture, économie et société protohistoriques dans la région nîmoise*, (CEFR 131), 2 vols. Paris
   (1990b) 'Chronologie des habitats de la Gaule méditerranéene des IIe et Ier siècles avant J.-C.', in Duval, Morel and Roman eds. (1990), 227–42
   (1992) 'Les fanums de Castels à Nages et de Roque-de-Viou', *Documents d'Archéologie Méridionale* 15: 44–49
   (1993) *Les Gaulois du Midi. De la fin de l'âge du Bronze à la conquête romaine*, Paris
Raepsaet-Charlier, M.-T. (1995) 'Aspects de l'onomastique en Gaule Belgique', *Cahiers du Centre Glotz* 6: 163–181
Ralston, I. B. M. (1981) 'The use of timber in hill-fort defences in France', in *Hill-Fort Studies. Essays for A. H. A. Hogg*, G. Guilbert ed., Leicester, 78–103
   (1988) 'Central Gaul at the Roman conquest: conceptions and misconceptions', *Antiquity* 62: 786–94
   (1992) *Les enceintes fortifiés du Limousin. Les habitats protohistoriques de la France non-méditerranéene*, (DAF 36), Paris
Ramage, E. S. (1973) *Urbanitas. Ancient sophistication and refinement*, Norman, Oklahoma.
Rambaud, M. (1966) *L'art de la déformation historique chez les commentaires de César²*, Paris
Rathbone, D. W. (1990) 'Villages, land and population in Graeco-Roman Egypt', *PCPhS* n.s. 36: 103–42
Rawson, E. (1985) *Intellectual Life in the Late Roman Republic*, London
Raynaud, C. (1990) *Le village gallo-romain et medieval de Lunel-Viel (Hérault). La fouille du quartier ouest (1981–3)*, (ALB 422), Paris
Rayonnement . . . (1965) Le rayonnement des civilisations grecque et romain sur les cultures périphériques, (Actes du 8ieme congrès international d'archéologie classique), Paris
Rebourg, A. (1991) 'Les origines d'Autun: l'archéologie et les textes', in Goudineau and Rebourg eds. (1991), 99–106
Recueil général (1957–) Recueil général des mosaïques de la Gaule (supplément à *Gallia* 10), Paris
Reddé, M. (1985) 'Le camp militaire d'Arlaines et l'aile de Voconces', *Gallia* 43: 49–79
   (1989) 'Vraies et fausses enceintes militaires d'époque romaine', in Buchsenschutz *et al.* eds. (1989), 21–6
Redfield, J. (1956) *Peasant Society and Culture*, Chicago
Redfield, J. *et al.* (1936) 'Memorandum for the study of acculturation', *American Anthropologist* 38: 149–52; reprinted in Bohannon and Plog eds. (1967), 181–6
Reece, R. (1990) 'Romanization: a point of view', in Blagg and Millett eds. (1990), 30–4

Reece, R. (n.d.) *My Roman Britain*, Cirencester

Renfrew, A. C. ed. (1973) *The Explanation of Culture Change*, London

(1975) 'Trade as action at a distance', in *Ancient Civilisation and Trade*, J. Sabloff and C. C. Lamberg-Karlovsky eds., Albuquerque, 3–59; reprinted in A. C. Renfrew (1984) *Approaches to Social Archaeology*, Edinburgh, 86–134

Renfrew, A. C. and Cherry, J. F. eds. (1986) *Peer Polity Interaction and Sociopolitical Change*, Cambridge

Rich, J. (1993) 'Fear, greed and glory: the causes of Roman war-making in the middle Republic', in *War and Society in the Roman World*, J. Rich and G. Shipley eds., London, 38–68

Rich, J. and Wallace-Hadrill, A. eds. (1991) *City and Country in the Ancient World*, London

Richardson, J. S. (1976) 'The Spanish mines and the development of provincial taxation', *JRS* 66: 139–52

(1991) 'Imperium Romanum: empire and the language of power', *JRS* 81: 1–9

Rigby, V. (1973) 'Potters' stamps on terra nigra and terra rubra found in Britain', in *Current Research in Romano-British Coarse Pottery*, A. Detsicas ed. (CBA Research Report 10), London, 7–24

Rippengal, R. (1993) ' "Villas as a key to social structure"? Some comments on recent approaches to the Romano-British villa and some suggestions toward an alternative', in *Theoretical Roman Archaeology: first conference proceedings*, E.Scott ed., Avebury, 79–101

Ritterling, E. (1906) 'Zur Geschichte des römischen Heeres in Gallien unter Augustus', *BJ* 114/115: 159–88

Rives, J. B. (1995a) *Religion and Authority in Roman Carthage from Augustus to Constantine*, Oxford

(1995b) 'Human sacrifice among pagans and Christians', *JRS* 85: 65–85

Rivet, A. L. F. (1980) 'Celtic names and Roman places', *Britannia* 11: 1–19

(1988) *Gallia Narbonensis, Southern France in Roman times*, London

Robert, L. (1977) 'Deux inscriptions de Tarse et d'Argos', *BCH* 101: 88–132

Roddaz, J.-M. (1984) *Marcus Agrippa*, (BEFAR 253), Rome

Rogers, G. M. (1991a) 'Demosthenes of Oenoanda and models of euergetism', *JRS* 81: 91–100

(1991b) *The Sacred Identity of Ephesos. Foundation myths of a Roman city*, London

Roman, Y. (1983) *De Narbonne à Bordeaux. Une axe économique au 1er s. av. J.C.*, Lyon

Romeuf, A.-M. (1986) 'Les ex-voto en bois de Chamalières (Puy-de-Dôme) et des Sources de la Seine (Côte d'Or). Essai de comparaison', *Gallia* 44: 65–89

Romm, J. S. (1992) *The Edges of the Earth in Ancient Thought. Geography, exploration, and fiction*, Princeton

Roth Congès, A. (1992a) 'Nouvelles fouilles à Glanum (1982–90)', *JRA* 5: 39–55

(1992b) 'Monuments publiques d'époque tardo-héllenistiques à Glanon (B.-du-Rh.)', *Documents d'Archéologie Méridionale* 15: 50–56

Roymans, N. (1988) 'Religion and society in late iron age northern Gaul', in Jones *et al.* eds. (1988), 55–71

(1990) *Tribal Societies in Northern Gaul. An anthropological perspective*, (Cingula 12), Amsterdam

(1993) 'Romanisation and the transformation of a martial élite-ideology in a frontier province', in *Frontières d'Empire. Nature et signification des frontières romaines*, (Actes de la Table Ronde Internationale de Nemours 1992, Mémoires du Musée de Préhistoire d'Ile-de-France 5), P. Brun, S. van der Leeuw and C. R. Whittaker eds., Nemours, 33–50

Roymans, N. and Derks, T. eds. (1994) *De Tempel von Empel. Een Hercules-heiligdom in het woongebied van de Bataven*, 's-Hertogenbosch

Rozman, G. (1973) *Urban Networks in Ch'ing China and Tokugawa Japan*, Princeton

(1976) *Urban Networks in Russia 1750–1800 and Pre-Modern Periodisation*, Princeton

Rüger, C. B. (1972) 'Gallisch-germanische Kurien', *Epigraphische Studien* 9: 251–60

(1983) 'A husband for the mother goddesses – some observations on the Matronae Aufaniae', in *Rome and her Northern Provinces. Papers . . . Frere*, B. Hartley and J. S. Wacher eds., Gloucester, 210–221

Rule, M. and Monaghan, J. (1993) *A Gallo-Roman Trading Vessel from Guernsey. The excavation and recovery of a third-century shipwreck*, (Guernsey Museum monographs 5), Guernsey.

Runciman, W. G. (1984) 'Accelerating social mobility: the case of Anglo-Saxon England', *Past and Present* 104: 3–30; reprinted in W. G. Runciman (1989) *Confessions of a Reluctant Theorist. Selected essays*, Cambridge, 121–147

Rüpke, J. (1990) *Domi militiae: die religiöse Konstruktion des Krieges in Rom*, Stuttgart

Rykwert, J. (1976) *The Idea of a Town: the anthropology of urban form in Rome, Italy and the ancient world*, London

Saddington, D. B. (1961) 'Roman attitudes to the "externae gentes" of the north', *Acta Classica* 4: 90–102

(1982) *The development of the Roman auxiliary forces from Caesar to Vespasian, 49 BC–AD 79*, Harare

Sahlins, M. (1976) *Culture and Practical Reason*, Chicago

(1988) 'Cosmologies of capitalism: the trans-Pacific sector of "the world system"', *Proceedings of the British Academy* 74: 1–51

de Saint-Blanquat, H. (1992) *Archeo TGV. 450 km d'histoire*, Tournai

Saller, R. P. (1982) *Personal Patronage under the Early Empire*, Cambridge

Saller, R. P. and Shaw, B. D. (1984) 'Tombstones and Roman family relations in the Principate: civilians, soldiers and slaves', *JRS* 74: 124–56

Salmon, E. T. (1982) *The Making of Roman Italy*, London

Salviat, F. (1977) 'Orientations, extension et chronologie des plans cadastrales d'Orange', *RAN* 10: 107–18

(1986) 'Quinte Curce, les insulae Furianae, la fossa Augusta et la localisation du cadastre C d' Orange', *RAN* 19: 101–16

Salzman, P. C. (1980) 'Culture as enhabilmentis', in Holy and Stuchlik eds. (1980), 233–56

Sauget, J. M. and Sauget, B. (1985) 'Réflexions sur le processus d'urbanisation d'*Augustonemeton* (Clermont-Ferrand). A partir de quelques observations chronostratigraphiques récentes', in Chevallier ed. (1985), 221–35

Schadewalt, W. (1973) 'Humanitas romana', *ANRW* I 4: 43–62

Schama, S. (1987) *The Embarrassment of Riches. An interpretation of Dutch culture in the Golden Age*, London

Scheers, S. (1977) *Traité de Numismatique Celtique* II. *La Gaule Belgique*, Paris

Scheid, J. (1985) 'Religion et superstition à l'époque de Tacite: quelques réflexions', in *Religion, supersticion y magia en el mundo romano*, Cadiz, 19–34

(1991) 'Sanctuaires et territoire dans la Colonia Augusta Treverorum', in Brunaux ed. (1991), 42–57

(1992) 'Epigraphie et sanctuaires guérisseurs en Gaule', *MEFRA* 104.1: 25–40

(1995) 'Les temples de l'Altbachtal à Trèves: un "sanctuaire national"?', *Cahiers du Centre Glotz* 6: 227–43; reprinted in Metzler *et al.* eds. (1995) 101–10 as 'Der Tempelbezirk im Altbachtal zu Trier: ein "Nationalheiligtum"?'

Schwartz, S. (1995) 'Language, power and identity in ancient Palestine', *Past and Present* 148: 3–47

Shaw, B. D. (1982) '"Eaters of flesh, drinkers of milk": the ancient Mediterranean ideology of the pastoral nomad', *Ancient Society* 13: 5–31; reprinted in Shaw (1995) ch. 6

(1983) 'Soldiers and society: the army in Numidia', *Opus* 2: 133–39; reprinted in Shaw (1995) ch. 9

(1995) *Rulers, Nomads and Christians in Roman North Africa*, Aldershot

Sherwin-White, A. N. (1967) *Racial prejudice in imperial Rome*, Cambridge

(1973) *The Roman Citizenship*[2], Oxford

Silberberg-Pierce, S. (1986) 'The many faces of the Pax Augusta: images of war and peace in Rome and Gallia Narbonensis', *Art History* 9: 306–24

Silverman, S. F. (1965) 'Patronage and community-nation relationships in central Italy', *Ethnology* 4: 172–89

Skinner, G. W. (1964) 'Marketing and social structure in rural China', *Journal of Asian Studies* 24: 3–42, 195–228, 363–99

(1977) 'Urban development in imperial China', in *The City in Late Imperial China*, G. W. Skinner ed., Stanford, 3–31

Slofstra, J. (1983) 'An anthropological approach to the study of romanization processes', in Brandt and Slofstra eds. (1983), 71–104

Smith, A. G. ed. (1966) *Communication and Culture*, New York

Smith, C. A. ed. (1976) *Regional Analysis*, 2 vols., New York

Smith, J. T. (1978) 'Villas as a key to social structure', in *Studies in the Romano-British Villa*, M. Todd ed., Leicester, 149–85

(1982) 'Villa plans and social structure in Britain and Gaul', in Chevallier ed. (1982), 321–36

Soricelli, G. (1995) *La gallia transalpina tra la conquista e l'età cesariana*, (Biblioteca di *Athenaeum* 29), Como

Spawforth, A. J. and Walker, S. (1986) 'The world of the Panhellenion II: Three Doric cities', *JRS* 76: 88–105

Sperber, D. (1975) *Rethinking Symbolism*, Cambridge (French original 1974)

Stead, I. (1967) 'A La Tène III burial at Welwyn Garden City', *Archaeologia* 101: 1–61

Stevens, C. E. (1933) *Sidonius Apollinaris and his Age*, Oxford

(1952) 'The "Bellum Gallicum" as a work of propaganda', *Latomus* 11: 3–18, 165–179

(1970) 'Roman Gaul', in *France, Government and Society*², J. M. Wallace-Hadrill and J. McManners eds., London, 19–35

(1980) 'North-west Europe and Roman politics, (125–118)', in *Studies in Latin Literature and Roman History II*, (Collection *Latomus* 168), C. Deroux ed., Brussels, 71–97

Steward, J. (1951) 'Levels of socio-cultural integration: an operational concept', *Southwestern Journal of Anthropology* 7: 374–90

Stewart, C. and Shaw, R. eds. (1994) *Syncretism/Anti-Syncretism. The politics of religious synthesis*, London

Strasburger, H. (1965) 'Poseidonius and the problems of the Roman empire', *JRS* 55: 40–53

Stuart, P. ed. (1971) *Deae Nehalenniae. Gids bij de tentoonstelling, Nehalennia de Zeeuwse godin, Zeeland in de Romeinse tijd, Romeinse monumenten vit de Oosterschelde*, Middleburg

de Sury, B. (1994) 'L'ex-voto d'après l'épigraphie: contribution à l'étude de sanctuaires', in Goudineau *et al.* eds. (1994), 169–73

Syme, R. (1958) *Tacitus* 2 vols., Oxford

(1986) 'More Narbonensian senators', *ZPE* 65: 1–24

Talbert, R. J. A. (1984) *The senate of imperial Rome*, Princeton

Tardy, D. (1989) *Le décor architectonique de Saintes antique*, (*Aquitania* supplément 5), Bordeaux

Tassaux, D. and Tassaux, F. (1983–4) 'Aulnay-de-Saintonge. Un camp augusto-tibérien en Aquitaine', *Aquitania* 1: 49–95; 2: 105–59

Taylor, T. (1991) 'Celtic Art', *SAR* 8: 129–32

Tchernia, A. (1983) 'Italian wine in Gaul at the end of the Republic', in Garnsey, Hopkins and Whittaker eds. (1983), 87–104

(1986) *Le vin d'Italie romaine. Essai d'histoire économique d'après des amphores*, Rome

Thevenot, E. (1968) *Divinités et sanctuaires de la Gaule*, Paris

Thollard, P. (1987) *Barbarie et civilisation chez Strabon. Étude critique des livres III et IV de la Géographie*, (ALB 365), Paris

Thompson, E. A. (1952) 'Peasant revolts in late Roman Gaul and Spain', *Past and Present* 2: 11–23; reprinted in M. I. Finley, ed. (1974) *Studies in Ancient Society*, London, 304–20

Tierney, J. J. (1960) 'The Celtic ethnography of Poseidonius', *Proceedings of the Royal Irish Academy* 60: 189–275

Toner, J. P. (1995) *Leisure and Ancient Rome*, Cambridge

Tortorella, S. (1987) 'La ceramica Africana: un riesame della problematica', in Lévêque and Morel eds. (1987), 279–327

Toutain, J. (1906–20) *Les cultes païennes dans l'empire romain: les provincees latines*, 3 vols., Paris

Travaux militaires . . . (1978) *Travaux militaires en Gaule romaine et dans les provinces du nord-ouest*, (*Caesarodunum* supplément 28), Paris

Trevor-Roper, H. (1983) 'The invention of tradition: the Highland tradition of Scotland', in *The Invention of Tradition*, E. Hobsbawm and T. Ranger eds., Cambridge, 14–41

Treziny, H. (1992) 'Imitations, emprunts, détournements: sur quelques problèmes d'architecture et d'urbanisme en Gaule méridionale', in Bats *et al.* eds. (1992), 337–49

Trixier, J.-P. (1985) 'Les temples du puy de Dôme', in *Les sanctuaires Arvernes*, G. Tisserand *et al.*, Clermont Ferrand, 12–46

Trow, S. D. (1990) 'By the northern shores of Ocean: some observations on acculturation process at the edge of the Roman world', in Blagg and Millett eds. (1990), 103–18

Tuffreau-Libre, M. (1992) *La céramique en Gaule romaine*, Paris

Turcan, R. (1972) *Les religions de l'Asie dans la vallée du Rhône*, (Etudes préliminaires aux religions orientales dans l'empire romain 30), Leiden

(1982) 'L'autel de Rome et Auguste "ad Confluentem"', *ANRW* II 12.1: 607–44

(1986) 'Les religions orientales en Gaule narbonnaise et dans la vallée du Rhône', *ANRW* II 18.1: 456–518

(1996) 'La promotion du sujet par le culte du souverain,' in *Subject and Ruler: the cult of the ruling power in classical antiquity*, Papers presented at a conference held in the University of Alberta on April 13–15, 1994, to celebrate the 65th anniversary of Duncan Fishwick, A. M. Small ed. (*JRA* supplement 17), Ann Arbor, 51–62

Untermann, J. (1969) 'Lengua gala y lengua ibérica en la Gala Narbonensis', *ArchPrehLev* 12: 99–163

(1980) *Monumenta Linguarum Hispanicorum. II Die Inschriften in iberischer Schrift aus Südfrankreich*, Wiesbaden

(1992) 'Quelle langue parlait-on dans l'Hérault pendant l'antiquité?' *RAN* 25: 19–27

Vaginay, M. and Guichard, V. (1988) *L'habitat gaulois de Feurs (Loire). Fouilles récentes (1978–81)*, (DAF 14), Paris

Van Andringa, W. (1994) 'Cultes publiques et statut juridique de la cité des Helvètes', *Roman Religion in Gallia Belgica and the Germaniae*, (Actes des Quatrièmes Rencontres Scientifiques de Luxembourg, Bulletin des Antiquites Luxembourgeoises 22), Luxembourg, 170–194

Van Dam, R. (1985) *Leadership and Community in Late Antique Gaul*, London

Van Ossel, P. (1992) *Etablissements ruraux de l'Antiquité tardive dans le nord de la Gaule*, (*Gallia* supplément 51), Paris

Vatin, C. (1972) 'Wooden sculptures from Gallo-Roman Auvergne', *Antiquity* 46: 39–42

Veblen, T. (1926) *The Theory of the Leisure Classes*, New York

Vernhet, A. (1986) 'Les ateliers du sud de la France: présentation générale', in Bémont and Jacob eds. (1986), 33–4

Vertet, H. (1986) 'Centre de production de Lyon', in Bémont and Jacob eds. (1986), 126

Veyne, P. (1975) 'Y' a-t-il eu un impérialisme romaine?', *MEFRA* 87: 793–855

(1976) *Le Pain et le Cirque: sociologie historique d'un pluralisme politique*, Paris; English abridged translation (1990) *Bread and Circuses. Historical sociology and political pluralism*, London

Veyne, P. (1983) ' "Titulus Praelatus": offrande, solemnisation et publicité dans les ex-voto greco-romains', *RA*, 281–300

(1993) 'Humanitas: Romans and non-Romans', in *The Romans*, A. Giardina ed., Chicago (Italian original 1989), 342–69

Vickers, M. ed. (1986) *Pots and Pans*, Oxford

(1994) 'Nabataea, India, Gaul and Carthage: reflections on Hellenistic and Roman gold vessels and red-gloss pottery', *AJA* 98: 231–48

de la Ville de Mirmont, H. (1904) 'Cicéron et les gaulois', *Revue Celtique* 25: 163–80

Les Villes de la Gaule Belgique. . . . (1984) *Les Villes de la Gaule Belgique au Haut-Empire*, (Actes du Colloque tenu à St Riquier (Somme) le 22–4 octobre 1982 (*Revue Archéologique de Picardie*, 3–4), Amiens

Villes et agglomérations . . . (1992) *Villes et agglomérations urbaines antiques du sud-ouest de la Gaule*, (Deuxième colloque *Aquitania*: Bordeaux, 13–15 septembre 1990, *Aquitania* supplément 6), Bordeaux

de Vries, J. (1984) *European Urbanization 1500–1800*, London

Wachtel, N. (1974) 'L'acculturation', in *Faire l'histoire*, J. Le Goff and P. Nora eds., Paris, 124–46

Wait, G. A. (1985) *Ritual and religion in iron age Britain*, (BAR BS 149), 2 vols., Oxford

Wallace-Hadrill, A. (1988) 'Greek Knowledge, Roman Power', *CPh* 83: 224–233

ed. (1989a) *Patronage in Ancient Society*, London

(1989b) 'Rome's cultural revolution', *JRS* 79: 157–64

(1990a) 'The social spread of Roman luxury: sampling Pompeii and Herculaneum', *PBSR* 58, 145–92; revised and rewritten in Wallace-Hadrill (1994), 65–174

(1990b) 'Pliny the Elder and man's unnatural history', *Greece and Rome* 37: 80–96

(1991) 'Elites and trade in the Roman town', in Rich and Wallace-Hadrill eds. (1991) 241–72; revised and rewritten in Wallace-Hadrill (1994), 65–174

(1994) *Houses and Society in Pompeii and Herculaneum*, Princeton

Walter, H. (1986) *La Porte Noire de Besançon. Contribution à l'étude de l'art triomphal des Gaules*, (ALB 321), 2 vols, Paris

(1993) *Les Barbares d'Occident romain*, (ALB 494), Paris

Walter, V. J. (1974) *The Cult of Mithras in the Roman Provinces of Gaul*, (Etudes préliminaires aux religions orientales dans l'empire romain 41), Leiden

Walthew, C. V. (1982) 'Early Roman town development in Gallia Belgica: a review of some problems', *OJA* 1: 225–36

Waltzing, J. P. (1895–1900) *Etude historique sur les corporations professionales chez les romains*, 4 vols, Louvain

Ward-Perkins, J. B. (1970) 'From Republic to Empire: reflections on the early imperial provincial architecture of the Roman West', *JRS* 60: 1–19

Weber, E. (1979) *Peasants into Frenchmen. The modernisation of rural France 1870–1914*, London

Webster, J. (1994) 'The just war: Graeco-Roman texts as colonial discourse', in Cottam *et al.* eds. (1994), 1–10

Webster, J. (1995) 'Translation and subjection: interpretatio and the Celtic Gods', in *Different Iron Ages. Studies on the iron age in temperate Europe*, (BAR IS 602), J. D. Hill and C. Cumberpatch eds., Oxford, 175–83

Webster, J. and Cooper, N. eds. (1996) *Roman Imperialism: post-colonial perspectives*, (Leicester Archaeology Monographs 3), Leicester

Wells, C. M. (1972) *The German Policy of Augustus*, Oxford

(1974) 'The ethnography of the Celts and the Algonkian-Iroquoian tribes: a comparison of two historical traditions', in *Polis and Imperium, Studies in honour of Edward Togo Salmon*, J. A. S. Evans ed., Toronto, 265–78

(1992) 'Pottery manufacture and military supply north of the Alps', *RCRFActa* 31–2: 195–205

Wells, P. S. (1987) 'Industry, commerce and temperate Europe's first cities: preliminary report on the 1987 excavations at Kelheim, Bavaria', *Journal of Field Archaeology* 14: 399–412

(1993) *Settlement, Economy, and Cultural Change at the End of the European Iron Age. Excavations at Kelheim in Bavaria, 1987–1991* (International Monographs in Prehistory, Archaeological Series 6) Ann Arbor

West, L. C. (1935) *Roman Gaul. The objects of trade*, Oxford

Wheatley, P. (1972) 'The concept of urbanism', in *Man, Settlement and Urbanism*, P. J. Ucko, R. Tringham, and G. W. Dimbleby eds., London, 601–37

Whittaker, C. R. (1980) 'Rural labour in three Roman provinces', in *Non-slave labour in the Greco-Roman world*, P. D. A. Garnsey ed. (*PCPhS* Supplement 6) Cambridge, 110–27

(1989) 'Supplying the system: frontiers and beyond', in Barratt *et al.* eds. (1989), 64–80

(1990) 'The consumer city revisited: the vicus and the city', *JRA* 3: 110–18

(1994) *Frontiers of the Roman Empire. A social and economic study*, Baltimore and London

Wiedemann, T. E. J. (1986) 'Between men and beasts: barbarians in Ammianus Marcellinus', in *Past Perspectives. Studies in Greek and Roman historical writing*, I. S. Moxon, J. D. Smart and A. J. Woodman eds., Cambridge, 189–201

Wierschowski, L. (1995) *Die regionale Mobilität in Gallien nach den Inschriften des 1. bis 3. Jahrhunderts n.Chr. Quantitative Studien zur Social- und Wirtschaftsgeschichte der westlichen Provinzen des römischen Reiches*, (Historia Einzelschriften 91), Stuttgart

Wightman, E. M. (1970) *Roman Trier and the Treveri*, London

(1974) 'La Gaule Chevelue entre César et Auguste', in *Actes du 9ième congrès international d'études sur les frontières romaines*, Bucharest, 472–83

(1975) 'Rural settlement in Roman Gaul', *ANRW* II 4: 584–647

(1976a) 'Il y avait en Gaule deux sortes de Gaulois', in Pippidi ed. (1976), 407–19

(1976b) 'Le vicus dans le contexte de l'administration et de la société gallo-romaine: quelques réflexions', in Chevallier ed. (1976) 59–64

(1977) 'Military arrangements, native settlements and related developments in early Roman Gaul', *Helinum* 17: 105–26

(1978a) 'Soldier and civilian in early Roman Gaul' in *Akten des 11 internationalen Limeskongresses*, Budapest, 72–86

Wightman, E. M. (1978b) 'Peasants and Potentates. An investigation of social structures and land tenure in Roman Gaul', *AJAH* 3: 97–128

(1984) 'Imitation ou adaptation? Une note sur les inscriptions dans le nord de la Gaule romaine', *Revue du Nord* 66: 69–72

(1985) *Gallia Belgica*, London

(1986) 'Pagan cults in the province of Belgica', *ANRW* II 18.1: 542–89

Will, E. L. (1987) 'The Roman amphoras from Manching: a reappraisal', *Bayerische Vorgeschichtsblätter* 52: 21–36

Williamson, C. (1987a) 'Monuments of bronze: Roman legal documents on bronze tablets', *Classical Antiquity* 6: 160–83

(1987b) 'A Roman law from Narbonne', *Athenaeum* 65: 173–89

Willis, S. (1994) 'Roman imports into late iron age British societies: towards a critique of existing models', in Cottam *et al.* eds. (1994), 141–50

Wissowa, G. (1916–19) 'Interpretatio Romana. Römische Götter im Barbarenlande', *ARW* 19: 1–49

Wobst, M. (1977) 'Stylistic behaviour and information exchange', in *For the Director: research essays in honour of James Griffin*, C. E. Cleland ed. (Anthropological Papers of the Museum of Anthropology, University of Michigan 61), Ann Arbor, 317–42

Wolf, E. (1956) 'Aspects of relations in a complex society', *American Anthropologist* 58: 1065–78

(1982) *Europe and the People without History*, Berkeley

Wolff, H. (1976) 'Kriterien für latinische und römische Städte in Gallien und Germanien und die "Verfassung" der gallischen Stammesgemeinden', *BJ* 176: 45–121

Wood, I. (1990) 'Administration, law and culture in Merovingian Gaul', in *The Uses of Literacy in Early Mediaeval Europe*, R. McKitterick ed., Cambridge, 63–81

Wood, M. and Queiroga, F. eds. (1992) *Current Research on the Romanization of the Western Provinces*, (BAR IS 575), Oxford

Woolf, G. D. (1990a) 'World systems analysis and the Roman empire', *JRA* 3: 44–58

(1990b) 'Food, poverty and patronage. The significance of the epigraphy of the Roman alimentary schemes in early imperial Italy', *PBSR* 58: 197–228

(1992a) 'The unity and diversity of Romanisation', *JRA* 5: 349–52

(1992b) 'Imperialism, empire and the integration of the Roman economy', *World Archaeology* 23: 283–93

(1993a) 'Roman Peace', in *War and Society in the Roman World*, J. Rich and G. Shipley eds., London, 171–94

(1993b) 'Rethinking the Oppida', *OJA* 12.2: 223–34

(1993c) 'The social significance of trade in late iron age Europe', in *Trade and Exchange in Prehistoric Europe*, C. Scarre and F. Healey eds. (Acts of the Prehistoric Society Conference, Bristol 1992), Oxford, 211–18

(1993d) 'European social evolution and Roman imperialism', in *Frontières d'Empire. Nature et signification des frontières romaines*, P. Brun, S. van der Leeuw and C. R. Whittaker eds. (Actes de la Table Ronde Internationale de Nemours 1992, Mémoires du Musée de Préhistoire d'Ile-de-France 5), Nemours, 13–20

Woolf, G. D. (1994a) 'Power and the spread of writing in the west', in *Literacy and Power in the Ancient World*, A. K. Bowman and G. D. Woolf eds., Cambridge, 84–98

(1994b) 'Becoming Roman, Staying Greek. Culture, identity and the civilizing process in the Roman East', *PCPhS* n.s. 40: 116–43

(1995) 'The formation of Roman provincial cultures', in Metzler *et al.* eds. (1995), 9–18

(1996a) 'Monumental writing and the expansion of Roman society in the early empire', *JRS* 86: 22–39

(1996b) 'The uses of forgetfulness in Roman Gaul', in *Vergangenheit und Lebenswelt. Soziale Kommunikation, Traditionsbildung und historisches Bewußtsein*, (ScriptOralia 90), H.-J. Gehrke and A. Möller eds., Tübingen, 361–81

(1997) 'Beyond Romans and natives', *World Archaeology* 28: 339–50

Wrigley, E. A. (1978) 'Parasite or stimulus: the town in a pre-industrial economy', in Abrams and Wrigley eds. (1978), 295–309

Wuilleumier, P. (1953) *Lyon, métropole des Gaules*, Paris

Zanker, P. (1988) *The Power of Images in the Age of Augustus*, Berkeley (German original 1987)

Zecchini, G. (1984) *I druidi e l'opposizione dei Celti a Roma*, Milan

Zoll, A. L. (1994) 'Patterns of worship in Roman Britain: double named deities in context', in Cottam *et al.* eds. (1994), 32–44

(1995) 'A view through inscriptions: the epigraphic evidence for religion at Hadrian's Wall', in Metzler *et al.* eds. (1995), 129–37

Index